Regional Horror Films,
1958–1990

ALSO BY BRIAN ALBRIGHT

Wild Beyond Belief! Interviews with Exploitation Filmmakers of the 1960s and 1970s (McFarland, 2008)

Regional Horror Films, 1958–1990

A State-by-State Guide with Interviews

BRIAN ALBRIGHT

McFarland & Company, Inc., Publishers
Jefferson, North Carolina, and London

Abridged versions of two of the interviews in this book originally appeared as "Drive-In Force: Florida Filmmaker William Grefé," *VideoScope* #67, Summer 2008, and "It Could Only Happen in Milpitas, California! How a Young Teacher Rallied an Entire Town to Make a Monster Movie!" *FilmFax* #117, April/June 2008.

LIBRARY OF CONGRESS CATALOGUING-IN-PUBLICATION DATA

Albright, Brian, 1973–
Regional horror films, 1958–1990 : a state-by-state guide with interviews / by Brian Albright.
    p.   cm.
Includes bibliographical references and index.

ISBN 978-0-7864-7227-7
softcover : acid free paper ∞

1. Horror films — Production and direction — United States. 2. Motion pictures — United States — History — 20th century. 3. Motion picture producers and directors — United States — Interviews. 4. Horror films — United States — Catalogs. I. Title.
PN1995.9.H6A63 2012   791.43'6164—dc23   2012037348

BRITISH LIBRARY CATALOGUING DATA ARE AVAILABLE

© 2012 Brian Albright. All rights reserved

No part of this book may be reproduced or transmitted in any form or by any means, electronic or mechanical, including photocopying or recording, or by any information storage and retrieval system, without permission in writing from the publisher.

On the cover: *The Evil Dead* (1981) (New Line Cinema/Photofest)

Manufactured in the United States of America

*McFarland & Company, Inc., Publishers
Box 611, Jefferson, North Carolina 28640
www.mcfarlandpub.com*

For Adele, Sam, Iris and Gabe

Acknowledgments

First of all, I owe an enormous debt to the people who helped me with my background research, contacts or photos, and who helped me refine the listings and focus the book: Gordon K. Smith in Texas, Ed Tucker in Florida, Fred Olen Ray, Tom Weaver, Bill Warren, Daniel Griffith, George Reis at *DVD Drive-In*, Rebecca Preston at the Dallas Producers Association, and Joseph Ziemba at *Bleeding Skull*. And a big thank you to Joel Sanderson at *The Basement Sublet of Horror* in Kansas for giving me the opportunity to see one of the rarest films in this book, *The Beast from the Beginning of Time* (1965), and to Johanna Perrino at WCTV in Wadsworth, Ohio, who sent me a copy of the only-slightly-less-rare *The Wednesday Children* (1973). Jean-Claude Michel and Jose Bogato in Spain deserve special mention for putting me on the trail of *Southern Shockers* (1985).

Extra special thanks to Chris Poggiali, the world's coolest librarian and curator of *The Temple of Schlock*, who not only pointed me in the direction of some of the more obscure entries in the book, but who also read through portions of the manuscript and helped correct my boneheaded mistakes. Likewise, the amazing Fred Adelman at *Critical Condition* granted me access to his mind-blowing archive of vintage movie advertisements and video box cover art, and the book would be a much poorer looking pile of paper without his significant contributions.

Thanks to J.R. Bookwalter for publishing my first work and letting me crib the title of his first feature for my blog (to be fair, he stole it from Billy Idol), and to Terry Maher for his opinions, photographic memory and access to his back issues of *Fangoria*.

And to all my editors: Michael Stein and Jim Wilson at *Filmfax*, Anthony Timpone, Chris Alexander and Mike Gingold at *Fangoria*, Steven Puchalski at *Shock Cinema*, Darryl Mayeski at *SCREEM*, and Joe Kane at *VideoScope*.

As always: Adele, my parents, Fritz the Nite Owl, Video Central in Columbus, Star Time Video in Circleville, and B-Ware Video (rest in peace) in Cleveland.

Table of Contents

Acknowledgments — vi
Introduction: I Hear America Screaming — 1

Part I: The Interviews

Harvesting the Dead: Ed Adlum — 17
Something Fishy: Donald Barton — 28
The Director Next Door: J.R. Bookwalter — 39
Nutriaman: Martin Folse — 55
All the President's Monsters: Milton Moses Ginsberg — 63
It Came from Florida: William Grefé — 76
Better Watch Out: Lewis Jackson — 96
Night Frights: Russ Marker — 108
Survivors Will Be Persecuted: Robert W. Morgan — 119
Left at the Altar: Tom Rahner — 130
Bayou Bloodbath: Albert J. Salzer — 135
Teen Terrors: Larry Stouffer — 144
It Could Only Happen in Milpitas! Robert Burrill — 158

Part II: The Films

State-by-State Listing of Regional Horror Films, 1958 to 1990 — 175

Select Bibliography — 321
Index — 323

Introduction: I Hear America Screaming

It's the summer of 1964, and you and your family have rolled into the Telegraph Drive-In just outside of Toledo to munch popcorn and watch a seemingly innocuous double feature of *Spencer's Mountain* (1963) and *The Wheeler Dealers* (1963).

Suddenly, up on the screen, a sweaty man in a suit appears against a red backdrop and ominously intones: "Ladies and gentlemen, you are about to witness some scenes from the next attraction to play this theater. This picture, truly one of the most unusual ever filmed, contains scenes, which under no circumstances, should be viewed by anyone with a heart condition or anyone who is easily upset. We urgently recommend that if you are such a person, or the parent of a young or impressionable child now in attendance, that you and the child leave the auditorium for the next 90 seconds."

Before you even have time to cover your impressionable child's eyes, let alone consider the logistics of leaving a drive-in for 90 seconds, you are greeted in rapid succession by images of a woman in her bra having her tongue gorily ripped out of her head, two lovers scalped on a beach, a heart plucked from another woman's chest, and a risqué bathtub leg amputation, all in dripping color and all featured prominently in the Herschell Gordon Lewis film *Blood Feast* (1963).

"Nothing so appalling in the annals of horror!" the trailer claimed. And nothing so appalling in the annals of Toledo cinema, apparently, since the local Armstrong Circuit canceled its scheduled screenings of the film after families complained about the unexpectedly grisly trailer.

This was not the first, or last, time *Blood Feast* (generally credited as the first American gore film) would run into legal problems. When the movie opened in the fall of 1963, drive-in audiences responded by lining up for miles to see it, and local bluenoses reacted with shock and horror at its crude gore and crass title. The film was banned in Sarasota after one showing. Newspapers in Pittsburgh refused to even run advertisements for it. A group of East Haven, Connecticut, police officers declared the film objectionable, and a Philadelphia theater owner was arrested for exhibiting an obscene film and contributing to the delinquency of a minor after screening it for an audience of teenagers.

The censors occasionally prevailed against *Blood Feast*, but the film's producers (Lewis and David F. Friedman) were hardly deterred. They followed *Blood Feast* with a string of similarly themed gore pictures, and were soon joined by other like-minded filmmakers who were willing to push the limits of good taste for a fast buck.

Blood Feast, in fact, was just the first of what would soon become a flood of horror films that over the course of the next three decades would shock audiences, flummox critics, and completely redefine the boundaries of the genre. In addition to their subversive content, films like *Night of the Living Dead* (1968), *The Last House on the Left* (1972), *The Texas Chain Saw Massacre* (1974), *I Spit on Your Grave* (1978), and *Friday the 13th* (1980) also shared a very similar production lineage: They were made far outside of Hollywood, produced in burgeoning film communities that had sprouted in Florida, Texas, Oregon, New York and all points in between.

The history of the horror film, at least in the last half of the 20th century, was made as much by enterprising independent filmmakers as it was by the major studios. But the films mentioned above weren't just independent horror films; they were *regional* horror films, conceived, produced and often distributed entirely in corners of the country not typically associated with the entertainment industry — from the backwoods of Utah to the bayous of Louisiana and the outer boroughs of New York. Made with little regard to genre convention, or in some cases even any basic knowledge of filmmaking, by the 1970s these regional indies were at the vanguard of horror cinema.

Before we go much farther, it might be helpful to provide a better definition of what, exactly, a regional horror film *is*. Opinions will probably differ, but for my purposes a regional horror film is one that

The Astra Video release of *Blood Feast* (1963) (courtesy Fred Adelman).

was (a) filmed outside of the general professional and geographic confines of Hollywood; (b) produced independently; and (c) made with a cast and crew made up primarily of residents of the state in which the film was shot.

I am *not* talking about runaway productions — films made by Hollywood production crews in other states. So while *Don't Look in the Basement* (1973), a film made in Texas by a Texan, is a regional horror film, *Race with the Devil* (which was made in Texas by Texas-born director Jack Starrett) is not, because it was a 20th Century–Fox production made with a (mostly) Hollywood crew.

This book is about regional horror and science fiction films, but there were literally thousands of independent films in almost every genre made all over the country between the late 1950s and late 1980s, produced by a mix of professional filmmakers and gifted (and not-so-gifted) amateurs. And while there were certainly regional films made before that period — and an unfathomable number made since the 1990s, when most independent filmmakers made the switch from film to video — the roughly 30-year period I've outlined here represents the peak of this type of indie production, when it was possible (thanks to a combination of economic incentives and trends in film distribution) for just about anyone with enough cash and courage to pick up a camera, make a movie, and actually find national distribution in theaters or (later) on video.

So Why Did I Write This Book?

Okay, so there were a whole lot of cheap horror films made in the boonies and boroughs a few decades ago. Why write a book about it? For one thing, it hasn't been done before (as far as I know). There have been thousands of books written about horror films over the years, and they've been organized almost every way imaginable: chronologically, by sub-genre, by studio, by director, by subject matter, by country of origin, and even by the amount of gore spilled per film. But you will find no other collection of movies so odd, so varied and (to me at least) so interesting as when you arrange U.S.–made horror films geographically.

A quick glance at the listings in this book will reveal that some of the most influential (and notorious) horror films of the past 50 years were spawned almost as far from the mainstream film industry as you could get. *Blood Feast, Carnival of Souls, Night of the Living Dead, Last House on the Left, I Spit on Your Grave, The Texas Chainsaw Massacre, The Evil Dead*— these were all shot independently in the South, the Midwest, even New Jersey.

Once you watch enough of these movies (and believe me, there were times when I thought to myself, "I have watched enough of these movies...") you also start to recognize the distinct local flavor present in each one. There is a certain look and feel to the horror movies made in Texas or Florida that not only couldn't be duplicated in Hollywood, but that also couldn't be duplicated in Mississippi or Louisiana or Wisconsin.

Which is all part of their unique appeal. These films represent not just regional film making, but a cultural regionalism that is going extinct. Art and life in the United States have rapidly homogenized over the past few decades — everyone is watching the same TV shows, listening to the same canned radio programming, shopping at the same department stores, and eating at the same chain restaurants, no matter where they live. Yes, there are pockets of distinct culture left, and yes, life in Massachusetts probably looks a lot different than life in Mississippi or on Long Island, but you can still travel from one end of the country to the other without eating anywhere other than Olive Garden or shopping anywhere other than Wal-Mart.

When most of these films were made, however, almost every area of the country had its own restaurants, its own grocery stores, its own television programming. If you got off the freeway, you could never be quite sure what you were going to encounter (which, come to think of it, is the premise at the heart of many horror films). Watching these movies gives you a real glimpse of New York or Arkansas as they existed at the time.

Finally, regional horror films (at least the interesting ones) radiate with a kind of unique

4 • **Introduction**

energy that you just can't find in most other films. There is something inherently and almost uniquely American — something downright *democratic*— about these films and the stories behind them; a sort of "let's put on a show" enthusiasm that shines through all the chainsaw maulings and decapitations.

Which is not to say all of these films are fun to watch. Many of them are quite bad. Others are passable, but clearly made by first-time filmmakers. In some cases, you get the impression that not only have these people never made a film before, it's quite possible they've never *watched* one, either.

Whatever their technical faults, these regional oddities are a testament both to the filmmakers' independent spirits and their sometimes warped artistic impulses. While the earliest of these films (like *The Blob* or *The Killer Shrews*) looked very much like their low-budget Hollywood counterparts, as time went on regional horror films just got stranger, wandering farther and farther afield of both genre and storytelling traditions. One of the reasons films like *Carnival of Souls*, *Night of the Living Dead*, and *The Evil Dead* remain popular and influential among modern horror fans is that they pushed the boundaries of the genre. It's safe to say, I think, that none of the above titles would have been quite the same had they been made by filmmakers already ensconced in Los Angeles.

That's important to remember, because independently-made horror films (not just the regional ones) rattled the cage, so to speak, infusing new energy in the horror genre at just the right time. In the 1960s, when independent films like these first started coming into their own, horror films had largely become an international affair. Between the release of *Psycho* in 1960 and *Rosemary's Baby* in 1968, the bulk of the horror and sci-fi films most people remember fondly were generated either by Hammer in England or Toho in Japan, or one of their many imitators overseas. In the U.S., the genre was largely represented by a

The walking catfish monster from *Zaat* (1975), filmed in Florida (courtesy Ed Tucker).

short-lived wave of *Psycho* knock-offs and Roger Corman's series of films based on the writings of Edgar Allan Poe (which were themselves modeled very closely on Hammer's period gothics). Most of the other low-budget horrors being cranked out in Hollywood followed the Corman model.

But out in the boondocks, fiddling around at the margins, interesting things were beginning to happen. First was Herk Harvey's *Carnival of Souls*, a downbeat thriller that built its reputation largely on late-night TV airings. Then came *Blood Feast*.

"*Blood Feast* is like a Walt Whitman poem," its director has frequently said of his first gore outing. "It's no good, but it's the first of its kind, and therefore it deserves a place." With its over-lit Miami locations, garish stage blood and ridiculous plot, *Blood Feast* was about as far from the cobwebby castles of Hammer and AIP as you could get. There really was not anything quite like it in the marketplace at the time, or for several years afterward for that matter, other than Lewis' own follow ups.

And in 1968, *Night of the Living Dead* arrived and pretty much turned the genre on its head. The film combined the documentary feel of a nightly newscast with Lewis' unabashed gore and some shambling ghouls that would have been right at home stumbling through one of those Hammer cemeteries — except that they were wandering through a distinctly modern, banal Pennsylvania landscape.

With *Night*, the American horror film re-asserted itself as a market leader, and the Europeans (especially the Italians) spent much of the next decade trying to recreate it. They mostly failed, unable to recapture what turned out to be a uniquely American blend of gore, nihilism and Yankee know-how.

The effect that the most outrageous of these films had on the genre and the viewing public was palpable. *Night of the Living Dead* was released in some markets on a kiddie matinee with *Dr. Who and the Daleks*, resulting in auditoriums full of wailing, traumatized tykes (most famously documented in Roger Ebert's scathing review of the film). When *The Texas Chain Saw Massacre* premiered at the Empire Theatre in San Francisco, audience members stormed out of the theater (some of them reportedly vomiting) and nearly started a riot in an effort to get their tickets refunded. Moviegoers in Tallahassee (led by a local Congressional representative) similarly vacated a theater during a showing of *Last House on the Left* in 1973.

The filmmakers were often inventively pushing boundaries out of necessity rather than by design; they were often at the mercy of forces beyond their control, and many of them were, frankly, winging it, which goes a long way toward explaining why some of the movies are so great (*Night of the Living Dead*, in retrospect, is exactly the sort of horror movie you'd expect from people that normally made commercials and safety films) and why many of them are so ... not awful, really, but almost inexplicable. What are we, as viewers, supposed to make of the likes of *Black Devil Doll from Hell* (1984), *Psycho from Texas* (1984), *Shriek of the Mutilated* (1974), *Janie* (1970), *Manos: The Hands of Fate* (1966), or the repulsive *555* (1988)? These films, in their own often awkward way, not only subvert our ideas about the genre, but the very notion of what a movie is.

That's a long-winded way of saying that I think filmmaking at this level is really folk art, in a way. Not that all of the films I'd classify as "regional" are necessarily primitive. There are plenty of polished, commercial films in this book, and there's definitely none of that "homemade" feel to the likes of *Alice, Sweet, Alice* (1976) or Frank LaLoggia's *Lady in White* (1988). These were professional films made by professional filmmakers, but they were still filmmakers who had to make their own way in an environment that was not always conducive to making a movie—which makes them, to put it in scientific terms, worthy of further study.

Most of these movies are triumphs of individual determination, completed and released despite financial hardship, technical difficulties, and a sometimes glaring lack of talent (or even basic competency) on the part of the filmmakers. That's why I can't watch something like *Satan's Children* (1975) or *Honeymoon Horror* (1982) without wondering, who were these people? Where did they come from? What were they thinking? How did these films ever get made?

Well, How Did These Films Get Made?

I'm about to launch into a truncated history of independent horror cinema, but before I do that I want to state for the record that I am fully aware that by starting this particular genre survey in 1958, I'm ignoring a significant chunk of that history. Thomas Edison, after all, got the ball rolling from his facilities in New Jersey and New York (where he produced an early version of *Frankenstein* in 1910), and plenty of films were made on the East Coast in the early days of cinema. Not to mention the local film clubs that sprang up across the country as soon as hobbyists could get their hands on camera equipment—many of these groups produced elaborate, sometimes feature-length projects, including a number of horror and science fiction films.

East meets West, with a notorious common tagline ("It's only a movie"): Texan S.F. Brownrigg's *Don't Look in the Basement* (1973) shares the bill with Wes Craven's Connecticut-lensed *Last House on the Left* (1972) (courtesy Fred Adelman).

And regional filmmaking was certainly not restricted to horror films. Earl Owensby, William Grefé and many of the other filmmakers profiled here made plenty of action films and car-chase comedies, and others around the U.S. mounted art films, dramas, safety and industrial films, and blaxploitation films, in addition to dabbling in other genres. Regional filmmaking encompasses a body of work that ranges from John Cassavetes' groundbreaking *Shadows* (1959) and the crude concoctions of Andy Warhol's Factory, to the subversive comedies of John Waters in Baltimore, Richard Linklater's Austin-based indies, and unclassifiable oddities like *Poor Pretty Eddie* (1975), a Georgia-lensed hixploitation film produced by a convicted murderer that featured the disparate talents of Leslie Uggams, Shelley Winters, Dub Taylor and Ted "Lurch" Cassidy.

Porn films, at least in the early days, were also a decidedly East Coast phenomenon before the adult film industry largely consolidated in Los Angeles. Thanks to free-flowing capital that was (allegedly) available from local criminal organizations, New York and Miami served as the smut nexus of the universe. Before hardcore, there were also hundreds of nudie cuties and roughies produced in New York and Florida, and quite a few of the filmmakers in this book (Andy Milligan, Lewis Jackson, Joel M. Reed, Doris Wishman, Roberta Findlay, Henri Pachard, Gerard Damiano) worked in both horror and adult films at one time or another.

Religious filmmaking also thrived during this period, and actually became one of the most vibrant DIY enterprises going at the time. Much like their counterparts in the porn industry (although I'm certain they wouldn't appreciate the comparison), Christian filmmakers created a production and distribution structure that existed completely independently of the mainstream movie industry, a system that has evolved, survived and thrived right up to the present day.

Independent film production companies (often associated with specific churches or evangelists) sprang up all over the country and distributed their films directly to churches through a network of Christian film libraries. Home video effectively killed this distribution method in the 1980s, but religious filmmaking has since grown into a multi-billion-dollar industry.

There was even some crossover between the religious and horror genres. The filmmakers behind *The Blob*, for instance, operated the religious filmmaking company Good News Productions, and exploitation vet Ron Ormond's *If Footmen Tire You, What Will Horses Do?* (1971) and *The Burning Hell* (1974) are two of the most off-the-rails religious films ever made.

Horror films, though, were the big regional money makers drawing crowds to local drive-ins and neighborhood theaters. And from the early 1960s into the mid-1980s there was a significant increase in the number of independently produced films in general (and horror films specifically) made in the U.S. because of a confluence of social and economic conditions that made it attractive for investors to finance these movies, and profitable for exhibitors to show them.

The first was the Paramount Decision of 1948, in which the Supreme Court held that movie studios that owned their own theater chains were violating anti-trust laws. The major studios were forced to divest themselves of their theaters (a process that was drawn out over much of the following decade), which had several significant effects on the industry. First, the studios began charging higher rental fees to theater owners for their films. Second, because the studios could no longer block book their product into their own theaters, they began making fewer, but more expensive, films. According to *The History of American Cinema*, production hit an all-time low (of 143 films) in 1963.

As the studios reduced the number of films made each year, they shifted some production overseas (where fewer unions and generous government subsidies helped further reduce costs), and served increasingly as distribution companies rather than production studios. At the same time, television (and other factors) led to a precipitous decline in movie attendance.

Since the studios were hanging their fortunes on a smaller and smaller number of blockbusters, all released to coincide with peak attendance seasons, independent theater owners were left with fewer options. As some of these theaters changed double features three or even four times per week, there weren't enough first or second-run studio films available to meet demand.

This was the void that American International Pictures and its competitors were created to fill. The independent production and distribution companies that sprang up in Hollywood and elsewhere in the late 1950s and early 1960s existed primarily to provide a steady stream of films to theaters struggling to fill screens *and* seats. Genre pictures drew crowds.

Many distributors and exhibitors, in fact, began bankrolling their own films (Joy Houck in New Orleans is a good example). In some states, resources already existed that encouraged independent filmmaking — a thriving television production industry in Florida, for example, or the presence of the NYU Film School (and a lot of out-of-work actors) in New York. In Utah and Texas, where a combination of picturesque scenery and anti-union/right-to-work laws drew film crews from Hollywood, professional production facilities and film laboratories (like Jamieson Film Company in Dallas) sprang up to help serve the out-of-towners, and spawned a local film industry in the process.

That takes care of the "demand" side of the equation. But in order for filmmakers, particularly independent filmmakers, to churn out enough product to meet that demand, they had to have access to capital. And at this point, I think it will be helpful to take a brief and hopefully painless detour into the history of the U.S. Tax Code.

Death and Taxes

Investing in a film is a risky proposition. There's no guarantee it will make a profit, or even get distributed. For independent features, the risks are even greater.

There was a time, however, when thousands of doctors, lawyers, dentists, grocers, real estate speculators and other people with access to large amounts of ready cash were lining up to hand their money to independent movie producers, thanks to amendments made to the tax code in 1963 that provided considerable write-offs for film production.

Prior to 1976, film investors could write down losses against income that were several times greater than their original investment. As Harold L. Vogel tells it in *Entertainment Industry Economics* (page 110), since the deductions and credits available were based on figures greater than the actual amount invested, these investors could "experience the fun and ego gratification of sponsoring movies and receive a tax benefit to boot."

Under a typical scenario, a producer would put together a partnership, and line up investors willing to provide around 25 percent of the budget in cash. The remainder of the budget would come through a non-recourse loan from a bank.

If an investor put up $25,000, he could deduct interest on his portion of the loan, and take an investment tax credit and a depreciation write-off on his share of the movie — which for tax purposes would be figured at $100,000 (the actual investment, plus his share of the loan). The write-offs in the first year could eliminate taxes on a significant portion of the investor's regular income. If a film lost money, the investors could write off "paper losses" via accelerated depreciation.

According to an article in *Time* magazine that appeared on January 19, 1976, six-figure professionals (especially doctors) were pumping as much as $1 billion per year into movie-related tax shelters, partly financing more than half of all the films shown in the U.S. And these weren't just cheap horror and action films — movies like *Shampoo* (1975), *Chinatown*

(1974) and *The Great Gatsby* (1974) benefited from tax shelter investors as well. But these tax shelters were especially important for regional films, since those productions depended almost entirely on the largess of local investors.

The good times couldn't last forever, though. The Tax Reform Act of 1976 placed new limits and requirements on the types of tax shelters used for film production through "at-risk" rules that limited individuals from claiming losses for some investments for which they had limited economic risk. The noose tightened again with the Revenue Act of 1978, which extended the at-risk rules.

This whole system of finance came crashing down with the Tax Reform Act of 1986 when the tax code was revised once again, effectively eliminating film investment tax credits. With the end of those generous write-offs, the era of indie horror films bankrolled by attorneys, grocers and insurance salesmen was over.

There were other factors at work, too. Independent film production crested from 1973 to 1977, then began a steady decline brought on by rising production costs (the average negative cost increased by 450 percent between 1972 and 1979), the crackdown on personal tax shelters, and the major studios releasing their own exploitation-style films. Exhibitors also began to consolidate, large chains like AMC became the dominant players in the theater industry, and the independent sub-distributors and exhibitors (who were more open to handling low-budget films) closed down.

This double-whammy of economic and distribution changes sent the indies into a long death spiral. By the early 1980s, companies like AIP, Film Ventures, Dimension, Fanfare, Independent International and others were either out of business or no longer distributing films theatrically. In July 1981, *Variety* noted that independent feature film production had dropped off by 16 percent in the preceding 12 months, reaching its lowest point since 1970.

That might have been the end of things, but some new technology was about to offer low-budget filmmakers a much-needed lifeline.

Video Violence

Theatrical distribution all but vanished for low-budget exploitation films by the mid–1980s, but like the zombies that frequently populated these movies, regional horror films were hard to kill. In fact, the brave new world of home video distribution helped them survive right on into the new millennium.

As the home video market took off in the early 1980s, distributors and video stores were hungry for new product to fill their shelves, and many otherwise forgotten horror films began turning up on VHS. Older titles like *Blood Feast, Don't Look in the Basement* and *God's Bloody Acre* found whole new audiences on home video (and probably did more business on tape than many of them ever did theatrically). Newer films that might have been released to theaters in the past were dumped into the fledgling direct-to-video market. (Such was the fate of William Wesley's quirky *Scarecrows*, for example.) And low-budget movies were increasingly made specifically for home video.

While all this was happening, there was a revolution going on in video cameras. In 1982, Sony released its first professional Betacam camcorder, followed in 1983 by a consumer grade model. JVC jumped into the market not long afterward.

For the first time, consumers were able to make home movies without the hassle of handling and developing film stock, which was becoming an increasingly costly process.

This opened up a whole new world of possibilities, and amateur filmmakers (and pornographers) across the country were quick to take notice. Anyone with a decent camcorder could now make a horror film, and as long as it had plenty of gore and made a marginal amount of sense, they actually stood a good chance of having it distributed nationally.

Thus was born the shot-on-video (SOV) horror film. One of the first of these films was *Boardinghouse* (1982), a bizarre slasher film that was actually screened theatrically at one point. *Boardinghouse* was followed by David A. Prior's *Sledgehammer* (1983), but it was United Home Video's *Blood Cult* (1985) that really opened the floodgates. *Blood Cult* was touted as the "first movie made for the home video market." It wasn't, but this Betacam epic was a rental hit and spawned several similar titles from United, as well as a burgeoning underground of camcorder films that included Gary Cohen's *Video Violence* (1987), the Polonia Brothers' *Splatter Farm* (1987), Wally Koz's *555*, the delirious *Black Devil Doll from Hell*, *Woodchipper Massacre* (1988) and hundreds (thousands?) of others.

These shot-on-video films, as well as their more professionally mounted direct-to-video counterparts, were made by a new generation of DIY filmmakers who had been inspired by watching either George Romero or Sam Raimi films. Armed with high-end video equipment, amateur actors, battered copies of Tom Savini's *Grande Illusions* or *Dick Smith's Do-It-Yourself Monster Make-Up Book*, and a sometimes over-inflated sense of their own talent, they unleashed a horde of Romero-esque zombie flicks, slasher knock-offs and other oddities that often confused and vexed unwary renters.

The filmmakers who arrived on the scene in the 1980s were a much different breed than their predecessors in the '60s and '70s, who had largely been journeyman directors or hucksters looking to make a fast buck. Most of the newbies were fans first, and approached their projects with a self-conscious enthusiasm absent from the older films. Filmmakers like J.R. Bookwalter in Ohio, Don Dohler in Maryland, Donald Farmer in Tennessee, Tim Ritter in Florida, Todd Sheets in Missouri, Brett Piper in New Hampshire, and the Polonia Brothers in Pennsylvania formed a loosely organized community that published their own fanzines, swapped tapes at horror conventions, and slammed each other in the *Fangoria* letters pages.

Although the filmmakers' hearts may have been in the right place, the flood of cheap horror films that hit the market during the video era was a mixed bag. Technology had now democratized the filmmaking process, but in many ways it marginalized the films themselves.

From a technical standpoint, shot-on-video films just didn't look very good. At their best, the picture in these SOV flicks was on the level of a daytime soap or a local newscast; at their worst, they looked kind of like that footage Uncle Murray took of your high school graduation.

More significantly, most of the films were just crap — and crap of the highest order, at that. The scripts were bad, the acting was bad, the lighting was bad. Where most of them did succeed, though, was in the special effects department. What these filmmakers lacked in artistry, they made up for in enthusiasm for blood and guts, and the gorier the film, the more attention it was destined to receive among fans and collectors.

After 1990, the number of SOV films exploded as camcorder prices dropped and new digital video recording technology was introduced. Backyard filmmakers (part of what is sometimes referred to as the microcinema movement) turned to self-distribution, hawking their films in magazine ads, at conventions, and (later) over the Internet.

While the pool of potential filmmakers got larger, the audience for these films got smaller. J.R. Bookwalter, who made a number of shot-on-video films in the 1990s, points out later in the book that as time went on, the audience for his films was increasingly made up of other people who also wanted to make shot-on-video horror films — a niche audience, indeed.

That's the primary reason I've chosen to end the book in 1990. In the 1990s, economic and distribution models changed significantly, and the glut of movies produced after that point has been so large that sifting through them would probably take another lifetime and a boatload of patience. Suffice it to say that there is still a thriving community of regional horror filmmakers, but the way they make and distribute their movies, by and large, is fundamentally different than anything described in these pages.

How to Use This Book

I have arranged *Regional Horror Films* into two parts. The first is a collection of interviews with directors and producers who made independent horror films during the period in question. I've tried to provide a good cross-section by selecting filmmakers diverse in chronology, geography, and biography. Thus, I've included Texan Russ Marker (who worked primarily in the 1960s) and Ohioan J.R. Bookwalter (who began his career in the 1980s); Louisiana native Albert Salzer and New Yorker Ed Adlum; and professional filmmaker William Grefé along with school teacher Robert Burrill.

Others I included simply because I really wanted to know more about them and their films, like Bigfoot researcher-turned-filmmaker Robert W. Morgan, or Tom Rahner, producer of *The Brides Wore Blood* (1972), a film I've seen more times than I could ever hope to justify.

The second part is a state-by-state guide to independent, regional horror films made between 1958 and 1990. To be included, the films had to be made outside of California; be produced independently of a major studio; and primarily have a local cast and crew.

Careful (and even not-so-careful) readers will note that I've played fast and loose with some of these rules. For one thing, I've included some films that were clearly financed by distributors like Troma, Hallmark and Independent-International. My rationalization there is that all of those companies were headquartered outside of California, and they were (mostly) much smaller operations than their Hollywood counterparts like AIP and Film Ventures.

A more glaring exception would be the made-for-TV horror films that Larry Buchanan made for AIP in the 1960s. These were clearly financed by an outside party and were only distributed to the small screen, but I've made room for them here because they represent the bulk of Buchanan's genre output, and with the exception of a couple of cast members, they were made entirely by Texans. (I'm justifying the inclusion of William Girdler's *Abby*, also financed by AIP, the same way. Plus, how could I *not* include *Abby*?)

I've also let a few runaway productions slide by, too, like the Illinois filmmakers who shot *Homebodies* in Cincinnati, or the folks from Jersey who shot *Track of the Moon Beast* in New Mexico. In a few cases, the genealogy of these films is a little unclear, so I've tried to err on the side of inclusiveness, figuring it would be a greater sin to leave something out than to put something in that might not belong.

I also struggled with whether or not to include any regional films from California. I know, I know — the whole point of the book is that these movies were made *outside* of California. But there were a host of films made in the Golden State in the 1970s and 1980s that certainly qualify as regional productions — the San Francisco-lensed films of Nick Millard (*Criminally Insane*, 1974; *Satan's Black Wedding*, 1975) immediately come to mind. However, trying to sort out which California films could be classified as "regional" would have muddied the already murky waters I'm wading through, so I left them out.

BUT: I just couldn't resist covering *one* California film, so I included an interview with Robert Burrill, the high school teacher who made a cheap-but-charming (to me, anyway) movie called *The Milpitas Monster* with the help of his photography students, their parents, the mayor, half the residents of Milpitas, California, the guy who did sound effects for *Star Wars*, and Tennessee Ernie Ford. *The Milpitas Monster*, whether you find it entertaining or not, is probably the best example of exactly the type of filmmaking this book is about. It wasn't just a regional horror film; it was a *community* horror film.

As for the listings themselves, I've included a basic synopsis, along with information and trivia about the films and/or the filmmakers. I've tried to take a "just the facts" approach here, but oh, those slippery facts.

Although we live in the information age, I've been surprised, frustrated and confounded at how *little* information is available on some of the films, and how unreliable much of the available history can be. I have read over and over and over again that *Manos: The Hands of Fate* director/star Harold Warren was a fertilizer salesman, but when I looked up the fairly voluminous newspaper accounts of the film's production and premiere in El Paso, I was surprised to find that he was actually referred to multiple times as the manager of an insurance company. (Please insert your own joke about insurance and manure here.)

I have tried to answer as many questions as I can in the limited space available, confirmed some legends and debunked a few others. Where question marks remain, I've acknowledged them. This is as accurate a portrayal of who made these films and, in some cases, why, as I could assemble. Is everything that follows 100 percent true? I think so, but if Harold P. Warren of El Paso, Texas, didn't really hawk fertilizer for a living, then I guess anything is possible.

One thing you won't find are actual reviews, something I avoid for a number of reasons. For one, I'm horrible at writing reviews. I've tried my hand at capsule reviews before, and they generally stink. And in this day and age, capsule reviews of old horror movies are a dime a dozen. There are thousands (possibly millions at this point) of Web sites of varying quality dedicated to the artless art of film criticism. In addition to the professional and amateur Web sites, there is the bottomless pit of bloviating on the Internet Movie Database, where users can comment on and argue about these films, in addition to hopelessly muddling their credits through incessant updating. Occasionally, the filmmakers themselves (or their children, or nieces and nephews, or next door neighbors) chime in, too. I have no interest in adding to the din. If you want to know whether or not *Redneck Zombies* (1987) is a good movie, go to Google. Better yet, watch it and decide for yourself.

If a movie is particularly boring or bad, I've tried to point that out so that you don't waste too much of your precious time. But frankly, the older I've gotten, the less inclined I am to trash old movies, particularly those of the distinctly hand-made variety.

There's another reason I avoid reviewing the films, and I might as well come clean now: I have not seen all of them. That's not entirely surprising since a handful of them are lost, a few have never been released legitimately on video, and others have been out of print for years (in some cases, decades) and are difficult to come by unless you want to pay $130 for a used VHS tape on eBay.

I *have* seen about 75 percent of them, which I think isn't too bad. Since I made the decision early on that I was primarily going to catalog the films rather than review them, I didn't feel any particular pressure to watch all of them. In some cases I worked very hard to watch the films I hadn't seen; others I deliberately avoided because I simply couldn't bear watching the complete *oeuvre* of every one of these directors.

What I really wanted to create with this book was a primer; a guidebook to map out some otherwise poorly documented genre acreage. Each of you is going to pick and choose which twisted paths to follow, just as I have. You may be satisfied merely with the knowledge that there is a shot-on-video movie called *Copperhead* (1983), and that it was made in Missouri by a professional photographer who once wrote a book called *The Insiders' Guide to Branson & the Ozark Mountains*. Or you may feel compelled to spend 90 minutes on *Copperhead*, and if that is the case then I say go forth, young adventurer, and when you are done report what you've seen to the rest of us.

One of my hopes for this book is that it will spur enough interest in these films and their creators that others might help clarify the boundaries of exactly what a regional horror film is (or isn't). I've likely included a few movies some readers will feel I should have left out, and omitted a few that should have been included. I'm open to suggestions, and I'm fairly easy to find online, so please let me know if I've made an egregious error, and I'll be sure to make corrections in any future editions.

(I have, in fact, set up a blog at *regionalhorrorfilms.blogspot.com*, where I've been posting some of the original research material that I used for this book, along with video clips, photos and other random bits of information. If you have thoughts on the project, complaints, or information to relay, that's the best place for it.)

I also hope the book will jog a few memories, and we can yet discover a few more forgotten oddities. One of the great joys of working on this project has been learning about some of the more obscure titles, and I'm proud to say this is the first print reference work (as far as I know) to include entries for *Demon from Devil's Lake* (1964), *The Beast from the Beginning of Time* (1965), *Silent Death* (1983), *Southern Shockers* (1985) and *The Hackers* (1988), films I'd certainly never heard of until I started my research.

It's kind of amazing, when you think about it, that with hundreds of published reference books and the seemingly bottomless pit of obscuria on the Internet, that there are *still* hidden or lost films from the latter part of the twentieth century floating around out there. We may yet shake some loose. George Barry's *Death Bed: The Bed That Eats* (1977) seemed like a weird message from another planet, transmitted via European bootleggers, until Barry himself was finally able to release his sole feature film on DVD in 2003. When I contacted Joel Sanderson at *The Basement Sublet of Horror* about *The Beast from the Beginning of Time*, he told me that while sifting through Herk Harvey's film archives he stumbled across footage for an unfinished film called *The Reluctant Witch*. And you can imagine my surprise and delight when someone overseas sent me a copy of *Southern Shockers*, a Mississippi film only released on tape in Spain, which I was then able to share with some of the filmmakers — several of whom had never even seen a complete cut of the movie. Who knows what else is collecting dust in the closets and garages of America?

It Takes a Village of the Damned

I've been speaking in the past tense a lot, but I'm well aware that the regional filmmaking movement has expanded probably a thousand-fold since 1990, in large part because of the availability of cheap digital video equipment. In fact, we may be poised to enter a new golden age of low-budget filmmaking in which moviemakers with a good idea, a decent camera, and high-speed Internet access can reach a mass audience.

In 2009, a film called *Paranormal Activity*, produced for $15,000 in the San Diego home of director/producer Oren Peli, was picked up by Paramount and received a nationwide theatrical release based, in part, on a viral marketing campaign very similar to the one that turned the $60,000 shot-in-Maryland flick *The Blair Witch Project* (1999) into a multi-million-dollar hit. Peli's film, likewise, grossed millions and prompted a sequel with a significantly higher budget. So it is still possible for one of these (literally, in this case) homegrown flicks to break into the corporate-controlled distribution system. None of these films may turn out to be the next *Texas Chain Saw Massacre*, but they might at least be the next *Alice, Sweet, Alice* or *Carnival of Souls*, or even the next *Black Devil Doll from Hell*, for that matter.

State governments, desperate for any sort economic stimulus, have also begun establishing new tax incentives targeted at bringing Hollywood production crews to places like New Mexico and Ohio. These programs are also helping local filmmakers via direct financial aid, and by providing opportunities to work with pros when they blow in to town to shoot something like, say, *Spiderman 3* (2007) in Cleveland.

My own home state of Ohio has seen an uptick in low-budget horror production lately, including everything from the goofy killer turkey film *Thankskilling* (2009), made for $3,500 in Newark, to Ohio native Rob Kurtzman's decidedly more elaborate *The Rage* (2007). Both of these films were widely distributed on DVD and on cable (and in the case of *The Rage*, even theatrically).

Of course, there are just as many films that don't make it past a few courtesy viewings by friends and family, or maybe a YouTube post, and some don't ever escape their directors' hard drives. Are these movies, which sometimes literally play to an audience of twenty or ten or two, something less than real films? Maybe, but that's not necessarily the point any more.

Bad local movies are kind of like bad local theater; they are more of a means to an end. I've seen a lot of crappy community theater, but the fact that the actors stink or the sets fall over doesn't mean the experience was any less fun for the people putting the play together, or the audience who came to cheer on their friends, neighbors and family members. In other words, the quality of the art is less important than the participatory nature of the medium. Local films, even awful ones, are a community building exercise, even if you're just talking about a community of people in your town who like scary movies.

It can be more than that, too. After Robert Burrill released *The Milpitas Monster*, he attempted to publish a book about the experience, and about the notion of community filmmaking. I thought a lot about my conversation with Burrill one hot September afternoon when I spent the day at a park here in Columbus, Ohio, watching a crew of local filmmakers prepare to film a bunch of undead pre-teens attacking an ice cream man for a (still uncompleted) zombie movie called *Book of the Dead*. As the crew waited for the arrival of a dilapidated ice cream truck donated by a local car dealership, and the special effects guy patiently stirred a five-gallon bucket of fake blood, dozens of kids in zombie make-up sat in the picnic shelter with their parents, having snacks and sucking down sodas. It looked like a family reunion gone horribly awry.

"It was all based on community involvement, and being in the position of a school teacher, it really became a model of cooperation — civic cooperation between the city and

The Milpitas Monster greets a gaggle of school children in 1976 (courtesy Robert Burrill).

the community," Burrill told me. I think it's that sense of community that has drawn me back to these films — as awful as some of them are — again and again. Whether that "community" was a literal one (Milpitas) or a community of horror film fans (the films of Don Dohler) or even just a community of yahoos drinking Black Label beer and making it up as they went along (I'm looking at you, *Invasion of the Blood Farmers*), you can catch glimpses of those moments when everyone pulled together to make a little movie magic.

That's what I'd like to see more of in modern regional horror films — a little magic, a little community spirit, a chicken in every pot, and a horror movie in every town. Is that too much to ask?

Now that we've reached the end of all the introductory jibber jabber, it's time for the fun part — the movies. So prepare yourself for a panoply of paranormal terrors the likes of which have seldom been seen in the annals of horror; a mad menagerie of bigfeet, blood farmers, giant crabs, giant spiders, moonbeasts, mutilators, maniacs, devil worshippers, devil dolls, deaf vampires, vampire cops, death beds, camping cannibals, cannibal mothers, kung fu gorillas, psychos in love, toxic children, toxic zombies, zombie rampages, jellyfish monsters, nasty nutriamen, bloody horrors, blood circuses, barbaric beasts, bog monsters, beast creatures and boogens. And like the man said, if you have a heart condition, or you are easily upset ... I think you know what to do.

Part I • The Interviews

Harvesting the Dead
ED ADLUM
New York

Movies with audacious titles seldom deliver on their lurid promises, but *Invasion of the Blood Farmers* (1972) is a rare, happy exception — there are farmers, they *do* harvest blood, and technically, they stage an invasions of sorts, even if it doesn't progress much beyond a few split-level homes in Westchester County, New York. Originally, the blood farmers were supposed to be aliens, but the low-budget precluded the building of a space ship, so they were turned into Druids, who (as everyone knows) are much less ambitious.

Not so for the film's producer, Bronx-born Ed Adlum. Before *Blood Farmers* came into his life, Adlum had recorded a minor novelty song with his band, The Castle Kings, had worked as an editor for *Cashbox* magazine, and was already on his way to establishing a lengthy and successful career in the publishing industry.

Adlum's first foray into film was *Blonde on a Bum Trip* (1968), which he co-produced with Jack Bravman. A few years later, he teamed up with playwright and journalist Ed Kelleher, corralled a cast of theater students, along with New York's reigning first family of porn at the time, Mike and Roberta Findlay, and churned out *Blood Farmers* over several weekends and numerous cases of beer.

The same team returned a few years later for *Shriek of the Mutilated* (1974), which unlike their prior effort, promised much but delivered very little — despite the potentially volatile mix of Bigfoot and cannibalism. Both films received limited theatrical distribution, but (because of their lurid titles) were staples of late-night TV and video store shelves for years.

Adlum, by that point, had had enough of the film industry. He later split from *Cashbox* to start his own trade magazine, *Replay*, which he still publishes today. He spoke to me from his offices in California.

Did you grow up on the East Coast?

Yeah. I was born in the Bronx and grew up there. I got married after the Army. I got married in my mid-20s and moved to Westchester County. In 1974, I relocated to California, where I've been ever since. But it was while we were in Westchester County that I made the movies.

You were in a band called The Castle Kings, which performed "You Can Get Him Frankenstein."

I started that band with a fellow named Jimmy Walker when we were young. We added two other guys, a guitar and piano. We were very lucky. While trying to get a contract with

Dot Records, which was in business in those days, we were walking down 57th street in New York on our way to Dot, and we were singing this song, "You Can Get Him Frankenstein," that we had created ourselves. A bald-headed guy with glasses and a beard stopped us and said he liked the song. Would we come up to his place of business the following day and sing it to his associate? The man we were speaking to was Ahmet Ertegun, arguably the most important person in rock and roll. The guy he wanted us to sing it for was his protégé, Phil Spector. We did, and we recorded it. It went nowhere. We did another tune for them, the old army hymn, "The Caisson Song," and that went nowhere. Ahmet sent us a little letter saying that he was not renewing our contract. That's when I went in the Army and Jimmy Walker went and joined a group called The Knickerbockers, and they *did* have a hit called "Lies." That busted up and Jimmy ended up as one of the Righteous Brothers when the original two boys parted company. The last I heard he's up in Napa Valley now, and he's still working Holiday Inns with some band he created.

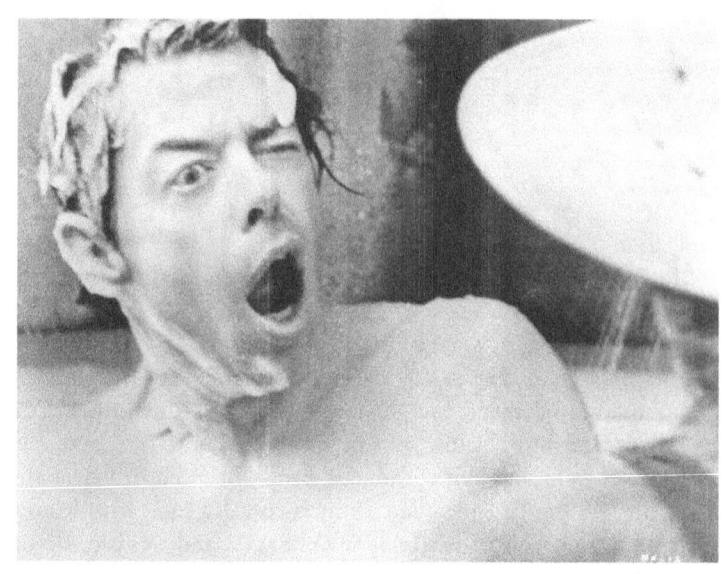

Producer Ed Adlum also doubled as the shower victim in *Invasion of the Blood Farmers* (1972) (courtesy Ed Adlum).

I've actually got a copy of the Frankenstein song on a CD compilation.

[Laughs.] At the end of the record, we go, "Frankenstein, Frankenstein, bring me back that girl of mine." And a voice says, "Hey Frankenstein, bring me back that girl of mine." That's Phil Spector. The original idea was that at the end of that, Ahmet Ertegun would say, "No," but he never did it.

It was great fun. But it was too much, too soon. We never had the talent to warrant a gig like a contract with Atlantic Records, which was hot-to-trot with so many rock and roll acts. All killers, too. It was a very laid back music-making kind of an organization. Very comfortable. But we were very childish, very undisciplined and very untalented. What happened to us — namely "Go away and don't come back" — was exactly what *should* have happened to us.

As history goes, though, I bought a copy of *Cashbox* magazine during that period, and after the Army I hit the streets looking for a gig and ended up taking one with *Cashbox* magazine. The fact that I had a copy of it seemed to impress the guy who was looking for help. He invited me down — this was in 1964 — and he said, "The job we're looking to fill is about pinball machines and juke boxes." I said I had noticed that little section in the back, and he said they needed somebody to help do that. That was in the spring of 1964, and that's what I've been doing ever since [*laughs*]. But of course, I did go the high road in 1975. I started my own publication for that business, which is called *Replay*.

Did you have any publishing background before *Cashbox*?

I studied journalism at Fordham College. I have a degree in that. Probably one of the few guys that came out of that school that went into the trade they studied for. I think that's the rule in any college. The genius in our class was guy named Denny Azzarella, who was in Fordham on a scholarship. He was a friend of mine who was, in fact, on the Frankenstein record blowing the saxophone. Denny was a boy genius out of Jersey City, and he got a scholarship to UCLA film school right out of Fordham. Then he got a gig with David Wolper Productions right out of UCLA. He was a top producer there for a year or two. He got killed while they were making a series called "Primal Man." He and his crew were in a plane up in Bishop, California, and the plane went down. He was killed. He was still in his twenties. He worked under the name of Denny Ross. I guess the titles were too expensive to write out Azzarella!

Did you meet Jack Bravman through *Cashbox*?

No, I knew Jackie prior to *Cashbox*. I worked for six months at *LOOK* magazine when it was in business. That would have been 1962. I started there in March, then I went in the National Guard for six months. Jackie was like me, working in the mailroom. Jackie had never heard of the idea of making movies until he met me. We chatted, and I told him that my dream was to make pictures. I got him interested. I don't if this is good bad or what, but Jackie's interest in film tended toward the kind of thing that was showing on 42nd Street in those days. Not me. My sensibilities were a little too strong for that. But Jackie was my friend. What had happened — and the place in time is difficult, but it was somewhere in the mid-1960s — Jackie got some money to do a picture, which he called *Sex in the Acid Bath*. He said to me, "Can you help?"

I said, "No. Are you kidding me?" A couple of months later he came back and said, "Look Eddie, we're not able to do this. We need your help." Which I found interesting, because I'd never made a picture! I said, "I will do it if you take the sex out of it and change that name." I rewrote the script, took out all the stuff I found objectionable. Instead of *Sex in the Acid Bath*, I named it *Blonde on a Bum Trip* (1968), which I thought was a pretty cool title.

We made this picture in black and white, and it was foul. Jackie said there was only one way to rescue this, and that was to put some inserts in there. I said, "That's terrific, but you can do that without me." My name is still on that picture, and it did play the 42nd Street circuit for a bit. Of course, there's no money it. I don't know what ever happened to it. I've never known.

Let's put it this way: after that rather shameful exercise in filmmaking, I wrote a script with a guy that was working for me at *Cashbox* at that time. His name was Eddie Kelleher. Eddie and I wrote this thing called *Invasion of the Blood Farmers*. The reason that I wanted to do this was because my good friend Ralphie Mauro, who was a struggling actor, perfectly fit the lead bad guy in that picture, a character I called Creton. Oddly enough, I never even approached Ralphie because he had gone to California. But Jackie and I got together, and he helped me produce that first picture. When it was all over, he said he would edit. When it came time to edit, I found out Jackie didn't know how to edit a picture. But what Jackie *did* do was introduce me to a guy named Mike Findlay.

Michael was to movies what Denny Azzarella was to television — a budding genius whose life was cut short. Michael and I spent a lot more time together than I ever spent with Denny. Michael was a consummate moviemaker, in that he was a guy who knew how to find raw film under a rock [*laughs*]. Who knew how to rent equipment for a dollar-ninety-eight that other people were paying ten thousand dollars for. Who knew technicians who knew all of the underside of the business, so to speak. I'm not talking illegal or anything like that. But Michael made porn.

Porn and horror, and even *Lawrence of Arabia*, are all basically the same exercise. You put people in front of a camera, you put film in the camera, and you push the button. Okay? I had made *Blood Farmers*, and needless to say he came in and saved the picture. I was so grateful to him. I said, "Mike, I'm gonna make a picture with you." I brought him up to the *Cashbox* offices on Broadway, and I got on the phone with some of my jukebox operator friends, and I raised money. I got Eddie Kelleher to write a thing called *Shriek of the Mutilated*, which was a total piece of crap. But we made it, and it was so bad I sold it. I think we made $12,000 on that picture. I sold it outright to a guy, interplanetary rights. I said, "I don't care what you do with it! Take it away, Jose!"

He did, and Michael was so angry with me for not consulting him on the sale of the picture that he never spoke to me again. That's true to this day, because several years went on with that Mexican standoff, and then I read in the *New York Times* that he had been killed on the top of the Pan Am building. It was the only time I cried over someone who died, and that includes my parents, sorry to say.

Why were you and Kelleher talking about doing a horror film in the first place?

Well, when you're sitting in the same office in a weekly magazine, you share a lot of stuff. Eddie had written a couple of scripts that were produced as off-Broadway plays. Of course, I'm telling him about this script I'm writing called *Invasion of the Blood Farmers*. Eddie and I started going desk to desk, coming up with zany ideas, basically laughing and having a good time. It's not a long stretch from that to, "Hey Ed, why don't we get together and knock this puppy out?" And we did — at my house over lots of Budweiser, by the way. I lived in Yorktown Heights, up in Westchester County, New York. I think in two weekends we had it done, and finished a couple of cases of beer in the process.

I brought it back to *Cashbox*, typed it up all nice and clean looking. Up comes a guy who was in the jukebox business called Mickey Greenman, who said, "Do you mind if I look at that?" A couple of days later Mickey called me up and said, "Listen, my boss would like to help you out making that picture. He'll put in $4,000." And we were on our way. I called up a few other people, got the money together. Eddie and Jackie Bravman, as I told you, were helping me. We got a crew together. We used that house of mine up there in Westchester County as the principal set.

That little white house was where I lived with my wife and two kids. All that woods up there is an hour north of New York City. We made it, and the rest is history.

It's interesting that that picture is kind of like a cult thing today. I certainly didn't start out to make a cult thing. You can't create camp. That one worked. It was so bad it's funny. It's like *Plan 9*. It's one of those great, bad pictures. *Shriek of the Mutilated* is one of those *bad* bad pictures. It should be burned. But the *Blood Farmers* is a monument to ineptitude, and I love to watch it. I can almost quote every line in that film, and I practically pee uncontrollably when that shit comes on the screen. I think it's funnier than hell!

How did you come up with the concept? Weren't they supposed to come from space?

The original idea was that the planet Hyanus had lost its sun, and therefore [*laughs*] the food supply was drying up. The leader of Hyanus (who was to be my friend Ralphie, a.k.a.

Creton), he and his boys get together and take their space ship to Earth in search of their fresh food supply, which — drumroll! — they find in human blood. That's the original idea. That was the script.

Now, fast forward a couple of months. We're now filming the very first weekend. At the end of the very first weekend, we shot this, that and the other thing, and I said to myself, "Eddie [*laughs*] there ain't no way we're gonna have the money to do this outer space stuff. We're gonna have to change the script." I grabbed a book called *The Black Arts*. I had it in my basement — this is an absolutely true story — and I'm leafing through it looking for ideas, keeping in mind what we'd already filmed.

I come across a thing called "The Druids." On the very first page it says, "There's absolutely nothing known for sure about the practices of the ancient Druids." I slammed the book shut [*laughs*] and said, "Is that so!" I'm serious. "If that's true, I'm gonna make it up!" I looked at the script and underlined the stuff we'd filmed already, and looked at the stuff we didn't, and changed these guys from planet Hyanus people to Druids who were wandering the Earth in search of a blood supply to revive their dead queen.

Well, she wasn't dead, she was in this glass coffin. Nice lady, by the way. Cynthia Fleming. That thing was a gas chamber. When we turned on the lights, we had her covered with flowers. Let me tell you, flowers stink! Poor Cynthia was cooking in the flower box after ten minutes, and never complained [*laughs*]. There's a great scene at the end of *Blood Farmers* where we finally let her out of the coffin after we give her the re-agent or whatever. Oh yeah, Jenny's blood. It's a very confusing story! Anyway, old Cynthia comes rising out of the box ready to smite her enemies, and she really should have come out of that box with a gun looking to kill me for having tortured her. I'm not kidding. It was awful. Every time I yelled, "Cut," people were instructed to take the lid off that coffin and let some air in there. That woman was cookin'! She did a great job. Playing a dead body is not easy.

You asked a question about the script. I hope I answered it. I guess the answer to the question, "Eddie, what's this business about you starting with one script and ending with another?" is that I had to change mid-stream because there wasn't enough money in my budget, or expertise in my staff, to create the outer space sets and scenes and costumes we needed. I changed it to something we could handle, which was a story about ancient Druids who were still alive like vampires, roaming around Westchester County, New York, in search of blood to get their dead queen going again so that they could rule the world. Makes no sense to us, but all the sense in the world to the Druids.

Watching the film, it's hard to see how the cast got through some of that dialogue without cracking up.

You can thank Budweiser. Those guys stuck to the script except for one guy, Dick Erickson. He played a character called Kinski. He couldn't remember his lines. We had to write it on giant pieces of white board with magic marker. The cop would come in and say, "Oh, hello, I'm investigating some strange shit." And Dick Erickson, playing Kinski, would go, "Oh yeah? Like what?" And the cop goes, "What are you doing here?" And Kinski would go, "Well..." And then he'd absolutely turn his head and look at the cue card off screen instead of at the cop he was talking to. And he'd go, "At present, we're involved in the examination of nonferrous metal alloys, when they get bombed to shit by solar waves in the omega grouping." Every once in awhile he'd dart his eyes back to the cop to make it look like he was talking to him!

The best part of the *Blood Farmers* is the part you can't see. If you sat down with me,

I can point and show you where light cables are visible on the screen. I can show you where a can of Black Label beer is right there next to the pot of boiling blood. There is so much shit going on in that picture [*laughs*]. The doors that won't open, so there were people on the other side pushing them as guys would open them. Oh, we had a good time making it.

When I interviewed Jack Neubeck, who played the mute Druid, I told him he was lucky he didn't have to recite any of that dialogue.

Jack is another guy that should shoot me. I made him limp. Absolutely no reason to do that. Please don't ever tell him! It had nothing to do with the film at all. We even had him running through the woods with a limp. Running with a limp! It's not done. We were chasing him with the dog that he ended up killing and eating.

He said you had to put dog food on him to get the dog to chase him.

I think that's an exaggeration. That dog's name was Akita, I think. It was a great big white husky. He was just a friendly pooch. That was one of the jokes we came up with: if that dog won't chase you, Jack, we're gonna have to spray you with Kennel Ration. But we'd say, "Here Akita, here Akita." He's running with his tongue out. Everything's nice in doggy land. And then of course you cut to this white sheepskin rug that we had gotten and stuffed with newspaper, which Jack ate and beat the crap out of. It was the end of the dog.

I didn't know how to end the picture. They said, "Bring the friggin' dog back." Because the dog had his blood drained, I had to replace the dog. I called a pet shop and said, "Do you rent dogs?" [*Laughs*] They said, "What?" I had a friend, who had a white poodle. "Can I borrow it?" That's the dog at the end of the picture. The dog's name was Fluffy, by the way.

What did your neighbors think of all of this?

They loved it. They're all in the picture. None of them could act. The cop was my next-door neighbor, Frank.

I wanted to know where he came from. He's a county sheriff, but he sounds like he just stepped off a subway in the Bronx.

Yeah. Frank Iovieno. [*In deep voice*] You know he worked for the phone company. I said, "Frank, I need you to play the cop." Poor Frankie took it all very seriously. He did. I told him to talk a little gruffer. And it didn't make sense because some of the lines of dialogue stuck into his mouth just didn't fit. But the saddest part of it was at the screening. I invited Frank and his wife and all his sisters and shit, they all come down. I had relatives of my own that came down from Brooklyn. It was really a mob scene when we showed this picture. Every time he came on the screen, people busted out laughing. He was terribly offended.

He said, "Why are they laughing at me?" I said, "Well, I didn't tell you, but it was a comedy role." He bought that. Then he said, "You think talent scouts and other people will see this and find me?" I said, "Maybe, Frank." I'm thinking there ain't nobody gonna buy this picture, Frank! I'm running away to Brazil [*laughs*]!

But Frank was cool. He worked on it. The funny part — I could talk forever about this picture, but I'll tell you this one more thing since you brought up Frank. We had another shot to do with Frank in it, and Frank had to go to a barbeque. I looked at the script and said there was only one thing we could do. I said, "Frank, we're gonna have to kill you!" So he says, "Okay, make it quick."

The advertisements for *Shriek of the Mutilated* (1974) gave away the film's "surprise" ending involving an "evil cannibal cult" (courtesy Ed Adlum).

And we killed him. He was walking in that little house. That was Jackie Bravman, by the way, in the black hood coming up with the hypodermic needle. He stuck it in poor Frank's back. And Frank died, then got in his car and went to his barbeque. He had some more stuff to do in that picture, but you can't keep the ribs waiting!

By the time you made the film, had you already talked to anyone about distribution?

Not until it was over. There were some obvious guys in those days, like Avco-Embassy, that handled crap. Semi-crap. I shouldn't say crap. A few other companies. Independents, people that put out blood pictures and stuff. I showed it to a bunch of guys, and people looked and said, "What, are you nuts?" One of them didn't, a guy named Nick Demetroules. If you want to know the truth, I wish he would have told me to go away. It was not a good relationship. But at least Nick did get it up on the screen and around the country.

I think he had something of a reputation in the industry.

Well, it's news to me. I don't know. He was Jerry Gross's partner.

What do you know about Jackie Bravman? Is he dead? Some of his films have turned up from Something Weird Video.

Some of that stuff has shown up. In fact, *Blonde on a Bum Trip*. But I don't know if he's still around or not. I'd heard that he died. I think Eddie Kelleher is dead.

I was trying to find Kelleher for an interview when he died.

What's interesting is when I've seen this on the Web, they say Ed Kelleher was my *nome de plume* and that *I* was dead. I got a call from an old friend of mine. He said, "You're alive!" I said, "Leslie, what the hell are you talking about?" "Somebody told me you were dead!"

I think that's what the story is. Eddie died and some people confused us. There was a lot of confusion about that. I remember an interview with Eddie that I saw in *CREEM* magazine where he claimed that he came up with the title *Invasion of the Blood Farmers*, which I thought was interesting because A) he didn't, but B) he probably thought he did. I remember doing it with Jackie Bravman. We were on the sixth floor of a building we were in and talking about poor Ralphie. He couldn't get an acting gig. I said, "Ralphie's this little skinny guy. There must be a part for him." I stopped right in front of the elevator. I remember like it was yesterday. I said, "Jackie, I've got it. We'll do a picture and we'll call it *Invasion of the Blood Farmers*, and Ralphie can be Creton the leader of this crowd that comes to Earth looking for blood." Ralphie was never in the picture [*laughs*].

How widely was the film distributed?

It got all over the joint. I've never seen it on TV, but I believe it's been on TV. Of course, it's been ripped off. I never sold VCR or DVD rights to anybody. Every single copy is a knock off. And what's funny about those knock offs, is they all begin with an FBI disclaimer. It's like counterfeiting money and then putting on there, "Counterfeiting money will put you in jail." So it' s a joke, but the whole thing is a joke. I never really chased anybody. That guy Nick Demetroules sold the film to some companies in Europe. I never sold him foreign rights. I said to him, "You cheated me," and he said, "Sue me." I was in that kind of a world, and if you want to know the honest truth, I knew that I had a piece of junk and I never saw any money from it. I never made a nickel out of it.

I had fun, and I made my money in the magazine business, not the picture business. Would I ever make another picture? Absolutely not. The effort involved is huge. Yet there's great fun. But if you really want to make a good picture, you've got to spend money. I didn't have any money to make that film. People got paid six packs of beer, the cast and crew ate baloney sandwiches at night. It was real nuts-and-bolts kind of an operation. It was a great way to learn how to make a picture.

The only guy in that whole crowd that ever went on in the picture business was the assistant cameraman, Freddy Elmes, who became Frederick Elmes the photographer [*River's Edge, Blue Velvet*]. Big deal in Hollywood. Freddie was a nice kid. But the guy he worked for was one of these hippies that knew everything better than the next guy. I was always considered a Nazi because I was always saying, "Come on, can we please work?"

Did you get to know Roberta Findlay?

Roberta is fun. If it wasn't for Roberta, we never would have made *Mutilated*. As I told you, I had written the script with Kelleher, and I had raised the money from the jukebox guys yet again. Michael was supposed to be the director. I was supposed to be the producer. In fact, Michael was everything. I was just assisting him. What happened was, Michael had some troubles in the head. I don't want to be disrespectful of his memory. I thought the world of the man, but he was troubled. Michael got real troubled the very first day we started filming. Just me and him, me in the gorilla suit cavorting in the trees. It was background footage for the titles. Michael got very squirrelly and ended up going to the hospital and getting his ass shot up with Valium. He came back to my house and crashed on the bed.

I called Roberta and said, "Roberta, you better come up and get him. As far as I'm concerned, that's the end of this picture." She came up, and Michael was out of bed by this time. We're all sitting down in that famous basement where I wrote all these scripts. I said, "I want to stop this. I don't think I've spent more than $500. I can afford that. I can send the money back to the investors, get all of this camera crap back. That will be the end of that. I'm not throwing any good money after bad."

And Roberta says, "Is the money raised?" Yes. "Is the script written?" Yes. "Have you cast the actors?" Yes. "Do you and Michael have a crew?" Yes, we do. "Then there's a picture to be made, let's make it."

She says, "I'll be the cameraman, let Michael direct, you produce and we'll make this picture."

Without her, we wouldn't have done it. She shot *Shriek of the Mutilated*. When it was all over, it was the biggest turkey that was ever created by man or beast. I knew I had a real pig on my hands, and I had a devil of a time. People I was sending it to would call me back laughing. "Why did you send me that crap?" The final place I sent it was American International Pictures, and they turned it down. But a guy by the name of Ray Axelrod, who had been sitting at the screening for some reason, he had a company called American Films Ltd. He liked it. He called me up at *Cashbox*, and we made a deal over the phone in ten minutes. He was there with the money. I gave him the negative and that was the end of that. Michael lost his mind when he found out how much I sold it for. Never spoke to me again.

I had no reason to speak to Roberta, since her husband wasn't speaking to me. When he died, I called her. I got her message machine, but she never returned my call.

I remember Roberta. That woman was a piece of work. She weighed about 18 pounds, she had hair down to her feet. She was fun.

She did more films with Ed Kelleher.

She worked with Eddie?

He wrote several horror novels, and they turned a few of those into movies that she directed.

No kidding! With Roberta and Michael, you're looking at a married couple making sex

Shriek of the Mutilated star Alan Brock (seated, far left) and director Michael Findlay (seated, far right) at a gathering after the film's first screening for distributors. Ed Adlum and his former wife, Tippy, are standing behind Findlay (courtesy Ed Adlum).

films. That was what was going on. I just assumed that that's what she stayed with. I had no idea that Eddie Kelleher went and worked with her. They made cheap horror pictures?

Most of them were distributed through Crown International. There were a few. She usually does not do interviews, but she did a few DVD commentaries.

I remember the Supreme Court came down on porno. Mike and Roberta had been making films for this guy, Stan Borden. So they tried every trick in the book to get around this law. One of them was medical films. Roberta was playing the sex doctor. You'd piss in your pants watching 'em! She's on the screen with this white pharmacy coat on, and the little circular mirror on her head that only shows up in the comic books. She says, "There is much sexual dysfunction in society today. Such sadness, because it can be relieved. For example..." Boom! They'd show something on the screen. I'm serious. It was Roberta playing Dr. Nussbaum or some shit.

[Note: Stan Borden was the founder of American Film Distributing, which distributed sexploitation films like the Findlay's Flesh trilogy (The Touch of Her Flesh, 1967; The Kiss of Her Flesh, 1968; The Curse of Her Flesh, 1968), Olga's Girls (1964), and John and Lem Amero's The Lusting Hours (1967), in which both the Findlays appeared.]

I'm telling you I didn't know Eddie and Roberta were making pictures behind my back. I'll be jumped! There was no love lost there. I was a Nazi. I got the pictures done. If I got up early, they did too.

Where did the idea for *Shriek* come from?

I don't remember. It was the abominable snowman idea. I don't know how that ever happened.

With the kids in the flowered van, and the fake monster, I always thought it was structured like an episode of "Scooby Doo."

Yes, it is. Totally accidental. Scooby Doo stole my idea! That's me running across the lawn as the abominable snowman. I thought it was great. I had a busted toe. Me and Roberta were in a traffic accident. She was sitting in the back with the camera. Some guy cut me off and I slammed into the side of him and dislocated my toe. We did the rest of the picture with me on crutches. That's when Michael was getting ready to kill me. I'm butting in. "I really think you ought to have Jack looking a little more to the right." I'm the sorry ass sitting on crutches with his foot in a cast! That's when he should have come over, and he did, and said, "Do me a favor and shut up!" [*Laughs.*]

Do you remember much about the big party scene?

Oh, yeah. We did that in an apartment in New York City. The crazy guy is Tom Grail. He was in the *Blood Farmers*. He was a real actor, which made everybody else look bad. That was a good scene. I got the "Popcorn" record from a kid who worked for Music Hall Records. Just for promotion. He gave me a piece of paper and said, "Go ahead and use it." Everybody's friends came up, we got a popcorn wagon in there. The guy making the popcorn worked for *Cashbox*. It was just a lot of people we knew. We jammed them into this apartment and filmed it. I liked that scene. It made the rest of the picture look worse.

They took the song out of the DVD release because of rights issues.

"Popcorn"? They never contacted me. I don't even know where that letter is. I got a letter from the kid. Whether he had legal rights or not, he said, "Go ahead and put it in the movie."

Did that second film get any more or less play in theaters?

I have no idea. I walked away from that. I walked away from the motion picture business. Michael walked away from me. I'm learning more about this stuff right now from you, and that was over 35 years ago.

Did you keep up with Ed Kelleher?

No.

He had an interesting background, too.

Did he get married or anything?

I don't know. He had a degenerative brain disorder, and was placed in a nursing home.

What a shame. If you're familiar with the *Blood Farmers* movie, he's the guy who plays Tex, the drifter with the leather cowboy hat.

He wrote for *CREEM* as "Edouard Dauphin." Where did that come from?

It's all silly stuff. I was once called the patriarch of the jukebox and games business, even though I was only in my forties. We were laughing at that at the job. If you're the patriarch, that makes you the dauphin, which is the crown prince in the old French royalty. That's where that came from.

When we made up the titles of the *Blood Farmers*, there are a lot of phony ones in there. I am "Pat Triarch," and he was "Edouard Dauphin." So I guess he kept that name going [*laughs*].

There are a lot of phony names in the credits. Some of the cast members worked on Broadway, like Jack Neubeck. The guy that played the lead passed away a few years ago.

The main girl's name was Tanna Hunter. Bruce Dietrich was the guy.

Who was Tawm Ellis?

That was a phony name. He was in the union, the actor's union. His real name was Tom Ellis, and he put it in there for that reason. He asked me to please spell his name Tawm, so that they didn't look and find him. We had that a number of times in my brief career; actors who wanted to be on the screen but belonged to SAG, and couldn't because it wasn't a union picture. You'd shoot the back of their head, or change their name. It's all very silly. I never liked unions. I was thrown out of the musicians union! I have a problem. Didn't pay my dues. Screw you!

So you left the film industry, and *then* moved to California.

I started the magazine and that's the rest of my life, you know. I had two kids, that marriage dissolved, and I remarried about ten years ago. I'm living in a farm up in a town called Camarillo in California. That's my weekend hobby. I go out and I get dirty. I have a good life. This business is okay. It used to be good; now it's okay. I still go to work. I'm 67. I don't do much work. I do mostly the administrative and bookkeeping things. I'm looking at the walls, and I have some pressbooks from *Mutilated* and some other artifacts of *Blood Farmers* around. I remember how it was. At least I had a small moment in a small sun, and that's what I look back on. That's probably more than most people, so I'm content.

The emotions, though, come up when we talk about these people. I didn't know that Eddie went on and made some more pictures. I think that's neat. That's almost like me finding out that some of the guys in the Castle Kings actually made more records. There's a certain jealousy there. I'm not gonna disguise it. How can anyone do anything without me there to help [*laughs*]?

Something Fishy
DONALD BARTON
Florida

Although it was not the most well known horror film to emerge from Florida in the 1970s, *Zaat* (1971) was certainly one of the most well traveled. Distributed regionally under its original title by Clark Film Distributors, then nationally under the name *Blood Waters of Dr. Z*, *Zaat* was still playing drive-ins well into the 1980s. It later turned up on video as *Attack of the Swamp Creature*, and in other markets under a number of titles, sometimes with the directing credit attributed to the mysterious "Arnold Stevens."

The film, about a scientist (actor Marshall Grauer) who transforms himself into a giant, homicidal catfish, was actually produced and directed by Donald Barton, owner of Barton Film Co., a Jacksonville filmmaker who specialized in documentaries and training films, many made for the state of Florida.

The monster from *Zaat*, a.k.a. *Bloodwaters of Dr. Z* (1975) (courtesy Ed Tucker).

Made for less than $100,000 and partly shot at Marineland of Florida, *Zaat* was Barton's first and only feature and he had largely put the film behind him when he was contacted by fan Ed Tucker, who arranged for a theatrical screening at the St. Johns 8 Theatre in Jacksonville in 2001, and helped Barton release a re-mastered video of the film, including outtakes and trailers.

Barton later turned his production company over to his sons (who continue in business as Barton Productions), and went to work in marketing and fundraising for St. Vincent's Medical Center in Jacksonville. Now retired, he maintains a Web site at www.holyspiritcomm.com. Tucker, meanwhile, has set up a tribute site to *Zaat* at *www.zaatmovie.com*.

Are you originally from Florida?

My background is right here in Jacksonville, Florida. I was born here, raised here, went to parochial schools, including high school. I graduated from Holy Cross College in Wooster, Mass. I was a radio announcer there and did sports programming. I came home and went in business with a fellow who was a pioneer in the industry. His name was Gerden Russell.

I went to a television school in New York after I graduated. That was the era of live programming, so that's a long time ago. The thought was that film was going to take over, so I wanted to come back to Jacksonville. I met this fellow who had made himself a 16mm processing machine. We were the only film company that could process black-and-white film in the state of Florida. To make a long story short, we had a partnership for many, many years.

I was in the business not to be a lab person, but to produce films. We started producing things, mostly documentary films, training films, a lot of work for the state of Florida.

This was the Barton Film Company?

It stated out as Russell-Barton, then the lab went its way and we continued in production, so it was Barton Film Company from then on.

We did some work for the Small Business Administration and other groups. It was a great learning experience, creating storylines to meet the customer's needs. We had a staff of eight people and we enjoyed some success. It was not really great in the financial sense, but we were always there ready to work on 16mm film. Now, of course, everything is electronic.

I have two sons who are in the business now. The Daughters of Charity out of St. Louis have a hospital in Jacksonville called St. Vincent's. I was a marketing person and then became the fundraiser for them. My sons bought our business. The boys do a lot of work, and they are called Barton Productions. That's basically my background. I retired from St. Vincent's about five years ago.

Your work with the commercial production company led you into making a feature film, then.

The first opportunity we sensed was during the era when the most popular television shows were westerns. All the TV shows in the evening would be westerns. We decided we could probably do a show about a sheriff chasing criminals on water, because that's what we had a lot of: this beautiful scenery. So we did a pilot film called *Seminole*, and we had a cast out of New York. We had a director by the name of Jack Gage who'd done a lot of serial stuff. We put this together, and it was represented by William Morris, but we never got the contract we wanted. In the meantime, the show *Everglades* came out, which was a sheriff chasing people in an airboat, along with several others like *Surfside 6*, which was another one based in Miami. We did that as a side project and we had separate investors. Some Baptists were in on it.

When did you make that?

I can't remember. It was way before *Zaat*, though. We just thought with the natural setting we had and with the success of monster movies, that maybe we could somehow come up with something, produce it and make some money out of it. We did create the monster, we did write the script, but we didn't make the money [*laughs*]! Here again, we had cash investors, and they knew the risk was very, very high.

Who were your investors for *Zaat*?

A variety of people. We had a TV executive, we had an insurance executive, we had a Caterpillar Tractor executive. We had a couple of lawyers. We were very diversified. They knew our reputation and the quality of our work, and decided they would roll the dice with us, knowing full well that it *was* a roll of the dice.

But we did finish the picture. Here again it was done on a real shoestring. We had a lot of people who dedicated a lot of extra time to the production of it. At that time the distribution for the Southeast was handled out of Jacksonville for the drive-in theaters and the small theaters. There was a distributor here [Clark Film Distributors] who was with us every step of the way. That's one of the main reasons we did it, because they had the contacts to actually get it in theaters.

Had you approached them ahead of time?

Yes. We made them a part of what we were doing, and they advised us on saleability of the idea, how it should be marketed, and what we could expect. The biggest problem you have with something like that is by the time the producer gets the film in the theater, and the theater manager takes his percentage, the sub-distributor takes his percentage, there's only about 15 percent left for the producer. There are charges for the advertising and the whole nine yards. You could write a book on it. But when you don't have the leverage, that's what happens to you.

I forget how many theaters we were in. I think we were in about 100 theaters. I would call some of the theaters because I knew it was booked there. I called Texas one night, I forget what city it was. "Oh my gosh, they're lined up outside!" And they reported the box office as being very successful. We knew there was good interest in the flick. That was the pleasant part of it. Then this distributor said, "I think I can set you up with a national release." Well, that was the beginning of the end. The national people were not very reliable. They were thieves, to put it mildly.

Then we found that some of the people in the business at that level may get a copy of your print, and go to a lab and make a copy of it, and make prints and distribute it themselves. I really got on the tail of a Houston distributor, and I said, "You have no right to show this movie in the theater. Where did you get the license?" He said, "I bought it from so and so in California." They didn't own it in California; we owned it in Jacksonville, Florida. This guy said, "Well, Mr. Barton, I was in Spain last year, and your movie was showing in Spain!"

So they're a bunch of thieves out there in that business, and that was a learning process for me.

Who came up with the original idea for the story?

That was Ron Kivett. He was a staff person from Barton Film Company. A very creative guy. He developed the costume. It was a basic rubber suit. I knew a fellow who was the monster in *Creature from the Black Lagoon* (1954) in Miami, Ricou Browning, so I called Ricou and told him we were doing a monster movie. I wanted to know how they went about making their monster suit. This was some years ago. He said it was made by a company in California. I asked him if he remembered the price, and he said it cost about $60,000. Well, that was our whole budget! We had more than that, but that was still a lot. We were able just to absorb that cost because we were still doing documentary work, and we were in no hurry to do the feature. We weren't going to take it on until we were ready. We worked on it as we could, until we got ready to shoot. We set up a schedule of 30 days, and on the 30th day we wrapped it up.

So you had to figure out on your own how to make a suit?

Yes. We experimented. We went down to Rainbow Springs and experimented with the suit, what kind of climate the compound would stand, and the depth.

This was around 1970 or 1971?

Yeah.

What was the budget?

We had a cash budget of about $100,000. We had another $100,000 or $150,000 in the effort that went into it, but we couldn't count that [*laughs*]! The shooting schedule was a 30-day schedule.

Was that continuous?

No. We shot six days and took Sunday off. The photographer was a fellow who had worked on a creature film in Miami.

Jack McGowan, who worked on *Children Shouldn't Play with Dead Things* (1972)?

Right. Jack McGowan. So he knew how to light a set quickly. We had to be able to move fast. He knew how to light for suspense. We didn't have nearly enough suspense, but he knew how to do it. He had a gal assisting him, an assistant cameraman he brought with him, and a make-up guy from Miami. The rest of the crew was from the Jacksonville area.

Where did you find your cast?

We started with the monster. Believe it or not, I put an ad in the paper. "Wanted: six-foot-five or taller to play monster in a movie." This is in the classified ads! This was not a big promotional ad. We had about six or eight people report. This one guy, Wade Popwell, was absolutely perfect. He had the right attitude, he was in good physical condition, he was a swimmer, he was six-foot-five, he was just perfect. We hired Wade. For the others, we did auditions for the different parts. The only out-of-town cast member was the fellow who played the federal agent [Dave Dickerson]. I think he was from Missouri.

Can you tell me about Marshall Grauer, who played the mad doctor?

Marshall was a real theater actor in Jacksonville. We went after him because we knew he had the look that we wanted. We knew his professional abilities. The sheriff, Paul Galloway, was just a delight. He was a professional guy. He's been in circuit theater for many, many years. He did commercials for us from time to time. A funny guy. We mainly cast locally. Some of the actors had very little experience, and I'm afraid it shows [*laughs*], but we did the best we could.

How did you handle the underwater photography?

We had done some underwater work, but nothing like trying to put a monster in the water. We were able to really pick up a lot of the sets that were called for in the script at Marineland. They had a big tank there. Some of the other stuff, like the gal who goes swimming, that was done at Rainbow Springs. We almost lost our monster in Rainbow Springs, I'm afraid.

How did that happen?

It's 40 feet deep. Even though they had worked out some kind of an air thing, his retriever had to retrieve him! Anyway, it was a little bit hairy there for a while.

Was there some kind of breathing apparatus?

Not originally. But then they worked out some kind of a thing that went in his mouth, and it went above the head. He was able to breathe that way. When they went to Rainbow Springs, they did devise a portable tank for him. It was not very sophisticated, believe me. We rolled with the punches, but we had some innovative people and they worked on it and got it done.

How did you communicate with Popwell while he was in the suit?

We would discuss it with him ahead of time. The fellow who actually built the suit really nursed him along. He communicated with him through the head [*laughs*]. Wade, fortunately, had a sense of what we were looking for, and he was able to deliver it. It was a combination of effort between me and Ron, and from Ron to Wade. If he had a question he'd ask Ron, and Ron would relay it to me. I was not able to talk to him once he got the head on.

Who provided the music for the film? It had a mostly electronic score.

Electronic and some stock music. It's all stock. Jamie DeFrates was a local musician here. Some of the prints do not have the sequence, but at one point a group of hippies are singing in a house. That was an original piece of music. The sheriff walked down the street with the hippies to the station to protect them and put them up for the night so the monster wouldn't get them. The rest of the music was from stock.

Other than almost losing your monster, how did the rest of the production go?

It went very well. We had time to scout the locations, since we weren't traveling all over the world. We had just great cooperation from people. We had to stage the sheriff on a flatbed truck telling everybody to get out of town. We got the Baptist Church in Green Cove Springs to help us. They got all sorts of people. Everybody who we contacted about doing the movie wanted to be a part of it, so it worked out real well. The Baptist Church furnished us meals [*laughs*]. They were very, very cooperative.

What did the Baptists think of the monster?

That's a good question! I don't know if we ever went back and asked them if they saw it. We heard second-hand that they loved it. By today's standard, it was a nice monster, really [*laughs*]. Except it tried to get even with everybody.

What about the people at Marineland?

They were delighted. We were not interfering with anything, because the area we shot in was not in use for the general public. And then they had a motel next door with a restaurant. We needed to do some overnight stuff there, and they were not very busy at that time of year we shot. They were delighted to have us, and we had full cooperation from them.

Were you able to stay on schedule?

Absolutely. We didn't vary it one bit. We had a lot of experience, because when you are doing documentaries you have to be able to bring the product in on time. We did a very good job of that. Everything that we did, we always brought a show in on time. This was no different.

Was the film shot in 16mm or 35mm?

It was shot in 35mm. The problem we had was the editor. The soundman was the editor, and he'd done a lot of documentary work. He was a really good, experienced, guy. George Yarbrough was a crazy guy, but really creative. He could only edit in 16mm. So we had to reduce the 35mm to 16mm so he could edit, then we had to go back and match the thing. It was not easy, but it was a way he could work, and I thought he did an excellent job with the material he had.

When you were finished with the film, what did you think of it?

I was pleased. We didn't make a lot of changes, but there were a few things that we did. I don't remember exactly what they were. George edited it. He had his own theater in Wyoming, and he actually edited it out there. When he sent it to me, rough-cut, he had samples of the music in there. We probably didn't cut more than about two minutes out of what he did. And I probably didn't make more than half a dozen changes, because he was

Zaat's impressive poster. According to director Donald Barton, the film was re-released under a variety of titles (occasionally with altered credits) by unscrupulous distributors (courtesy Ed Tucker).

with us all the way. He understood what our goal was, he understood what he had to work with, and he very creatively put it together.

What did the original *Zaat* poster look like?

The *Zaat* poster was originally in color, and it had the Zaat monster on the full page. Then around it there were a few little clips from the movie, like the fellow who was in the airboat, the gal who was being lowered into the vat. We had about five or six little scenes in there. It was a really good poster. It was made by a group out of New York.

What happened with the national distributor that ripped you off?

We furnished them with prints. The negative was always in the possession of the California laboratory. We think they probably took a regular print and made a negative, and then made prints off the negative. It was being distributed around without the people who we'd signed the contract with involved.

I got a call from the attorney general from the state of California. He said there was somebody in California that took a print of the movie and proceeded to raise money to produce a sequel [*laughs*]. His name was Ron Barton. There's nobody called Ron Barton attached to that movie. They were going to take this guy to court. Apparently he had done this before with four or five other movies. I never knew what the end result of that was, but they were going to try and prosecute this guy.

How long ago did that happen?

That was a long time ago. That was during the national distribution of the film.

The film had several different titles.

It was *Zaat* originally. When the original distributor made the contact with the California distributor [Capitol Films], they wanted to develop a new campaign, which I had no problem with. I thought *Blood Waters of Dr. Z* was a good title. They prepared a press kit. Here again, they didn't last as a company. They were the ones actually that we delivered the prints to for distribution nationally.

And then a lot of these prints went missing.

Of the 20 we sent out there, we got back about 13, because the bankruptcy court had them.

Then it started showing up on TV. When did you first start hearing about the unauthorized distribution of the film?

I think that probably was from a distributor called Aquarius. We never got one single report of a TV showing by Aquarius. The reason I knew what was happening was that I had a friend in Tallahassee, and he called me one day and said, "I just saw your movie last night." On television in Tallahassee? That was the type of thing they did. They booked it, pulled in some money, and we never saw it.

Some of those prints had different credits on them, right?

I never saw that, but that's what I understand.

What was different in the TV versions of the film?

The Sci-Fi Channel used it as part of that *Mystery Science Theater* show. They made fun of it. It was funny, and they did a good job. That's the only one I know of. The guy who

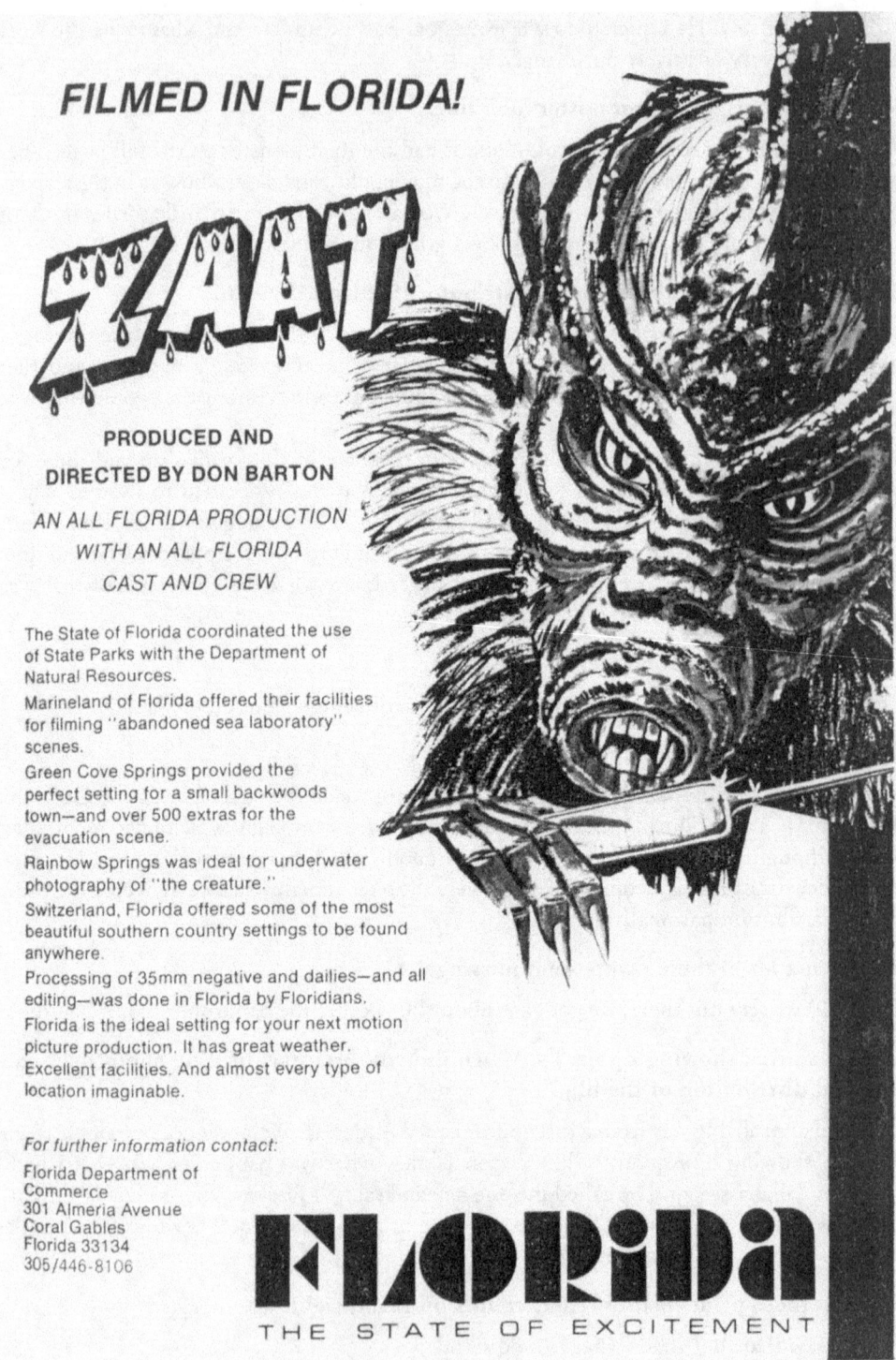

A *Boxoffice* magazine advertisement touting *Zaat*'s regional roots (courtesy Chris Poggiali).

talked me into doing the reunion, Ed Tucker, follows these things, and he got us really great publicity in some of the horror magazines.

I'm not a horror flick fan, but Ed is. And he has been the one to kind of push and shove me into doing what we've done here.

Didn't you wind up filing suit against the cable channel that played the movie on *Mystery Science Theater*?

Yeah, we did.

That was just a rights issue?

That's correct. They ran it on television without our permission, and we owned it. They ridiculed it. It cost us a lot. Anyway, we did a lot of heavy talking, but when it came right down to it, the settlement was not that much. We could have pushed it, but we might have had to push it in a New York venue, and I didn't want to do that.

You wound up going back and getting the negative, didn't you?

The lab retained the negative, but they made us a scene-by-scene, color-corrected internegative. I forget whether it was 16mm or whatever. We used that for making the videos. I forget the technicalities of it. That was very important to us that we had a good quality video. We packaged it. Ed is the one who put together the package on it. It's very sharp.

You had a screening of it in Florida.

We had a 30th anniversary screening. You would not believe the publicity we got from the local radio and television and newspapers. We had rented a theater, and it was a double. They could show the same print simultaneously on two screens, and each theater held about 300 people. The night of the event, these people started lining up at five o'clock! We sold out and turned away people for two theaters! It was absolutely unbelievable. We had all this memorabilia for sale, and everybody bought something.

A young man and his wife had flown down from Philadelphia. I don't know how in the world they knew they were having a showing, but I guess Ed put something on the Internet [*laughs*]. But that was quite a boost, and we really felt good about that.

What kind of memorabilia did you make?

We had coffee cups, t-shirts; you name it, we had it. Anything you wanted.

Does the monster suit still exist?

It's in my garage. A couple of Halloweens ago we put it out in the driveway. These little kids came by and said, "It's Zaat!" How did they know anything about Zaat [*laughs*]? We had a little light from down below looking up at his snout. They loved that.

What kind of shape is Zaat in?

According to Ron, it would need some more of the stuff on it, the skin flakes. But somebody could get in there and wear it. Somebody could wear the head. When we did the reunion, the fellow who wore the monster outfit [Wade Popwell], in response to some people in the press, said that he'd do it again in a heartbeat. Unfortunately, he died last year.

You also started a *Zaat* Web site.

I think probably Ron Kivett or Ed did that. When we had the orders coming in for the memorabilia, you could order it through the Web site, I think. We ended up selling over 300 videos.

There was a group of young people who heard about or knew about *Zaat*. They found me in my home, and were wondering if I had any old *Zaat* stuff I wanted to get rid of. I had a couple of cans of outtakes that I had no use for. I told them to take it. I don't know what they were doing with it. Low and behold, Ed says, "Guess what? Someone in Switzerland or Sweden has got clips of *Zaat* that they are selling on eBay!" And these people, I don't know where they came from, but they were supposedly central Florida residents. Maybe one of these guys was from Scandinavia! We notified eBay that they had no right to the material and they took it off, but can you believe that? They were selling excerpts of *Zaat* on eBay.

Have you done any other screenings of Zaat?

No. We went into three other theaters and had good crowds at all of them. Nothing since then. We just kind of burned out, but it took a lot of effort to put together that whole thing. The only way we were able to recoup any cost was through the sale of memorabilia.

Do you think you'll put *Zaat* on DVD?

We talked about it, and we just haven't gotten around to it. I think we will. Particularly if it looks like we might do a sequel.

What are you doing now?

I've been enjoying not having to wear a coat and tie. We are occupying our time with our 23 grandchildren, and our nine kids. Six of them live very close by.

Actually, this may sound a little bit strange to you, but I have a background of asthma. A few years back I couldn't breathe, and sitting up in a chair I had an idea for a movie. That never happened before in my life because I wasn't a script writer. This was a synopsis of a story line that was very clear. My dear wife typed it up, and the story is that a computer nerd wants to generate a rally in Jerusalem to try and bring peace on earth.

We happen to be Catholic, so the Holy Sprit is very much involved in our church work. The Holy Spirit was the one who inspired this guy in the story to do this thing. It just evolved into a nice little movie. But I'm not a script writer and I didn't want to even attempt a script. I tried to market the synopsis. A lady that I met in California had represented a gentleman who we saw in one of those swashbuckling B-movies, and who eventually played Jesus in *The Passion of the Christ* (2004). I was in contact with her before that. I sent her the synopsis of this story, which is called *Rally*.

A week later I called and asked if she read it. She said it was fabulous, but it will never sell in Hollywood [*laughs*]. Things have changed a little, but not that much.

That put us into a little non-profit corporation, which we call Holy Spirit Communications. We send out a newsletter and we have a Web site.

After *Zaat*, why didn't you make any more features?

We didn't try to do any more work. It was not the type of business we were in. Then the move from film to electronic was a big move. The progress of electronic and the cost that it has taken is just immense. It put a lot of people out of business. We decided we didn't want to go that route. That's when we elected to do something else, and my sons really took over. They are electronic people. They can edit something, and what might have taken me a week, they can edit it in two days. It's just awesome.

Didn't Ron Kivett actually write a sequel at one point?

I think he wrote a synopsis for a sequel. We have had several suggestions. We're really kind of looking at the possibility of a sequel now. We're not saying anything about it, because everything depends on who wants to roll the dice. Anyway, there are some horror flick people out there who might want to do it. I think there could be a sequel. The story that I tend toward in my own brain right now would be Zaat encountering the terrorists! Terror against terror...

The Director Next Door
J.R. BOOKWALTER
Ohio

Horror fans have been making their own films ever since cheap 8mm and 16mm cameras first appeared on the shelves at the local department store. But in the 1980s a number of enterprising fan/filmmakers began making full-length features, first on Super 8 and later on videotape. As home video sales boomed and distributors searched for more titles to release, more and more of these backyard films began popping up at video stores across the country.

Ohio's J.R. Bookwalter was one of the pioneers in this new world of ultra-low-budget monster movies, and first gained national exposure when he made what may be the most expensive Super 8 movie ever, a George Romero homage with a six-figure budget called *The Dead Next Door* (filmed in 1986 and released in 1989). That film, which was financed (without credit) by nearby Michigan wunderkind Sam Raimi, launched Bookwalter's two-decade career directing and producing dozens of low-budget horror films.

From his dinky office in Mogadore, Ohio, Bookwalter made a series of films on 16mm, VHS and digital video that included *Robot Ninja* (1989), *Humanoids from Atlantis* (1992), *Ozone* (1993), *The Sandman* (1995), *Polymorph* (1996) and *Bloodletting* (1997). After moving to California, Bookwalter worked for Charles Band at Full Moon, where he produced, directed and edited even more features.

Along the way, he started his own distribution company (Tempe), and published the magazine *Alternative Cinema*. (Full disclosure: once upon a time, the author was a regular contributor to the magazine.)

Now living in the Akron area again, Bookwalter has dedicated the past few years to producing and distributing horror films from a new generation of filmmakers, and remastering and re-releasing his own back catalog to DVD.

www.tempevideo.com   *www.jrbookwalter.com*

How did you get started making films?

When my sister and I were kids my mother bought a Super 8 camera, much like anybody else who was born in the sixties would have had. I think that was more of an inspiration than anything else, because she would always shoot these home movies. Back then you had to set up the projector and it was a big deal to watch them. That was always very inspiring. There were also these little Super 8 reels you could buy at Kmart, which were cut down scenes from different movies and cartoons.

My friends and I were making little magazines and little fanzines. Seeing *Star Wars* (1977) was probably the thing that inspired me, and billions of other people, to pull my mother's camera out of the closet and start making stuff. That was initially just with old *Star Wars* action figures, little stop-motion animation things. Eventually I roped in the kids in the neighborhood, but I was mostly doing little sci-fi things, *Darth Vader Lives* and *The Incredible Shrinking Man*.

Then *Fangoria* magazine came out, and the first issue had a *Dawn of the Dead* (1978) article where they showed the head blowing off the shoulders. That's when I said, "Wow, I've got to do that." Then I was into splatter, and all my movies took this horrific turn that I'm sure my parents were not thrilled about. How much blood can we throw around? That was the progression.

I probably made 40 or 50 Super 8 short films from age ten or 11 to when I was out of college, around the time *The Dead Next Door* came along.

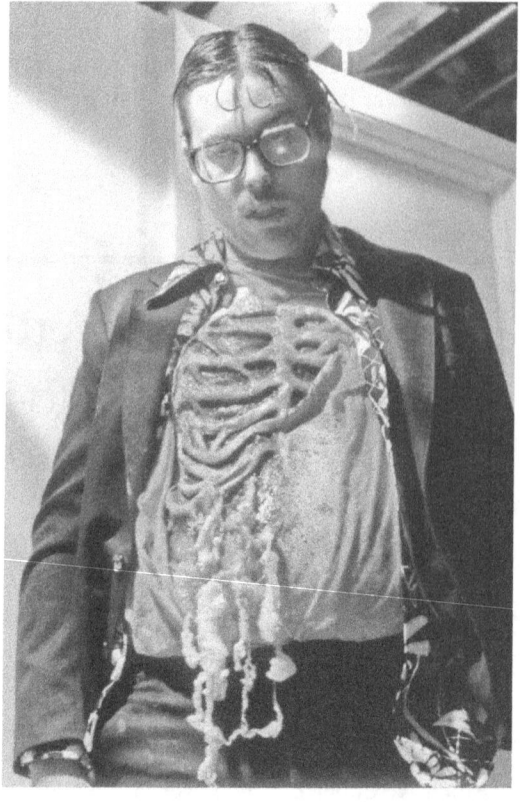

Director/producer J.R. Bookwalter appeared as a doomed Jehovah's Witness in *Skinned Alive* (1989) (courtesy J.R. Bookwalter).

Didn't you make some homemade music videos?

That was later. When I got into high school I was in marching band, and I had a bunch of friends who were willing participants in doing that. One of the first ones was this country song called "Swingin'" that became legendary at my high school. We would show it at the talent show, at band reunions. This thing got played all the time. Then I took footage from a copy of *Psycho* (1960) that I never returned to the library. I cut it up into a video for Rockwell's "Somebody's Watching Me." It was really cool, and one of the things that I showed to get *Dead Next Door* made. That was something of an editing exercise — and I'm just afraid the Summit County Library is still going to come after me. I think I did one for "The Beautiful Ones," the Prince song from *Purple Rain* (1984).

There were less of those than the earlier movies. That was more just trying something different. The technical dilemma of doing those was more creatively challenging.

Did you go to film school in Pittsburgh?

They didn't have a film program. My mother wanted me to go to college, and I didn't really want to. We settled on the Art Institute of Pittsburgh because they had photography classes, and I had an interest in that. I figured I could take photography, and since I'd be in Pittsburgh I could maybe do something with George Romero.

As it turned out, I couldn't work for Romero when he was doing *Day of the Dead* (1985) because of my school hours, but I did wind up being an extra. I quit at the beginning of the second year because my apartment was robbed. I figured that was a sign of things to come. I should just cut my losses. I really wasn't learning anything. The money my mother would send me for food I would just spend on Super 8 film and processing.

Was your camera equipment stolen?

My Super 8 camera wasn't, but I had a 16mm Bolex that I had invested in with a friend, and we never even got a chance to shoot anything with it. I think my stereo and some other stuff got stolen.

How did you connect with Sam Raimi?

I think I left school in mid–July of 1985. I was just bumming around for the first couple of weeks, not really doing anything. I was flipping through some back issues of *Fangoria* and stumbled across the article with the *Evil Dead* in it. I thought, "These guys are in Detroit, and that's only four hours away. Maybe I can get some work with them." I had no aspirations to get a movie made; I was just looking to maybe be a production assistant.

I was living with my mother and being a bum, so I had to do something, especially since I quit college, which she wasn't excited about. I called up there, got the answering machine and left a message. A few days later the phone rang, and it was Sam Raimi. I about dropped the phone and fell over. That would not happen these days [*laughs*]!

Long story short, that led to me going up there and meeting all those guys. I showed them a bunch of my short films. He was sort of pushing me. He said, "What do you want to do?" I told him I thought I'd make industrial videos in my hometown, take the Romero route. Who knows? I was basically trying to interview for a PA position. They were starting *Evil Dead 2* (1987).

He actually was the one who encouraged me to make my own movie. He said if I got started on something, maybe he'd kick some money into it. I'm thinking, "Shit, you don't have tell me twice!" The whole four-hour drive back I started coming up with these crazy ideas. I starting putting together a script, and put together this little investment proposal that was basically stolen from a book that I had, and I sent it up to him. The rest is sort of history, I guess. At least B movie film history.

How long did it take you to get started on the actual film?

I think we got the first check in September of '85, and the thing wasn't finished until April or May of '89. It was a good four years in there. The bulk of it was shot over the summer of '86. We would keep going back and getting pick ups and effects inserts that we had missed from the main part of the shoot. At some point we started editing the film, and as there was stuff that I didn't like, I'd discuss it with him. He was always pretty willing to send us a few more bucks if I wanted to reshoot something.

There were a lot of mistakes made and a lot of down time. In between, I was shooting wedding videos and dabbling in music and doing what ever else I could do. By December of '88, we had a locked picture on a one-inch video master of the finished movie. Just the sound remained, which wound up happening the next spring.

Did you originally plan on shooting in Super 8?

Before Sam got involved with it, my brilliant idea was to shoot on VHS video, because it was what I had available to me. I was going to raise $8,000. My God, it sounds like a luxurious budget compared to what most people are shooting their movies for now! My father's neighbor had a little VHS editing system, and he had a pretty decent camera for the time.

It was Sam's idea to double the budget. Actually, I think I was going to shoot for four grand, and he was willing to double it to eight. My memory is getting foggy on the details now.

Pretty quickly, we decided that VHS video wasn't really going to cut it. I think *Blood Cult* (1985) had just come out on home video that fall, and that was shot on Betacam, which was the new format. That was much higher-end than what we were shooting on.

We actually wound up shooting a day of footage on three-quarter-inch video as a test, and nobody liked the look of it. It just looked like a soap opera. That's where this decision came in to do Super 8, which threw a few monkey wrenches into things. I was fine with it because I felt more comfortable with the format. He was comfortable with it because he had shot all his short films on Super 8, and I think he liked the idea of shooting a feature on Super 8. That was something he'd wanted to do.

How much did it wind up costing?

Only God knows. I don't think anybody does. The best estimate I could come up with was $125,000. Of that, I would say a good 50 percent was absolute waste, nothing that's even on the screen.

Where did the waste come from?

For whatever reason back then I always insisted on having these dumpy little offices. We were only paying like $200 a month rent, and we had phone lines and stuff. We were trying to be like a real production company, which was just humorous. I wish I could go back in time and slap myself in the head.

It wasn't *so* impractical. We actually had to have a lot of that stuff. You're talking about a movie that just mushroomed over that summer of '86. This was going to be just a little thing I was going to do with a handful of friends, and we wound up enlisting a lot of people from all over the place, 1,500 extras and a big cast and crew.

It was ridiculous, because everyone was on a deferred salary. There wasn't any money going out to anybody. But it was just stupid waste. We sent our first set of film-to-video transfers to this house in New York that did a horrible job, and that was a five- or six-thousand-dollar waste of money. There were a lot of mistakes like that. There were some mistakes in the initial editing, the way that I was cutting stuff. It's all technical stuff. Sam had to fly me out to L.A. to relock the cut after we were already done. It was a big nightmare. It wasn't all totally my fault. Neither one of us knew what we were doing with electronic post-production. I'll put some of the blame on him, too [*laughs*]! I'm just kidding.

That was my film school. I never had any formal training in any of this. You get a little bit of money early on and think, "I need this and this," and before you know it that money is gone, and you're like, "Oh shit, now I need more money. What are we gonna do?" We did some creative stuff along the way to cut down on that budget, but over time it just got away from us. If we'd had that money up front, we could have shot that movie on 16mm, at least. The problem was it was really being piecemealed out, a few thousand here and there. And the money would just get spent on living expenses and office expenses, and stupid things that didn't need to be paid for.

Was it difficult to keep Raimi engaged during the lengthy production process?
That was my biggest frustration. After the principal photography was done, I think we did the editing maybe in the fall or early winter. Once I started getting into some of the cutting I was able to stay occupied. After that is where things started to really slow down. Part of that was because he was busy with *Evil Dead 2* (1987), and he was shopping himself around Hollywood. He ultimately wound up doing *Darkman* (1990).

It would be weeks or months before we got any feedback on it. That's when I was turning to wedding videos just to keep busy.

The people who were working with me on the movie gradually, over time, just disappeared. By the end of it I was the last man standing. That was the most frustrating part, because it just felt like when we started shooting it, the video market was in a place where a movie like that would have been pretty viable, and by the time we finished it the video market was heading into the toilet. We kind of blew our opportunity to even see any of that money back.

What did Raimi think of the film when it was finished?
Good question! I think he was less impressed than some of his collaborators. Scott Spiegel, I remember, was a big cheerleader for that movie. He saw it in fragments and he was into it, and he had a role in the movie, but when he finally saw the whole finished movie he was more excited than anybody. At that point my enthusiasm was so low from fighting with everything just to get it done, it was nice to hear that.

I think Sam was kind of like, "I don't know what to do with this." When it started he wanted me to make more of a scare movie. It was never intended to be that. It was this weird, epic Romero homage. I don't think he knew what do with it, and his mind was elsewhere, anyway. I know Rob Tapert, who at that point had kicked in a few bucks along the way, was not impressed at all [*laughs*]. Bruce Campbell was like, "Nice try, kid," but I don't think he was that impressed. Although he was willing to cash a check to come aboard and supervise the post-sound. It's easier for me to look back on it now and see it through their eyes than it was at the time, but I just wanted it done. I wanted to get as far away from that movie and that whole situation as possible after all that time.

You shot part of the film in Washington, D.C., and initially did so without permits, right?
Yeah. When you're young you do foolish things. Early on in the prep process I had called the film office down there, and said, "We want to do some shooting in D.C., and here's the idea of what we want to do." The woman was nice enough to run down the costs for all the permits and the police, and she said, "You absolutely, positively can't have zombie extras on the White House fence. That's not going to work."

Not only could we not afford that, but what I thought would be the coolest stuff in the movie, we couldn't even shoot. I turned my attention to just getting the rest of the movie shot. The D.C. stuff was much later in the process.

When it finally came down to it, we had to deal with this problem. Are we going to do this or not? That material had worked itself into the plot so much at that point that we had to do something. So we decided to do it guerrilla-style. We took the Zombie Squad station wagon and a rental van that somebody had loaned to us, and the hardcore members of our production team to dress up as zombies, and we just went and did it. We didn't ask anybody. We just drove down there and said, "Okay, let's set up here."

We started with the zombies on the White House fence, because I figured this was most likely where we were going to get into trouble. To make a long story short, we had driven around the Ellipse after finishing that stuff, and they had shut off the roads. We had FBI, Secret Service, drug-sniffing dogs, the Washington police, everybody was there. And the only thing that got us off was my producer, Scott Plummer, still had his Akron University student I.D. We just passed the whole thing off as some stupid student movie.

They didn't take the film or anything. They just said, "Okay, you can't shoot anymore. If you do, you have to go talk to such and such at the film office." I immediately recognized the name because it was the woman I had talked to.

We went to the film office and I introduced myself to the woman, and told her what we had done. She was so floored—first of all, I don't think she realized our production was so small, so that worked in our favor. She gave us permission to shoot some of the other stuff that I wanted to do around D.C., with the directive that we couldn't bother anybody, and we couldn't close anything. That's how we got away with doing the rest of the filming.

At the time the police had told us they thought we were terrorists climbing over the White House fence. You can imagine if somebody attempted that now [*laughs*]! As it was, we were probably 30 seconds away from a warning shot, at least. They were coming after us, and we jumped in the cars and took off.

It's something I look back on now, as an adult, and I would never do that again. I'm glad I did because it's a once-in-a-lifetime story. I wouldn't attempt it now, though.

Did you use a helicopter for that big aerial shot of the zombies?

Everybody thinks it's a helicopter because we put the sound effect in the movie. It actually was an airplane. We put 300 extras out in the field, and we would take off and circle around, and when we'd start to land I'd film a take. Then we'd take off again. We did four or five takes that way.

Because we had the extras, we also shot at the Soap Box Derby and outside the Goodyear Blimp hangar. We called it our "big day," because that was our big day with all the extras where we got all that footage.

That actually went very smoothly. We had permission to shoot everywhere. We did everything the right way. The only thing we did that was low-end or no-budget was we had gone to Radio Shack and bought these really nice walkie-talkies. I paid by check and walked out with them, with the sole intention of taking them back for a refund when we were done. Radio Shack—I don't know if they still have it, but they had a very liberal return policy. We did that a lot over the course of that movie. We couldn't afford the stuff, but we needed it. It never occurred to us to go rent the stuff from some place.

How many people wound up working on the film?

The count that I remember was 1,500 extras. There were maybe another 40 or 50 people in the crew and principal cast.

Was it difficult to corral that many people for a film shoot?

No. It's funny, because the one thing I hear from low-budget filmmakers all the time is how they have such a problem getting extras and even their cast to show up. We really never had that. On all my movies, we never had any of those problems. There was just nothing else going on that summer or something. People would show up and sit there all day in this sticky makeup in the heat. Some of them would come back three or four times. It got to the point we had so many people who wanted to do it, we had to turn people away.

That part of it was totally unexpected. I actually had to put two or three phone lines in the office because you'd take a call from somebody who wanted to be an extra, then hang up and the phone would ring again with another person. It was pretty crazy. Who knew that Akron was so boring?

What was your original plan for getting the film distributed?

I don't think there *was* a plan initially. I know at one point we had entertained the idea of blowing it up to 35mm because there was some kind of theatrical market then. Sam had actually done a test and had a reel of Super 8 to blown up to 35. We took it to a theater here in town and watched it, and it was pretty dismal. We had some scenes transferred from Super 8 to 16mm, and from one-inch video to 16mm, and those ideas were scrapped.

By the time we finished, Sam was on to *Darkman* and he had some connections to Universal, which operated MCA Home Video at the time. I know he approached them with it, but it wasn't their cup of tea, although they were releasing all kinds of bizarre stuff back then.

I had hooked him up with Dave DeCoteau at Cinema Home Video, and they actually had a meeting, DeCoteau pretty much blew it by suggesting that Sam call it *Evil Dead III* or something, some crazy thing. That was the end of that!

He wound up licensing it to this guy Tony Elwood, who had Electro Video, and that was the initial video release. Tony was also a filmmaker and had worked on the crew in some capacity on *Evil Dead 2*. He was trying to get his own label started, and he had his own movie called *Killer* (1988). It was also a Super 8 film. He was basically selling *Killer*

Bookwalter poses with one of the zombies from *The Dead Next Door* (1988) (courtesy J.R. Bookwalter).

and *Dead Next Door*, going through the mom-and-pop stores and advertising in *Fangoria*. You could buy it through Marshall's Discount Video.

Not too much came of that, and then eventually I took it over. Not much happened with it after that, either [*laughs*]!

Raimi's name doesn't appear on the film. Was there any problem with him being associated with *Dead Next Door*?

He didn't want his name attached to it. He wanted to go under this ridiculous "Master Cylinder" name. Back then I refused to use it, and I just decided to leave out an executive producer credit. A local writer named Dave Kuehls had spent a lot of time on the set talking to people, and he kept hearing Sam Raimi's name. Everybody knew. Sam had actually come to visit for a couple of days and watched some of the shooting here in town. It was no secret. It was just a matter of time before it came out. I didn't realize Dave was going to make a whole sidebar out of it in *Fangoria*. He quoted me talking about it, and Jolie Jackunas, the producer that Sam had hired to help with the movie, and Scott Spiegel. So all three of us were talking about him. The cat was out of the bag, and Scott and I both got very angry phone calls the day the issue came out.

Was his name ever on any of the video releases?

When I remastered it three years ago for the Anchor Bay release, I did put the Master Cylinder credit back in there. Looking back, I was being juvenile. I actually saw a *Fangoria* magazine or something years ago where they asked him about it and he did admit that he helped with the movie, but he kind of downplayed it. I don't think anybody would watch that movie and think Sam Raimi had all that much to do with it, except for writing checks. It's certainly not this style of filmmaking.

Did he ever make his money back?

Noooooo. It's been so poorly handled over the years, and it was released in deals where we got ripped off and all kinds of crazy stuff. Now with DVD they're selling it for so much cheaper than VHS that even for a company like Anchor Bay, while they moved a reasonable number of units, it wasn't enough to cover the cost of something like that.

It was a case of a lot of first-time filmmakers not knowing what they were doing. Sam told me *Evil Dead* never made its money back until they made *Evil Dead 2*, and they used a chunk of that money to pay back the investors.

Have you talked to Raimi since then?

We've had a little correspondence, but not much. I had written him shortly after I first moved to L.A. When Anchor Bay picked up *Evil Dead* I was trying to encourage him to pull some strings to get them to look at *The Dead Next Door*. Years later I wound up being approached by Anchor Bay about it.

After *The Dead Next Door* you shot two films on 16mm, *Robot Ninja* and *Skinned Alive*. How did those projects get started?

Technically it was three if you count *Ghoul School* (1990), which was originally supposed to be produced here.

I had gone to L.A., and my friends David Barton and Dave Lange were working on makeup effects for this film called *Beverly Hills Corpse*, which wound up being called *Murder*

Weapon (1989). That was how I met Dave DeCoteau. He kept showing up everywhere. I'd meet him when he'd come over with Linnea Quigley, who was co-producing and starring in that movie. They would come over to the house where I was staying, where they were working on the effects. The sound house in Hollywood where we were doing the sound mixing for *Dead Next Door* was where DeCoteau had done *Creepazoids* (1987) and all his stuff. So he just kept popping up and we kept seeing each other.

David Barton said DeCoteau was looking for movies, and I should hit him up and see what we could do. At the time I was talking to Jon Killough, who had a project called *Maggot Man* he wanted to do. There was another filmmaker, Tim O'Rawe (who wound up doing *Ghoul School*), who had an anthology thing called *Basement* that he wanted to do. It just was sort of a weird thing where I somehow got involved in taking those projects and pitching them to Dave DeCoteau for those guys. He was less interested in those and more interested in having me do something. He had seen a good chunk of *Dead Next Door* at that point.

I went over the short list of projects that I wanted to make. He wanted to make something for $10,000 or $15,000, but just coming off of *Dead Next Door* and spending all that money, I wanted to do something a little bigger, ideally. He threw out the title *Robot Ninja*. I was so eager to make anything else that I said, "Sure, I can do that." The basic deal was $15,000 cash, he was gonna cover the film stock and lab cost, and I was gonna get paid $2,500 for the whole show.

We went out and made that, and regretted it immediately [*laughs*]. In the course of finishing *Robot Ninja*, I think I was trying to get him on the hook for another movie. Jon had come up with this project called *Skinned Alive*. He'd given up on this *Maggot Man* thing. I threw that out to DeCoteau and wound up talking him into two other movies, including this *Ghoul School* thing that O'Rawe had.

Those movies didn't cost that much more. I basically got the same amount of money to produce them that I did to do everything on *Robot Ninja*. He coughed up a few extra bucks to cover some other expenses and the cost of the directors.

Why did you regret *Robot Ninja*?

Actually, I didn't regret it right away. I think I was sort of despondent when I cut it together. We were cutting it on film. There was a place in Cuyahoga Falls that did some film stuff. We cut those on a flatbed. It just wasn't coming together the way I wanted it to.

It wasn't until Cinema Home Video sent me a few copies of the finished artwork and the packaging, and I sat down and watched it, that I got really depressed about it. I didn't like the packaging. The sound was all screwed up. I wasn't that crazy about the movie.

Although I had the stupidity to actually defend it. *Fangoria* gave it a pretty nasty review and I wrote in defending it, and then they slapped me again on the letters page. I learned a valuable lesson [*laughs*]. And now I view it as my absolute, hands-down worst movie.

I thought that was supposed to be *Humanoids from Atlantis*.

Yeah. I used to think *Humanoids* was the worst, but everybody kept telling me it wasn't as bad as *Robot Ninja*. *Humanoids* at least — I can't say that it saves itself, but it's got the fake ending, which everybody seems to like for some reason. I don't know why. Neither one of them are good movies. It's like comparing two piles of dog crap [*laughs*].

But *Robot Ninja* wound up being popular in Germany, of all places, I guess because it's so violent. It's probably the goriest movie that I've made.

How did you get Burt Ward and Linnea Quigley into *Robot Ninja*?

Scott Spiegel was in that scene, too. That was planned from the beginning. That was because DeCoteau had Lyle Waggoner from "The Carol Burnett Show" in *Murder Weapon*. There were agents who had lists of these actors from the 1960s and 1970s, and putting them in a movie would help sell them in New Guinea or somewhere. DeCoteau wanted to do the same thing with *Robot Ninja*, and he was willing to foot the bill for it and fly me out to California to shoot it.

Adam West was my first choice, because I'd grown up on "Batman." There were other people on the list, too. Erik Estrada, and I think they had the professor from "Gilligan's Island," Russell Johnson. There was a list of guys like that we could use. Adam West was too expensive and considered hard to deal with. Burt Ward was on the list, so I figured if I can't get Batman, at least I can have Robin.

Linnea ended up in there because she had this partnership with DeCoteau at the time. I think she got paid a hundred bucks for the day and just did it as a favor to him.

I wrote this scene with the three of them in mind, and Burt Ward was just awesome to work with. I'm sure he was mortified when he saw the actual film, but working with all three of them was great.

We were supposed to do the same sort of stunt with *Skinned Alive*. There was a scene that was ultimately cut out of the movie with a sheriff and the deputy, and Scott Spiegel was supposed to play the deputy. He was just going to come down from Michigan and do that cameo. There was talk at the time of having somebody like Donald Pleasance come out and play the sheriff, but it wound up not happening. When we decided to cast Scott as Snake, that whole scene got scraped.

By that time, DeCoteau figured these weren't selling enough units with these marginal names, so that was the end of that.

Was working in 16mm much different than working in Super 8?

We really had the same pains in the butt. We were dumb enough to write all these big night scenes. We didn't have enough lights to pull it off. We could have shot half of that movie just putting people against a black screen, for all the image that we got out of the film. We used to call Mike Tolochko, the cinematographer on those first few movies, the Prince of Darkness because everything wound up being underexposed. It wasn't his fault, but we didn't have enough lights to pull it off.

At the time it was exciting because we were so close on the heels of finishing *Dead Next Door*, and by June we were shooting another movie. Going from Super 8 to 16, even though it was less money, felt like an upgrade. On *Skinned Alive* I found a new cheap office in Mogadore. We were going to do two shows back to back. It felt like we were actually *doing* something again after being idle so long waiting for *Dead Next Door* to be finished. It was a deception. The end product wasn't what anybody wanted.

Was it difficult for you to act as producer instead of directing?

It was tough because I think I was still too used to being the number-one guy, and there was a difficult adjustment. Jon had a very specific vision of what he wanted, but unfortunately he didn't have enough experience to pull that off. I tried as best as I could to be there and help him, but as the process went on and we had a shooting schedule to get done, there were starting to be casualties of war during the process. I was literally standing there threatening to pull pages out of his script if he didn't get things moving. I had to become a bit of a dictator, and I wasn't particularly well liked on that set. I really hadn't had any experience being just producer, so it was a learning experience for me, too. I can't say that I was the best person for the job.

It really came to a head because by the time we started cutting it, Jon and Mike Tolochko were doing day and night shifts. I would come in in the morning when Mike came in, after Jon had left. We'd watch the cut so far. There was a lot of stuff missing and a lot of problems. We wound up doing some reshoots, and Jon was so disgusted with everything that he quit and walked off the thing. I wound up having to step in and finish it. I can't blame him, looking back, because he was between a rock and a hard place. It wasn't the best of circumstances.

What did you think of *Skinned Alive*?

I always thought it was better than *Robot Ninja*. Scott Spiegel, who did not originally play that character [Snake], came in at the last minute after we had already shot a few days with another actor. He basically saved that whole movie with his performance. That, and the fact that it's pretty bloody. I'm happy with it for what it was. Even today I view it in a much more positive light than I do *Robot Ninja*.

Why didn't you produce *Ghoul School*?

I did, until it became a three-way struggle. There was the director who had written the script, and there was me, and DeCoteau, who was financing it. DeCoteau had realized by then that he had to keep releasing something every few months to keep things moving along, and he just wanted to get the thing shot. Tim and I kept working on the script, and I wasn't happy with the way it was going.

We had set up that Tim would just come in from New Jersey and we would shoot it in Ohio with the same people from *Skinned Alive*. I showed the script to some of the people who were gonna work on the movie, and they weren't that crazy about it. We were all trying to do better. I just said, "Let's walk away from that and hopefully we can maybe do the next one with DeCoteau." I just told him I was not interested, thinking he was probably gonna kill the movie and we'd do something else. But he said, "Let's just make the movie anyway." Tim had convinced him somehow that he could get it done.

That wound up being a horrific nightmare. Tim and I remain friends, and I was still trying to help him any way I could. I think we had set them up with the camera rental. He needed somebody to do some location sound mixing. I wound up going out there to do that. The day I arrived his special effects guy got put in jail. I think he was spending like $5,000 on make-up effects, and this guy walked off with four grand. He had nothing to show for it.

He was just despondent. I called Mike Tolochko and Dave Lange, who had done all the make-up effects for *Robot Ninja* and *Skinned Alive*. They drove out to New Jersey and looked at what we could do for a thousand bucks, which wasn't much.

We got involved in that aspect of it, and then DeCoteau was so disgusted with the dailies that he saw after everything was processed, that he just decided to take the movie away from Tim and hired me to oversee finishing it.

In the 1990s you moved into video distribution. How did you get involved in that?

Initially it was just like a mail order kind of thing. Dave DeCoteau was doing the Cinema Home Video stuff with our movies, so I was sort of just watching what he was doing, and

I wanted to do the same thing. It really sprang from being unhappy with the way the movies were being sold.

The thing that existed then that doesn't now were the mom-and-pop video stores that were eager for product. You also had all these sub-distributors around the country that had little boiler room operations where people would just sit on phones all day calling video stores, trying to sell them cheesy B movies for high prices. This was back in the days when you'd get seventy or eighty bucks for a VHS tape. They'd turn around and buy this stuff from distributors like me for fifteen or twenty bucks, and sell it for $50 or $60. There was a lot more money in it for them [*laughs*]. I don't know if it worked out for us! This was in the days before you had to have UPC bar codes and all that stuff on the boxes.

You eventually wound up distributing other directors' movies through Tempe.

I started with this old *Basic How-To Halloween Make-Up* video that I had experimented with in 1987. We shot that and tried selling it to local costume shops. That was the first effort at making and distributing it, which was an abysmal failure. After I had gone to L.A. for a year and come back, I decided I was going to make some more movies and sell them. That's when all the Cinema Home Video stuff started. Initially it was through mail order and conventions and stuff. There was actually a business there back then, because people were eager to buy stuff. You were talking about $15 or $20 VHS tapes, where they had been paying $50 or more.

That led to picking up other stuff after I had done all those productions for Cinema Home Video. I used other people's movies as a test market. By the time we got to *Ozone*, which was the first movie I made with the intention of distributing myself, I had already put out a few other releases.

How did you find those other films?

One of the first ones I put out was *Winterbeast* (1986/1992). That guy had known Brett Piper, who is an effects artist, and Brett was getting our newsletter, *The B's Nest*, which was the predecessor to *Alternative Cinema* magazine. I think he had shown them that and suggested they talked to me.

I think it was the same way for a lot of those projects. Some people I would meet at conventions and they would give me their movie. Every convention I've ever gone to in my life, people are always giving me movies to watch. Much like now, there's no problem finding the movies; it's finding *good* movies that's the problem.

Were these mostly shot on VHS or on film?

Winterbeast was 16mm. It was bad 16, but that was part of its charm [*laughs*]. We had *Heartstopper* (1989), which was 35mm, and *The Majorettes* (1986), which was 16mm. But the rest of them were shot on video at that point.

Some of them were better than others. There was one called *Zombie Army* (1991), and I think those guys shot on Betacam, which was much higher-end than most of the other stuff.

There were a lot of other people making little shot-on-video movies by that point. Did you encounter any of those guys, like the Polonia Brothers or Jon McBride?

Yeah, that was a little bit later. We started this thing called Tempe Video Wholesalers, where we were selling *Murder Weapon*, *Robot Ninja*, *Skinned Alive* and *Ghoul School* to local stores.

I think they had some other tape, maybe *Linnea Quigley's Horror Workout* (1990). That was really our first step into distribution, but it didn't get us too far.

DeCoteau had his own mail order business. He was finding all these places to get cheap product. He would get tapes for five bucks and sell them for ten bucks. I was doing his catalog design. I would do his video box covers and his catalogs, and he would pay me with these tapes. I would turn around and sell them through my own mail order business, which makes it sound like we were competing, but I was actually going to conventions and stuff, where he wasn't. He gave that up eventually, and I kept doing it.

I don't think I ever spoke to Jon McBride, who made *Woodchipper Massacre* (1988), but I was selling that movie as well as *Cannibal Campout* (1988) and *Splatter Farm* (1987), which was the Polonias' first movie. I think there was a magazine called *Independent Video* at the time that a lot of us were in.

A lot of that stuff seemed very marginal at the time. Is it strange now to see a two-disc special edition DVD of something like *Splatter Farm*?

I guess it's not that strange. You figure as time goes on people tend to remember things more fondly than they probably thought of them originally. That's not an aspersion on that movie, necessarily. I remember when I started putting together all of these special edition DVDs of my own films, people were like, "Is this guy insane?" I was completely remastering them from the ground up. It was not really financially viable, but I did it mostly for my own personal reasons. I wanted to restore this stuff for the future.

I think we've reached the point that DVD has been around for twelve years, and it's way past the saturation point. People are just scrambling for stuff to pick up. Anchor Bay would have never put out *The Dead Next Door* in 1998 or 1999, but by 2005 they were running out of stuff to release. I'm not saying they're scraping the bottom of the barrel, but that's the implication. They can only put *Evil Dead* and *Halloween* out so many times [*laughs*].

You've worked in almost every format. What were some of the limitations to working on video?

I've shot on everything except 70mm or Pixlevision. As far as video, I never had enough money to have a proper camera. When I first moved to L.A. and came back in 1991, and started doing those Cinema Home Video movies, I had bought what I thought was a good quality Super VHS camera that was affordable for the money that I had available to me. I think we're only talking about maybe $2,500, which nowadays is nothing. You can buy an HD camcorder for less than that now.

The requirements that I had were that the image not be so harsh, and that the camera had three chips, because that was the big thing back then. They were able to more accurately reproduce the color.

The major flaw was more on the post-production side. The way we had to edit them seriously degraded the quality. The minute you go down one generation, and you have to do that again to add sound effects, you're lucky if anything looks worthwhile at all by the time you get to the actual dubs. Especially by today's standards.

For DVD, I was able to go back to *Ozone* and all these movies, go back to the camera masters, pull them into Final Cut Pro and finish them that way. They looked so much better, but still can't hold a candle to today's stuff. Even from 1991 to the time we did *Polymorph* (1996) on MiniDVD with the Sony VX1000, that's only a five-year period of time. The technology leaped ahead pretty dramatically.

There seems to have been a whole new boom in low-budget filmmaking thanks to these new, cheaper cameras.

We did the last couple of shows here on MiniDVD. When I started with Full Moon they were still shooting 35mm. By the time I started producing movies for them, I convinced them to shoot on DVCAM. I actually bought this $18,000 camera with cool lenses and all that stuff. That's what we were shooting those movies with. By the time we shot maybe the third or fourth one of those, [George] Lucas came forward with the first *Star Wars* prequel. That's when the HD thing kicked in. It's not even worth shooting on standard definition anymore.

The last show I actually did for Full Moon was on HD. We went from the DV camera to that era, even though it wasn't really "finished" HD. It didn't take long. So much happened in that amount of time, and now you have all these offshoots of HD where the cameras are very affordable compared to back then. It was like what happed as VHS hit a wall, and MiniDVD replaced it.

Now we seem to be back to where we were in the 1980s and 1990s, where anyone can make a movie. The downside to that is that *everybody* makes a movie, whether they have any talent or not.

There's nothing special about it. More than just getting distributed, everybody wants to be a YouTube star now. You have two camps: the people that are content with being on YouTube and having that audience, and you've got the guys that are still trying to pound out movies the old way and sell them. Even more so than when I started, there's way more product than will ever find a home. Obviously you have avenues for self-distribution now, which a lot of people are taking to.

Amazon.com has this space where they will do manufacturing on demand of DVD-Rs that you can sell on Amazon. You are limited with what you can do with those. It's semi-legitimate distribution. There are more avenues to sell stuff, but there is less interest in seeing what's being made. Everybody is out making stuff.

I always used to joke that my audience was mostly composed of people who want to do what I'm doing. And looking back over time, it's really true. Most of the people that grew up watching my stuff are now making their own movies, and finding out the same thing: that their audience is mostly comprised of people who also want to make movies [*laughs*]!

Fan is a very relative term in this day and age! You don't want to let any of that stuff get to your head. When I grew up watching George Romero's stuff, I wanted to make movies. I wasn't just watching it purely for entertainment. I guess it's just a watering down process over time.

How do you decide what you will distribute?

I put some titles up on the wall and throw a dart at them — I'm just kidding. Not that far off, though. I don't pick up outside movies as much as I used to. Last year I decided I'd just throw some chunks of money at people and have them make some movies exclusively for my label. In between that, I have to pick stuff up. The problem with having a distribution business is that if you have a couple of releases a year, you will never get paid by your distributors. They want you to have a steady stream of releases. I've been forced to release some stuff I wasn't as crazy about, as well as the few titles I wanted to get behind and push. It

Bookwalter at his desk during the production of *The Dead Next Door* (courtesy J.R. Bookwalter).

becomes more of a factory mindset. I hate to say that, but that's the reality. I have to put something out every so often, or I'm not gonna get paid.

How do I choose them? I think every movie is different. There's an example I'll give you of a zombie movie I picked up last year. I wasn't that crazy about the movie, but I admired the guy's spirit and what he did. In talking to the filmmaker I thought this guy deserved a chance. There was something to his movie and I thought people would like it. It wound up being one of my better sellers last year. Every case is different. I can't say there's a formula behind any of it.

What was your best experience working on a film?

I don't think any of my experiences were good, really. I'm one of those people — and this is one of the reasons I haven't shot anything in a while — who hates being on set. I love the prep work and I love the post work, but I don't like being on set. That's the opposite of everyone I know, because everybody thinks it's the greatest thing in the world to be standing there yelling "Action!" and "Cut!," but I just hate it.

I've always said if I could get a robot to program with everything, and send him out to get the footage and just bring it back to me, I'd do that. My experiences on set have ranged from absolutely miserable to tolerable, I guess. Probably one of the best experiences I had was *Witchhouse II* (1999), with it being my first 35mm movie and shooting in Romania. They put us up in a Hilton hotel, and I had my own driver who would drive me to set every day. It was like being on a real movie. Unfortunately, the whole time I was sick with the flu.

Witchhouse 3 (2001) was probably another one. It was a different experience than *Witch-

house II, but it probably was a better experience ultimately. I wasn't even planning on putting my name on that movie; it was something I was doing on a dare with Charlie Band. But it wound up turning out okay.

Dead Next Door would ultimately be the number one, because I'll never have an experience that would duplicate that again. Just the amount of time involved and the number of people who came out and just worked their butts off for nothing. That's a once-in-a-lifetime experience.

What was your worst experience?

All of them! My worst experience on set was probably *Deadly Stingers* (2003), the last one that I directed. It's still unreleased, thank God. That was my first HD show. That was the one that was almost all night shoots, which is always miserable. We had this awful scorpion puppet. We wasted hours and hours trying to light it to look halfway decent, and it never worked.

I was sitting there on set just wishing I was somewhere else. There were positives, too. The cast was pretty good and they were really into it, and [cinematographer] Mac Ahlberg shot it, so working with somebody like that who had shot tons of other movies was a great experience. It wasn't all bad. It should have been a better experience than it was, but I knew going into it that there was only so much I could do. In fact, I told Charlie Band that my magic hat was out of rabbits, but he said it would be fine. That was his answer to everything: it'll be fine. It's not the worst movie I made. It's certainly no *Robot Ninja*. Coming out of the *Witchhouse* movies I had higher expectations. I should have known better.

Do you think you'll get back into directing again?

What was the line The Eagles used — when hell freezes over [*laughs*]? Maybe. I don't feel any motivation to do it. It's such a pain in the ass. So many people want to make movies, and they are clamoring to make movies. When I was out in L.A. the last few years, I really started to feel like Tim Robbins in *The Player* (1992). There's that scene where they're at lunch and they're all talking film and shop talk, and he didn't want to talk about it. He says, "We're intelligent people. Can't we talk about something else?" and they all laugh at him. That's what I felt like the last few years in L.A., because I just wasn't as hungry to go out and make anything. I didn't know what I wanted to do when I moved to L.A. in '97, but I wound up making all that stuff for Full Moon and burning myself out. I was less interested in making movies.

I just wanted to take a break from it. I didn't have any stories I was burning to tell, and I didn't want to deal with all the egos and bullshit that goes along with making these movies. Unfortunately, there is always crap you have to deal with.

What was the last thing you worked on?

We did these wraparounds for this thing called "Bad Movie Police" that I produced. Those were shot shortly after the last film I directed. I just produced them. We did this documentary called *Something to Scream About* (2003).

Was *Deadly Stingers* (2003) your last directing gig?

That was finished right around the same time. It's been five years, but it hasn't felt like that because I've been putting all these old movies on DVD and I've been executive producer on a few projects. I guess I've kept busy, but boy, I'm surprised it's been five years.

As far as the last time I've been on a film set, it's been awhile. I don't miss it yet.

You're back in Ohio now. What do you plan on doing next?

I get asked that all the time. I've fallen into a dangerous pattern of just putting out something new on DVD every month or two. I can't say I have any ambitions to start anything new.

Last year I started a series of little movies where I pay the people to do these small films. Some of them were things that I wanted to do for a while, and we started with the *Kingdom of the Vampire* (2007) remake, which Brett Kelly did in Canada.

Brett had approached me and we actually rewrote the script. He found a really cool house and asked what I thought about doing it up there. He was willing to do it for the deal that I offered. That was the beginning of that series. I had the Campbell brothers [Andrew and Lucas] here in Ohio do one for me called *Poison Sweethearts* (2008).

There's another one called *Platoon of the Dead* that I've had kicking' around for years, and John Bowker, this guy out in Oregon, shot that one. We got Ariauna Albright to co-star in that one. That one's gonna come out probably in early 2009.

The Polonia brothers did a thing called *Forest Primeval* (2008) for me. All three of us liked *Equinox* (1970), and this was sort of our homage to *Equinox*—not that the world needs such a thing. That came out in February.

I was talking to them about doing a horror anthology called *Blood by the Fire*. John Polonia passed away earlier this year, but Mark still wants to do it. That's an old script I wrote around the same time as *Dead Next Door*. I think we're gonna change some of the stories a little bit. I'm cleaning out the closet of old stuff.

Strangely, a bunch of people have approached me about doing remakes, or doing a sequel to *Skinned Alive*. I keep telling them nobody wants to see this besides you guys [*laughs*]. So who knows? I don't know the merits of doing a remake or sequel of something for the same measly money as the original.

With *Kingdom of the Vampire* we actually had less money than the first one, but because of the technology advances it turned out a lot slicker. And it ultimately is a better movie than the original.

I sometimes joke that I should do the Roger Corman thing, and pull these old scripts out and have people remake them word for word, just with different titles on them.

I'm so unfocused with my own stuff, and now we just found out I'll be a proud father here come February. After 20 years of just these movies being the absolute obsession of my life, I've turned that around and I'm more interested in my personal life now.

Nutriaman
Martin Folse
Louisiana

As home video began to surpass drive-ins as the primary venue for low-budget horror films in the 1980s, certain titles appeared with a comforting regularity on the shelves of mom-and-pop video stores across the country. You were pretty sure the films had played only a few theaters (if any), and you'd never heard of any of the actors, but no matter what video store you walked into you'd see that same box art over and over again. *Terror in the Swamp* (1985) was one of those titles, an obscure monster flick from Louisiana that remains the solitary film credit of producer and screenwriter Martin Folse.

The enterprising Folse is the owner and operator of Houma and Morgan City, Louisiana's local television stations, KFOL/KJUN TV 10. The colorful and controversial Folse hosts his own news program and is active in local politics — particularly in trying to get improved levees for Terrebonne Parish, which suffers frequent hurricane damage.

But in the early 1980s, Folse was a 22-year-old college graduate who decided to shoot a horror film about a Bigfoot-like hybrid of man and a nutria (a large, semi-aquatic rodent native to South America that has bred uncontrollably in Louisiana after being released from local fur farms).

Not long after completing *Nutriaman* (as it was then called), Folse moved into television and was soon operating Houma's only station. I spoke to Folse not long before Hurricane Gustav ravaged the Houma area, knocking down the KFOL tower during one of Folse's broadcasts.

How did you get involved in the television industry?

I was a graduate of Nicholls State University in broadcast journalism. To be quite honest with you, I'm one of those guys that knew what I wanted to do when I was eleven years old. I loved sports and I used to play around with broadcasting. I would pretend to broadcast games while they played on TV. I just developed a love for it. I got a degree, and when I got out I decided to make the movie. I was 22. I was 21 when I got out of college, and I was 22 when I started writing the movie and raising money and getting it all together. I made the movie, and after that is when I really switched toward the TV industry.

Did you buy a station right away?

I had gone to work for the local cable company. A few months later I flew to New Jersey and met with the owner of the cable company, and told him I would like to lease a channel from him. They made that deal happen, and a few years later the license to this area became available. I went to the bank and bought the license. Ever since then I've been building my station. That's the very short version [*laughs*].

How did the film project get started?

It's sort of funny. Right out of college I'd bought a professional video package, the old three-quarter-inch decks you had to carry on your side, and the big cameras. I started filming people's houses for insurance purposes. They would lay all their jewelry out and I would do an inventory, but I'd put it on video. They would sign it and I'd send it to the insurance company, and the owner also put a copy in their safety deposit box.

I did that for a while. I loved to film different things. One day I was hunting with some friends and I was filming all the nutria that were around the duck blind. One of my friends wanted to shoot one of the nutria. I stopped him. It hit me right there, and I said it would be a great movie to have an overgrown nutria protecting the wildlife from hunters and all. We laughed about it, but that led to the idea for the film. The process started from there.

How did you finance the film?

I started writing the script. Before the script was done, and I had a pretty good idea where it was going, I went around and started visiting with people who had made it pretty well.

Doctors, lawyers, business people. I was pretty young and raw at the time. I would go to them and say, "I've got this crazy idea. I don't know if it will work, but would you want to put some money in it?" We formed a limited partnership and started raising money. In those days, it was a pretty good tax write-off for business people — sort of like the state has now, so there can be more incentives to invest in movies.

It was one of those situations where either I was crazy enough to go out and do it or it just wouldn't happen. But they put their faith in me, they gave me a few bucks and we went out and got it done.

What was the budget?

The total budget was probably a little over $200,000. Back in those days, that was a lot of money.

What format did you shoot in?

We shot it in 35mm film, which was a high standard for a low budget film.

Where did you get your crew?

The crew was from New Orleans, basically. They're still in the business. I had talked to a lot of people from different crews, but I found a crew out of New Orleans that had shot some of the Journey videos, they shot *The Toy* (1982) and some other Richard Pryor movies. I went to them one day and said, "Look, I'm trying to break into the business, and I don't have a whole lot of money. Would you help?" And one of the guys who owned the company said, "Yes, I think we can help." So he got involved in the process.

What about the cast?

We just did some casting. We put an ad in the local paper and said, "If you would like to try out for some parts for this horror movie we're about to do, we'll have casting calls at this place and this time." I was shocked at how many people actually showed up. The whole block was lined with people.

It was pretty funny. Some people came in bikinis or dresses. My brother was helping me and I just looked at him and said, "I've created a monster!" It was pretty funny.

What about the hero, Billy Holiday, who played the fish and game warden?

He's dead now. He passed away. There have been several people in the movie that have passed away. Not that its' a *Nutriaman* curse, because the movie is almost 30 years old. I don't even know how old it is! It's one of those things that it just happens. A few people pass away.

He was from New Orleans. He did a lot of acting on Bourbon Street. He was actually a stand-up comic, but he played some bit roles in different movies at the time. Really nothing I can even remember. He would play different parts. Because it was low-budget, the character actor became the lead role. He was our lead guy.

The other two actors I wanted to ask about were those massive poachers, Chuck Bush and Michael Tedesco.

I called them "The Condo Brothers" [*laughs*]. Chuck Bush, who was the taller of the two, was in *Fandango* (1985), the Stephen Spielberg movie. He was a very good friend of mine. We went to high school together. When we were looking for a couple of big old guys to play in the movie, I called him up. I figured after *Fandango* that there was no way he'd bite on this. But he said yes. He came down and played his role. The other one was Michael Tedesco, who was one of the investor's brothers. He came in and he was just a great guy.

Who handled all those explosions and pyrotechnics?

That was done by Joe Catalanotto from New Orleans. He's an explosives expert. He would use littler detonators to blow up stuff. He was a would do all that.

He's listed as the director.

It's sort of funny how that goes. He got the director's credit, but actually a guy name Joy Houck, whose daddy owned all of the Joy Theaters, did a lot of the directing. Billy Holiday did some of the directing. It was a joint effort. But Joy was the one who came on board in the beginning. Joe didn't care if other people put in their say-so. But Joy sort of took over that role. He had directed a couple of creature flicks before. One of them was *Creature from Black Lake* (1976). Gerald McRaney got his start on one of his films.

As a matter of fact, when I was flying to California for the editing, Gerald McRaney was in the seat next to me. We got to talking and I started showing him pictures from the movie set. He said, "Is that Joy Houck? He directed my first movie!" So he showed me a couple of pictures in his briefcase, and it was ironic that was even happening. I didn't know him from Adam; I just recognized him from "Simon and Simon."

Did you direct any part of the film?

No. I did the screenplay and the script, and to be honest if I would have had time, I would have loved to have directed. That would be a dream of mine. I'm fairly creative, and I write country songs and music now. I learned that once I was on that set, my job was mostly producing, getting things ready, calling people up if we needed boats or barges or airplanes. I was doing that. Getting all the logistics set up.

I had no idea Joy Houck had anything to do with your film. What was he like?

Joy was very knowledgeable, and had a pretty good temperament to direct. That's how I found him, anyway, but I was young. What the hell did I know?

Did you meet his father?

I did. They put the movie in some of their theaters. Teddy Solomon and Joy Houck, Sr., were partners. I had a chance to meet both of them. It was Gulf States Theaters, I think. I had to go show the film to Mr. Solomon and he agreed to put it in all the local theaters. At one point, up until a few years ago, *Nutriaman* in Houma was the second top grossing movie in its first week. The one that beat it was *E.T.* (1982) [*laughs*]. Not that we made a lot back because the theaters got their big cut, but it did pretty well. People get a little nostalgic about it. The governor, Edwin Edwards, came to the premiere. I still have pictures of that.

Corky Fornoff flew the plane in the movie that was spraying all the people in the canals. Corky flew the jet in *Octapussy* (1983). He was a local guy from Houma. I asked him to fly the plane in *Nutriaman*. He didn't know me. He had seen me play sports in high school and all that. He said he'd help us. People were stepping up left and right to help. They were gonna get a cut on the end if it became a blockbuster, which it just never did.

Did the local police force participate?

Absolutely. Everybody in the town got involved. The sheriff was involved. As a matter of fact, the current sheriff actually had a line in the movie. It was the talk of the town. They would block streets off, block bayous off. The wildlife and fisheries people helped out. The local police helped out. The parish president's office helped out. Everybody responded.

When was the film made?

I want to say it was October of 1983. The reason we picked October was because I had an 18-day filming schedule, and it was an outdoor movie. Rain is pretty scarce in October. We didn't want to go over budget or over schedule, because I had no budget. So we picked October. Believe it or not, we had 18 straight days of beautiful weather.

What was the production experience like for you as a first-time filmmaker?

It went well, but I'm gonna tell you it was one of the biggest learning experiences of my life. Here I am in my early 20s, dealing with chaos (which movies are). There was a lot of changing and moving on that film. At some points it got very harrowing. I thought, "Oh my God, what have I gotten my self into?" At other times it was a pleasure to be around.

The VHS cover for *Terror in the Swamp* (1985), the only horror film about a mutated nutria ever filmed in Houma, Louisiana.

The guy that actually played Nutriaman was one of my good friends. Putting him in that water in October was pretty cold! That was something.

I'll tell you this, if I had to do it again, I would do it much differently because I learned so much. To me that was just a tremendous learning experience.

What were the hardest things for you to do?

Just keeping up with the cast and crew. There were so many personalities. I had to learn each one's personality and get them to a place where the environment was not falling apart. As you well know, actors and people who make movies are very temperamental. They want it done their way. The challenge was trying to work that puzzle together to where everybody felt like they won. At the end of the day I guess it worked out, but it's tough sometimes to pull it together.

Who made the creature suit?

Dr. David Rau, who is one of the finest surgeons in Terrebonne Parish today. His hobby was making costumes and creatures. He was one of my brother's best friends, and I went to him one day and said, "Look, do you think you can make a nutria suit with a mask and a face?" Sure enough he went to work on it. In fairness to him, he did it mostly for free. He put his heart and soul in it. I didn't have any money. When I first was gonna do it, I sent a letter to Rick Baker, who did *An American Werewolf in London* (1981), and I asked if he would give me a price to make a nutria man suit. They sent me back a quote of $50,000 or whatever. That was almost my whole budget! Naturally I couldn't go that route.

[Rau's] ability to make costumes and all probably paid off, because he's one of the most meticulous surgeons around. He's a great surgeon.

Was the whole thing shot in Houma?

Yes.

Jaime Mendoza-Nava did the music. How did you get connected with him?

Here's the funny thing: Joe Catalanotto tells me that he's got a guy in California that's gonna do all the music. In those days, it wasn't like it is now. I've got seven editing machines here that we can edit movies on. We just use them for TV. You can do everything by computer now.

We flew to California and I thought I was going to this big studio to do sound. I walk into some little hole in the wall in South Hollywood. Here's a guy walking on gravel with a microphone. They get a dog howling and slow it up to make the Nutriaman. I think he had a lot of this already. I remember watching one of those *Boggy Creek* movies or whatever it was, I think a year later, and I could swear the music was the same! They were probably using music back and forth. I don't know who got the bad end of that deal, me or the guy who made *Boggy Creek* [*laughs*]. All I know is that I paid a lot of money for music and sound effects.

He worked on a lot of films, so I imagine he re-used quite a bit of his own music.

He made a lot of money [*laughs*]!

What was your original plan for distribution?

I had no plan. The original plan was finish it first because I'd read several articles that said only 11 percent of people who start movies actually finish. They run into financial problems or the crew quits. Once we made it to the editing, I was thrilled to death that we had at least made it to that point.

The first thing I did was meet with Mr. Solomon and Mr. Houck. There were two separate meetings if I recall correctly. We made a little money back from that. They made most of the money! Then I flew to California and I met with a guy from 20th Century-Fox. He said, "No, we can't use this kind of film." He was one of their buyers.

So then I was in California. I bought a suit and I walked into Universal Studios, unannounced. I walked right past the guards, and they didn't stop me. I was in Universal Studios for about a day.

This lady, I think her name was Diane Maddox, was an executive there. She was an executive or a vice president. I had the can of films with me. I dropped it off to her. She called me back a few days later and said, "We don't do low-budget films, but I appreciate the fact that you snuck in to see me." That amazes me!

It was funny. I was trying to move it. Finally we got a bite from a company called Shapiro Entertainment. They gave us a little front money, which never paid for the whole movie. They put it through distribution in foreign countries and it went on video. But they changed the name of it to *Terror in the Swamp*. It went from *Nutriaman: Terror in the Swamp* to *Terror in the Swamp*, because nobody knew what a nutria was. There were two posters.

New World Pictures ended up buying the rights or part of the rights from Shapiro. They did all the domestic stuff, and then Shapiro did the overseas stuff with the movie.

Did you ever see any money back from the video distribution?

No [*laughs*]. We just about broke even. We were probably short of breaking even, but in those days everybody could write the rest off. Nobody lost. Today it would be a different thing. I think we got right around the break-even point. Everybody sort of chalked it up as one big experience.

The film was made right before the tax laws changed.

I think so. Each person who put in their money was dealing with that with their accountant individually. I don't know how they were doing it. I know I wasn't doing it because I didn't make any money!

I was supposed to get 30 percent of any of the gross proceeds. If the movie made $200,000 I was supposed to get $60,000, no questions asked, but I put all my money back to the investors. They all got their money back before me. I never made a penny. To this day, I've never made a penny.

When people tell me, "Boy, you must have made some money on that," I say, "No, I didn't." I got a t-shirt, a ticket to the movie, and I got a poster hanging up in my office. And I got experience. That's what I made.

You had t-shirts?

As a matter of fact, my mama gave me one for Christmas last year all framed up. Thanks for bringing back the memories, mama!

I take it the lack of financial return was the reason you didn't make a second film.

The follow-up film I had planned on was along lines of, "Just when you thought it was safe to go back in the marsh...," but I got involved in TV right after. My schedule was so hectic that I just never went back into the motion picture end of it.

Who owns rights to the film now?

I do. It reverted back to me. I'd have to look at the contract. As far as I know it reverted back to me. I think at least domestically I could do what I wanted to do with it. I could be wrong on that. That's such a past part of my life that I can't remember everything that's on the contract. I don't even know where the contract is now. I've sort of moved on in the TV industry and the music industry.

You still operate the TV station there in Houma.

I'm the sole owner. I've been writing music. I've got about 130 songs that I've written and put on CD. I've had four of them that have hit the radio. I'm mainly trying to get other artists to sing them. I had one that went overseas and played the for troops in Iraq and Afghanistan. The military network liked it and played it for all the troops.

What song is that?

"Three Minute Love Song" is one of them. It's about a little girl whose daddy goes to war. She's missing him and she's going to buy snowballs with her mom. It's a real patriotic little song.

The other one is called "Does He Know," a real slow ballad, about a soldier who comes back who had his legs blown off in the war. He can't dance with his lady but she still goes home with him every night.

You've also been active in trying to get better levees in your region. How has that effort progressed?

We are still trying to get our levees. We have a pretty dynamic new governor [Bobby Jindal] who is in contention for the vice president slot, but I don't think he'll get it. He's a friend of mine. I've interviewed him many times. I've become an advocate for the levees. I've covered many hurricanes over the years. We've had big rallies. We want to bring public awareness about our levees, and about the fact that south Louisiana is responsible for the nation's fuel. We're responsible for over 30 percent of the nation's oil, which comes right out of where we live.

We're also the number-one supplier of seafood. Without coastal Louisiana, the nation would be in a crunch.

Does *Nutriaman* ever get shown in Houma?

No. But as a matter of fact I showed it on my channel 20 years ago. So many people to this day say, "Why don't you play it on TV?" I'm past that point. Let's let Nutriaman retire. I'm proud of it, but I've moved on. Not that I would never do another movie, because I have an inkling that I would probably do one in the next couple of years. But I'm getting mentally ready for it. It's in my blood for whatever reason.

What kind of film do you want to make?

I want to make a tearjerker. I've got a script I've been working on called *Five Minutes*, about a set of brothers close in age. One of them gets killed in a car accident, and the family becomes distraught. The other brother is distraught because they had a major fight before he got killed. He's praying to God to have five minutes to talk to his brother. An angel appears, and throughout the film he's talking to the angel, but the family thinks he's gone crazy.

That's a lot different than *Nutriaman*.

Much different. I'd like to think I'm a little deeper than *Nutriaman*. I'd love to do it again. I'm glad I did it, but I couldn't have made a living making low-budget horror flicks!

All the President's Monsters
MILTON MOSES GINSBERG
New York

Milton Moses Ginsberg has directed only two feature films in his career, and they couldn't be more different.

An editor by vocation, New York native Ginsberg toiled in television for several years while studying the works of filmmakers like Michelangelo Antonioni and Alain Resnais. His first feature, *Coming Apart* (1969), was a single point-of-view experiment about a psychoanalyst (Rip Torn) secretly filming his encounters with a succession of women via a hidden camera in his loft. Critics at the time were divided about the film (some praising it as a work of genius; others calling it borderline pornography), and *Coming Apart* was a commercial flop.

Unable to mount any of his more personal projects in the aftermath of *Coming Apart*, Ginsberg made what he thought would be a more commercial project—a political satire about a lycanthrope in the White House called *The Werewolf of Washington* (1973).

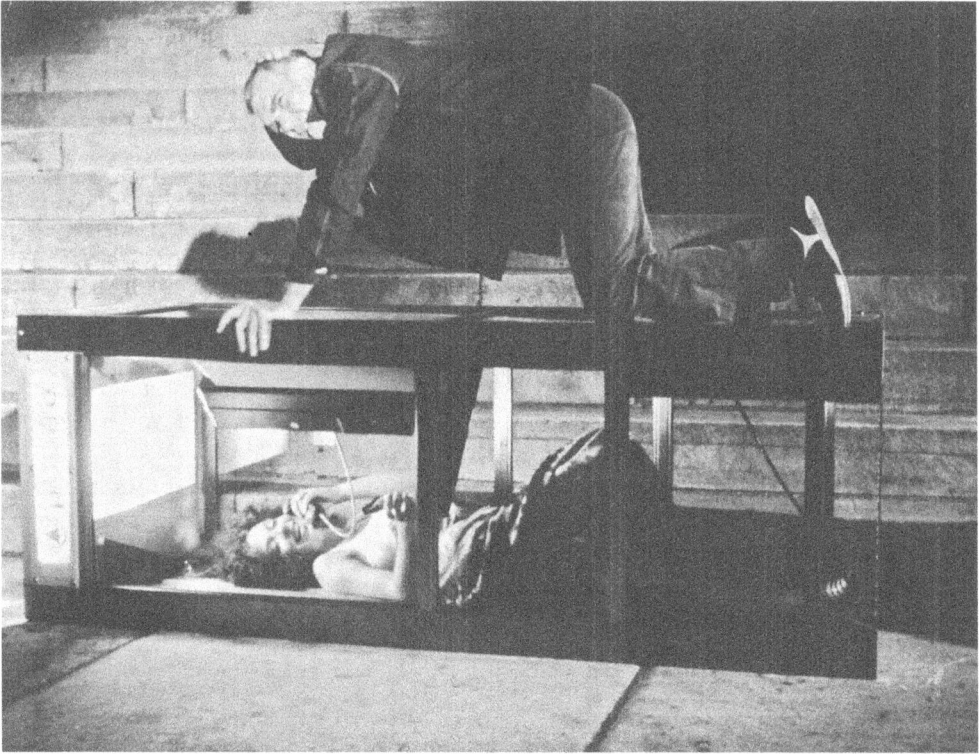

Milton Moses Ginsberg demonstrates the art of werewolfery while actress Barbara Spiegel reclines in a phone booth (courtesy Milton Moses Ginsberg).

The film, about a presidential press aide (Dean Stockwell) who is bitten by a werewolf, was conceived and filmed before most of the details of the Watergate scandal were known to the public. Its prescience did not help its box office, however, as it was spottily distributed and dismissed by critics.

Ginsberg is still active as an editor, and in recent years has made several short films with his wife, artist Nina Posnansky. When we spoke in 2008, the University of California, Berkeley, had just played *Werewolf* as part of its Halloween film program.

Tell me a little bit about your background. Where did you grow up, and what did your parents do?

I grew up in the Bronx, not far from Yankee Stadium. I went to the Bronx High School of Science. At the time I was interested in engineering. In my last year at Science I had an English teacher — we all have one teacher along the way who just kind of inspires us and often changes the direction of our lives. And I remember him. I had gotten into Columbia, and I loved his course and I began to love literature. He said, "Mr. Ginsberg, I don't want to impact too much on your life. My sense is that if you come from the Bronx your parents may not be well-to-do, and engineering is a practical thing for you to pursue, but I really don't think you want to do that."

In my first year at Columbia I was taking courses with Lionel Trilling and all the literati. I have never regretted that.

I was a kind of a loner as a kid. At eight or nine years old my favorite activity was going to the movies on Saturday. I was addicted to going to the movies on Saturday. When I was ten I saw *Spellbound*. I went into the theater, this little kid who was there to see the three features and the ten cartoons, and I came out an acolyte of Freud.

But one of the things I saw at the time was *The Wolf Man*. It was the only horror film I saw. I never saw *Frankenstein* or *Dracula* back then. *The Wolf Man* traumatized me. We can talk further about that in a minute.

By the time I got to university, I was no longer interested in movies. I had loved movies, but I became interested in literature. I would take a girl to the movies every now and then. I would see films that impressed me, but I wasn't interested. I was interested in the novel. I was obsessed with Faulkner, obsessed with Dostoevsky. I wanted to write novels. I graduated university and took odd jobs, tons of odd jobs, doing anything, trying to learn to write.

I couldn't write the great American novel because I couldn't get past the great American first sentence [*laughs*]. I remember the first sentence to just about every novel that moved me, but no first sentence was ever adequate enough for me to build on.

I was doing this for years and really drifting. I had a buddy who was also interested in writing. One day he says to me, "I have a job as an assistant editor. Do you want to do that?" I asked him what publishing house it was at. He said, "No, it's as an assistant editor in movies. I'll teach you how to do that, and you can work half a year. You make enough money in half a year that you can goof off the rest of the year and write."

That was all around the early 1960s. At the same time a friend of mine, a hustler from the Bronx who used to supply quiz shoes with prizes, came into twenty 35mm cameras. He would sell them really cheap. He sold me this Olympus camera for $25. I found I loved taking pictures. I'd always liked taking pictures as a kid.

Then within one week I saw *L'Avventura* (1960) and *La Dolce vita* (1960). They opened in New York at the same time. I was stunned by *L'Avventura*. Absolutely stunned. It was like an epiphany. If I ever had a religious experience, it was seeing that movie. I thought, "Wow, this guy [Michelangelo Antonioni] is doing in cinema what I only thought novelists could do." He was crystallizing the same kind of emotions, and it was totally visual. Extraordinarily visual.

That had a tremendous impact on me. In those days there were theaters in New York, the Bleecker Street Cinema and the Thalia, that were like repertory theaters. They would change their program two or three times a week.

I remember once, early on, somebody said, "*Citizen Kane* is playing at the Bleecker. You ought to see that. It's the greatest movie ever made." I went to see *Citizen Kane*. I didn't think it was the greatest movie ever made. It was brilliant and contrived. I wondered whether to stay to see the other film on the bill, which was *Open City* (1945). When I saw *Open City*, it was just an extraordinary experience. I wanted to make films like *Hiroshima, mon amour* (1959), because of the way [Alain] Resnais was treating not only human emotion, but time and space.

All of that just really blew my mind. As the sixties progressed, all of these filmmakers were working all at the same time. There must have been ten Italian filmmakers whose work was just extraordinary. Fellini, Emanno Olmi, who did a film called *The Fiancés*. A whole bunch of them. Dino Risi, Luchino Visconti, Roberto Rossellini. The French had their filmmakers: Resnais, Godard, Truffaut. They were at the peak of their careers. They were turning out these movies at the rate of one a year, but there were so many that every other week there was a film opening in new York that just really expanded your sensibilities and expanded your heart. Those were the kinds of films I wanted to make.

I think I came close with *Coming Apart*. I had never worked on a feature film in any capacity before that.

But you had edited films, right?

I was an assistant editor for years. Then I began to do camerawork. I became a cinema verite cameraman. I had never worked on a feature film until the day I showed up to do *Coming Apart*. I had written a few scripts.

In *Coming Apart*, I tried to do something that was a reflection of my experience and the experience of the people that I knew. But I tried to do it with the formal values that I had picked up from French and Italian cinema, Japanese cinema; maybe Bergman influenced me more than I like to acknowledge, with films like *The Silence* (1963).

The response to *Coming Apart* was very mixed. People either said it was a masterpiece or they said it was dreadful.

The reviews were highly polarized.

That's a good way to put it. About three or four years ago I read a review from Gene Siskel that I hadn't seen before, and his review started off, "If you have never considered suicide, you will not connect with this film. The value of this film will elude you," or something like that. When I read that I froze and thought, "Jesus, look what he's revealing about himself!"

But the reviews were indeed polarized. I couldn't get another gig. I was writing, but I couldn't do any films. I thought, "You know what? I'll do a horror film."

When you began writing screenplays, was that process easier for you than it had been when you were trying to write novels?

Absolutely! It was absolutely easier because I wanted to direct, and I couldn't afford any properties. I couldn't buy a novel. So I decided to write something. The very first one was based in the art scene in New York. My closest friend at the time was a painter. I wrote a script based on that.

I sat down and decided that, judging by the films I'd seen, there were roughly 40 or 50 scenes in a film. I thought of how I would place them across a landscape. Where would the action go? Who would the characters be? I was establishing a kind of grid. What would be the flow through space, through action? What would the characters be, and who were they? As soon as I did that, then I wrote. I forced myself to do it.

But you're right, living within the restrictions, not trying to achieve immortality, just trying to do what was necessary to make a film, was in fact very liberating. And I was a good writer. The first screenplay was optioned, the second screenplay was optioned, and the third one was *Coming Apart*.

How long prior to *Coming Apart* did you work as an assistant editor?

I must have been an assistant for four years or so.

You also worked in television, including on "Candid Camera."

Yes, I very briefly worked on "Candid Camera." That had a very strong impact on *Coming Apart*, that concept of the hidden camera. It was fascinating because I realized people were addicted to the show. It's amazing. It was so far ahead of its time in terms of concealed cameras and ubiquitous cameras. The guy who did the show, Allen Funt, was truly a lunatic. He had closed-circuit television in his offices so he could watch all the editors at work. That's how nuts he was!

Otherwise, I worked on very political shows for NBC like "Death of Stalin" and "The Rise of Khrushchev" (1963). I remember I was working with an editor named Jack Kaufman, and Jack had a real great visual sense. The producers had all come from radio in the early years. I remember once we were working on the end of the Khrushchev show, and he had found a rare speech by Lavrentiy Beria, one of the henchmen of Stalin. They wanted that speech to be the end of the show. Jack said, "No, I'll cut you something else." Somebody had sent him pictures of a blizzard in Moscow with all these Russians walking through the blizzard and cars not able to move. He cut a final sequence with that. The producer asked what he was doing, and Jack said, "I'm giving you the context of all of this. Never forget these guys are operating in an arena of human beings, and some of the human beings are us, and some are them." He said, "This is not picture radio, this is cinema," and they went with it. That was the phrase he used that made quite an impression on me.

I was learning. I think I have a gene for editing. It's something I've avoided all my life, but when the landlord knocks, the jobs are there. But I try to avoid them.

So in the aftermath of *Coming Apart*, you decided to make a horror film.

After *Coming Apart* I tried to do additional films. I wrote about similar subjects. Films about people professional people, filmmakers in the midst of their life. Realism born of neo-realism. The way Antonioni came out of neo-realism and went into modernism. I was trying to do those kinds of films. *Coming Apart* really did not do well because of some of the hostile reviews, and I couldn't get the other projects off the ground. I thought, "I'll do a horror film."

The Wolf Man was hiding in my unconscious. There's no doubt about that. I'm quite serious about it. I look at it now and I see why. I was obsessed with werewolves.

I went to the producers of *Coming Apart* and said, "Give me an advance; I'll do a werewolf film for you." They said, "Great. That's perfect." I remember somebody gave me a house on Fire Island in May, and it rained for about ten days. I wrote the script in ten days.

I was obsessed with Nixon. There had been this break-in at Watergate, and at the time Nixon was trying to push through his Supreme Court nominees. There were incredible struggles with the Democrats over the same kind of creeps the Republicans put up now for Supreme Court nominees. He was engaged with this and arguing with the press. At the same time there was this Watergate break-in in the back pages of the newspapers.

During the ten days on Fire Island, I needed an armature, some kind of plot for my werewolf movie. I set it in the White House. Not with the president being a werewolf, but this press aide being a werewolf. I almost anticipated John Dean. The guy was like John Dean, but John Dean didn't exist yet, so to speak. He wasn't in the public eye at that point. I came back to the producers. They read the script and said, "You want to attack the president? You've got to be nuts. Keep your money and don't ever show your face here again! You're dangerous."

Then I found a producer, who had been an ex-girlfriend of mine, who was in the film business. That was Nina Schulman, who recently died. I hadn't been in touch with her for many years. She was no longer my girlfriend, but she was a practical person and we were still friends. She said, "I'll try and produce that for you."

We needed a lead. We needed a werewolf. We came up with this plan where we would get an 8 × 10 photo of the actor we were looking for — and among the early ones were Gene Wilder and George Hamilton. We had friends who were art directors in magazines. They would do eight or ten copies of the photo, and in each one the actor would gradually become more of a werewolf. If we sent the script to Gene Wilder, every ten pages there'd be a photo of him transforming into a werewolf. What actor could resist?

Another actor at the time we did that with was Donald Sutherland. Donald Sutherland was very anti-war during the latter stages of Vietnam. His girlfriend was Jane Fonda. He absolutely loved the script and wanted to do it. He said, "I have to see your work." We had a screening of *Coming Apart* for him, which he loved. He took the film home to Jane Fonda, and she said, "This is sexist. You can't do *Werewolf of Washington*."

So we lost Donald Sutherland. His agent said he would try to get around it, but he didn't really. Finally we got Dean Stockwell, who I think was a brilliant choice.

As all this was progressing, the Watergate story was getting bigger. But we filmed in, I believe, September of '72. Nixon was running for president. He was re-elected in November of '72. The story hadn't broken yet. So far, I was ahead of my time. One of the problems with the film, aside from its obvious deficiencies, was that when Watergate broke, it was something no fiction could encompass. The reality was just so much bigger than any fiction that my film looked tame.

Who came up with the title?

I did. I'm very good with titles, and the title was a grabber. Whoever heard the title, whether they knew it was about presidential politics or not, wanted to at least read the screenplay or do the film.

Why were you so affected by *The Wolf Man*?

It has a very interesting structure. The original move was written by a guy named Curt Siodmak. Naturally, Curt used his unconscious to fill out the character and came up with a lot of the mythology. What's interesting is it's set in England, I think, although it was not really set in England. It's set in some European country. There's an English estate with Lon Chaney's father, Claude Rains, but there are gypsies going through the countryside. So God knows where it is.

But Lon Chaney comes there, and he's this lumbering American. Chaney was a big awkward guy, which qualified him for the Steinbeck piece, *Of Mice and Men* (1939). He's this kind of lumbering guy, the son of this aristocrat. He has no mother. He falls for somebody else's girlfriend, and she falls for him. Immediately it's this heavy Oedipal overlay, with his father finally killing him to save the girl. His mother is the gypsy woman. She's a surrogate mother, but when he kills her son, she takes him on as a son. She says, "You didn't kill him; you released him." I borrowed all those lines because I wanted to stay true to that in the beginning of the film.

***Werewolf of Washington* was filmed in Glen Cove and partially in D.C. Tell me about the locations.**

I'm going to ramble on again. You may have to focus me. What happened was we finally got $100,000 to make the movie. It's a pretty big script for $100,000. You had the White House and all these locations, and make-up and helicopters and everything else. I've always said that I set out to do the impossible, and I achieved it, but I neglected the possible.

In fact it was the scope of the production — a scene or three a day in disparate locations, *all within a month for a hundred grand, even*— that caused me to neglect the artistry of the piece. We spent more time driving to and from locations and setting up each morning than actually rehearsing and filming.

Even in the script, I tried too hard for laughs and not hard enough at making the characters believable. And the "horror" aspect I thought was too politically implicit to bother developing cinematically. Both fatal errors, even in a low-budget horror film.

When you're shooting that ambitiously in a short schedule, you must get everything the day you set out to shoot it. If you don't shoot it on Thursday, it's not gonna be in the film. I think the film suffers a lot from the focus of my ambition in this thing.

Because we had very little money, I couldn't bring the cameraman down to Washington. I had done a lot of camerawork as a verite cameraman. I rented equipment, and Dean and I and a couple of production assistants went down to Washington. I shot all of the stuff going in and out of the White House (or the illusion of going in and out of the White House), and I shot the moon coming from behind the capital dome with bats flying. In the end I was not happy with this DP's camera work. But once we set down that path, there was no changing it.

I was using a cameraman who just used too much light, and it slowed everything down. It's another reason why I couldn't bring all of the performances to the right pitch, but also some of them were not written adequately.

We had interviewed several cameramen. I saw this fellow's work, I liked it, but in the end.... Let me put it this way: initially I thought we would do it in 16mm, fast, not necessarily hand-held, but with a very mobile crew. I think the film suffered from our trying to put too much production value in it.

Then there was Glen Cove. I had a very good production manager named David Appleton. He and the associate producer, Steven Miller, who had put up the money, knew where to go and who to approach. There was this fashionable girls' school in Glen Cove that we used as the interior of the White House. We used the grounds to shoot the gypsy camp, Stockwell getting bit, and the fight between the president and the wolf after the helicopter sequence. We used people's homes in Glen Cove.

Some of the interior filming was done in New York. The scene at the end where Dean is in the seat, where he's chained up. Then he comes back to his apartment after the helicopter sequence. Those were done in New York. Some of the moon rises I shot from the roof of the building I was living in, which was over by the East River.

The bulk of the film we shot in and around New York. The Capitol steps scene was shot at the Brooklyn Borough Hall with a borrowed telephone booth. The helicopter exterior we shot at LaGuardia, and the interior was done in a vast Pan Am hangar at JFK.

All of the Michael Dunn scenes were shot in a power plant at JFK. Its vast windows opened it to view from the road, and I always loved its vividly-painted pipes and dynamos. We shot one angle of the party scene in an apartment on Sutton Place, and had to shoot the reverse angle in a home on Long Island a few weeks later. The back and forth edits matched perfectly.

When you shot in D.C., did you get permits?

I thought we hadn't, but after we spoke the first time, my brother Arthur (who acted as a second production manager) reminded me proudly and rather testily that he had obtained location permissions for everything. Even in Washington, we shot the exteriors of the Capitol and White House in plain view from the street. Life was easier then!

My brother was also the second art director. He designed the gypsy symbolism on the surplus army ambulance. We offered to re-paint it, but the owner of the ambulance loved it.

How long was your filming schedule?

It must have been about 20 or 25 days. I don't remember.

Tell me about working with Michael Dunn.

I think I almost wrote Michael Dunn into the script. Michael was, at the time, the premier dwarf, a brilliant actor.

I think I knew him through mutual friends. Michael was in bad shape when we were filming. He was getting very sick because of his condition, and he would die soon. Some times he didn't have the energy to do scenes. I would say, "You know what, let's forget it." He'd say, "No, I want to do it." He could not do the scenes sometimes. I figured out that if he had the first line of the scene, that was not good. But if I had a triggering line for him, he'd respond. He'd perk up and go right into it. He really loved working and he loved the project.

But that was true of so much of the cast. There was an actor named Beeson Carroll, and he just was great to be around. He had a perfect manner. I guess I haven't done enough movies. I've done three. There was a lost film I did after *Werewolf of Washington*. But that happens. Certain people in the cast you just develop a tremendous camaraderie with, and you just really get along very well and you grow to love people. Then you all go your separate ways.

What was the other film you did after *Werewolf of Washington*?

I had done a film with Rip where Nick Ray was supposed to do a film, and he got very sick or died. The producer called me up and said, "I'm doing a film with Rip Torn, and Rip says you're the only guy who can do this film for a limited budget. He trusts you and he likes you, but I don't think we're gonna finish the film for the money we have. We're just going to shoot and then try to raise money."

So I came into a very bizarre situation where he thought we would shoot twenty percent of the film. I said, "If we can confine it to certain scenes, if we don't do the car chases or shoot outs, which are gonna burn up film and money, we can do the other stuff." We strung together about 60 percent of the film. The well ran dry. I didn't like the script, and I had to rewrite it. The initial contracts were so Byzantine that whenever somebody would say, "We'll give you the money to finish the film," they'd take a look at the contracts and then back off. It was tremendously frustrating for Rip and for everybody involved.

The other two recognizable names in *Werewolf* would have been Clifton James and Thayer David.

Thayer David had a small role as a police inspector in the Romanian part of the film. I am Romanian, and my grandparents were Romanian. Maybe that has trickled through. We cast a lot of people out of Actor's Studio. It suited the politics of most of the people.

Dean was very angry with me at the end that the film didn't do better. He and his agent felt that I could have edited it differently, and they were right. The one thing I couldn't

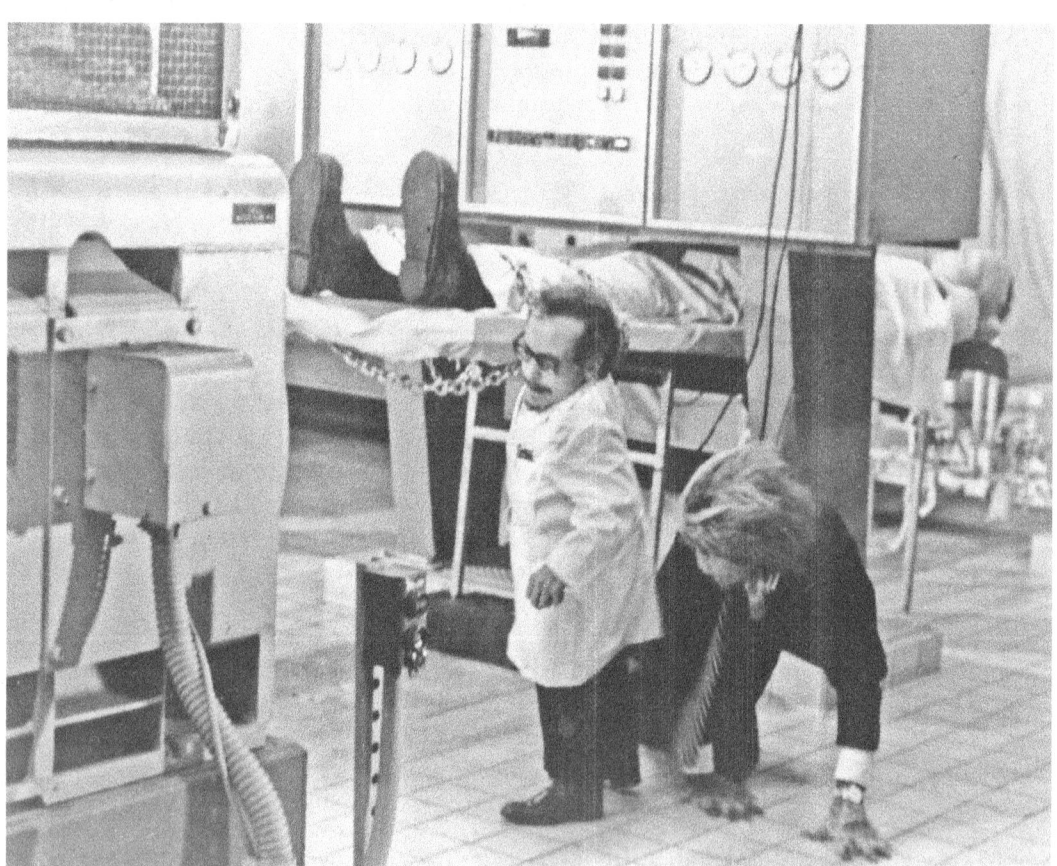

The late Michael Dunn shows Stockwell's werewolf around the laboratory (courtesy Milton Moses Ginsberg).

do was make it shorter to accelerate some of the scenes, because our contract called for delivering a 90-minute film. If I didn't deliver a 90-minute film, the producer and I wouldn't have made any money — not a cent! Everybody was working for next to nothing. I would have lost my percentage of the film. But because the film was certainly a failure by box office standards, I didn't make any money anyway! It would have behooved me to make a better film. It's a film I have very mixed feelings about. I enjoyed doing it, but it doesn't impress me. I tell people, very frankly, it's one of the worst films ever made with three of the funniest scenes ever shot.

You mentioned that to me before. What are the three scenes you think worked?

The telephone booth scene I love. People remember it. People feel that I did that as a comedy sequence, but it is really horrific. The scene where he transforms in the helicopter, and the president can't see him but the Chinese ambassador can. The bowling alley scene is great, with the hand enlarging in the ball. We shot that in the basement of a church in Princeton, New Jersey. I was laughing so hard and loud I thought I was killing the audio, but I couldn't stop!

I also liked the bit in the bowling alley where Stockwell and Biff McGuire waddle down the bowling lanes.

Oh yes, that's right. The other scene I like is the one when he comes out of the Pentagon complex and he wakes up in the cemetery. He has a meeting before he's chained up. I loved the scene where he's chained up. From there all the way through to the end, it works for me. From the Michael Dunn scene on, it almost works for me, although I think the Michael Dunn scene went a little too long. The scene where he's in the Attorney General's office, and is having a conversation with the attorney general and Commander Salmon [Beeson Carroll], plotting the points of all the killings in Washington in the form of a pentagram. I love the acting in that.

I also love the scene in the restaurant where he's trying to explain to the Naval psychiatrist that he's a werewolf, and they go into the bathroom. I like the interchange between the actors in that.

But there's a lot I don't like. I don't have a gift for horror films, because unconsciously I'm not interested in them. I enjoy them occasionally, but I enjoy the more primitive ones. The original *Dracula* I think is scary as hell. Coppola's *Dracula* (1992) was not. I love *Frankenstein*, and the DeNiro *Frankenstein* (1994) is not bad because it's so faithful to the novel. But my unconscious doesn't get off on doing horror films or creating horror sequences. The rather favorable article in *Film Comment* pointed out that I was more interested in the psychology of the werewolf, Whittier, than anything else in the film, which I think is true. I liked the effect in the helicopter and stuff like that, but I don't think my sensibility really reaches in that direction. What I do, I do well — the *Coming Apart* kind of thing. There is so much horror in real life that for me to work in it metaphorically doesn't seem to happen.

***Coming Apart* was first time you set foot on feature set. *Werewolf* was more challenging from a logistical standpoint. Were you prepared for that more complicated style of filming?**

I think I was. I think if we'd had two months to shoot the film and use more dolly shots and that kind of thing, it would have been a better film. I really think the fault of the film comes in the writing of it. The minor characters are too minor, too cliché, too patterned after living people. Every one of those characters was based on somebody in the political world at that time, Katharine Graham the publisher, Nixon, John Mitchell, the Attorney General, were all based on real people. Some of those minor characters were one beat too short of taking on flesh. If you don't identify with characters, you're not going to pull off the horror. It's too gratuitous. And the horror is just too slapdash. My unconscious doesn't get off on it, as I say. It's like you're asking Antonioni to do a werewolf movie. I'm not Antonioni, and I don't have his limitless sensibility, but I *do* share his limitations.

What was it like working with the special effects?

We had to shoot all the transformations in one day. The one in the helicopter, the one after he is shot and comes back to human form, the one where he's sitting in his apartment before he goes out to the telephone booth.

But that's a massive amount of work. The way I did it was, you only go through the make-up once. The guy is only going through the make-up from beginning to end only once. That means when he changes back, I have to reverse the shots. It was all done in that rocking chair, so that I had to put a blue cloth behind him for the transformation in the helicopter, and put a red cloth behind him to put him for the transformation back in the final shot on the floor.

The make-up man, who did a brilliant job under the circumstances, would apply a little makeup. I'd shoot it with three different backdrops. Then he'd put on a little more, and we'd do it again with three backdrops hoping that Dean could keep his head in the same place.

Dean was a trooper, and it was a long day. We filmed that in New York in a friend's apartment in the building I was living in. In my apartment, the actors were rehearsing the scene for the climax in the film. They waited around all day to do that scene where everybody rushes in as the werewolf dies and transforms back to Whittier. That's the name of Nixon's home town, by the way.

Presidents! Some other producers were interested in another script I had, a serious piece about the last weeks of Marilyn Monroe. This is around 1990, 1991. They optioned it, but again it was about the Kennedys, about presidential politics, and it made people nervous. It never got going.

Your cinematographer, Robert Baldwin, had done stuff around New York and New England like *Let's Scare Jessica to Death* (1971).

That's the one I had seen.

Did you know the rest of the crew?

No. I didn't' know anybody. You just go out and by word of mouth, you put together a crew in those days. You asked people, "Do you know anybody?" They'd come in with their resumes.

I want to ask about the initial distribution. Diplomat Films released *Werewolf*. How did you get involved with them?

Initially, a fellow named Don Rugoff was going to distribute it. He was a major importer of great European films. He had Cinema 1 and Cinema 2 in New York. He wanted to distribute this, and for some reason his business and health began to fall apart.

There was a guy who I knew called Sam Lake, who was using the adjoining editing room where we were cutting this thing. He was a theater owner who had made tons of money with *Deep Throat* (1972). He decided to wanted to be legit. He paid an advance on the film. At the same time HBO was really coming into their own, and they wanted the film to show on HBO. Sam's theatrical run did not work out well. I think he was trying to put it in the same theaters where he showed *Deep Throat*, and the *Deep Throat* audience did not respond to this. But it went on HBO. I was very pleased with that because it just about made its money back.

Nina Schulman and I were working for other people. We were salaried. The owners of the film evidently sold a print to German television. This was in the early or middle 1970s. In those days in Europe there were generally two channels to a country. So if somebody bought the film, they showed it. And apparently for German television it was kind of a kiddie movie. They would show it initially every week, then every other week, then once a month. Having invested in the print, they were not going to lose their investment. Every kid who grew up in Germany in the seventies saw it. When I talk to Germans, they say, "Oh, yeah, *The Werewolf of Washington!*," and they giggle.

The film died pretty quickly. Then it was pirated off God-knows-what to make these murky DVDs. You can tell people that I do not recommend anybody looking at this film under the only circumstances they seem able to see it.

You told me the negative was destroyed.

I let the negative go because I was in the process of moving and I just did not want to move the negative. I thought the lab would survive a little while longer, but they didn't. When I gave a 35mm copy of the print of *Coming Apart* to the Museum of Modern Art, and told them this story, and they became heartsick. They said, "Never destroy the negative of anything." Of course, well after the fact I've been regretful about it. But we like to burn bridges and move on some times.

I want to mention two other things, if you care to explore them, because we were talking about my favorite scenes. Over the years I have evolved a cut from a three-quarter-inch videotape. So the director's cut on this film is 24 minutes. I have some kind of vague narrative with all of my favorite material in it.

I have, over the past two years, been trying to locate a print so I could do a recut on this thing. It's an ambition. I don't know if I'm going to have time for it, to put it off on some kind of digi-master and re-edit it using after effects and maybe more streamlined editing techniques. I could maybe come up with something that runs an hour and 15 minutes instead of an hour and a half that I will be happy with. But I think there's a limit to where my happiness with this film can go.

The University of California at Berkeley showed the film in 2008. Do you know where they got their print?

I have no idea. There must have been about 30 to 50 prints made. I'm surprised. It's the first time I've heard of any print, and you're the one who found it for me. They said I could borrow it. I won't be able to fly out for Halloween to see the quality of the print, but I'll borrow it and put it off on a DigiBeta. It's probably sending good money after bad, but it is my child and I have some responsibility to it.

What kind of changes would you want to make?

I would use black and white for some of the scenes. I think I can montage the transformation scenes much more effectively or more humorously. Maybe change the music, although the music is not bad. Maybe I could make the music more pervasive. Maybe start off with one of the better scenes, like the helicopter scene, and go into flashback and bring it up again. Something to make the beginning of the film more dynamic.

Just generally do a lot of shortening. Some of the shots go on too long; some of the scenes are superfluous and boring.

Watching it again today, I thought that, although a lot of the minor characters are very topically referenced, that the overall themes in the film are still very relevant: the knee-jerk impulse among politicians to engage in cover-ups, or the fact that many of us have an ideological bent that can blind us to the facts in front of our faces.

That's a key to the movie: the ideological bent that blinds you to the facts. Clearly this guy feels guilty about killing people and he wants to have himself revealed, exposed and locked up. Nobody wants to hear about it.

Once the rest of the facts about Watergate came out, was the film out of release already?

It went into release after the facts began to come out.

What was your response after having concocted this plot based on the early facts of Watergate?

Did I feel prescient? I was proud that I knew that the Watergate thing was bigger than everybody thought it was. I was very concerned about the film being successful so I could get some traction in the business, which seemed to be separate from my own discomfort about getting rid of this guy as president. But who knew that we would get subsequent

Ginsberg and Dean Stockwell filming a scene for *The Werewolf of Washington* (courtesy Milton Moses Ginsberg).

presidents who would be far worse? That's totally unimaginable. You thought the dark ages were over when Nixon resigned. Clearly they weren't. They were just beginning.

Have you revisited the film much in the ensuing years?

No. I looked at it a couple of weeks ago after you called. I just went through it looking for the places I would make changes. I revisit the making of it in my head. There were people I appreciate after the fact. I appreciate that guy, David Appleton, just working so hard and killing himself to bring all the elements together every day that we had to shoot. I remember Michael's effort and his pain, and the pleasure of working with Beeson and the pleasure of working with Dean.

Did you ever cross paths with Dean Stockwell again?

Not really. In a sense maybe he was right to be angry, and I'm sad about that.

I was surprised to see that Clifton James is still alive.

Clifton is still alive. I see him at the Actor's Studio, and I think he, too, was pissed with me. He was close with Dean.

An actor we haven't talked about, who gave an extraordinary performance, was Biff Maguire who played the President. Shepperd Strudwick came in for the role of the president, and a very good actor from the movie *Joe*, Dennis Patrick—but Biff had the part as soon as I met him. He brought a comic genius to his characterization.

A rough storyboard for the opening wolf attack scene in *The Werewolf of Washington*. This was the only storyboard used on the film (courtesy Milton Moses Ginsberg).

Except he had this mustache and there hadn't been a president with a mustache since Teddy Roosevelt. But if we asked Biff to take it off we'd have to live with what he looked like sans mustache, and he seemed kind of perfect. Then I remembered a candidate named Tom Dewey, a governor of New York who ran against FDR. He had a mustache. That cinched it.

Like I miss Beeson and Michael Dunn, I miss Biff. Biff and I stayed close and we planned to work together again on a novel I had optioned — Robert Coover's *The Universal Baseball Association, Inc.* Never happened. I dropped into oblivion.

Michael and I stayed in contact until he died not long after from his painful ailments. But generally it was a strange ending to a production, very unlike the experience of *Coming Apart* where Rip and I became like brothers. Viveca Lindfors and I just loved one another right until the time she died. I would encounter her and she would grab me and say, "Milt, when are we gonna make another film?" I did not have that experience with *Werewolf*.

There's another aspect of it that doesn't relate to any of this. In those days it was much easier to cast a film. When I cast *Coming Apart*, I didn't go through agents. I had to deal with agents, but I would go around to off–Broadway theaters in New York and say, "Jesus, you'd be great for this. Would you be interested in reading this screenplay?" There was still some of that with *Werewolf*. It is very hard to do a film, and $100,000 was a lot more money in 1973, but not when you're shooting 35mm color. Even then it was expensive. It was a burden; I'd forgotten we'd filmed all the transformation scenes in one day. That's quite extraordinary.

As I say, it's not a great film, but it has three really very funny, imaginative scenes. Not nearly enough [*laughs*]!

It Came from Florida
WILLIAM GREFÉ
Florida

Florida has long been a hotbed of oddball exploitation filmmaking, with luminaries like H.G. Lewis, Doris Wishman, Fred Olen Ray, Bob Clark and many others producing a wide array of horror, biker and nudist camp films there over the years. One of the most prolific and successful directors to call the Sunshine State home, though, is Miami-born William Grefé. Although he began his career as a writer, Grefé (born in 1930) was unexpectedly drafted to direct his first feature (*The Checkered Flag*, 1963) when the original director took ill. Since then, he's directed more than a dozen films, produced many others, and helmed innumerable commercials.

While he's directed biker films (*The Wild Rebels*, 1967), racing films (*Racing Fever*, 1964), and comedies (*The Godmothers*, 1973), Grefé is probably best known for a string of outré horror films he made in the 1960s and 1970s, starting with the were-jellyfish flick *Sting of Death* (1965) and its co-feature, *Death Curse of Tartu* (1966). In the 1970s he jumped on the nature-run-amok bandwagon, directing *Stanley* (1972, with Chris Robinson using his pet rattlesnakes to do away with his enemies) and *Mako: The Jaws of Death* (1976, with Richard Jaeckel telepathically controlling some killer sharks), along with the William Shatner psycho tour de force *Impulse* (1974).

During that same period, Grefé served as president of Ivan Tors Studios, the Miami-based outfit that had produced the TV series "Flipper" and "Daktari."

Still in Florida, Grefé continues to work with independent filmmakers and maintains a Web site at *www.williamgrefe.com*.

A lot of independent films have been shot in Florida. Why is that?

Well, basically because it's the Sunshine State. A lot of people like Herschell Lewis came down from Chicago to film here. Herschell came down from Chicago. He and Dave Friedman called me

William Grefé and Rita Hayworth on the set of *The Naked Zoo* (1971) (courtesy Daniel Griffith).

up and I helped them get crews and equipment. In fact, I think on one of their commentaries they gave me credit for helping them.

People just sort of migrated to Florida. Ivan Tors was the one that really got Florida going when he first he did "Sea Hunt," and then he expanded to "Flipper" and "Gentle Ben." He had a studio in North Miami. Prior to that, there were very few trained crews. In other words, there were guys that could do newsreel stuff, but Ivan more or less trained the crews, and that started the real influx of various equipment houses and so forth. That was in the real early 1960s. The independents just started springing up from there.

A lot of people don't know it, but prior to Castro, Cuba was like the Hollywood of Latin America. They had very experienced cameramen, soundmen, etc. When Castro took over, the film community fled to Miami.

When I did my second film, *Racing Fever* (1964), which I wrote, produced and directed, I couldn't afford union crews or anything. A lot of these guys were working as dishwashers and parking cars or whatever they could do. I gathered them all together, because my sister spoke perfect Spanish. We shot on weekends, because they weren't working weekends. The first two or three films I did, I used Cuban crews. In fact, I used one cameraman, Julio Chavez, on at least ten of my films. He was a very good DP.

In any event, that's basically it. A lot of the porno guys came down here and knocked out stuff. New York and California were so heavily unionized that it was hard for them to sneak around. I think they came down here to sneak around.

You actually worked for Ivan Tors, didn't you?

I went in as head of production at Ivan Tors, and six months later they made me president of the studio. What was interesting about that, I'd been independent and I didn't want to be an executive sitting on my ass, doing nothing except running and making deals. I had it in my contract where I was allowed to make one independent film a year, and Ivan had first shot at it. If he turned it down, then I could go to other sources. When I came up with *Stanley* (1972) I offered it to Ivan, and Ivan said, "I'm into family and animal stuff." So he turned down *Stanley*. I made that over like six weeks, and I took leave from Ivan to make *Stanley* independently.

What was your background before that? How did you get into filmmaking in the first place?

I first thought I wanted to be an actor. After high school I did summer stock; I did off Broadway. I worked in Woodstock, New York, and Chatham on The Cape, and Cherry Lane Theatre in Greenwich Village.

And then the Korean War came along — I guess I'd seen too many John Wayne movies and I joined up. After the war I got married, and I figured being an actor wasn't very secure for a family guy. I just started writing. I wrote and wrote and wrote and wrote screenplays. I've got all the rejection slips to prove it! Finally, I sold one called *The Checkered Flag* (1963) to a guy down here that had a little studio and did nothing but commercials. We went to Sebring, and they had me on the set for rewrites. The first day the director had a nervous breakdown and collapsed, and panic set in with all the investors. The director of photography [DP] was an old DP from L.A. who had retired to Florida. We're in a motel room in Sebring, and everybody's panicked. We've got to get a director — what are we gonna do?

Finally the old DP said, "Look, first you've got to find a director, and there's none in Florida, so you've got to get one out of New York or California. By the time you find the guy, he can't just fly in and direct the movie stepping off the plane. What the hell — the writer knows all about it, make him the director!" They drafted me at one o'clock in the morning in a motel room in Sebring.

Naturally I knew the script, and I knew actors. But I didn't know a 75mm lens from a 30mm lens. Nothing technical. So I sort of leaned on this old DP to help me. I think very visually, and I would think of a scene, let's say it should have had a 35mm lens on it. He'd put like a 50mm on, and when I'd see the dailies it was not exactly what I had in mind.

So I knew right then and there that I had to get a crash course in the technical end of filmmaking. I just picked everybody's brain; there was no film school. Most people keep diaries and write what they should do. I wrote a diary on all of the mistakes I made and what you should *not* do. So every time I made a mistake, I kept a whole log of stuff. Fortunately, *Checkered Flag* went out and it played top of the bill above a picture called *Trigger Happy* (a.k.a. *Deadly Companions*, 1961), with Maureen O'Hara and Steve Cochran, who were at that time pretty well-known Hollywood actors. The thing was a success, and that led to me being behind the camera. So that was it. That's how I got started.

You also did second-unit work on Del Tenney's zombie film, which was later retitled *I Eat Your Skin* (1964).

Del came down from Connecticut, and he called me up and asked if I'd help out. I helped him with crews and equipment.

How did he know who you were?

I don't know. I guess at that time I was the only act in town. I think I might have known him because I knew Joe Sugar, who was the head of Twentieth Century–Fox distribution in New York.

I don't know if you know the story of Del, but Del really lucked out like a bandit with Twentieth. He did those two horror movies [*Horror of Party Beach* and *Curse of the Living Corpse*] at the time Twentieth was doing *Cleopatra* with Liz Taylor. They were tens of millions of dollars over budget, and Twentieth was hanging by their fingernails. In those days, all the majors had like 30 offices and 30 exchange cities around the United States. They had no product. Del shows up at Joe Sugar's office in New York. Twentieth, just to keep their distribution busy, picked those two pictures up as a dual bill. So that's how Del lucked out because of *Cleopatra*.

Del was a guy who liked the studio, but he didn't like the heat of Florida. He didn't like working outside. I did all the second-unit exterior stuff, and actually took some of the actors out and worked with them.

One of Del Tenney's radioactive mutants menaces a beach bunny in *The Horror of Party Beach* (1964).

Do you remember anything else about the film? Did you work with the zombies?

I did something on a cliff with the zombies. I forget now. I haven't seen the picture in 25 years. I remember there was a cliff scene near some water somewhere. Then we did some stuff out on Key Biscayne. There were no houses or anything out there because they had a big swamp.

One funny thing happened when Del was there. There was a scene in the movie where the people were outside having tea or lunch or whatever. One of the women in the film had a couple of little poodles. Del was sort of a nervous type of guy. Del directs the scene. It was one take. Del said, "Perfect. Let's get to the next set up." I said, "Del, you don't want a take two?" He said it was perfect. I said, "Del, look at the dogs." The two dogs were humping like crazy during the whole thing! Del was so interested in the actors that he didn't even see the dogs.

As a director, the first horror film you did was *Sting of Death*, which was a for-hire job. Tell me about the producer of that film, Richard Flink.

Richard was a building contractor, and he'd never produced a movie before. He knew nothing about it, but he wanted to be in the film business. He got hold of the writer, and the writer talked him into doing this. I guess, again, I was about the only act in town that knew anything about directing movies, so they hired me to direct it.

What was funny about that was the house in *Sting of Death* was Richard's house. I knew enough that when a crew moves into a house, it is absolute chaos. It's a place to work, you know. Anyway, I told him, "Richard, we should go out and rent a vacant house." He wanted to save money. "Okay, Richard; whatever you want." At that time he had super expensive rugs. We're dragging cable across the rugs; everybody smoked, and there's cigar ash everywhere. His wife is having a heart attack. The crowning blow was they had a thousand-year-old antique Chinese vase mounted on the wall. The boom man is following the shot, watching the actors. The end of the boom hit that Chinese vase and the thing crashed and broke. They carried the wife away in a basket [*laughs*].

Another crazy thing he did was when we did the underwater stuff. We were going to shoot out at Soldier's Key, which is right off Key Largo. He rents this big 80- or 90-foot boat. Real big boat. He pulls up and the forecast is 12-foot seas, 30-mile-an-hour winds. I said, "Richard, there's no way in God's world we're gonna do underwater work." He said, "I'm paying for this boat, and we're going out." It was like the George Clooney movie, *The Perfect Storm*. My God, everybody was seasick. We get out there and couldn't even hold an anchor it was so rough.

One of the divers — we had a couple of bikini babies on the thing. One of the guys was mucho macho, and he's gonna show off to these broads. He says, "Richard, I'll go down. It should be calm underneath." He dives down, and when he comes up he's like 25 or 30 feet from the boat, swept out to sea. "Help! Help!" We're throwing him donuts and ropes. I said to him, "Richard, now will you believe me? Let's go up to Rainbow River, which is all clear water." We went and did all the underwater stuff up there.

Richard, even though he was married and all, he wanted to be the big producer. He had some bikini babies in the film, so he takes two of these girls out. He gets a second camera and he's gonna direct them. He's telling them to do this, do that. And the cameraman said, "Richard, there's no film in the camera." He said shoot it anyway! He was just playing. He never shot a foot of footage.

How did you know Doug Hobart, the special effects artist?

Doug came aboard on that because, if you know Doug, I think believed he was the reincarnation of Lon Chaney. Doug loved anything horror, and he had worked with K. Gordon Murray on some of these Mexican horror movies. He hired Doug to go around and promote them. Doug wanted to play the jellyfish monster. In the movie, remember where they find the dead guy that's covered with sores and everything? That's Doug. So after that, when we did *Death Curse of Tartu*, Doug wanted to create Tartu. He did a beautiful job creating the make-up for Tartu. On *Impulse*, with William Shatner, Doug was there and he begged me to lie in the casket when we were doing the scene in the funeral parlor. That's Doug. Doug lay there, and I bet you by the time we lit the thing, it took an hour. Doug lay there like a corpse. He didn't move a muscle. He was in his glory being in that casket.

What did you think of the jellyfish monster?

In those days, you saw the feet with the flippers on them. Now if you tried to release that in the theaters they'd stone you to death in the lobby. Back in those days, it wasn't too bad. You could get away with a lot of stuff on the low-budget pictures.

Didn't Doug have some trouble breathing with his head inside that jellyfish mask?

We had to fill that with air to blow it up, and then put a plug in there. If you watch the thing, it's starting to go down. He's breathing all the air, and as he's breathing all the oxygen out of the air, he collapsed. We had to tear that thing open to get some air to him. We didn't have anything sophisticated like shooting oxygen into the thing. Just pump it up and work as long as you can.

That film, and all of those early films in Florida, had very striking cinematography and really vibrant color, which was not always the case with low-budget films made elsewhere. The Florida films had a very distinctive look to them.

There were two reasons for that. Number one, in Florida, we have no smog whatsoever. The glare off the ocean really lends itself to beautiful photography. Number two, most of the cameramen back then believed in putting color in. If you ever watch *Racing Fever*, there's a scene in a locker room or something. The DP said we had to get some color. He hung up an orange life jack or something. They always liked to put color

The Seminole mummy (Doug Hobart) and witch doctor in Grefé's *Death Curse of Tartu* (1966) (courtesy Daniel Griffith).

in. The only black-and-white film I ever did was *The Devil's Sisters* (1966). That's a lost film. We shot that in black and white. All the rest were in color.

The films always looked very cheerful, and then a monster would come out and kill everybody.

There was one other thing on *Sting of Death*. We had a shoot with the monster out in the Everglades. It's near the beginning. Richard had a friend that had a hunting camp in the middle of the Everglades. To go into the middle of the Everglades is a logistical nightmare, because you have to drag everything way out on the trail, then we had to get an airboat to haul the crew and everything out there. Because I'm from Florida, I knew you could find beautiful Everglades-like locations by just driving. I kept saying, "Richard, why are we spending hours doing this?"

We go out on the trail and all of that jazz. We get all the way out to the island after like three hours. The cable to the battery for the camera had fallen overboard. Now we have to go all the way back in an airboat, drive into Miami and get a cable. We didn't shoot until like three in the afternoon.

When I did *Stanley*, the only thing I did in the Everglades were a few second-unit shots. On *Stanley* I just did locations that I could drive to. I knew logistics will kill you, and visually it doesn't look any better.

The most beautiful shot that everybody commented on was at the end of the movie where he's taking the girl out in a boat to his cabin, and there is a long shot I did with the birds all flying, hundreds of birds. I did that right in the park in the heart of North Miami. But it was the most beautiful shot. Everybody in California said, "Oh my God, the Everglades are beautiful." We were just in a county park!

You worked with William and Harry Kerwin on those early films.

Rooney Kerwin. We called him The Rooney. That was William Kerwin. He was also an actor. He was the best all-around film guy I've ever met in my life. You name it—he was a cameraman, a soundman, a grip, a gaffer, props, costumes, directing, producing. He could do anything. He had what was called a Rooney Kit. We called him The Rooney. We never called him Bill. You could be in the middle of Afghanistan, and you'd say, "I need some purple thread and I need a gold thimble," and he'd go to the Rooney Kit. He had everything in there.

My one daughter is in the film business. She's a first assistant director in the DGA. I've made her fill up the Rooney Kit. You could have sweaters and raincoats and everything in the Rooney Kit. When you're out there, you don't know what's gonna happen.

Betty Kerwin, who was Harry Kerwin's wife, she was my script girl on a lot of the films.

Another guy you worked with was Gary Crutcher.

Gary was a great guy. In fact, I just talked to him fairly recently. He moved to Las Vegas. Gary was a wild and crazy guy. I'll never forget. He was in the writing department at Columbia. A friend and I went over to visit him one day. I hadn't seen him in a couple of years. I said, "Gary, how's it going? Are you writing anything?" He said, "Oh yeah, I just did a screenplay. It was produced." Just then the phone rang. He said, "Excuse me, I've got to go. I had to shoot the producer." He just walked out. My friend said, "What did he say? My God, he shot the producer!"

Did he actually shoot the producer?

Yeah! Gary had been with Columbia for years. When everybody was going public with these public issues and raising tens of millions of dollars, some company wanted him to head up their writing department. He said, "I've been with Columbia so long, I don't know." He negotiated a golden parachute in case anything happened. He left Columbia and went with this other company. After about two years they folded, and he got a bloody fortune. He went out to Vegas and bought a six- or eight-unit apartment house.

Rita Hayworth starred in Grefé's *The Naked Zoo* (1971).

Did I tell you how I met Gary? When I was in L.A. one time, I was looking for writers. I was with Ivan Tors. Someone said, "You've got to meet Gary." I was staying at the Hilton there on Sunset. I called him up. He comes up and he didn't look like a typical Hollywood guy. He had short hair and a suit and tie. I said, "I'd like to read a couple of your scripts." He opens up his briefcase. He's got a .45 automatic, he's got a dagger, and it's lined with pills, uppers and downers. I never hired him, but when I made the *Stanley* deal, I called him.

You only had a few weeks to prepare for that film, correct?

I wrote the story. I had it all in my head. I didn't have time to write the screenplay. I had to produce and direct this thing. I called up Gary. This was a Friday night, and I was taking the red eye back to Miami. I said, "Gary, Tuesday morning I have to have a screenplay in Miami." Back then there was no fax. He had to finish it Monday and put it in overnight FedEx. Gary just popped pills the whole weekend, stayed up for 70 hours or whatever. He wrote *Stanley* over the weekend and just followed the whole outline. I told him when I called to meet me at the L.A. airport. He met me there and I just sat with him in the airport and wrote down what happened in every scene. I just wrote it all out on a yellow pad. He followed that and wrote the screenplay in one weekend. That's Gary. He's a wild and crazy guy.

You made *Death Curse of Tartu* (1966) to fill out the double bill with *Sting of Death*.

Back in those days, all horror movies were released as a double bill in the drive-ins and neighborhood theaters. We had made *Sting of Death* and the distributor, Thunderbird, couldn't find another horror movie. They couldn't pick one up. He said the magic word. "If you guys can do a horror movie, I'd finance it." This was like a rush thing, because they had to get it in theaters April 15. Back in those days, all the theaters opened up North on April 15. It was a nightmare not only shooting, but it was nightmare editing back in those days. It was so time consuming. Not like today.

Long story short, I wrote that screenplay in 24 hours, and we shot *Tartu* in seven days. I thought, "What the hell can I write about?" I took the ancient legend where the Egyptian pharaoh says if anybody disturbs the tomb, he'll come back and kill them. So I just moved that to the Everglades and made it an ancient Indian witch doctor. It was the format of the Egyptians, just moved to the Everglades.

How much did those films cost to make?

Death Curse of Tartu cost $27,000 [*laughs*]. We shot it on 35mm. Now this is the mind blower: About a year ago I was looking at my notes. This was a 90-minute film. There was 8,100 feet of 35mm. I shot 11,000 feet, which means there was like 1.5 to 1 ratio. So what is in there is what we shot. There were no second takes. That was it. Some of these major pictures my daughter's been on, like *Waterworld* (1995), they shot 900,000 feet of film. She did *Six Days, Seven Nights* (1998), the Harrison Ford movie, and they shot 600,000 feet. I shot 11,000, out of which we used 8,100. By the time you figure a short end or a false start, that was it. What you see is what we did!

Tell me about Brad Grinter.

He was in the beginning of *Tartu* in the cave. Brad also directed a couple of films. Brad worked with me on a couple of films. His son Randy Grinter did a film with me called *The Psychedelic Priest* (1971), which we did out in L.A. during the hippie days.

He would do anything to make a dollar. Brad was in nudies, he was in regular films. He directed some. Brad always liked the young girls. He was like 55 or so. I kept telling him, "Brad, you're such a good looking guy, you ought to go over to one of the yacht clubs on the beach and hit up some multi-millionaire widow. You'd be set for life."

Do you know Charlie Martin? He was in *Racing Fever* and *Checkered Flag*. Charlie was half-actor, half-gigolo. He'd get his tuxedo on, and he'd also be with wealthy women. Did you ever see *The Shootist* (1976) with John Wayne? Charlie was the bartender at the end that Wayne blows away.

Charlie was out in L.A. one time. He called me up and said, "Bill, I want you to meet my girlfriend and come over for dinner at her place. Her name is Happy Starr." I thought, "Happy Star— my God, that must be a stripper." I go over to dinner, and it ended up that she was married to Gene Starr [Eugene G. Starr], the guy that invented and held a patent on the cross-drilling of oil wells. When he died, she sold out for sixty million dollars. Back in the late sixties, that's like $150 million today. Charlie kept saying to me, "She said she'd give me a couple of

Soap actor Chris Robinson with his scaly co-star in *Stanley* (1972).

million dollars, but she's afraid my ex-wife will get it." I said, "Forget about getting the million, just set up a trust fund and you can live off the two million dollars the rest of your life."

So he goes to her with this trust fund thing, and she says, "Terrific, I love the idea. We'll meet with my attorney Monday." Over the weekend, old Charlie serviced the account and she died of a heart attack! He never got the two million dollar trust fund.

Another time I went to bed with Gloria Swanson and George Hamilton. Here's the deal. Charlie said that he was dating Gloria Swanson. Did I want to come up and meet Gloria? We went up there, and she had rented the old Douglas Fairbanks estate in Beverly Hills. We go to the door and Gloria Swanson says, "Quick, come in. I'm going to be on television with Buster Keaton." I think it was a show called "Hollywood Palace" or something. We go up to her bedroom and she had this giant four-poster bed. The TV is there. So Charlie Martin and myself and Gloria Swanson are all laying there watching TV. I don't know what the deal was, but George Hamilton was living with Gloria. He walks by and she says, "George, come in here quick." So George Hamilton gets in bed with us. The four of us are laying in this gigantic four-poster bed watching her and Buster Keaton. I like to tell people I went to bed with Gloria Swanson and George Hamilton!

In the earlier films, you primarily used local actors. When you did *The Naked Zoo*, you had Rita Hayworth and Steve Oliver. How did that project come together?

The first one that I used some real good Hollywood actors was *The Hooked Generation*, prior to *The Naked Zoo*. In *The Hooked Generation*, at that time the lead actor, Jeremy Slate, was a big drive-in star because he had done a couple of films like *Born Losers* and some of those. I went out to California, and I was able to negotiate a deal for Jeremy and then John Davis Chandler. Johnny is a terrific actor. He played the druggie. Johnny Chandler was a seasoned pro. He'd done a couple of Peckinpah movies. His first movie was with Burt Lancaster, and he played a killer [*The Young Savages*, 1961]. Then Willie Pastrano was the light heavyweight champion of the world. I used Willie in that, and he was like a natural born actor.

Wild Rebels was the first time I used Willie and Steve Alaimo. Steve Alaimo was like a bubble gum idol. He had his own show on CBS, which Dick Clark produced, called "Where the Action Is." Steve was on *Wild Rebels* and *The Hooked Generation*. Willie Pastrano was completely insane. All the trouble I got into with him was unbelievable.

Was working in California much different than working in Florida?

Not really. What I did in California, that was the hippie days. I shot that film [*The Psychedelic Priest*] with no script whatsoever. We just winged the whole movie.

The story on that one: This producer I knew [Terry Merrill] called me up and said, "Bill, the hippie scene is what's happening. Get out here. I want you to direct this movie." I told him to send me a script. He stopped. He said, "Look, I'll send you a roundtrip ticket. Just get out here." As it turned out, at that time they had what they called trading stamps. Instead of cash, if you owned a TV store and I owned a garage, and you needed your transmission fixed, you'd give me trading stamps. When I needed a TV, I could go get a TV from you. He'd raised about 100,000 in trading stamps, but no cash!

I asked to see the script. He said, "Bill, I'm in serious trouble. I don't have a script. I raised these trading stamps." He discounted like 50 cents on the dollar to get me out there. I was at the Ramada Inn on Sunset, and that ended up being a trading stamp deal. Well, after three days of eating every meal at the Ramada Inn, I said, "I'll buy, let's go across the street to The New World," which was a restaurant right on the Sunset Strip. At that time all the hippies were living in doorways up in the Hollywood Hills. The Strip was just full of hippies.

We go to dinner over there, and here's this long-haired hippie girl with her boyfriend. She had a long flowery dress on. I said, "She looks like a typical hippie." He runs over there and says, "Do you want two points in my movie? You can star in my movie." So now we had this hippie girl that had never acted in her life. The next morning we're having breakfast in the Ramada Inn, and this actor comes in. I said, "He looks like a young priest." The producer said, "I know why I need you to direct this movie. You're brilliant!"

Now we had a our cast and no script. We used to go out every day and just wing the whole thing. We'd go up to Topanga Canyon, which was a hippie stronghold. We shot out in the desert. The soundman was like an alcoholic that hadn't done a film in I don't know how long. The gaffer was on an acid trip the whole time.

The wildest thing is he comes in one night, and this producer was on an acid trip. He said, "I just met a great witch." I didn't pay much attention to it. The next day we're riding down Sunset in the convertible with a hand-held Arri, and we're shooting the hippies, second-unit stuff. He says, "Lita is calling me."

Well, Lita Radner was a headliner in like *Esquire* magazine, and they had a five-page write up about this witch. She has this castle like in the hills. We go to the door and knock, and this big guy — six-seven, looks like pro football player, a 300 pounder — answers it.

The producer said, "We'd like to see Lita. She's calling me." It was myself and this producer, Terry, and Brad Grinter's son, Randy. We're standing out there, and Lita comes out. She's in this big flowing, chiffon gown. She looks at this producer and says, "You're putting off bad vibes." She looks at me and says, "You're putting off good vibes." She grabs both of us and yanks us in, leaves Randy standing there and slams the door right in his face.

We go into this room, and she's got this big throne. This is the truth, and it just blew my mind. She claps her hands and this little guy comes in with a silver tray full of tea. I said, "Oh shit, she's serving tea. What the hell's in the tea?"

I finally said to her, "Our friend is still standing outside." She claps her hands again, and the big guy comes and brings Randy. This is what blew my mind. Randy comes in, and he's 17 or 18 years old. He's grooving and he's really wiggling around. She just pointed her finger at him and said, "Sit." He froze like he was hit by a bolt of lightning, and he just sat. He was frozen for half an hour. She hypnotized him some way or something. I don't know how, but it was like a bolt of lightning hitting him.

But that movie turned out halfway playable. Something Weird Video is now releasing it.

When I finished the picture, it wasn't edited yet. I became president of Ivan Tors. I took credit as the director of photography rather than director and writer, because Ivan Tors was strictly kid stuff, you know. Family fare. I didn't want some wild hippie drug movie with my name as director and writer. It's an interesting film if you ever get to see it.

Back to *The Naked Zoo*. Was that shot in Florida?

In Florida. Rita Hayworth, Ford Rainey and Stephen Oliver. Ford was a seasoned Hollywood pro. The way that came about was I had a $250,000 budget, which was a pretty good budget for me back in those days. I went to L.A. and I wanted to get Rita. I went in to her agent, and the agent wanted $250,000 for Rita. We fought, and I told him the most I could afford was $50,000. Forget it, no way. We fought back and forth for three days. Finally, I called up my investors and I said, "You guys have got to trust me on this. Wire me $50,000." They wired it to me and I got a cashiers check. I walked into that agent. I said, "You and I have been fighting for three solid days. There's $50,000. I will put that in any bank in the state of California in escrow, end of story." He said, "You've got a deal!"

Stephen Oliver was one of the stars of "Peyton Place." The minute I got Rita aboard, Stephen jumped on. I was able to get Ford Rainey, who was an established Hollywood character actor.

What was Rita Hayworth like to work with? She'd mostly been doing films overseas at that point.

Handling actors, as a director, you have to be an amateur psychiatrist. I knew Rita was from the old Hollywood school of doing 15 or 20 takes. I'm a two- or three-take guy, tops, on the budgets I had. I budgeted the film so the first day I did ten takes to one. The second day I was down to seven takes to one. After three or four days she got her confidence in me as a director. That's the way I handled her.

What is amazing about Rita is she was super, super shy. A very shy person. My poor wife was driving her one time, and her husband Aly Khan had died in automobile wreck. She was scared to death of automobiles. My poor wife would be coming to a stoplight, and she'd hit the brakes a little bit and Rita would dash to the floor. It was really amazing, because you think of her as this gregarious, outgoing person. The minute the camera rolled she was in character, but in person she was very shy.

She was starting to get Alzheimer's a little bit. One time she held up production for a couple of days. I thought she was drunk, because back then nobody knew about Alzheimer's. About five or six years later was when she really got it full blown.

What about Steve Oliver?

The original title of that movie was *The Grove*, which was Coconut Grove. That was sort of a hippie stronghold. Steve was on drugs and all that. He just loved the Grove, and he was in the whole Grove scene. But he had trouble with the whole drug thing. He wasn't a pretty boy, but he was a good-looking guy and had a TV series. He should have been a big star, but drugs knocked him out of the box.

Joe E. Ross was also in that film. He made a lot of movies Florida.

Joe E. hung out there. He was a cash guy. If you went to his agent, hypothetically he'd want $5,000 for the day. You hand Joey $700 cash, and that was it. He was also in my movie with Mickey Rooney, *The Godmothers*. We used Joe in that. Whenever he was in town doing nightclubs, you could get Joey if you had cash money.

Who produced *The Naked Zoo*?

I produced it, and the executive producer was a guy named Robert Robertson. There was a big thing called Pirate's World [a theme park near Dania, Fla.], and they had a studio there they built near Hollywood, Florida. He and a guy named Pearlman put up the money for the picture.

I was producing and directing. I was having a nightmare in pre-production. I'm a fanatic for prep, and everything's got to be signed, sealed and delivered. We had built the set of Stephen Oliver's home in the studio. I assigned my assistant to rent the furniture, because you could rent furniture from the store. He didn't get a deal in writing. He makes a verbal deal. We're shooting Monday morning, and this guy shows up Saturday. I can't remember the exact figures, but it was like $1,500 bucks to rent the furniture. He comes and says, "I've changed my mind, it's $5,000." Well, we didn't have a contract.

I said, "I've got two words for you: Fuck you." I threw him out of my office. Everybody panics. What are we gonna do? I got the whole crew and secondary cast in and said, "You have a couch, you bring it. You bring a chair. You bring a nightlight." I assigned like 25 people to bring a piece of furniture, and Sunday we furnished the whole set.

[Note: Robertson may have been C.T. Robertson, producer of Santa and the Ice Cream Bunny (1972) and Jack and the Beanstalk (1970), also filmed at Pirate's World by Barry Mahon.]

You've said in the past that *Stanley* was inspired by a dream you had.

I was president of Ivan Tors at the time. I was out there on Ivan's business in L.A., and *Variety* came out with *Willard* as the biggest grossing independent film. It just dawned on me: animals for the next horror movie. *Willard* was really the first one. I went to bed that night, and I don't know what the hell I ate but I dreamt *Stanley* just like I'd been to the theater.

I woke up in the morning and thought, "Jeez, this is a pretty good idea." I went to see Mark Tenser and Red Jacobs, who owned Crown International Pictures. They'd handled *Wild Rebels* for me.

Red Jacobs was a crusty old guy, and had a cigar about a foot long. I said, "Hey Red, I've got a great idea for a movie." He said, "Leave me the screenplay." I don't have a screenplay. He said, "Leave me a synopsis, I'll read it over the weekend." I don't have a synopsis. "Get the hell out of my office!"

He had a big box of Cuban cigars on his desk. I opened up the box and grabbed a handful. He said, "You son of a bitch, put those back." He's screaming at me.

I said, "Just relax. Get Mark Tenser in here and let me tell you the story." I told him the whole story, and he asked how much I could make it for. I told him $125,000. He shook hands with me. He was from the old school. He was a tough old bird, but if you shook hands with him, it was a deal. He said, "I'm only gonna put one monkey on your back. I have to have it on the drive-in circuit April 15." That was the magic number. Here it was almost the end of November. I had no script. Back in those days it was a nightmare to edit because it wasn't computerized. It was a nightmare to do the final mix of the music and effects. I was really under the gun. I knew Gary Crutcher, and so I met him at the airport and told him the story.

We started shooting like ten days later. I brought it in Christmas Eve. I had to edit like crazy to get it in the theaters. It's really become one of the big cult classics.

Chris Robinson had done a lot of movies in Florida during that period.

Chris was an established Hollywood actor when he moved to Florida. He was in "Twelve O'Clock High" and a lot of movies. Chris was a very good actor, and a good director. He directed a couple of films.

He did a couple of films with Ted Cassidy.

He did one himself that he directed. I think he wrote it, a Civil War story where he's an albino or something.

That was *Sunshine Run* (1972).

Chris was such a good actor. After *Stanley*, he got onto a soap opera. He was making good bucks, and he ended up owing the IRS like $200,000. I don't know if he ever settled or they threw him in jail. After that, he dropped out of the film thing and went into the Indian movement. I have not heard anything about him since.

Was it easy or difficult to get your money back out of the films, especially ones where you were serving as producer?

With the theaters I always tried, as a distributor, to get cash advances. I'd been around. Did I mention to you how I made my first distribution deal on *Racing Fever*?

No. How did you do it?

Fortunately, as a young filmmaker, I'd learned the name of the game is distribution. I directed *The Checkered Flag*, which was a quirk of fate where I was drafted in the motel room. The next film I did, I wrote, produced and directed *Racing Fever*. I was responsible for the distribution on it. In those days all distribution was in New York. I went to New York and I ended up at Allied Artists. The vice president liked the movie. I found out that the vice president never makes a decision, because if he makes the decision and the movie bombs, it's his ass. They jerked me around for a week in New York.

I called up Steve Broidy, who was president of Allied, and I told him I had just made this movie. He said, "Jump in a plane and get out here. If I like it, I'll make a deal with you immediately." I'd never been to L.A. in my life. I knew one person in L.A., an actor I did summer stock with in Woodstock, N.Y. I screened the movie for Steve Broidy. He said, "Come to my office in the morning and I'll make a deal." I called up this actor, Dan Magnum. I said, "Dan, I just produced this movie. Do you know any attorneys that know anything about the film business?" He told me about a friend of his who had just opened his own office.

I said, "Gee, I want some attorney with a little gray hair. I don't want some kid right out of college." He said, "Oh no, he just opened his own private practice, but for seven years he was chief legal counsel for Allied Artists." Talk about luck! So the next morning I walk in with my attorney, and everybody's jaws dropped open because he had written a distribution contract, and he knew every zinger there was. Instead of net this was a gross deal, a cash advance versus a bankable guarantee, etc. So I learned right there the name of the game was distribution. Steve Broidy thought I was a genius, but it was pure, dumb luck.

The lead snake from *Stanley* was later made into a wallet, which director William Grefé claims to still own.

What about on films where you worked with other distributors, like Crown?

With *Wild Rebels*, they bought the film outright and paid cash. We doubled our money. I was sort of against that deal, because it was the second motorcycle picture out. Corman had come out with *Wild Angels*. I was against it, but the investors said whenever you can double your money within four or five months, it's a good deal. We sold it outright.

On *Stanley*, they financed the movie, and they put up all the money for that. I got a nice salary and a few dribble drabbles, but all distributors are notorious thieves. All of them. Every one of them. You have to know how to get around it. When we get to *Cease Fire* (1985), I'll tell you how I handled distribution on that.

Did you really have the snake made into a wallet?

Yep. Still have the blood stains on poor old Stanley. If you ever come to Florida and see my house, Stanley built my house!

Impulse **was the film that you did with Socrates Ballis. Tell me about him, and how that film got made.**

Socrates was an actor, basically. In *Hooked Generation*, he played the Cuban at the beginning of the movie, and he got shot through the chest. Soc had worked with me on a couple of films as an actor and as an assistant. He wanted to be a producer, so he went over to Tampa and he was trying to raise money. I read the script, and the script, in my opinion, needed a lot of work. We changed a lot of it when I finally got the money and came on board. I was a hired gun on *Impulse*. Soc and I were going out to L.A. to talk with agents and try to do some casting.

We're in the Miami airport, and here comes Bill Shatner walking down the ramp. I said to Soc, "Shatner would be good in this." We stopped, talked to Shatner, made a deal in the airport and never got on the plane. We never went to L.A.!

That's how Shatner got in. Harold Sakata was wrestling over in Tampa. He was a professional wrestler. That's how he got *Goldfinger* (1964). He was wrestling in London and Cubby Broccoli saw him wrestling on TV. Jenifer Bishop was sort of Socrates' girlfriend. She was a pretty good little actress.

Was Jenifer Bishop in *The Godmothers* (1973)?

No, but Socrates was on that. If she did it, it was just a little bit thing. Socrates played one of the godfather's henchmen. There's a real well-known Italian actor out of New York that's been in so many big movies — remember *The Professional* (1994), about the little girl and the French actor? The guy that more or less deals the contracts out and held the money for him. What's his name? He's a well-known actor.

Danny Aiello?

Danny Aiello! He's been on more damn talk shows and interviews, and he keeps talking about being in *The Godmothers*. I don't remember him. The only thing I can think of is he might have some little extra part in the background. I've never seen him, but he keeps talking about being in Florida with Mickey Rooney in *The Godmothers*.

Jenifer Bishop told me that Harold Sakata loved to go dancing.

Sakata was a very gentle guy. I've been out to dinner and lunch with a lot of name actors, but none of them turned heads like when I walked in with Sakata. He had a neck as big as a guy's thigh. He was such an unusual looking guy.

Shatner is very over the top in that film. Did you have to rein him in at all?

I did. Shatner has a tendency to over-act. I tried to calm him down a little bit. Did I tell you the Ruth Roman story?

No.

She'd worked with Alfred Hitchcock, she did *Champion* with Kirk Douglas. Ruth Roman had balls about as big as an elephant. She was a tough broad. Fortunately for me, I'd directed maybe ten movies by then. I knew how to be an amateur psychiatrist.

The first scene we shot is where they're over the fish tank. Shatner said to me, "Bill, this guy is sort of a nutty character. What if I reach in the fish tank and grab one of the fish?" I said that was fantastic. Do that.

Well, this was the very first scene that Ruth Roman was in. Ruth Roman knew that was gonna steal the scene right out from under her. She said, "That's not in the script, I'm not gonna do that." She storms off the set. A lot of inexperienced guys would have gone and begged for her to come out. I just let her stew for about ten minutes. I got the first assistant director, a guy named Gayle DeCamp. I went right outside of her dressing room.

I said, "Gayle, I'm sick and tired of this shit. Get the producer out here immediately." She's in there, and I know what she's thinking: "Jesus, he doesn't have me on film. This crazy son of a bitch is gonna fire me!"

A few minutes later she comes out and says, "I'm ready to do the scene." I said to her, "Miss Roman, you might be ready to do the scene but I'm not. Look, if you come up with a good suggestion for your character, and I like it, we'll use it. If Mr. Shatner comes up with a good suggestion for his character, we'll use it. But I'm directing this movie. Do you understand me?" She said, "Yes sir." And we were buddies from then on. They always test you and run over you like a bulldozer if you let them.

Didn't Shatner break his finger trying to keep Sakata from being hung?

Shatner came down that rope and broke his finger, and to this day his finger is still crooked. He never got it set properly. The harness slipped and Sakata was actually choking to death. Shatner is yelling for us to cut the rope, and he's trying to pick Sakata up. He's like 250 pounds or whatever. Just recently, 16mm footage surfaced of that hanging happening behind the scenes. The guy that's got it said he's gonna send me a DVD on it, but he's going to burn in the thing, because he said it's such valuable footage he doesn't want it pirated.

Wasn't that shown on *The Tonight Show*?

Yeah, when Shatner was on with Johnny Carson.

Do you know if it did very well?

It got distributed, but I think with them handling it, they got stolen blind by a lot of the distributors. But it did pretty good in theaters because it was an unusual thing for Shatner.

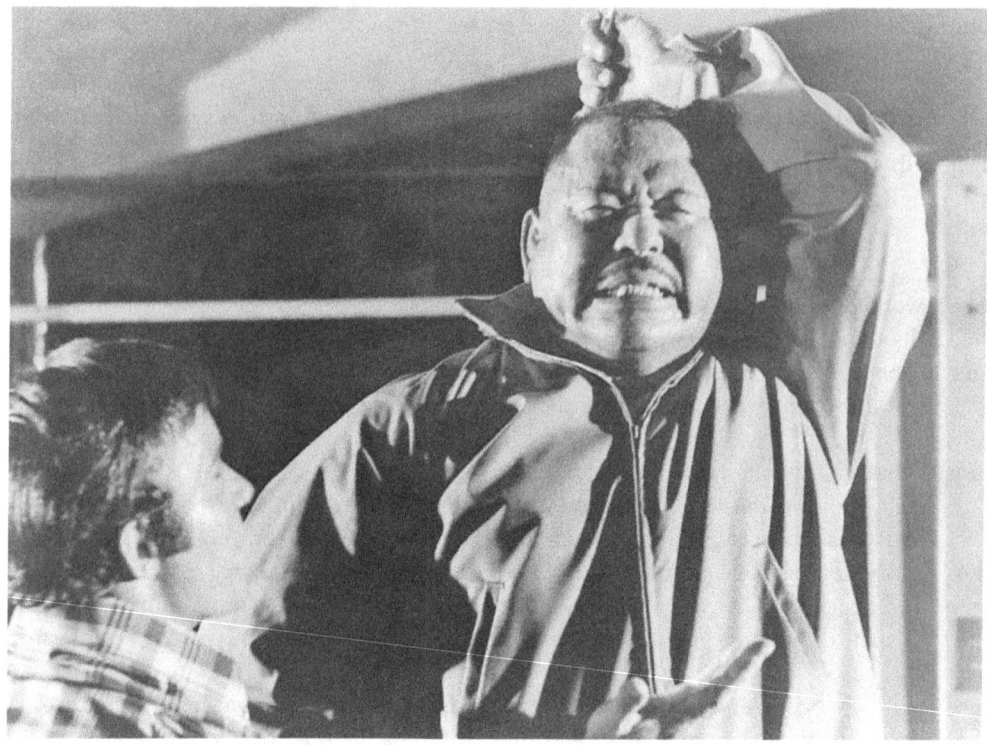

Psycho William Shatner gets the best of Harold "OddJob" Sakata in *Impulse* (1974). Sakata was almost injured during this sequence when his harness failed (courtesy Daniel Griffith).

Shatner knocked that film in interviews for a long time, but he seemed to soften up on it in his part of that *Gods in Polyester* book. Tony Crechales told me that Shatner really got into the character, and added a lot to the script.

As I said, we changed a lot of the stuff. I had known some con-men like that, and I told him, "Look, let's develop this guy like he's a smooth talker, and he doesn't come right on and ask people to invest in this deal. He almost makes the people beg him to invest." So Tony was able to address that theme. That scene in the cemetery, I forget where that was, so I suggested we shoot the cemetery. Tony rewrote that scene. It turned out to be a playable movie.

Who picked out Shatner's wardrobe?

God, I can't remember.

He had some crazy jackets.

That one jacket I remember was pretty wild. Shatner is a funny guy in person. I directed about 25 movies for Bacardi Rum, and they were like half-hour films. We were doing one in Puerto Rico, and I called up Shatner and said, "Do you want to do this little half hour film for Bacardi in Puerto Rico?" He calls up and all he needed was a shirt and a pair of pants. He calls me up and says, "Bill, how much are we gonna spend on wardrobe?" I said about $100. There was silence. He said, "Maybe I could go to K-mart and find something...." I guess he's used to spending a lot more on his shirts!

Another funny thing happened on that. The old Cuban custom is, if they had a wristwatch and you said, "Oh, what a beautiful watch, I'd love to get one like that," they would literally take the watch off and hand it to you. So the head of Bacardi distillery was all excited Shatner was in town. We go up to guy's office. The guy had a little old keg of Viejo, which is the top Bacardi rum. The average Viejo is aged for seven years. This was a 25-year-old Viejo. The head of the distillery says, "Would you like a sip of it?"

He takes out a jigger about the size of a woman's thimble. He gave us just little teeny taste of it. Shatner says, "Man this is great, I'd love to get a keg of that." The president of the distillery turns pale white. I knew what he was thinking, and it was gonna kill him to give that to Shatner!

But anyway, Shatner's a funny guy. The last time I saw him was in Tampa in his office. He's got a hundred-horse farm up in Kentucky. I said, "Bill, how are the horses doing?" He looked at me real serious and he said, "Let me tell you this Grefé—you never invest in something that eats while you're sleeping."

He's really like the Energizer bunny. He never quits. Now he's on that "Boston Legal." He finally switched completely to more or less almost comedy, the way he does it.

Everyone thinks *Mako* was a *Jaws* rip-off, but that project actually pre-dated *Jaws*.

It was written about three years before the Peter Benchley thing. I shopped it around and I couldn't get arrested. Nobody wanted to invest in it. So I put it in a drawer and forgot about it. When *Jaws* came out it was the biggest grosser in film history, so the phone rang off the hook because of all of these distributors and professional film people that had read the script knew I could get it out right away. "Bill, buddy, how the hell are you?"

I had the money almost immediately. After I shot it, we did not edit the film. I edited a seven-minute promo reel. I don't know how old you are, but at the time with *Jaws*, everything was sharks. *LIFE* magazine, *Time* magazine, shark, sharks, sharks. The publicity was so great that we literally beat *Jaws* out in Europe with that promo reel. We took that seven-minute promo reel, and all the European distributors made deals on the movie. It made a lot a money off that little promo reel.

You had just worked with some sharks a few years prior.

On *Live and Let Die*. There was a harbor in South Bimini where we used to wire off the harbor and throw all the sharks in there. The way you catch those sharks is you go out on the reef at night and throw out a cement block with a long rope on it. You take a big old snapper or that kind of fish, put a shark hook through the tail, and throw out maybe ten cement blocks. Every night the sharks will come on to the reef, and in the morning you'll lave at least two big ones. They get hooked, and they swim around dragging that cement block until they get tired, and then they swim in a circle.

Many people have commented that that's the best shark footage ever filmed. Can you think of any movie where a guy literally grabs a ten-foot tiger by the dorsal fin and is towed along? No movie I've ever seen. Spielberg used a million-dollar mechanical shark. We didn't have the money, so we used real ones.

Had you worked with Richard Jaeckel before?

I never had, but the guy was 100 percent pro. I think Richard was probably the most professional, best actor I ever worked with, bar none. The guy was in almost every scene. He was in 90 percent of the whole movie. He only blew one line in the whole movie;

he was that well prepared. That first day was the biggest nightmare I've ever been in on a film.

The first day of filming, Richard was not in the first shot. I was rehearsing Sakata and Johnny Chandler, and my whole directorial plan was based upon the new Arriflex BL, which was a lightweight camera. Prior to that we used a big old Mitchell, which was a 200-pound monster. The Arri had just come out, this Arriflex BL. There were only two of them in the United States. One was in L.A. and one was in Miami. The very first day the assistant cameraman had it on the tripod, and he cross-threaded the thing. He picked it up and broke the housing. We wiped out our camera. They're rehearsing the actors and the first AD came in and said, "Bill, we just wiped out the Arriflex."

I didn't completely panic, I just told them to get a Mitchell out there. I said, "Look, we've got a wild Arri we can shoot with, but you can't do sound with it." We had a shot where a boat approaches, and we could use that to get the approach shot. We could loop the sound.

They go out, and come back again. "Bill, are you sitting down." Now what? He said, "We were bringing the boat in and it got stuck on a sand bar. It will be two hours before we can shoot because we can't get the boat off the sand bar."

I was getting a little uneasy. I said, "Ask Richard Jaeckel to come in here." I said, "Richard, I apologize, but can you get ready because we're going to shoot this wild and we'll loop it until the Mitchell gets out here?" "No problem, Bill." He rushes out to get wardrobe and make-up.

Now we're in the trailer, and the first AD comes in. "Bill, are you sitting down?" *Now* what? "We just rushed Richard Jaeckel to the emergency ward. He split his head open jumping on a prop truck." So now I have no lead actor, I have no camera, and I got no boat. Then I started to panic!

Like an hour and a half later Richard comes back with eight stitches in his head, and insisted on working. The guy was a super pro. Really a great guy. When we were finished with the movie, I said, "Richard, I just want to thank you. You're a great pro and I appreciate your cooperation." He said, "Bill, when I walk on to a movie or TV set, the first thing I say is thank you dear Lord for letting me work today." The guy never stopped working. He was in every western, every war movie ever made.

And he always looked about 15 years younger than he really was.

He was in great shape. He was a surfing kid, from L.A., and he got that damn skin cancer. Melanoma is what killed him. But he was a great guy.

Were there particular advantages or disadvantages to working in Florida?

Definitely. Number one, you could go with minimum crews without the whole Hollywood entourage type stuff. Plus, once you get established, you can more or less live anywhere. I had three young kids, so I didn't want to get into the L.A. scene. Steve Broidy at Allied Artists had asked me to go to California for the studio and be a contract director out there. I turned him down. To raise three little kids in L.A. in the hippie era? Forget about it.

I made two films in North Carolina. We did *Whiskey Mountain* and *Escape* (1990), because I have a home in the mountains of North Carolina. We shot a lot of that on my property up there. The way that came about is one of my hobbies is the Civil War. I have a Civil War collection, and I know a lot about the Civil War, and I was always dirt biking in the mountains. So I just combined the dirt biking and Civil War, and ended up doing *Whiskey Mountain*.

What's interesting about that was this guy, Lewis Perles. He was on *Impulse*. He was a music guy. And Lewis was really into drugs and all this. We're editing *Whiskey Mountain*, and he's looking over my shoulder on the Moviola. He says, "Bill, this movie looks perfect for Charlie Daniels to do the score." I said, "Yeah, lots of luck. How am I gonna afford Charlie Daniels?" He said, "Charlie's a good friend of mine, I could probably get him."

He gets Charlie on the phone. He said it sounded interesting, but he was booked solid. He was doing like three concerts a week. That was the end of that, I thought. Two weeks later Charlie calls him up and says, "I was just opening a walnut, and the knife went right through my guitar hand and cut my nerves. I had to have an operation. So we had to cancel everything. You want to take a look at this movie?"

We had a rough cut. We flew up to Nashville. I'd never met Charlie before. We come in and Charlie looks just like he does on the stage, with the big cowboy hat. He's chewing tobacco. He said, "You must be Bill Grefé," and he spits in a tin can. So that's how we got Charlie to do all the music.

You said you wanted to tell me about the distribution for *Cease Fire* (1985).

That came about when there were companies going public. People were raising money that way.

I found a company to put up the print and ad money. I made a separate deal for us, theatrical only. We kept all of the ancillary rights. We got $325,000 just for the home video rights to it. Don Johnson was hot as a pistol. HBO gave us $525,000 in advance against the HBO and cable rights, plus it did really good theatrically. We ended up making separate deals on various foreign countries. I probably ended up with 20 distributors, with cash advances against it.

The way that happened is Don got "Miami Vice" because of *Cease Fire*. When we were shooting, Michael Mann and those folks developed "Miami Vice." They were in Miami to look at locations. Back in L.A., they were having a cattle call. They wanted two unknown actors that weren't really big stars. Don's agent kept calling Michael Mann. "I've got this guy working in Miami, blah, blah." So Michael Mann called me up and said, "This agent is driving me up the wall. Can you show me some dailies on this Don Johnson?" I showed him dailies. It's the best thing Don's ever done in his whole life, bar none. The rest is history.

When "Vice" came out, we had just finished the editing and were ready to go to distributors. Now the country was crazy about "Vice." I told the investors I thought we sit tight for three or four months. The show might be cancelled. But if it really took off, we had a big name actor in here. We sat on it for four or five months. When Don was the biggest thing happening, that's when we made the distribution deal. When "Vice" first came out, it probably wouldn't have done near the business.

Did you appear in a movie called *Dark Universe* (1993)?

For Fred Olen Ray? No, that was Steve Latshaw. I think my photograph appeared in that. He wanted some guy with a safari outfit or a gun, and he wanted to use me.

Then there was another movie that Latshaw did, but Fred Olen Ray produced it. Freddy is a good friend of mine. He talked me into doing some drunk scene. I forget the name of that thing.

What else have you been up to last couple of years?

I do a lot of commercials and that kind of stuff. Did I tell you about the film in Jamaica? This is the wildest. I've had a lot of wild things happen, but this is a wildest. This young director out in L.A. I know, he met this Jamaican lady that wanted to make Jamaica the Hollywood of the Caribbean. They hired a California producer to go down to Jamaica.

When you shoot in the islands, you might as well be shooting on the moon. It's completely different. Everything was disorganized, nothing was ready. They fired this California producer and called me up. This lady said, "Bill, you come highly recommended. We'd love you to produce this movie for us."

I told her it didn't quite work that way. So three days later, a roundtrip ticket comes. The check comes, and the check is from a college in Los Angeles. My wife said, "What the heck is this college check?" I said, "What do I know? Maybe they're investing."

I cashed the check and it cleared, so I'm off to Jamaica. I won't bore you with the problems we had, but it was a nightmare. In Jamaica, we really shot great from like eight in the morning until noon. It was a 90 percent Jamaican crew, and they were all into ganja. After lunch, everything was slow motion. It was a tough, tough shoot.

The young director takes it back to L.A. and edits it. He calls me up and says, "Bill, are you sitting down? This lady embezzled $1.2 million from this college. She was a comptroller of the college and the *Los Angeles Times* says she's sitting in jail. The college has taken a lien against the movie. She stole all the money from the college to make this movie."

[Note: This was Jean Thorbourn, former fiscal administrator for the L.A. campus of Hebrew Union College-Jewish Institute of Religion, who was arrested for forging numerous checks between 1989 and 1997. She embezzled at least $1.179 million from the college and used the money to finance a number of independent films, including Jamaica Beat (1997).]

That's just one of the little crazy things. It was called *House Next Door* (1996). I did one in Chicago called *Shooter on the Side* (1996).

It's a situation where there's always a deal in the works, which is 100 percent bullshit. I've got literally three different deals in three different movies that might happen, or might not. Who knows? I'm still active. I'm a chameleon. I do my own thing. I direct for other producers, I produce for other directors. I just love the business.

Better Watch Out

LEWIS JACKSON
New Jersey

Over the years, dozens of filmmakers have attempted to use Christmas as a backdrop for a horror film, with mixed results. Holiday-themed horrors have ranged from the sublime (Bob Clark's *Black Christmas*, 1974)) to the ridiculous (*Elves*, 1989), but if there was to be an award for the best Christmas horror film, it would have to go to Lewis Jackson's *Christmas Evil* (1980).

Jackson, a product of the film program at NYU, began his career working in low-budget sexploitation films, eventually helming the obscure (and apparently lost) films *The Deviators* (1970) and the bizarre *Transformation (A Sandwich of Nightmares)* (1974).

His magnum opus, though, was *Christmas Evil*. Originally shot as *You Better Watch Out* during a cold New Jersey winter, the film concerns a fragile toy factory employee (Brandon Maggart) whose obsession with Christmas leads him to don a Santa suit and dole out fatal holiday justice on those he's deemed naughty, while rewarding the lucky souls on his "nice" list.

Weird, melancholy, funny and whimsical, *Christmas Evil* stands as one of the finest films ever made for the exploitation market. Unfortunately, it was overshadowed in the Santa-suited-killer genre by the more gruesome *Silent Night, Deadly Night* (1984), and its reputation was further eroded thanks to rampant bootlegging of sub-standard prints during the video era.

Jackson reclaimed the film in 2006, however, and oversaw a stellar DVD restoration via Synapse Films, complete with a commentary track featuring the movie's number-one fan, Baltimore filmmaker John Waters. Now living in California, Jackson frequently appears at holiday screenings of his most famous film.

The cover for Synapse Films' DVD release of Lewis Jackson's *Christmas Evil* (courtesy Lewis Jackson).

Where did you grow up, and how did you get involved in filmmaking?

I grew up in Brooklyn, New York. To me, movies were *it* from the very minute that I can remember going to the movies. That's all I ever wanted to do. My parents are basically kind of working class, and thought that it was completely ridiculous.

I was basically sent off to school because I was going to be a doctor, of course; I'm from a Jewish family. I spent all my time going to the movies. I went to school at the University of Pittsburgh. Jonas Salk came out of the medical school there.

There were two art houses in Pittsburgh, and a lot of Midnight shows of genre stuff. That's where I was all the time. Eventually I transferred to NYU and was in the film program there before there was a School of the Arts.

That was in the mid-1960s. It was a year or two before the School of the Arts opened. I'm post–Scorsese and people like that who went to the school. At the time I was there, the school was really concentrating on a lot of documentary stuff. It was that period of cinéma vérité. Everybody was interested in making black-and-white movies about jazz performers and social issues and stuff like that, with a handful of people doing avant-garde things as well. There was all that underground filmmaking going on in New York at the time.

What kind of films did you watch?

I watched everything. The only thing I didn't like were certain kinds of overblown Hollywood movies, but basically when I moved to Greenwich Village, which was just at the same time I was going to NYU, I discovered real revival houses. There were no DVDs or anything; you had to go to the movies. One in particular was the Bleecker Street Cinema, which God bless them, showed triple features every night. It was a tiny little theater with these hard, wooden chairs and I would just go in for the duration. And I mean duration! They would show Franco Rossi movies, and this one and that one all in a row. You would just sit there all night long. It was an education. I can tell you that there are very few movies that I have not seen. I was so obsessive about this for so many years, and still am. I have a DVD collection you wouldn't believe.

I watched just about everything. When I was kid I actually loved horror films. That was when I really loved horror films. That was something that had a calling for me. As I grew up, with the New Wave and all the other things that were going on in film, that began to stretch my appetite for movies and the things that I wanted to do. I no longer could see making just a straight genre film without applying something else to it.

What kind of work did you want to do?

I just wanted to do what was in my head. Before I made this movie, I production managed low-budget films, I production managed porn films. I worked on so many different things I can't tell you, just to get the experience. In 1970, I got hired to make a softcore porn film. It was before *Deep Throat* (1972). I got it into my head that I would make a comedy about sexual perversions. It was called *The Deviators* (1970). It was shot in five days on 16mm. It had such a minuscule budget. I went slightly over, and it wound up costing $13,000. My producer thought that I had stolen the extra money! No one needs $13,000 to make a movie! How is that possible? At some point he took the film away from me and he added some hardcore scenes [directed by Eduardo Cemano], and it was released in New York. It played in New York as *The Deviators* because he didn't want to spend money on new titles.

Who was the producer?

I don't even remember. He just came out of the woodwork. Which, by the way, led to something that didn't get made.

That was a horrible experience, and I had to run away to San Francisco for a couple of months because I couldn't believe what a nightmare this had turned into. I come back and I get a phone call from some guy who says he wants me to make a movie for him, another sex thing. This time I come up with, of all things, a sex film based on *The Tibetan Book of the Dead*. He was all gung-ho about it, but he only wanted to spend $6,000 to make the movie. The thing was, this guy had made his money selling porn films all over the country. I go into his office, and he weighs about 250 pounds or something, and he's on crutches. He can't really walk. He's the strangest guy. Years later I pick up a newspaper and find that he went to prison.

Who was that?

I couldn't tell you his name anymore. But he did go to prison for sending pornography across state lines. This is many years after I had met him.

The Deviators was 1970. In '73 I made essentially a drive-in movie that was originally supposed to have pornographic elements, because *Deep Throat* had come out. I had partnered up with a guy [Elliot Krasnow, a.k.a. Kenneth Elliot] who was in advertising, and he wanted to become a producer. The year before he had made the first black porno.

When *Deep Throat* came out, it was so successful that there was money to be had from anywhere. He found these guys in Florida, flew down there and came back with a paper bag with $80,000 in it. He was gonna make the first black porno musical. He hired a guy named Bernard "Pretty" Purdie, who was Aretha Franklin's drummer, and he wrote the score. I produced it for him.

What was the title of black porno musical?

It was called *Lialeh* (1974). It came out on VHS. It was actually widely distributed. I don't know where it exists now, but I found it in my video store in New York.

The director [Barron Bercovichy] was a guy who had come out of Hollywood, and he had such a bad experience on this film that he quite the industry and went to medical school. It didn't do the kind of business they expected. There was a giant billboard on Broadway for this. It was a big deal. It made just enough money that he could get some more money, and this time I was gonna direct the movie.

I found a story in a comic called *Insect Fear*, one of the earlier underground comic books. It was a story about a guy who meets this beautiful girl and she sings in a nightclub. It turns out that she's like a snake woman or something, and that gets him killed. So I decided I would do this and we'd put some sex scenes in it.

The film wasn't really long enough. I couldn't stretch it out long enough to be a feature. What I did was, I shot a documentary simultaneous to shooting the movie and I called it *The Transformation (A Sandwich of Nightmares)* (1974). It opened up with the documentary of the prepping for the movie, then the movie played, and at the end was the wrap-up that showed you everything that went wrong. The documentary parts are fabulous. They really are fabulous. The movie itself is quite mediocre because I couldn't get decent actors. I had written a lot of dialogue, and the actors were just bad.

That wound up getting some distribution but then fading into the ozone. I'd love to get hold of it. I had prints of *The Deviators* and I had a print of *Transformation*, and they were snuck into storage by an ex-wife. They disappeared. That's really painful.

Between the first movie and the second, I got a job as a film critic at the *Independent Film Journal*. That was an industry magazine, but I became syndicated in other papers.

Did you write under your own name?

I wrote under my own name. The thing was, in the industry magazines, just like in *Variety*, you weren't getting many credits. But I was getting paid ten dollars a review. I would have to review upwards of 20 or 30 movies a week to live. At first it was like a dream. What could be bad about that? But within about two and a half years I thought I would kill myself. There was so much crap! Finally I went to a screening of Elia Kazan's movie *The Visitors* (1972). I *hated* it. I started screaming at the screen, walked out and quit the job [*laughs*].

That's between 40 and 50 hours of viewing a week.

I did nothing else. This magazine had to cover every movie released. That was its mandate. I would walk up and down 42nd Street and I would go pick out stuff that no one had seen. Italian westerns, anything, just to get my money. I can't tell you I sat through everything. But I could write a better plot than the filmmakers were providing.

You mentioned you worked as a production manager. What were some of the films you worked on?

A lot of very low-budget things that you wouldn't know. They all have disappeared from view. In the early to mid-seventies, a lot of people were making low-budget films.

You know who I did work for? Radley Metzger. I did several of the upscale Henry Paris pornos, as well as being the liaison on a lot of Italian and Yugoslavian movies that came over and needed to do location work. I worked on *Maraschino Cherry* (1978), and I forget the others. Maybe *Barbara Broadcast* (1977). I don't remember the titles so much anymore. I worked on a Yugoslavian film about Nikola Tesla. I did a lot of things.

While this is all going on, I am planning my epic movie. My story, and I'll always stick to it, was that one night in 1970 after smoking a joint, I had this image of a Santa Claus with a knife in his hand. I thought it was great. I had to do something with it. I basically wrote a draft during the time I was reviewing for the magazine, but I hated it and stuck it in a drawer. I took it out again and wrote another draft.

That went on for about seven or eight years until finally I had a screenwriting gig out here [in California]. I sold a script. Through one of the people I met through that experience, I met a guy who had been one of the wealthiest players in the stock market during the go-go years in the sixties. When that market crashed he had lost everything and he owed $60 million. He repaid all the money. He was one of the few people who had done that, which made him a mythic character. That was Burt Kleiner, who started the *L.A. Weekly*. He produced the movie version of *The Secret Life of Plants* (1979). He decided that I was gonna be his ticket back to the big time with the Christmas movie.

When you were doing work as a production manager, did you work on any horror films?

No. I worked on a pilot for television show starring a monkey, where the monkey is supposed to be anthropomorphized. You would hear the monkey getting electro shocks in the back before each new scene, and that was more horrifying than any experience I've ever had in my life.

What was the script you sold in California?

That was something that I'm gonna make now, if you want to know the truth. It's a script called *Chiller*, and I wrote it with somebody else. It's a science fiction script.

It was not produced. Eventually there were problems with the guy behind it. Do you know who Rudolph Wurlitzer is? He wrote *Two-Lane Blacktop* (1971). He met a guy out here who wanted to go into the movie business, and he hired Rudy to hire five other writers to write original scripts. One was Sam Shepard, this guy Steve Katz, and my partner and I were among them. We came up with an idea about a guy who goes into space and gets hit with radiation. He comes back and turns cold. They think he has hypothermia, and by accident he discovers that electricity makes him warm and he becomes an electric junkie.

I put that away, and then a few years ago I had the thought that this was so contemporary now. I changed it into a movie about solar energy. How much physical electric power do you need? That's what I've been doing.

In the DVD commentary you mentioned that between the time you came up with the idea and made the actual movie, you accumulated all this Christmas paraphernalia.

I had done that from the time I had the idea. Every time I saw something I bought it.

People would give me things. In terms of Harry's apartment, no one had to do any art direction. I had more than enough stuff. And the crew absconded with everything!

Did you have an interest in Christmas outside of this film?

Being Jewish I was always fascinated in the other sense of Christmas. Not the Christian sense of Christmas. As a kid, to go to Manhattan from Brooklyn and see the Christmas light and see the city decorated — to me Manhattan was my Oz. Do you remember that scene in *Saturday Night Fever* where John Travolta crosses the bridge into Manhattan? That was my life. Manhattan was the world I wanted to conquer. My father was a caterer, and he catered for television and movie stars. I worked parties for him. It just created this fantasy in my head. I wanted to be part of all of it.

But that was part of the attraction. I was interested in this idea of a totally non-religious Christmas.

Did Burt Kleiner bankroll *Christmas Evil*?

He didn't have a bankroll, but he had access to people with money. I was very ambitious about this.

The other thing that Burt did was he brought in Ed Pressman. He wanted a name as an executive producer. Ed really didn't do anything except provide the family toy factory, Pressman Toys.

We had a $450,000 budget. There was a cinematographer in Europe named Ricardo Aronovich who had worked with all these great directors. I had just seen *Providence* (1977), the Alain Resnais film. It's a fabulous movie, but beyond that, it's the most beautifully shot movie in the world. I wrote him a fan letter and asked him if he would shoot my movie.

Lo and behold he said, "Come and meet me." He was shooting a movie in Vienna. I flew over. I had storyboarded every frame of the film. I had a gigantic book. There's not a scene in there that isn't boarded. I showed him the storyboard and told him the way I wanted it shot and the lighting styles I wanted, and he thought it was fabulous. He agreed to do it.

He flies over. We've given him an apartment and set a salary. He comes up with his lighting bill. He tells us the lights he wants, and someone comes and

Harry's mother (Ellen McElduff) about to be very naughty with Santa (Brian Hartigan) (courtesy Lewis Jackson).

knocks on my door and says, "I think you should know his lighting bill is $200,000 more than you imagined."

I went to Burt. He had this friend named Pete Kameron who as a very famous person in the music business. He produced The Who and had managed The Weavers. Pete became very wealthy because before the law had changed, he took all the public domain folk songs, things like "Goodnight Irene," and he copyrighted them. They weren't copyrighted. The Weavers then recorded them and he became incredibly wealthy. He had just retired. I had to go to them for more money. They were out of their minds, but Burt agreed.

When I had to get the film back from the bootleggers, I had to go to Pete, who was still alive. Burt had died. I had to make a deal with him so that I had rights to fight the bootleggers. He tells me this story that I never knew. They needed all this money now, and Burt had no more people to go to. Pete knew all the right people. He borrowed the money from those right people. It turned out that when the film had all these problems with distribution, Pete had to bring in cash from Switzerland to repay his debt.

This film wound up costing $850,000, which for that time for an independent film was an extraordinary amount of money. The other incident that caused this was that I'd hired this woman as the sound editor. We go into the mix and they put up the reels, and there are no sound effects. There's no sound. She'd been so coked up she never laid anything in over a period of two months.

This is a non-union show. We had to go and hire union sound people for three or four days over the weekend. It wasn't just golden time, it was double golden time, and they worked around the clock, 24 hours for three days, and did all of the sound. That again increased the budget.

The thing about working on low-budget films is that by the time I got to my film, I knew how to cut corners and I knew how to make things happen. I had done 14 or more films like this and I knew how to do it. I knew how to schedule, I knew how to hire the right people, I knew how to get things done for little bits of money. That was really helpful. Even though it sounds like I spent a lot of money, there was a lot of production value and a lot of excess. I was really going for something fairly elaborate. Whether it looks it or not, the attempt at shooting outside in the dead of winter and trying to do these elaborate things was extremely costly.

There are lots of popular Christmas songs in the film. How did you handle the song clearances?

If I tried to do this now, the song clearances would have cost five times as much as the movie. I used stuff that was so old or archaic that it didn't mean anything. In other instances, I kept pulling back the amount of notes so that the things you think are so popular, you are only hearing for a second.

The band that's playing in the scene with the dance, that's being led by Danny Federici from the E-Street Band. He died [in 2008]. But he's leading that band, and they are just doing a kick-out arrangement of "Jingle Bells." There's a lot of stuff like that. I wanted to use "The Christmas Song," but I couldn't possibly afford it, so I have the character just hum a couple of bars.

There wasn't a thing about music back then. It took me a very long time just to find old Christmas music on LPs. Now there is a much greater awareness of all that stuff. Now you can find anything instantaneously. But I searched, and every once in a while would come across a fabulous old R&B Christmas album recorded by people you never heard of.

How did you get the footage of the tree lighting and the Thanksgiving parade?

The one shot of the tree lighting in Rockefeller Center? I saw a photograph in *New York* magazine of this angle on the tree, and we researched it and found out it was shot from the roof of Saks. For some reason Saks let us on the roof and we shot the tree lighting.

I shot the Thanksgiving Day parade. That's all my own footage. Instead of shooting at Macy's, we shot in Times Square. I had people with cameras and we covered the entire parade, much better than you would see it on TV. For the shots where Harry is staring at the television screen and he's looking at the Santa in the parade on the float, and the Santa turns to him, I was standing at the recruiting station in Times Square. Now it's a police station, but there was an army recruiting station there. The floats were going by me ten feet away. I started screaming at the top of my lungs at the Santa, screaming to get his attention, and I finally got it. He turned to me with a start. That's how I got that shot.

You actually filmed near Christmas, while the streets were all still decorated.

We did, about half of it or a little more. I wanted that feeling. We shot all those exteriors outside in January in the dead of night, in temperatures that were about 20 degrees below zero. Hardest shoot that everybody who worked on it ever had worked on, in that regard. It was a nightmare, but I wanted perfection.

How long did it take you to finish filming?

About 45 days. Somewhere between 45 and 50 days, with a few pick up shots later.

You had very carefully storyboarded the film. Was it difficult, given the shooting conditions and the schedule, to get the look that you wanted?

I could get the look, but I couldn't necessarily get the impact. When I wrote the scene of the mob chasing him, in my first version it was really a *mob*. There were hundreds of people, and you were seeing it from the sky, and it looked like a bloodstream flowing through the streets. By the time we shot those scenes, which were the last days of the shoot, we were basically out of money. The mob was my crew. I was down to sticks and stems. We're trying as best we could to cheat the shots.

I was very embarrassed about it when we shot it. And when I looked at what we had, I was devastated by it. When I look at it now, though, it seems fine. Time has kind of healed that.

How did you cast the film?

Through casting directors, actually. I had a casting director and she cast a lot of the movie. By the way, I couldn't afford to have my casting director bring people in and sort them out. I met every single person who came up for every single part in the movie. That was a three-month process. It was the most exhausting thing I've every done in my life. Everybody who comes in tries to sell you on themselves. They put on a show. It's a nightmare. I would never do that again.

I basically went through everybody. The leads were all originally different. The original cast was gonna be George Dzundza, the bartender in *The Deer Hunter* (1978). He's a fabulous actor. We started working and he began telling me how we were gonna rewrite the picture. I suddenly realized that he thought it was *Marty*. So that fell apart. The original wife of Jeff DeMunn was going to be Lindsay Crouse, who has been in a thousand movies. She used to be married to David Mamet. But she wound up meeting David Mamet just as we did that, and she got married and did a play.

I found everybody, but I couldn't find the lead. Someone introduced me to Vic Ramos, who was one of the top casting guys in New York at the time. He took it on for nothing. And he got me meetings with Peter Boyle, but he wasn't interested. There were a whole bunch of really well-known actors. Then he said he knew a guy who was mainly on Broadway. He was a musical comedy star and had actually been in "Sesame Street" the first year. He said, "I think he's somebody you should meet."

That was Brandon Maggart?

Yes. I met him, and I saw something. It was a gamble, because basically his looks were not like a movie star. But he brought something to it. When I look back now, there were some moments with him in the screen test where you see the performance completely whole. He brought that musical comedy quality to it. It comes from another place. It's off kilter. It appealed to me. I cast him and we started shooting a couple of days later.

What was he like to work with?

He was fine. He was a real pro. He'd been around. He liked to cut up a bit on the set, drop his pants and stuff like that. But other than that he was fine. He was one of those actors who could do something horrific, psychotic, and then you'd call cut and it didn't mean anything. He wasn't that person. He was back to the other guy.

I've heard stories about Judith Anderson, one of the great actresses, who would go onstage and do parts that were amazing, and she would walk offstage and she'd just smile and go about her business. There are certain actors like that who aren't so inner-driven. That was a good thing, to tell you the truth.

Was it difficult maintaining the correct mood or tone to the film? It's a melancholy film, but there are sequences that are also very funny.

I think that part of setting that tone was involved having all that Christmas stuff. The first scenes we shot were in his apartment. It kind of set a tone immediately. A friend of mine was the assistant director, and had set the scheduled up. He was very good at scheduling the movie in a way that the scenes that set that tone would come at the right time. The early scenes telegraphed who he was.

What were some of the most challenging things for you to shoot?

It was very difficult to shoot the scene where Harry goes into the bedroom and slices that guy's throat. I had this idea in my head and it was very hard to figure out how to make it come to life. My original idea was that the suffocating of the man and the bouncing in the bed would cause the wife to have orgasms in her sleep, so she'd be moaning. It was very hard to pull off!

The conclusion of that scene saved it, where he slices his throat and the blood lands on her and she can't scream. I wanted a lot more out of that. There's only so much time to shoot, though. That was very difficult.

The two scenes I thought were the most gratifying were the line-up, which was an idea I had I my head, and it was wonderful to see happen. And the scene where he climbs up on the roof and gets stuck in a chimney. We had a stuntman go up on the roof and do that whole thing. The close ups in the chimney were done in the studio. Ricardo, the cameraman, was such a great technician that he was able to pull this off and knew how to create these angles that you totally buy into.

I always loved the line-up scene; it should be on a Christmas card. Was that one of first ideas you had?

That's how I see things. I create scripts out of pictures, as opposed to out of a story, and then try to link them together. John Waters really likes that, too. That's one of his favorites. Did you listen to his commentary on the DVD? To him this is a whole movie about cross-dressing. He used to have a Christmas party every year, and this was the film playing at the party.

The other sequence I like a lot was the Christmas party, because it's so wrought with tension.

It's a very dark scene. It's a very melancholy scene. There's a sadness about the whole thing. I think a lot of people thought it was kind of out of place in this kind of movie, but the things that were influencing me at the time were very much at cross purposes. The movie comes out of the influence of horror movies, Fritz Lang, Douglas Sirk and Fassbinder. All these things were crossing paths for me. I was trying to incorporate all these different kinds of feelings.

Did you have any trouble securing locations because of the subject matter of the film?

No one knew. We didn't tell them. As I said, the film is totally secular. I will tell you that after it was over, a few years later, someone told me that someone who worked on the film, an assistant editor or somebody, was furious at me. She was saying, "This Jew is putting down my holiday?" She never left the film, but she was bad mouthing me plenty. She saw it as an attack on Christianity. The film certainly isn't; it's an attack on materialism.

Where did you get the toys that are featured in the toy factory?

We had to make them. We weren't allowed to use Pressman toys. There are certain things I didn't research. When we got to the Pressman toy factory, I found Hispanic women working on the line, and all they were doing was putting chess and checker things in boxes and shrink-wrapping them. All very simple board games. It had no relationship to what I had in mind, which probably goes back to a much earlier period of toy making.

We made the soldiers. We had to actually have somebody make these soldiers and stick the sword in them. I'm sure you saw it in the outtakes. There was a very elaborate subplot about the fact that Harry got the promotion because he came up with the idea for the toys, then they made them cheaper than he wanted. That's one of the scenes in the outtakes.

The ending of the film is very whimsical. Was that how you originally envisioned it?

No. The first time around I had this pathetic ending with him running around Central Park with helicopters shooting at him. It was just awful. I couldn't come up with an ending. Then I finally did come up with that ending. In its initial telling I wanted it to be much more elaborate, but it actually kind of worked in its own cheesy little way.

One of the cute things we did was when he's in the truck and he's roaring up and smoke is going by him. They rigged a vacuum cleaner hose to the exhaust pipe, ran it around and then put the hose sort of under the window. So every time he hit the gas pedal, streams of smoke like the clouds would go by. It was a wonderful, cheap special effect. The whole flying thing — I called special effects houses and they quoted me like a quarter million dollars to do a couple of seconds of flying. We figured out how to do it for $10,000 or $20,000.

How did you do it?

A combination of models and set pieces. Just being very careful and economical. It was before the digital age when you could do full special effects very easily. I personally am not so thrilled about that. I like the older effects.

Once you completed the film, what did you producers think?

They didn't know what to think. In a normal situation, you would basically have a couple of screenings and think about where to make a few cuts and trim things. That was where my game bit me, because I spent so much money that they couldn't give me that time. Burt basically threw it out there without any testing. I don't mean testing as in market research. I mean just showing it to people so I could get some feedback about where it might be a little long. They just threw it out there.

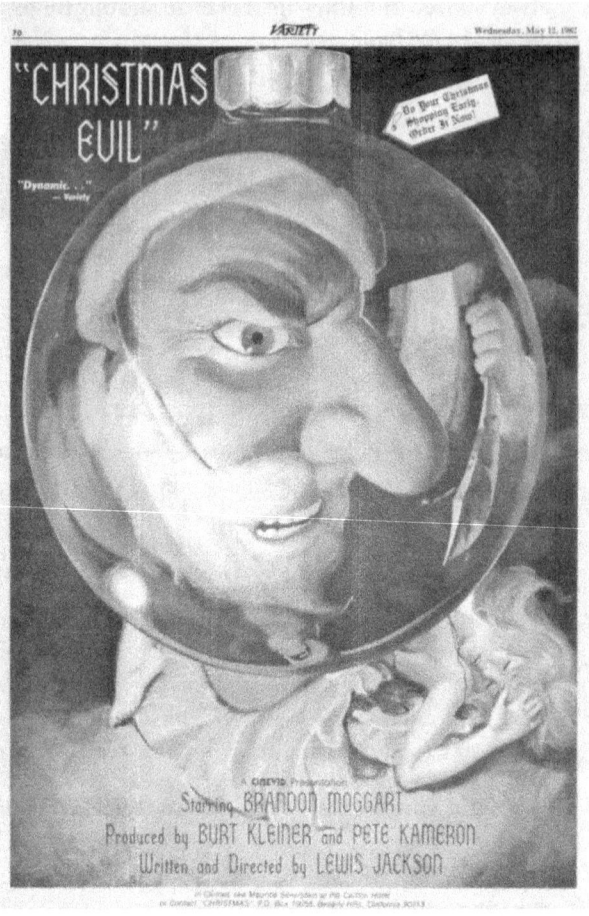

A *Variety* ad for *Christmas Evil* (courtesy Fred Adelman).

It took so long for the first murder to occur that it became a problem. While I was still cutting the film, Warner Brothers arranged to fly me out with the print. I only had seven reels. I showed the work print to Warner Brothers. They didn't take it. They watched up to the first murder, but they didn't take it. I think they thought it was slow and there wasn't enough violence.

Someone actually said to me, "You know, if you had Santa cut off a kid's finger and eat it, you'd be a multi-millionaire." I obviously didn't want to be so gross about the whole thing. I was trying to do this with a great deal of integrity.

What happened with distribution at that point?

It took awhile, but a company called Academy in Hollywood took the picture and they were very good distributors. They had good pictures. I was very excited. I went out to meet with them. I go into the meeting with head of the company and she says to me, "You know I've got to tell you this. Burt has been tying all his personal business dealings into this deal, and he's done this six times now. He just did it for the seventh time and I told him I'm out. I can't do this."

I went out to Hollywood to find out that the deal has collapsed. That's when I wound up in the dark. I came back, I didn't hear from Burt. Suddenly I find out that the picture has been sold to some company, and then there's another company and another company, and I find it playing on 42nd Street. This is where the bootlegging started. So many people had access to it, people were ripping off copies.

I took back the movie and spent three years with a lawyer, with Pete's help, stripping everybody of the movie. I could show you a stack of illegal copies of this thing. I insisted in each case that they send me everything they had. They wouldn't send me the actual DVDs, so I had stacks of boxes of broken DVDs. I thought I'd make an art piece of them at one point.

Were than any entities that still had claim on the video distribution rights?

It wasn't just video distribution. It was the rights, period. Red Suit was a company formed to make the movie. So Pete and I brought back Red Suit.

When the film was originally released, was there any controversy about the idea of a Santa Claus killer? The film *Silent Night, Deadly Night* (1984) caused a stir a few years later.

You know what the controversial part was? All of the newsletters, those little magazines for horror films, couldn't understand how I could make a movie with so little blood and gore. There wasn't a controversy about Santa Claus. In the early eighties, the film was gonna open one summer all over the West Coast. It was at the time that *Silent Night, Deadly Night* came out. So that film, which came out after mine, caused all that controversy. They basically told the distributor that the ad he had for this thing was not acceptable to the MPAA. For some reason that I'm not clear about, my film never got that release. He couldn't afford to start the whole thing over again.

These other films were just about psychotic Santa Clauses killing virgins or something. My film is so different, so much more serious about the notion of Santa Claus and based on real historical detail.

The film played eight years, every year, on 42nd Street. It was the perennial of 42nd Street. The first year it played I went to a screening. I was sitting there with the audience, and when he flies off at the end they all threw stuff at the screen. They threw popcorn, sodas. The audience went wild. They threw everything they could get their hands on.

Once the film was released, what did you want to do afterward?

I had some projects to do. The problem was this had become such a bad experience in terms of the genre, that I basically decided that I would give up on horror and I tried to make a *real* Douglas Sirk film. That was a mistake, because nobody was making Douglas Sirk films. They could care less. I spent a couple of years on that, then I wound up working as a screenwriter out here. That was an even a worse experience. I wound up on a project where I had to do seven versions of one script in one year. I kind of backed off a bit. I needed time to kind of think things through. I did things. I made some videos for commercial companies and stuff like that.

When this whole thing with John Waters started and I took back the film, that's when I decided I was ready to do this again. That's when I brought back *Chiller*. I've been working on that.

How has your opinion of *Christmas Evil* changed in ensuing years?

I like it a lot more. Part of the problem was, again, when I made it I couldn't edit it. It needed a little editing. There was a moment in time where there was a revival house in New York called the Thalia, and the guy there was dying to play the movie. He said, "You should make a few cuts. Why don't you do that up here at the theater." So we made a few trims to the print. It made the print better. It was small stuff, but it made the print better.

That was one thing, but the fact of the matter is that I could never see the film unless I was looking at these terrible bootlegs. Part of the whole raison d'etre of the film was having this cameraman who would create this heightened look that was so much a part of the movie. I couldn't ever see that on those bootlegs.

When the Synapse print came out, I could embrace the film again. I could see what I was doing. I've been doing a lot of screenings at Christmas. John Waters also had an art show that toured. There was always a film program with that. He invited me to show the film in several places as part of the program. The first one was at the Andy Warhol Museum in Pittsburgh. The audience just had a fabulous reaction to the film, which really re-awakened me to the movie. The years had actually made the film resonate with the audience. Rather than see it as slow here or there, the black humor in the film suddenly had real consequence for people.

I made it on the cusp before Reagan got elected. I could just envision what was happening with unions and working people and the dismissal of quality. I just saw it all happening. And it became the reality. The film actually played to people who didn't find it strange. They found it to be realistic, but funny. This film that had I had made with a sensibility that was probably out of its time—suddenly that sensibility was right.

Night Frights
RUSS MARKER
Texas

Russ Marker has been a part of the Texas filmmaking scene for more than four decades, with credits stretching back to the Dallas-lensed *Beyond the Time Barrier* (1960) right up through the Chuck Norris series *Walker, Texas Ranger*.

Born in 1926 in Oklahoma, Marker started acting in college and soon began picking up roles in movies and TV series shot around Texas and Oklahoma in the 1950s and early 1960s. He began production of his first film as writer and director in 1964, but *The Demon from Devil's Lake* (shot in Oklahoma) was never completed. His next film, the obscure *The Yesterday Machine* (1966), was shot in Dallas. The film, about a Nazi scientist who creates a time machine so that he can resurrect the Third Reich, received limited distribution, but appears to have played Texas drive-ins as late as 1974. Marker's brother, James Britton, appeared in both films.

In 1967, Larry Buchanan's cinematographer James Sullivan re-filmed Marker's *Demon from Devil's Lake* idea as *Night Fright* with John Agar. It's not clear if this film was ever released theatrically, but it became a staple of late-night television throughout the 1970s and 1980s.

Marker continued acting throughout the next several decades, appearing in *Bonnie and Clyde* (1967), *Two-Lane Blacktop* (1971), *Dillinger* (1973), *Dust to Dust* (1994), *Finding North* (1998) and multiple episodes of "Walker" before retiring.

Did you grow up in Texas?

I grew up in Okalahoma. I'm an old Okie boy. After I got married, we moved back down to Dallas. We've lived here ever since. We've been married 56 years.

How did you get involved in acting and working on films?

When I was in college I did a lot of plays, just kind of fell in love with acting. I didn't really like stage work that much, but it was the only thing happening in a small town in Oklahoma in those days. Later on they got to shooting quite a bit of stuff up there.

Yesterday Machine was with based on an idea I got right after the Second World War. I was reading an article about all these secret weapons that the Germans had been working on. The war ended before they got to use most of them, but they had some real amazing things.

I got to thinking about these weapons in Germany, and I thought, hell that would be something to base a story on. And so that's kind of where I got the idea for the *Yesterday Machine*.

It kind of stayed with me, the memory of it, because I wrote that about a year after I read the article. I thought, what if they had a damn time machine? This mad scientist had built it in order to bring Hitler back to power and re-establish the Third Reich. That's why I wrote that.

How did you get the film financed?

At that time, I was friends with several extremely wealthy millionaires here. Most of them were pretty nice guys. They weren't uppity and didn't act almighty like a lot of poor people think they do. I was a good friend of those guys, so I think one or two of them put up the money for it. I told them about it, and the war hadn't been over that long. Two or three of them were veterans. They though it was a damn good idea for a movie.

On the credits, Dan W. Holloway is listed as the executive producer.

It was Dr. Dan Holloway. He put up quite a bit of the money. He was from Houston.

Was he a physician?

Yes, he was a doctor. But he was living down in Houston, which is quite a little ways to drive from Dallas. Me and my brother, who was in the film, went down there and met with him. We got to talking to him and he liked the idea, and he put up the money.

What's your brother's name?

James. He used the name James Britton when he was acting. He's been dead for a lot of years now. He was one of the handsomest young men I've ever seen. Everywhere he went, the girls would just swarm all over him, but he was happily married. He didn't play around on his wife.

Once you got the money, how did recruit your cast and crew?

I knew many actors and crew members by that time; a lot of people in Dallas that were in the business. We just had auditions and invited all the actors. Of course, all of them knew me and I picked out the people that I liked for it. I knew the cameraman, Ralph Johnson, who was the cameraman on *The Yesterday Machine* and one of the others. He died right after that.

You mentioned Larry Buchanan. Did you know that he died about a year ago? I don't know if I told you much about Larry. He was a big tall guy. We were good friends. Sometimes he'd lose somebody from his crew or something, and he'd always phone me and say, "Hey, I'm missing a cameraman. You got one you can loan me?" We swapped out a couple of times like that. But Larry, the way he got his money was he was big and tall and handsome, and he'd just charm the pants off these old gals in Dallas. He knew a bunch of these rich women around Dallas, 'cause they'd just flock around him wherever he went. That's how he got funded.

In *The Yesterday Machine*, the top-billed actor was Tim Holt. His career was slowing down at that point.

He was working for a radio station in Okalahoma City. I was from Okalahoma. I went up one day to talk to him. Hollywood didn't want him much at that time. I showed him the script, and asked if he'd do this with me. He said, "I'd love to. Nothing's happening up here. I can't get a job." I said, "Well, you've got a job now." He moved down to Dallas and stayed during the filming of the movie for about three months. Then he got a call from the Coast and somebody had a part for him out there, so he left. He was a real nice guy.

The man who played the doctor, Jack Herman, was a drama coach, wasn't he?

He was. He taught at a school in Oak Cliff. Jack Herman was one of the nicest guys I've ever met. He was Jewish, and he'd been through some dangerous stuff over in Germany during the war, when the Nazis were putting them to death and in concentration camps and all that crud. So he heard somebody say I was doing this thing, and he wanted to be in it. He wanted to play the mad German scientist who wanted to bring Hitler back in his time machine. He did a heck of a good job in that thing.

Actor James Britton in Russ Marker's *The Yesterday Machine* (1966). Britton was actually Marker's brother (courtesy Russ Marker).

How did you come up with all that crazy scientific dialogue?

I just read all these articles. Mostly from this book or article I had read about all their secret weapons and things they were developing to use against us in the war. They had one — this is the truth, but I couldn't work it into the script — they had a weapon where they could fly over with their bombers, and drop thousands of gallons of water all over the battlefield. Usually armies know where the next battle is going to be. Anyway, they could electrocute entire armies on the field. When you get to thinking about it, that's pretty damn terrifying. At the end of the war the Russians captured a lot of the German scientists, and we captured a bunch of them. One of them helped us get to the moon. We never would have gotten to the moon or done all these things up in space if it hadn't been for him.

In addition to directing and writing *The Yesterday Machine*, you wrote the song in the nightclub scene. Did you have a musical background?

My dad was a musician, and he had an orchestra when I was growing up. I went to a few things with him. He could do all kinds of dances, play the piano. He was just very talented. A lot more talented than I was. I grew up interested in writing songs and things like that.

Ann Pellegrino was from New York City. I wrote this song for the movie for her to sing in this scene, and when it was over she just loved the song. She lived in New York, and was always performing up there. She took this song back up there with her, and later on she wrote me a note and said, "Everywhere I appear up here, they ask me to sing this song of yours. They just love that song." That kind of tickled me, because New York City to me, in those days, was the big time.

Tell me about Bill Thurman.

Billy Thurman and I were good friends. He was an interesting person. He and Stephen Spielberg were good friends because Stephen used him in a movie one time [*The Sugarland Express*, 1974] and just fell in love with Billy. Billy was a policeman here in Dallas. He was really a policeman. And he drank a lot.

There was a bar that was here in Dallas, run by an ex–FBI man. He had a bunch of Texas friends, so he moved down to Dallas and put in this bar. Billy Thurman would come out there to his bar and just get drunk as a skunk. And when Billy got drunk, he'd start arguing with people.

This ex–FBI agent and I got to be good friends, and he told me one time, "You missed the excitement out here yesterday." Billy got mad and started raising hell with somebody, and started a fight, and he and this guy were fighting all over the darn place, tearing it up. He was tearing up parts of this FBI guy's bar, and the guy didn't like it. He said, "You know how many cops it took to get Billy Thurman quieted down? It took *five* of 'em. He damn near whipped the hell out of three or four of them!" So that was the way Billy Thurman was. He never did fight with me or anything. Billy was a good actor, a damn good actor.

He always reminded me of Ben Johnson.

Yeah. I knew Ben Johnson pretty well at one time, when he was working more around here in Texas. He was a hell of a good actor. He won an Academy Award. Ben's been gone a long time.

Do you remember anything about Olga Powell, who played the Egyptian girl in *The Yesterday Machine*?

Not much. She was really from overseas somewhere, though.

Who distributed *The Yesterday Machine*?

We took it out to Hollywood. At that time there was a man here named Robert O'Donnell. He was a multi-millionaire, and he was head of Interstate Theaters. He owned damn near every theater in Dallas at that time, and was one of the nicest old guys I'd ever seen in my life. Every time I'd write a script or something, he'd send it off to someone he knew in Hollywood.

He sent one of my scripts to Audie Murphy. I went out there, and I was with Jody McCrea. I had met him out there and we got to be good buddies. One night he said, "Have you ever met Audie Murphy? He's a Texas boy." I hadn't, but I told him a friend of mine in Dallas had sent him my script. He said, "Why don't we go over to Audie's house, and you can meet him."

We went over there. Audie answered the door, and he had a beautiful home. A mansion. He had a six-car garage in the back, right behind the house. After we went to leave that night, we walked around the side of the house to see the garage. There was a Lincoln Continental in every damn one of those six spots in the garage.

Anyway, we went into Audie's house. He had a pair of cowboy boots on that were the gaudiest looking things I've ever seen in my life. I glanced at them and

Olga Powell as the Egyptian slave girl in *The Yesterday Machine* (courtesy Russ Marker).

thought, "What the hell is he wearing those awful boots for?" He was talking about my script, and he noticed me look down at his boots. He was grinning at me, and he said, "You noticed my boots, huh? Aren't they the ugliest damn things you ever saw in your life? You know why I'm wearing these? A little old lady came to the door one day, and she'd seen every movie I was ever in. She said she had me a gift. She bought this pair of boots for me." Then he said, "Russ, I don't give a damn how they look, I'm gonna wear these till the day I die."

It sounds kind of funny when you talk about it, but from that moment I thought, "There's a hell of a nice guy with a good heart." His wife at that time was named Pamela, and she was just a gorgeous gal. Sweet as she could be. It was kind of late when we got there, so she said, "You guys would like to have a little supper, wouldn't you?" She went in there and fixed us supper. She was a hell of a good cook.

So did O'Donnell distribute the film?

He's the one that went to bat for me and had Interstate Theaters distribute it.

Did *The Yesterday Machine* just play around Texas?

I really don't know. I don't know much more than just what I've told you. Bob, like I say, he owned damn near every theater in town at that time. Just as sweet as he could be. Everybody loved Bob. So he's the one that got it distributed, but I don't remember now how it came about. I remember when they had the premiere of one of the pictures at the Majestic Theater in downtown Dallas.

Were you able to make any money?

I made a little. Those people in Hollywood, sometimes they make sure your contacts are set up so that they're gonna get most of the money. I made a few thousand dollars off of it. Not a hell of a lot.

What did you do for a living?

I was a commercial artist and an illustrator. I illustrated several books. That's what my main job was. I had a studio in my home where I did my painting.

What was the first film you worked on? You appeared in *Beyond the Time Barrier*.

I'd done some things before that, but I can't remember what all they were.

Were they shot in Texas?

And some of 'em in Oklahoma. One we did in Oklahoma one time, it was about when Abe Lincoln was a young guy and he traveled on these flat boats down the Mississippi and saw the first slaves. That was the first time he got turned against slavery. He saw how cruel it was. They were shooting part of this movie up there. They had a few of these old trains. Some rich guy had collected these old-time locomotives. He had all of this narrow-gauge track that he'd built up there, and he collected these trains. That's one of the reasons they filmed up there.

When they shot *Jessie James* (1939) up there in Missouri, they brought some of those old trains up there. I didn't do any acting in that, but I went up and watched them shoot some of it. My uncle was a good friend of the director, Henry King. Me and my dad watched them shoot about 75 percent of *Jessie James* up there.

A lot of these things you just kind of stumble into. You go up and audition and ask around, and the first thing you know, you're working on it.

The people that made *Beyond the Time Barrier* also made *The Amazing Transparent Man* and *Date with Death* (1959) in Texas. Did you work on either of those?

No, I didn't work on those.

How did you get your part in *Beyond the Time Barrier*?

I played a pilot in that. I knew a lot of these producers and directors and other actors around town. I'm trying to remember who produced that darn thing. It may have been Wally Clyce.

It was produced by Robert Clark, Robert Madden and John Miller.

Bob Madden was a good friend of mine. I think Bob was involved in real estate for a while. He made a lot of money some way. Bob called me one day and said, "I've got a part you might want to do." Anything kind of strange or unusual, I enjoyed doing. He said it was a story about a pilot who's testing this new plane that's been developed. The plane is supposed to be super powered, and the damn thing goes so fast it flies into another time period.

Do you remember the director, Edgar Ulmer?

Edgar was a hell of a good director. He was a pretty good cinematographer, too. We were shooting a western on this big ranch in West Texas. It was a humongous ranch. The guy had like 10,000 acres or something out there. Edgar had come in from Hollywood and had been hired by this rich rancher that knew him.

A lot of these people weren't in the business, but still interested in it. Those were the days when there was a lot of interest in motion picture production. I wish there was still that much interest around here. It's kind of lagged lately.

The producer, he and his wife had moved down here from New York City. He had been with ABC up there. It was Joe Graham and his wife Jane. There was an old Jewish tabernacle in Dallas at the time that had been sitting vacant. They bought that thing and built two soundstages. It was as good as anything I've been inside of. They had a smaller stage where they did television commercials and lower budget movies and stuff like that.

[Note: Graham ran a company called Dallas Film Industries that was set up to produce TV series and theatrical films. In 1957, the company announced production on a half-hour television series called "Indemnity" starring Richard Kiley as an insurance investigator.]

Ulmer called me one day and said, "Russ, I'd like to have you on this show to help out. You've been around ranches a lot and ride horses." I drove an equipment truck out there. I'd never driven a big truck before. I had my wife come out with me.

Joe Graham was the director or producer, and he could get a high temper some times. They had a big scene that called for a bunch of cowboys — actually, cowboys in the old days didn't like to be called cowboys, because that suggested farmers. They preferred to be called drovers. So they had a bunch of drovers out there to drive this big heard of cattle across this narrow river. It really wasn't much more than a creek. It was four or five feet deep. They wanted them to start up on this hill and drive this herd of cattle across this creek and up on the bank.

I happened to be standing right behind Ulmer. He and I had been chatting. They're getting ready to drive these cattle across there, and all of a sudden I glanced up on top of this hill, and silhouetted against the sky was this beautiful shot. Two big bulls were fighting.

Joe was standing there looking at these cattle. I tapped Ulmer on the arm said, "Edgar, look at that." I pointed up there. He just took one quick glance and swung that camera around up there. Took it clear off the cattle. Joe saw that, and God he blew up. He said, "Don't ever do that to a director when they're directing a picture." What I started to say was, "If you were directing a picture and were any good at it, you'd have seen that damn shot!" But I didn't.

We get back to Dallas two weeks later. There were some other shots we got at a rodeo. I lived about two miles from the studio. I think I went there to pick up my check. I started down the hall to see Joe, and I really didn't want to talk to him. I figured he was gonna be pissed off about what happened out there.

I walked up and kind of timidly knocked on the door. He was at the editing machine and he kind of glanced up at me with a big smile on his face. He said, "Russ, come in here. I want to show you something." And he had that damn scene of those bulls fighting on the screen. He said, "Russ, this is the most beautiful scene in that whole damn film."

Do you remember what the movie was?

I can't remember the name. It had a rodeo in the title or something. It was shot in Stamford, Texas, out in West Texas. There were two big ranches this guy had.

They had a cabin where we were staying. The owner rolled up in front of the cabin in his pick up. He asked us if we'd ever eaten off a chuck wagon. We got in the truck with him. He said, "This old cook has been cooking on this ranch for years and years. His father was a cook on a chuck wagon on one of the old trail drives." It was a lot of fun. We were sitting around on the ground eating with a whole bunch of these cowboys who'd been working on this ranch for years.

Before *The Yesterday Machine*, you made *Demon of Devil's Lake*. Was that film ever completed?

I don't think we finished it. I think what happened was we ran out of money, and we couldn't get any more.

Who put up the money?

I think that was probably Frank Phillips. He was with [Oklahoma-based] Phillips Petroleum Company, and owned a bunch of oil wells and oil fields up there. He was very rich and he was also interested in movies. I met him at a party one night that my wife and I went to, and I think he backed that thing.

Veteran actor Tim Holt portrayed the detective in *The Yesterday Machine* (courtesy Russ Marker).

Where was it filmed?

That was shot up there around Lake Texoma. It's a huge lake up there, about 20 miles west of my hometown of Durant, Oklahoma. So we shot a lot of that around there.

How much of it did you complete?

Not much. I remember now what happened. We had an actress in that thing, a beautiful girl, just as sweet as she could be, and all of a sudden her mother got involved. Her dad didn't mind her working on it, but her mother was dead set against it. She thought all actors and people in the movie business were just sorry no-accounts. Of course, some of 'em are! But anyway, she wouldn't let her daughter be in the thing anymore, so we just had to end it right there. That's how that happened.

Do you know what the monster was supposed to look like?

I'll tell you something funny about that. I designed the monster. I had it in my mind how I wanted him to look. I wanted him to look different than anything else you'd ever seen. I made sketches of him until I got him the way I wanted him. There was an actor here named Byron Lord. You've heard of Lord Byron? Byron Lord took the name because he needed an acting name. I can't even remember his real name anymore. He just turned it around, and instead of Lord Byron he called himself Byron Lord, which was a pretty good actor's name.

Was the monster in the first film supposed to look like the one in *Night Fright*.

No, it wasn't. We had a different idea on that. Somebody else came up with that. I think one of my set designers came up with that idea and brought me a sketch of it. At that point I was not real interested in that movie. I was kind of getting tired of it. You spend so many 12- or 15-hour days on a movie. I mean, on that "Walker, Texas Ranger" series, I don't know how many sixteen-hour days I worked on that damn thing. I was on that show for eight years, and when I got through with that I was tired. I was worn out.

What happened to the footage from *Demon*?

I don't know. There were some guys here in Dallas that had put up some money for that, and I don't remember their names. When I discontinued it and wrapped it up, I didn't want to mess with it anymore. They were not too happy about it, because they had money in it. Things didn't end too happily between me and them. I can't remember who they were now, but that kind of ended that deal.

How did *Night Fright* come together? There was a gap of two or three years between your two films.

I was just doing some acting in some films. I don't remember what. I wasn't too interested in directing any more at that point. I was getting more acting parts.

Did you actually work on any of the Larry Buchanan films?

No, I didn't. Larry was an orphan. He was raised here in Dallas at an orphan's home. I always kind of felt sorry for him, knowing that he'd been an orphan.

I shouldn't talk about the dead. Larry was really — and I hate to say this, but it's true — he was not much of a director. There are so many things about directing that you have to know. You don't cut from a close-up to a long shot that's half a mile away. You have to have intervals. Or he'd shoot a couple of people talking, and he'd shoot over one shoulder and shoot one person, and then shoot from behind the other person, and he'd be shooting over the wrong shoulder or something.

Who was Wallace Clyce, who produced *Night Fright*?

We called him Wally Clyce. He was wealthy guy who traded mostly in real estate. He lived across town from us, but one day we got a call from him and he'd read my script. He said he wanted to produce it. That's kind of the way we got together. I don't remember a whole lot about Wally. He wasn't around the set much. I think he came once or twice and stayed a little while. I think he learned that the movie business is not as quite as exciting as he thought it might be. When you shoot a movie, it is kind of dull if you're not an actor or something like that.

How did James Sullivan, the director, get involved?

He just was a good director, and they hired him. He was a pretty darn good cinematographer.

Robert Jessup was the cinematographer on *Night Fright*.

I think he was Canadian, and he'd done a lot of work up there before he came to Texas. I think he just heard about us doing some stuff down here, and he always wanted to see Texas. Some of these people you're talking about I'd forgot about! This brings back a lot of memories.

Did you know John Agar?

I never had met John before. He was a real nice guy, and a darn good actor. Somebody had known him in Hollywood, but I don't remember who it was.

He'd worked for Larry Buchanan.

He was in several movies around Texas.

There was somebody in the cast named as Brenda Venus. Do you remember who that was?

I don't remember her at all. There was one scene in one of the pictures, a nightclub scene, and I think they had a dancer or two in that. She might have been one of them. The name suggests to me that maybe she was a streetwalker [*laughs*]!

How did you cast the college students in the film?

We just held auditions in those days. Of course, the newspaper carried it in the entertainment section. They'd come flocking in there. They'd come from everywhere. If they were good enough and fit the part, they got hired.

Were you on the set of *Night Fright*?

Oh yeah. I was around the whole time.

Did you appear in the film?

I think I played a deputy sheriff or a policeman.

Do you remember how long it took to film?

I think we were on that picture about two weeks.

Did filming go smoothly?

Yeah, it did. There were a couple of actors on there that were always clowning around. They were good actors, but they kept me in stitches.

Do you know if the film was distributed theatrically?

I believe so, but I don't remember much about that.

During the 1960s, what other acting work did you do?

That was just about it. I think I told you I went up to Oklahoma and did two or three up there, but it's been so long ago I can't remember what all I did. I worked on one called *Dillinger* (1973) with Warren Oates. Warren and I got to be pretty good buddies on that. I did some work on one called *Two-Lane Blacktop* (1971).

What part did you play in *Two-Lane Blacktop*?

It seems like I was a cop in that one. They liked me as a cop! I did one out there one time with Rory Calhoun, too. I hate to keep saying I was a cop, but I think I was a cop in that one, too [*laughs*]!

You and Bill Thurman could have been your own police department.
Bill and I got along pretty well. I'm glad I never had to fight that son of a gun. He was pretty well organized. We called it "organized" when you got too drunk. When he got drunk he really wasn't too organized, though [*laughs*]. He'd fight at the drop of a hat, and most of the time he'd drop the hat.

I saw him have a tussle with the police one day. It didn't develop into a full fight. I heard a row going on, somebody hollering. I stepped in the other room and looked, and there was old Billy getting upset about something. Two of 'em had a hold of him saying, "Billy, calm down. We don't want to have to arrest you." He said, "You'll play hell ever gettin' me in jail." Finally this cop that was a little bigger than Bill, a strong son of a gun, said, "Billy, I hate to do this, but you caused it." He whipped out this sap from his hip pocket and popped him over the head. It just knocked old Billy crazy. It brought a little blood, but not a whole lot. I tell you, we had some exciting times!

I did a few episodes of "Route 66." We were out on Church Road here in Dallas, way out in the country. We're doing this scene where we're supposed to get in this car and take off and chase some bad guys or something. One of the leads, and I can't remember which one, was standing there leaning up against this equipment van. I'm standing there talking to him, and about that time this bird sitting up on a limb above him just shit on him [*laughs*]. I heard this bird up there in the tree singing, and about that time I saw it hit his hand. He looked at me and looked up at that bird. He said, "That goddamned bird shit on my hand. For most people, they sing!" I'll never forget that.

What did you think of your films when they were finished?
I like *The Yesterday Machine* better than any of them, because it was about a time machine. That idea still fascinates me — how somebody could build a machine where you could climb in it and see what things were like long ago.

It had a great score.
I don't remember who did the music. I can't remember any of the musicians.

It looks like Robert Kelly, who was in the cast, had a music studio.
Bob Kelly. I think he had a studio in Dallas. He moved from here. I lost track of him.

Are you still acting?
I haven't done any in a while. I got into doing more writing, and it takes a long time to write a book, as you know. After so many years of acting, I got a little tired. When you're 80 years old, you get tired of going to those damned auditions [*laughs*].

But you did quite a few "Walker" episodes.
I worked on that series for eight years. I did 29 shows with them. Chuck Norris and I got to be good buddies. He was real nice guy. We got along fine. Anytime any episode came up that had some good exciting scenes he thought I'd like, he'd call me and say, "Come on down. We've got a part you'll like." It was always something good.

Survivors Will Be Persecuted
ROBERT W. MORGAN
Florida

Of all the filmmakers interviewed for this book, Robert Morgan may have the most eccentric biography. Best known to horror fans as the director, writer, producer and star of *Blood Stalkers* (1976), Morgan already had a lengthy and diverse resume before he started making low-budget films.

Born in Canton, Ohio, Morgan was serving in the Navy when, in 1956, his life took an abrupt turn. Morgan claims he had a chance encounter during a hunting trip in Washington with a creature he would come to call a Forest Giant — Bigfoot. After resigning from a post at the Federal Aviation Administration in the late 1960s, Morgan began organizing expeditions to search for Bigfoot, and over the course of the next several decades established himself as a leading authority in what was then the burgeoning field of cryptozoology.

Short, with a shaved head and a goatee, Morgan was an instantly recognizable and sometimes controversial figure in the Bigfoot community, who insisted on a no-kill approach to studying the elusive American yeti. At the height of his career, Morgan appeared in a number of films, including *The Mysterious Monsters* (1976), *Monsters! Mysteries or Myths?* (1974), and *In Search of Bigfoot* (1976). The latter two films documented Morgan's 1974 American Yeti Expedition into the Pacific Northwest, at the time one of the most elaborate of its type.

By the mid–1970s, Morgan was in Florida working alongside William Grefé on *Impulse* (1974) and *Mako: Jaws of Death* (1976).

Robert W. Morgan (wearing the fake Bigfoot arm) and John Meyer prepare to film a scene in *Blood Stalkers* (1976) (courtesy Robert W. Morgan).

Teaming up with Irv Rudley of Creative Film & Sound, he directed *Blood Stalkers* (a.k.a. *The Night Daniel Died*), a backwoods stalk-and-slash film starring Kenny Miller, Toni Crabtree and Morgan himself as homicidal hillbilly Jarvis. Oddly, given Morgan's background, the villains of the film are a gang of swamp dwellers who use the Bigfoot legend as a cover for their poaching activities.

Morgan now hosts and Internet radio program ("The AARF Show") dedicated to paranormal topics, and is in the process of publishing a number of books, including *Soul Snatchers: A Quest for True Human Beings, Citizen Spy* and *Lies Our Fathers Told Us*, about his relationship with Watergate burglar Frank Sturgis. His group, the American Anthropological Research Foundation, has a Web site at www.trueseekers.org.

What were you doing in Florida in the 1970s?

I left the FAA in Washington, D.C., and I moved to Florida because my wife, soon to be ex-wife, wanted to live there with my child. So I moved down there and got involved in the motion picture business. I was writing scripts. I worked with Bill Grefé. We shot *Impulse*. I watched how he did it, and also another film he did that I can't remember the name of. I figured if he could direct, I sure as hell could.

How did you meet Grefé?

He called me. I had done the American [Bigfoot] expedition that was on TV quite a bit. I had no clue who the hell he was when he contacted me in Miami. I was getting some press because of the Bigfoot expeditions I was doing in the Pacific Northwest, and also in the Everglades. I was working with Ted Ernst quite a bit. He became a great close friend and my attorney.

In the meantime, Grefé invited me over and asked me to write some scripts, which I did. He botched one so badly [*Mako: The Jaws of Death*] that I asked him to take my name off it. He asked me what name I wanted on it, and I picked up a phone book and chose the first name I saw [Robert Madaris]. I did get it registered in my name, and I still get royalties from it.

A fellow by the name of Irv Rudley, who owned Creative Film & Sound, heard about me and asked me to do a screenplay for him. I started making commercials with him, and we concocted the idea of doing our own film.

I looked at the minimum budget we had and I looked at the Everglades. I ran into poachers out there that used the Bigfoot — they called it Skunk Ape — to keep people out of the area.

Didn't Stan Webb, who appears in *Blood Stalkers*, tell you about the poachers?

The poachers actually stopped by the set, and they were some tough-lookin' bastards. They came in to watch us film, and I said, "Yeah, you can watch, but don't talk." They came in very quietly and they watched the scene with Celea Ann Cole. She was one good lookin' woman, and these guys were drooling. I thought I was gonna have to put a pad under them [*laughs*]!

Finally we started talking about this one scene where we were going to throw these bundles of skins to reveal that these characters in the film were poachers. One of these guys said, "That don't look like no alligator skin to me." So he goes back to his truck and comes back with one. The real, bloody thing. He loaned it to us. But they were very polite, they left when I asked them to, and it worked out pretty well.

You worked with Grefé on *Impulse*. What was that experience like?

I was supposed to be a grip, because I had no bloody clue what I was doing. This was my first time on a set. I had no idea how a film was made. On the very first night they put the whole crew together and everybody was introduced to everybody else. Bill Grefé is naming people off as they stand up. I'm just sitting there with my mouth open, thinking, "Wow, look where I am!" Then Grefé said, "Bob Morgan is our prop master," or something like that. I'm looking around like, Jesus, there has to be another Morgan here some place. I had no clue what he was talking about. So I stood up and he pointed at me. All of a sudden I'm a property master? I didn't even know what the hell that was.

So Gayle DeCamp, God bless him, he came walking by and said, "Don't worry about it; I'll take care of you."

I ended up driving truck for Grefé. I had just come out of the Pacific Northwest where I had worked with the loggers. I had always heard on the Bigfoot expeditions that if Bigfoot existed, the loggers would know about it. But none of them would come forward. Only that one guy, Ray Wallace, ever did, and nobody believed him anyway.

[*Note: Wallace owned a construction company, and one of his employees found the tracks in the famous Bluff Creek Bigfoot sighting in 1958.*]

I thought, "Why don't I go out and get a job as a logger?" Here I have thousands of hours of classroom instruction in electronics, and I was at that time a computer specialist for the FAA. When I was on duty I had the maintenance responsibility for the entire air traffic control complex in Washington, D.C.

So here I am, fairly well educated, and I go out and get a job through a friend of mine out there as a logger. I was a choker setter on the high line. After they realized that I had a bit of an education, they came up and just flat asked me why I was there. I told them I wanted to find out why nobody ever sees Bigfoot. They said, "We see it; we know all about it. But we're a bunch of 'dumb hillbillies.' If we talk about it, all those city people just make fun of us."

I was in fairly good condition after a season of that. The stunt guys on *Impulse* were getting ready to crash that car in the scene where the dead girl was in the water. They had the car up on a hill. The crew and everybody needed some water up there. They were going down and getting little buckets. I went down and picked up the whole container and ran it to the top of the hill. You should have seen the looks on their faces!

I got to know Harold Sakata. He was doing some exercises. I had my belts in karate, tae kwon-do and judo. I joined him. We ended up bashing each other around, and William Shatner is just staring at us, like what the hell is with these guys?

You know how actors give you those head shot pictures? The one from Shatner reads, "To Bobby, for higher kicks." It was really apropos. He came out and joined us a couple of times. We ended up being pretty good friends.

An accident happened, because Grefé doesn't give a rat's ass about anyone, during that one scene where Sakata is being hung at the car wash. If you look at that one shot, you take a look at Harold Sakata's tongue coming out of his mouth. We're all down below and we suddenly realize that that harness had slipped. He was literally strangling. Shatner grabbed him down below and tried to pick him up a little bit. A couple of us scrambled to the top and cut him down. He was in serious trouble. Well, that bonded us, believe me. As a matter of fact I still have that goddamn rope. Sakata came over and gave it to me. I have a picture of myself, Shatner and Sakata right after that, with that rope around his neck. I want to get that rope and photograph and have it mounted in a frame.

We were all over there in Tampa, and we would have parties in the evening. We were in a motel that was split in half, with one building on side of the road, and the other building on the opposite side. I was in the cheap seats. I happened to have with me a girl who was a Playboy Bunny. One night we're having this party and Shatner invited everybody up to his penthouse or whatever it was. But Sakata, for some reason, didn't want to go. This girl, Lisa, and I watched him walk across the parking lot across the road and back to the cheap rooms where he was staying. He had been in the bar, and as he left everybody went out of their way to bump up against Odd Job. He was the real star. But when he left the party, everyone had a girl except him. When he walked away, I wish I'd had a camera shot of it because the parking lot was full of cars, but no people. He was walking from lamppost to lamppost. Lisa said to me, "My God, he's the loneliest man I've ever seen."

Sakata and I were close. He would call me drunk as a skunk in Hawaii, and I'm up in Montana. One year I didn't get a phone call or a Christmas card. I wrote to his home, and his daughter wrote back thanking me for having written such a lovely script for her dad, but he had died of stomach cancer.

Jump forward 20 years. I'm walking into a bar in some ski town in Colorado. I just got into town. I had my kid with me and a girl I was dating. I'd never been there in my life. I hear some one say, "Bobby Morgan!" I turn around and this red-headed girl comes running up and throws her arms around me. It turns out it was the sister of my childhood love in Canton, Ohio. The girl that I had cared about in high school had died very early of nephritis. But her sister's name was Nancy. She said, "I've heard all about what you've done." She started telling me about the film. As it turns out, she was the nurse in Honolulu that took care of Odd Job. That's beyond bizarre. Sakata didn't want anyone to know he was dying. I guess he went down to just a little over a hundred pounds before he died.

The other film you worked on for Grefé was *Mako: The Jaws of Death*. Did you write the finished script?

I wrote the original story, but Grefé botched it. On that script I went into the motel where he kept his cast and crew. All I did was go up to see Sakata and Jenifer Bishop. I lost contact with Jenifer, and it breaks my heart. She was a sweetheart. Anyway, this was a public restaurant. Grefé comes up and tries to bully me because he's really tall. He comes over and does that routine on me. That's embarrassing. But Richard Jaeckel gets up, walks over and takes me aside. I think it was because of his presence that Grefé backed off. Jaeckel said, "Let me apologize to you. I signed on to this film reading your script. That's the script I wanted to do. But what am I gonna do? I'm an actor. I have to do whatever the director says."

John Chandler and myself and Odd Job had a date. We all jam into my little Volkswagen. Getting Sakata in and out of that Volkswagen was a blast! We go over to this restaurant — do you remember the scene with the Greek belly dancer in *Impulse*? The dancer's dad owned that place. They gave us a table right in up against the dance floor. They took Sakata and put him in the center of it and made him the sultan. Each girl would try to belly dance around him to win the prize. Sakata was blasted. We're eating dolmades. Chandler is shitting his pants laughing. We're having a great time.

What we didn't know was there was a Greek ship that had come into Ft. Lauderdale, and most of the sailors were there. They loved Sakata. Sakata is laughing and is drunk as shit. He's trying to dance with this girl. When Greeks get excited they break plates. Everybody is breaking plates! Then the bouzouki player gets carried away and leaps onto our table. Crash! Bang! He's playing the theme from *Zorba the Greek*. What I didn't know was that he was the guy that had originally been hired to play that theme in *Zorba*. No matter which way I turn I bump into some neat people. That was quite a night.

Prior to *Blood Stalkers*, you had been involved in a documentary called *The Search for Bigfoot*.

I'm virtually positive it was the very first serious expedition that was put together using some pretty well qualified people. A lot of the people that were involved in that '74 expedition had already been with me on two or three trips prior to that.

Nowadays you hear people talk about going on an expedition, and they're out for a weekend. I went out that year on the first of May and I was still in the field at Thanksgiving. It wasn't nonsense.

I had recruited a science advisory board. I had seventeen men and women I conferred with. Most of them had their Ph.D.s in a variety of complementary sciences. I did all my homework. I already knew the primary movement routes, and the people there had established a certain amount of trust in me.

The first part of it was in Dallas, Oregon, but that was a bust. It was a pass-through, overnight thing. It wasn't where they dwelled for any period of time.

It was quite expensive to do, as you can imagine, if you put that many people in the field for that many months. It wasn't cheap. Everybody was paid something. We compiled everything.

Insofar as the film was concerned, I had no intention of filming it. I had work to do. We were contacted by Bostonia. They offered to come out and wanted to go with us. The thing for the Smithsonian series (*Monsters! Mysteries or Myths?*) was shot about a month before the Bostonia crew came up. So we actually had two films going.

While we were out there, Tom Snyder had just started out on television. We got a call and they said I had two invitations to shows. They were going to fly me to L.A. We had just finished the Bostonia film and the Smithsonian series.

I had two choices for these talk shows. I took a poll of the crew, and they said I should go do it. One was Tom Snyder. There was another guy, but I didn't think he'd last, so I didn't go. It was Johnny Carson! He had the biggest show going ever, but I chose the other guy [*laughs*]. I'm one of the few people in the world to ever turn down Johnny Carson.

Another funny story: I had just gotten back from the expedition, and I was one tired puppy. I got this phone call early in the morning. This guy wanted me for a brief talk on his show. I was in no mood. I was tired, and I kept asking him his name because I wanted to write it down. It

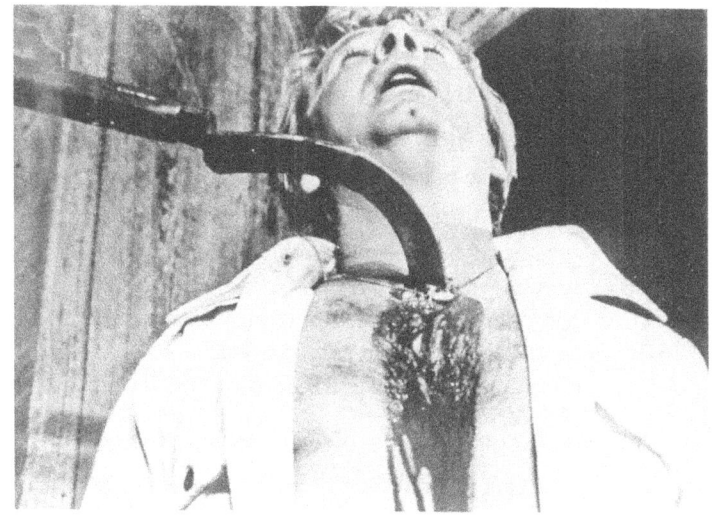

Kenny Miller meets his demise (courtesy Robert W. Morgan).

was Howard Cosell. I think I'm the first son of a bitch that ever made Howard Cosell spell his name on his show.

He never called me back. No sense of humor. See why I disappeared for a while? Nobody wanted to talk to me!

I believe the Lawrence Crowley documentary was later re-edited and titled *Bigfoot: Man or Beast?*

Probably. Crowley was with Bostonia. He probably re-edited the hell out of it. I didn't get along too well with him. They ran out of money. They had already left, and I kept telling them, "This is all build up. We're not there yet." Of course, he made it seem like the expedition ended when the forest fire hit. That's the end of the movie.

But we continued straight on. About five or six weeks later, I got a report and we found 161 tracks in a row over varying terrain. [Noted Bigfoot researcher] Grover Krantz drove from the other side of the state to spend the day with us. Grover was the kind of kid who used to run around and poke holes in people's balloons. Very dour guy, but very professional. He was on his hands and knees all day long. The entity had come out of the woods above a campsite where they had been logging in the area. These guys who were on 24-hour fire watch felt something strange. There were two of them out there. They discovered these tracks the following morning, and they called me. They didn't mess with the tracks.

The tracks came out of the woods up above, down a log drag. Then they did a curious thing — they walked almost a semi-circle. I realized the creature was walking out of the rim of the light. You could see toe movement, compaction. Everything was perfect. There was even one area at the top that confused me. All of a sudden they are striding along and the stride shortened abruptly. Why? Well, it wasn't until I was walking along side of it and one of my people at the base called out to me. I turned out to see what she was talking about. That was the first time the creature making those tracks had seen the firelight. I was observing an emotional reaction. That gave it even more credibility.

I called Larry Crowley and said, "Get your ass on the plane and get out here now." He thought he was being hustled. He was from Boston, and everything was a hustle with that guy. He said, "We don't have any money, and we've got everything we need." I said, "You don't have anything like this." I think he thought we invented it. Well, good luck. I couldn't have invented that in a million years. So he missed the best part of it. But he came up with something that was entertaining to people.

There were a lot of those documentaries and docudramas that came out in the 1970s. Did you watch many of them?

I had no clue. I don't care what other people do. I don't mean to be an arrogant ass, but I only have so many heartbeats, and I'm not going to spend them worrying about what somebody else is doing. It's not a competition. I don't care what anybody else does. They get things that I don't have. The whole idea is to get these mysteries solved. It doesn't matter who does it. Let's just get it solved, identify what they are permanently, scientifically, and get them into protection so jerks don't go out shooting monsters.

Once you decided to make *Blood Stalkers*, **how did you find financing?**

We got financing through Ben Morse, who was our executive producer. He was an accountant, a World War II vet. Nice guy. He went to private people, and we ended up with $60,000. That was all the cash we could raise. However, that wasn't too bad because Irv

Rudley owned the studio, we had the recording studio, we had a place to shoot interiors, we had the camera equipment. We already owned that. You have to factor that in. We had 21 days to shoot it.

I had written what you would call a close script. I scoured the everglades and tried to see what I could use. I fit the screenplay to the environment. Kenny Miller was in town. I'd never heard of him at the time, but I found out he'd been in a hell of a lot of movies. We started doing the casting. I had promised Jerry Albert when we were doing *Impulse* that if I ever did a film I'd use him. I got all the people I'd known and gave them all shares of the film.

I'm co-producing, writing and directing. A heavy load. The night before we're supposed to leave, the lead bad guy — I can't for the life of me remember his name. Who was the guy in the opening scene of *Impulse*, the guy with the sword?

William Kerwin?

Kerwin, that's it. It was a friend of Bill Kerwin's that was supposed to play the bad guy, Jarvis, in *Blood Stalkers*. He was supposed to play that part. Bill had guaranteed me this guy was good, and he was ugly enough to do it. The son of a bitch calls me about eight o'clock at night, and wants me to send him a thousand dollars. He's in jail. My lead bad guy is in jail, and he wants me to bail him out so he can come out and play the part!

Stan and I were sitting around, and I said, "What the hell am I gonna do?" Stan said, "I don't see where the problem is ... Jarvis. You're the only son of a bitch out there that doesn't have a part. We can't use Irv because he has to shoot the film, so it has to be you." I said, "I've never acted in my life! I don't know what you're talking about."

I stayed up all night reassigning all my dialogue to somebody else. Everybody else had dialogue. If you watch the film I think I have three lines in the whole damn thing. I had no intention whatsoever of ever doing that part. But I must have done something right.

When we had the premiere of the film, I took my daughter. Of course the audience hadn't seen the film so they didn't know who we were. When I finally get killed, the audience cheers, including my daughter. I looked at her and said, "What are you doing?" She had completely gotten absorbed in the story. My kid cheered when I got killed [*laughs*]!

Was it your plan from the beginning to direct the film? Was it difficult for you to act and direct at the same time?

Not really, because I had a good cast. Since I got rid of all the dialogue, it wasn't difficult to stand around. I relieved my frustrations through the part, actually [*laughs*]. It wasn't that difficult. Also, Irv Rudley was an excellent as a cinematographer, so we walked through the shots and he knew what we wanted. Our vision was pretty much the same. As a consequence, when he set up and we lit the shot, there were only very few corrections or adjustments that I made. It was a pretty smooth running crew. The professionals had all worked together before on *Impulse*.

Do you remember what year you made the film?

It was released in 1975 or 1976.

Where did you shoot *Blood Stalkers*?

There was a place called Loop Road. All the action scenes were done there in the Everglades. I think that area is called Pinelands. I can't remember the name of the bloody town we were in. There's a little town north about 15 miles. It was a small village.

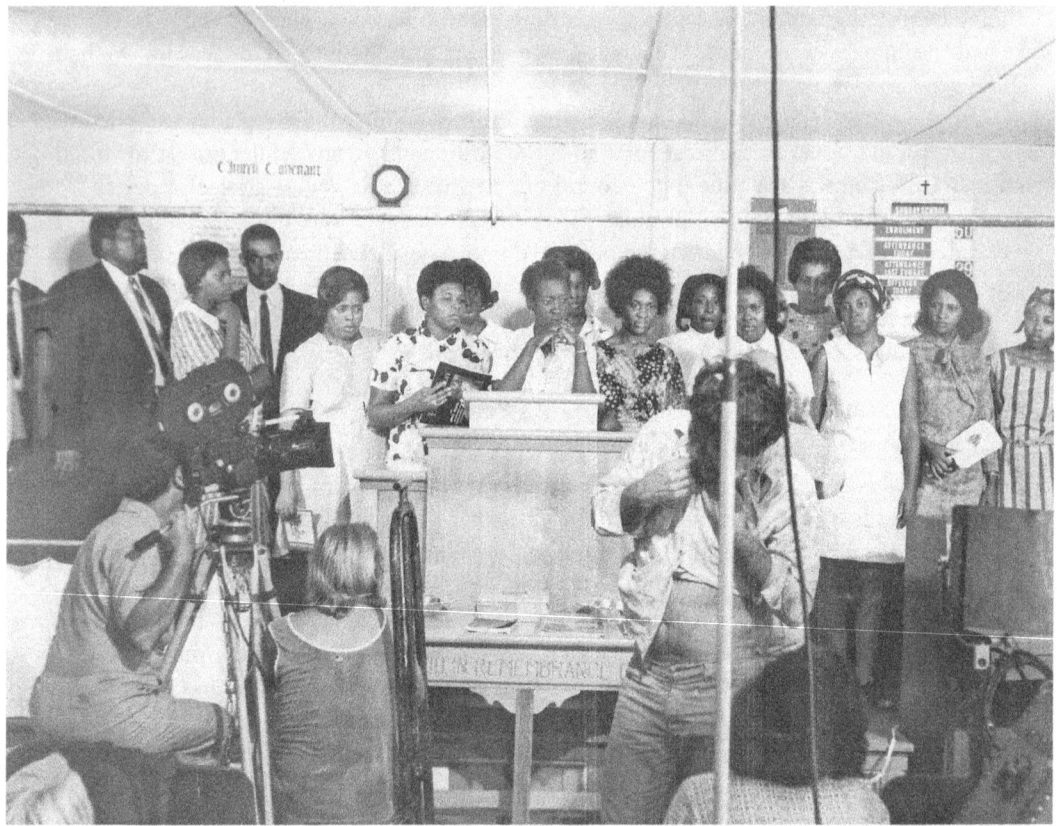

The crew of *Blood Stalkers* prepares to film the gospel choir that appears in the film's off-the-wall finale (courtesy Robert W. Morgan).

The strange thing about that village was I never saw a single living human being there. Really. You saw the shacks and the houses. I never saw a resident. Not one. The church choir that came out and the reverend were from Miami. We just walked into the church and did it. Nobody bothered us. I think we saw a dog once. Those signs—"No Trespassing, Survivors Persecuted"—were real! We did not make those. When we were scouting I slammed on the brakes and said, "Grab it!"

Tell me about Mike Polesnek, the animal wrangler on the film.

He had had a Bigfoot sighting, or something happened to some of his horses. He lived north of Miami. He had called me about it. I visited him at his ranch. Turned out he was quite the outdoorsman, he was a carpenter, all sorts of things. He and I bonded really quickly because he's a no-nonsense guy. If he says it, he believes it. After that I found out that he was an expert tracker. He used to collect snakes and things like that. He worked with Frank Weed, who was an importer of exotic animals. Mike knew his stuff.

But he and I bonded, and when I did the film I just asked him to come along. Almost everyone on that cast and crew were friends.

Who distributed *Blood Stalkers*?

I don't know. I had a call into L.A. I had to leave after we finished the film, and that was all in the hands of Irv Rudley and Stan Webb. I have no clue. I was out of Dodge in no time flat. I had other pressing commitments.

But you made it to the premiere.

In fact, I've got photographs of my daughter and I going to the theater with David Legge and Mike Polesnek. We watched it through and everybody laughed at the right times, everybody cheered at the right times.

As the people were starting to file out and they saw us sitting there all in a row, you should have seen the looks on their faces. A couple of young kids started scuffling. They didn't see us. They were holding up the theater. It was only a couple of rows down. I went down and grabbed this kid by the neck and said, "I don't think you ought to do that." You should have seen the look on this kid's face! It wouldn't surprise me if he peed his pants. He didn't know what to think. By the time we walked out, it looked like the whole audience was still out there waiting for us. It was fun.

What was good for me was to hear an audience that didn't know I was there react the way I wanted them to react. That was a compliment.

Was the film actually released under the title *The Night Daniel Died*?

It started out as *The Night Daniel Died*. The distributor changed it. They couldn't get it on the damn marquee. It played the drive-in theaters, too, come to think of it. I came back about a year after that, and it was playing at the Coral Drive-In in Miami. I took some people out to it. It seemed to do pretty well. I didn't think it would last two weeks.

I flew into Seattle once to see my daughter. She said, "Come on Dad, I've got to show you something." She took me to a video rental place, and there's the movie. They didn't have one; they had six of them in a row. It surprised the hell out of me.

The last part of that movie is pretty unhinged. Did you have any idea that it was going to come out that over the top?

Over the top? What are you talking about [*laughs*]!

It's a wild 15 minutes.

That was pretty much planned. It was in the editing, of course, that it all was put together. I think spice was added to it with Stan's music and all that stuff. It was pretty well planned to have a bunch of quick shots to wrap it all up. It's the last 15 minutes, let's wrap this up, kill everybody off and go home.

***Blood Stalkers* is about a Bigfoot hoax. Did you catch any flak from other researchers, or have concerns about making a movie about a hoax?**

No, and there's a good reason for it: A hell of a lot of people *do* commit hoaxes. All I'm doing is exposing the rationale behind one facet of it. There are so many. I can't even tell you how many times somebody calls and says there' a report. I don't go. I don't care. I spent so much time and hard-earned dollars chasing someone's fantasies. I think there are a lot less hoaxes now, but in those days there were a hell of a lot. It was a cry for attention.

Some of the people that are supposed researchers, I don't want to be seen with them. Like I said, we have so many heartbeats, and I don't want to waste a single one on bullshit.

There was a pretty well known guy in Ohio. This guy couldn't find his ass with both hands. He told me he'd found a prime location and that he was in "communication" with them. Like a dummy I go with him. Sure enough, you'd hear knocks on the trees. There was something too convenient and too cute.

I got suspicious. By this time, I was stuck in Ohio. I was waiting on the Gorbachev coup to go one way or the other. There was a film I wanted to do in Russia. It was supposed to be the first legitimate co-production between the United States and the Soviet Union. I'd already cast the film and all that jazz. I'd been over there four or five times. It was going to be one hell of a nice film.

But I had an ill aunt in Ohio, and I had some time on my hands while I was waiting to see what was going to happen. I went back to Ohio, and this is where this guy was. I got spotted. Why don't you come down? I went down and he was doing this knock-back thing.

I stopped in his hometown at a local bar. A couple of guys were playing pool and recognized me. They started telling me this story. His high school buddies had been doing this to him for years. They knew where he was going, because he'd come back and run his mouth. He'd go out and hit a tree, and they'd hit a tree right back using an axe handle. Just driving him nuts.

Then he called me up and said, "They're throwing rocks at this one guy's house and we've got a handprint." I went down to Newcomerstown, Ohio, and sure enough the Bigfoot had allegedly walked up to this guy's house and peeked at his wife through the window, and there was this handprint. I met his wife, and I think Bigfoot must have had a sense of humor! You could charge admission [*laughs*].

Morgan poses with actresses Celea Ann Cole (left) and Toni Crabtree (courtesy Robert W. Morgan).

Then I looked at the print. I said, "I guess this Bigfoot must have been a mechanic. That's goddamn motor oil!"

He told me I had to interview the people, especially the young girl. I'm trying to put on a nice face. I don't want to insult these people. Then the woman says to the little girl, "I think you should tell Mr. Morgan the real secret about your dolls." She said she had dolls that would fly across the living room and float around the house. I'm measuring the distance between myself and the front door. They had this shack across the way, and they said they could see in and see Bigfoot's red eyes glowing inside. This Bigfoot expert has some film on it. He showed it to me. Gee, there's' two red eyes, about eight feet high, and they go back and forth like two red flashlights. And they never blink. This crazy bastard thinks they're real! Need I say more? I stopped chasing sightings years ago.

You host an Internet radio show. What else have you been up to recently?

My book *Soul Snatchers: A Quest for True Human Beings* is being released on August 15. Right now I'm editing *The Bigfoot Observer's Field Manual*, which is a step-by-step guide to having an encounter. If you follow the steps, it will take you a year to get ready, at least. There's a hell of a lot of research to do if you want to put yourself in the path of a forest giant.

Tell me about the sequels to *Blood Stalkers* that you have planned.

What I have never understood was, how in the hell did that little film last so goddamn long? Last year I think I sold a couple of hundred DVDs that I had to autograph. This is crazy! I don't get it. Finally someone told me that you've got all these big-budget explosions and all these computerized monsters around, and they felt that the swing was coming back to the real guys. Real people. This is what seems to be the trend.

For 20 years everybody has been telling me I've got to make a sequel. How am I gonna make a sequel? I killed everybody off! But I found a way. Right now, the idea is to do all three sequels back-to-back, so there's complete continuity between the characters and everything else, and then release them one at a time over a period of year or two. That's where we are right now.

My character and Kenny Miller will be back. Kenny is not in the best of health. The poor guy wants to play it and I think he'd do a fine job, but I'm going to have to figure out what to do with the second and third scripts in case he's not around. But I'm hoping to God he makes it all the way.

When do you think production will start on the sequels?

The first script is nearly finished now. I had to go back and rip it apart because there was a guy, this rapper, who met my partner on a flight, and he wanted a part. He's a Haitian out of Miami, so I tailored it toward him. He's a big guy; he used to be a football player. But the guy was so flaky, he wouldn't return phone calls and all this other stuff. I can't deal with someone I can't rely on. So I bailed out of that, and I'm completely rewriting it for that purpose.

My original idea was to shoot one film in the U.S., and then shoot in the Isle of Man during their races. Then we would go to Calgary in Canada for the stampede, and we'd end the film there. But none of that's going to happen. We're discovering that with the weakened American dollar, it's not advantageous anymore. It's actually cheaper to shoot here. Now I have to go back and re-do those ideas. But that's the business.

Left at the Altar
Tom Rahner
Florida

The Brides Wore Blood (1972) is a good example of the contradictory nature of regional horror films in the video era, in that for many years it remained simultaneously obscure and ubiquitous. If the film played theatrically at all, it was probably for just a handful of engagements in Florida, and for many years it's very existence wasn't even noted by most of the major genre reference books. At the same time, thanks to distributor Fred Olen Ray (who purchased the film not long after its director passed away) it was widely available on video, and at one point could be purchased for just $3 at many K-Mart stores.

Brides was the first (and last) horror movie from Florida filmmaker Bob Favorite, who primarily made his living as an industrial and documentary filmmaker until his death in 1978. He had previously made two nudie films, *Riverboat Mama* (1969) and *Indian Raid, Indian Made* (1969), starring Morganna, a well-endowed actress who would go on to later acclaim as "The Kissing Bandit," interrupting sports events to smooch the athletes.

Tom Rahner not only helped to produce *Brides*, he also worked on the special effects and played a vampire during a flashback sequence (his wife, Jean, played his victim). As chair of the theater department at Flagler College in St. Augustine, Fla., Rahner also helped Favorite secure locations around the school's impressively designed campus.

Now retired, Rahner was both amused and a bit perplexed that *anyone* had any interest *The Brides Wore Blood*.

Who was Bob Favorite, and how did you know him?

Bob Favorite was a filmmaker in Jacksonville. He made short films, commercials, things for TV, industrial films. That sort of thing. He was one of the first people in this area to have open-heart surgery, and he made a documentary about the procedure that was shown on television and gained him a fair amount of notoriety.

Do you know what it was called?

No, but it had to be done in the late 1960s.

How did you meet him?

He contacted me as chairman of the theater department of the college, because he wanted to use the college and its environs for his film project.

Did he ever come to the college looking for help on his commercial/industrial films?

No, not really.

He contacted you specifically about *Brides*, then.

Exactly.

Do you have any idea why he wanted to make this film?

To make money! He had it in his mind that he wanted to make a feature-length film, because what he had done before were short films, commercial films, that sort of thing. He wanted to do a feature. Bob was a little on the frail side because of the heart surgery, and I think he felt he wanted to do something before he died, although he was in relatively good health. He still smoked, and sometimes his breathing was affected. He was very game, though. He wasn't looking for pity or anything like that at all.

So once he came to you asking for assistance, what was your involvement? You have writing and associate producer credits.

I don't know where the writing credit came from, because it was one of these deals where we'd get together and say, "What are we gonna shoot today?" It was pretty loose, although he did have something of a script. I was mainly the liaison with the college administration to use the buildings. The film was shot over a period of two years. He could only work on the film on weekends, so everybody that was involved in it worked Saturdays and Sundays for two years, 1970 to 1972. We all did it on spec. The idea was if the film sells, then we'll all get paid. Well, it didn't sell during his lifetime, so nobody got a dime. Nothing.

So there wasn't much of a script?

No.

The plot was a little confusing.

Turgid, I think, would be a good word for it.

Were you present for the entire shoot?

Oh yeah. I was in it, as was my wife. There's a sequence, if you recall, when the elderly Mr. DeLorca goes to see the medium, and he has this flashback of an earlier time. A bearded vampire chases a beautiful young woman up to a tower and bites her throat out. The bearded vampire was me, and the one that got her throat bit was my wife. Those were non-speaking roles.

Did Favorite mostly use people he'd worked with before on this film?

People he had worked with, mainly in Jacksonville. As I recall, he had two cameras. He used an Arriflex mainly for the outside shots, and an old Mitchell for most of the interior shots because it was a lot quieter. The Arriflex sounded like a threshing machine.

The sound engineer was Neil Mengel, and he still lives in Jacksonville. I saw him about a year ago. A gal named Liz Blanda was sort of the director's assistant, and also did sound. I can't remember the grips' names, but I'm sure they're all on the credits.

There was a Lee Hansen and a Peter Jannott, and Rick Voight was the camera operator.

Right. They set up lights and stuff like that. Worked real hard, all for the love of it. It was fun. But after a year it got pretty tedious giving up almost every weekend.

Where was it shot?

Mainly at the college. All the old fancy architecture, the towers, the stained glass windows, that's all part of Flagler College.

All the interiors of the castle were filmed there?

Yes. The college was designed by John M. Carrere and Thomas Hastings, who were the architects who did the New York Public Library, the Library of Congress and Grand Central Station.

The sets were the best thing about the film.

Absolutely!

Where did the cast come from?

They were locals from St. Augustine and Jacksonville. A number of them are still alive, although the film is 37 years old.

Who was the man who played the older DeLorca?

That was Paul Everett, and believe it or not, he was the dean of the college.

Was he involved with the theater department?

I had used Paul in one or two stage productions. He had a wonderful voice and a great look, and of course was a very intelligent man. He was former diplomat with the State Department in Southeast Asia. He spoke several languages. He was a Ph.D. from Harvard. Quite a guy.

What about the other actors?

The bride, the blonde who was probably the most prominent, was Dolores Heiser. Her real name was Jasbeck. She was married to a Jacksonville physician. I guess Heiser may have been her maiden name. Chuck Faulkner played the younger vampire. I don't know much about Chuck. He did a few things in Jacksonville, and maybe he'd done other things for Bob Favorite.

Jan Sherman played one of the victims; she was the very slender gal with the British accent. Delores Starling was the brunette victim who was invited to the castle.

What about the fellow who played the mute servant?

That was Bob Letizia. He played the role of Perro. Bob was from Jacksonville, and his family was in the restaurant business. I don't know if he did anything after that or not. He worked hard on the film. He had a lot to do with it.

How did Favorite finance the film?

I think Bob did it primarily out of his own pocket. One of the ways he saved money, which was one of the things that kept the film from being released for so long, was that at that time there were quite a few mini-theaters around that used 16mm equipment. Of course, after a few years, it became evident that 16mm just did not have enough substance to hold up like the old 35mm format. But Bob shot the film in 16mm, with the idea of later having it blown up to 35mm, or marketing it through these mini-theater chains that used 16mm.

After he made it he couldn't afford to blow it up to 35mm, and it just languished for years and years. It was never sold, never released to my knowledge until well after he was dead. Then I believe his wife, Dottie Favorite, sold it. I don't know who bought it, but it wound up on DVD.

Didn't Favorite also make some nudie films?

Oh yeah. Before he shot *The Brides Wore Blood*, he made several sexploitation films, or soft porn.

The titles I have are *Indian Raid, Indian Made* and *Riverboat Mama*.

I never saw any of them [*laughs*]. I was not connected with that. The only semi-nudity in the beginning of *Brides* was the young couple lying together, and she shows a little breast. All that was shot afterward. I guess Bob figured he needed to spice up the film a little bit, and make it a little more racy.

That scene did seem tacked on, and didn't even make sense in the context of the rest of the film.

It was a real stretch. The whole thing was pretty much patchwork.

Do you remember the scene with the demon in the basement?

The original video box cover art for *The Brides Wore Blood* (1972), shot on the campus of Flagler College in St. Augustine, Florida.

He shot all of that in Jacksonville. I wasn't present for any of that. That was not in the College. That was an entirely different location.

Bob Favorite passed away in the 1970s.

Yeah. I can't remember exactly when.

What was his wife like?

Dottie? She was a very nice person. Attractive, vivacious. She worked on the film, did most of the straight make up. I did most of the special effects makeup, like the pumping blood, the gore, and when Chuck Faulkner corrodes. She was just a nice person. I think she remarried, but I'm not sure.

Does she appear in the film?

No.

Were you familiar with special effects makeup from your theater background?

Right.

So what did you think when you saw the finished film?

We all laughed [*laughs*]. *Ahhhhhh, okay.* Better than *Plan 9 from Outer Space*, but not by much!

Once he actually finished the film, did you keep up with it?

Not really. He had everybody over to his house for a really nice steak dinner. Then we all went to a hall, and he showed the film. We had drinks and shot the bull, and then we all went home. And that was it! We waited, and waited, and waited. We were all like, "Are you gonna sell it, Bob?" We all would have liked to have gotten a little bit of money. But it just sort of faded away, sad to say.

When did you finally learn that it was on video?

Years later at a homecoming, a former student said, "I saw *The Brides Wore Blood* on VHS." I knew nothing of that. She got a copy for me, and then several years ago a friend of ours said, "Guess what I found on the Internet?" And he got me the DVD. It was purely by accident that I got a copy. There was nothing from Dorothy Favorite, ever. Not a word. I think when she sold it she kept it secret because she was afraid that all the people who had worked on the film — and there were quite a few — would jump on it and try to get something out of her. Nobody did.

Did you keep up with the other people you worked with on *Brides*?

I know a lot some of them are still here. Jan Sherman lives in Jacksonville. She works for Sally Industries. Paul Everett died years ago. Ben Robinson, who played the young stud on the boat, still lives here in St. Augustine. Robert Carberry, who was the coroner in the film when they go and find some remains, he and Jim Billington still live here in St. Augustine. Art Schill, I can't remember what he did in the movie, but he died recently. My wife is here, and she's very active.

Two others listed, Ken Pacetti and Mike Sherman, were the guitarists in the dance sequence playing Spanish guitar. They still live here in St. Augustine. The medium, Madame von Kierst, she was the dean of students at Flagler College at the time. That was [Mary A.] Billie Jensen, but Billie's long gone. She died years ago.

Those are the only ones I've kept up with.

Did you ever work on any other films?

No, not with Bob. When I was in college I was an extra on *Revenge of the Creature* (1955), which was shot in Marineland of Florida. But nothing of any consequence. I hate making films. You stand around and wait.

Florida, of course, used to be the film capital before Hollywood in the silent era. There were many films made in St. Augustine because of the architecture available and different types of terrain. They shot desert movies in the sand dunes on the beaches, and things in the swamps and around the old fortress. It got a lot of use.

I also did a couple of promotional films as part of an advertising campaign for the city. I have no real film career [*laughs*].

Bayou Bloodbath
ALBERT J. SALZER
Louisiana

New Orleans has always been a magnet for weirdness; wander the streets of the Big Easy long enough, and you're sure to see something or someone that you'd never encounter anywhere else on the planet. The city's local film industry is no different, and the homegrown horror films that have emanated from the region are some of the most peculiar ever made.

Case in point: *Night of Bloody Horror* (1969), a tawdry tale of murder, psychosis and matriarchal madness that veers wildly in all directions at once, and features a show-stopping early performance by "Major Dad" star Gerald McRaney.

The film was made by two men who would become, in their own ways, fixtures of the Louisiana film industry, Joy Houck, Jr., and Albert J. Salzer.

Houck, a prolific writer and director, was the son of local theater magnate Joy Houck, Sr., whose distribution company (Howco) had helped introduce the world to *The Brain from Planet Arous* (1957) and *The Legend of Boggy Creek* (1972).

Salzer, a theater graduate and New Orleans native, teamed with the Houcks for two other pictures, the melodrama *His Wife's Habit* (*Women and Bloody Terror*, 1969) and *Night of the Strangler* (1972). Along with *Night of Bloody Horror*, these films would be retitled and re-released multiple times on double and triple bills for more than a decade.

After *Keep Off My Grass!* (1975), a counter culture comedy directed by Shelley Berman, Salzer slowly worked his way into mainstream productions, first as a location manager on *The Autobiography of Miss Jane Pittman* (1974) and then as a producer on *The Dukes of Hazzard*.

Since then, Salzer (who splits his time between L.A. and New Orleans) has produced dozens of TV series and movies, and opened Crescent City Productions in his hometown, specializing in low-budget, direct-to-video productions.

Did you grow up in New Orleans?

I grew up between here and Los Angeles. I'm a New Orleans native. I'm back here right now. I produced my first picture, *Night of Bloody Horror*, in 1968.

How did you get involved in filmmaking?

I'd known Joy Houck, Jr., as a kid. We lived in the same neighborhood. I ran into him again one night, it must have been around 1967 or so, on my birthday. He said he had a script and I told him I'd like to help him make it. He and this other fellow [Robert A. Weaver], who was a camera guy, had written it. We just borrowed some equipment and went about our business. We filmed *Night of Bloody Horror* mainly on weekends.

We used people from the Southern Repertory Theater and Gerald McRaney, who turned out to be rather a big television star. He was a roughneck or whatever you call them. He had to go out on the oilrigs to make a living during the week. We had to shoot when he had time off. We just kind of got it together and it turned out pretty well.

Tell me about Joy Houck and his father.

Joy's father was an exhibitor. He owned theaters. He also distributed little pictures, and he distributed *Night of Bloody Horror*. He wound up buying it. We would have made a lot more money if we'd held on to it. He wound up with the lion's share of the money. But we all made a profit. We were all happy. I was only 24 years old, and Joy was like a year older, so we were glad to get going. We produced a few other films in a row that didn't make a dime!

Was Joy, Jr., involved in his father's business?

Not really. He was involved a little bit, but not really. In those days, the old man would put up money for the prints and advertising, but they basically used subdistributors in different parts of the country. I don't even know if that system exists anymore. He put up a certain amount for advertising, he bought prints, and the subdistributors would work them in the different markets around the country

Night of Bloody Horror made a lot of money. It probably made him a million dollars. That's what I was told. It certainly didn't make us anywhere near that.

You were listed as executive producer.

I don't know why I got executive producer [*laughs*]. Joy really produced and directed and wrote it. I was a producer/soundman. We did everything. We didn't have much of a crew. We'd pick up a little help every now and then. I learned how to run sound on that movie. I didn't get very good at it, but it didn't turn out too badly, I guess.

How long did it take to film?

I don't remember. I'd say around three months, maybe closer to four. We'd shoot on and off and run out of money, let Gerald go off to the oil rigs and make some money. He was already married; he was only 18 years old. He had a little baby, as I remember. We just kind of did it when we could get it together, then we'd stop, and then we'd do it some more.

Was McRaney already working as an actor at that point?

He was just starting out. That was his first movie. He was in theater, in the original Southern Repertory Theater down here. He was a member of that company.

The script was pretty crazy. What did the cast think of it?

The script was pretty much locked before we started. We knew what the script was all about.

It did seem a little—whatever it was, it worked. It kept people on edge. We just cast our friends. My friend Gaye Yellen, who I went to school with (I had just graduated from Tulane) played the young ingénue. This older guy, Herb Nelson, he was from Southern Repertory Theater, a New York actor. Evelyn Hendricks I knew from local theater. It was just local kids getting together.

What did you study at Tulane?

I was a theater major at Tulane, so I had a strong background in the stage. But there were only a couple of film schools in the country back then, and I didn't go to any of them. My film school was *Night of Bloody Horror*.

Did you have any trouble getting permits to film around the city?

Oh, there was no such thing back in those days. There still aren't very many permits in New Orleans. They're very hospitable in the whole surrounding area.

But back then, the most money we paid anybody was for a policeman when we needed one, and they only cost $25 for like 12 hours. No, we didn't have any trouble.

A lot of the picture took place in one house. It was a friend of my family. They let us a big house on St. Charles Avenue. We told them we'd be there maybe two weeks. We stayed three months! They'd come home and we'd be shooting, and we'd have to stop because they wanted to go to bed.

Where did you film the bar scene?

That was shot at a bar in the French Quarter.

Which one?

Several bars. One was a disco sequence, and that was at a bar in Chantilly someplace. The other bar sequence was shot at The Seven Seas. I don't even know if it's still there anymore. I think it's been gone a long time.

How widely was the film distributed?

It did very well. It kind of hit at the right time. It was in color, and it was right after *Night*

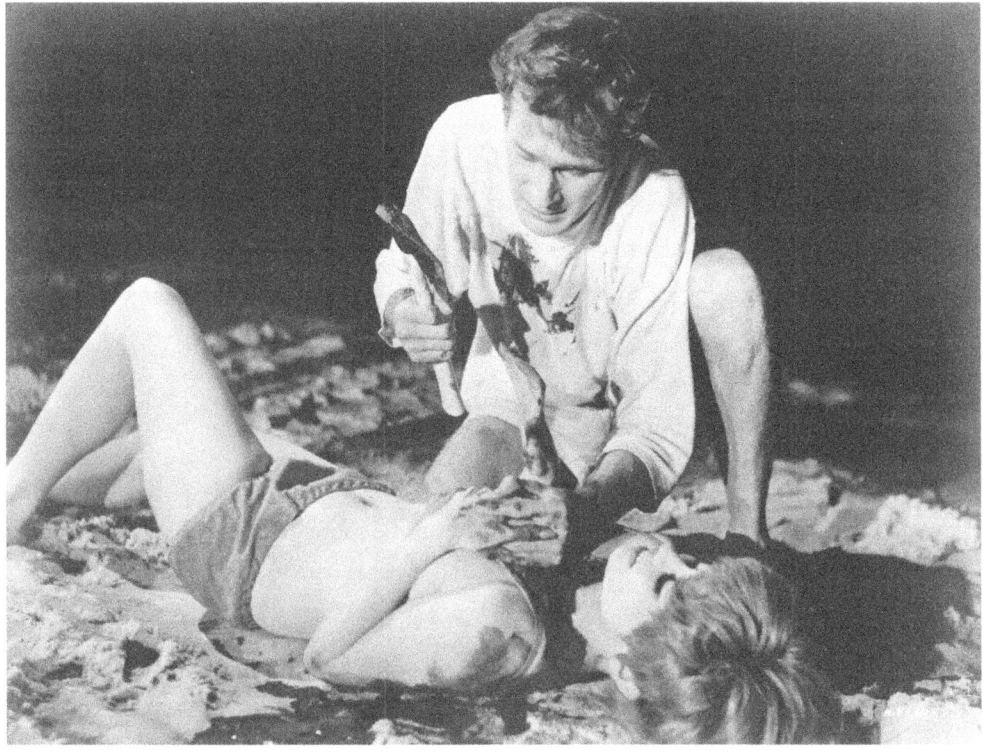

Wesley (Gerald McRaney) discovers the mutilated body of friendly nurse Kay (Charlotte White) in *Night of Bloody Horror* (1969).

of the Living Dead (1968) had made a little money as a horror movie. Drive-ins were big back then, and it was a huge hit at drive-ins.

Who came up with the title?

Probably it was Joy Houck, Jr., and I think it was probably because of *Night of the Living Dead*. "Night" seemed like a catchy phrase to use. I don't take credit for it. I imagine it was Joy.

How much time passed before you did the second film, *His Wife's Habit*?

That was huge flop. It was about a year, or maybe a little over a year. That was an idea Joy Houck, Sr., had. We all got together and wrote a script. It wasn't very good. Then we followed up with another picture that wasn't very good, either [*laughs*]!

What was the problem with the film?

It wasn't much of a story. It was about this older woman who likes young guys, and a motorcycle gang or something. It never made too much sense to me. It was really the old man's picture. Joy Houck, Sr., had all then money in that, and I don't think he got his money out of it. He would change the tile, and he spent a lot of money changing advertising, changing titles, and re-releasing the same pictures. Most of the time they still didn't make any money.

In that case, he changed the title to *Women and Bloody Terror*.

Was that the one he did that too?

He ran it on double feature with *Night of Bloody Horror*.

I think you're right. I know years later, when McRaney made his first big hit with "Simon & Simon," he re-released *Night of Bloody Horror* as a period piece. He put a little legend on it that said "New Orleans: 1968" or something. It was so outdated, but because McRaney was a television star he reissued the movie. He [Houck] lived to be 100. He didn't die that long ago. He was mean son of a bitch. It's possible he took all the money with him [*laughs*]!

The lead actress, Georgine Darcy, was in *Rear Window* (1954).

Oh, yeah. That's right. I forgot about that. I hadn't thought about that in a long time. Very nice lady.

Was she brought in from out of town?

Yeah, we brought her in from Los Angeles.

Who was Marcus J. Grapes? He appeared in a number of your films.

He was a friend of mine, local guy. He turned out to be more of a poet than an actor. He published some books of poetry, I believe. He moved to L.A. and I lost track of him.

You made two movies with Mickey Dolenz after that.

I did one, *Keep Off My Grass!*, which the Houcks had nothing to do with. It was another big flop. Shelley Berman directed that. That was another one of my worst bad ideas.

How did that get started?

I don't know. A friend and I wrote the treatment. We had some writers in California [Austin and Irma Kallish], and they wrote the script. They knew Shelley Berman. Somebody said he was a good director and he wanted to do a movie. And it all came together, and turned out to be not so hot.

That movie cost a few dollars. *Night of Bloody Horror* never had more than about $40,000 or $50,000 in production. Post production and prints and advertising were a different story. But *Keep Off My Grass!* cost about $175,000. I invested some of my profit on *Night of Bloody Horror* in that, and I lost all my money.

What were you doing for a living?

I was not doing too much of anything else. I was still kind of living at home.

That was when I met Mickey, and we're still good friends today. I went back to the old man and did another movie that he was in. I forget the name of that one. They changed the title so many times. It didn't make any money, either.

That was *Night of the Strangler*.

He changed it to a weird title. One of the leads was a black priest, and then he tried to turn it into a black exploitation picture [*Is the Father Black Enough?*]. That didn't work either [*laughs*].

I haven't seen *Keep Off My Grass!*, but I take it that it was some kind of counterculture film.

It was a cute premise, but it didn't work. It was kind of boring. It was sort of like these hippies start their own town, and they become the establishment that they were trying to get away from. But it took 90 minutes to tell the story, and it wasn't that interesting.

What was Shelley Berman like?

He was horrible. He didn't know what he was doing, and he was paranoid. He was crazy. He should have stayed doing stand-up, but then again he was crazy doing that, too [*laughs*].

Who came up with the idea for *Night of the Strangler*?

I did that with the Houcks again. I guess it was Joy, Jr. I didn't have anything to do with the writing.

The premise, about an interracial couple, was still fairly racy at that point.

I guess it was. It had black people in it and that was avant-garde, I suppose. I don't know [*laughs*]!

Do you remember much about the filming of that movie?

There was one guy cast in the lead. I don't know how he got cast, but I was against it. We had to shut down because he just couldn't cut it. That was when I brought Mickey in. I remember that. I brought Mickey in and he did a nice job. Mickey's a very talented guy. He still out there performing. I saw him last June. He was doing a couple of nights in one of the gambling casinos with his road show. He still goes out on the road with his nightclub act.

I thought he was pretty good in that movie.

He's a good actor. He was so famous for being Mickey Dolenz, everybody always just wanted him to play himself. He is still famous. It's ridiculous. This guy's over 60, he walks down the street and people are like, "Mickey! Mickey!"

What was Gerald McRaney like back then?

He was just a nice young man. We've been good friends all these years, and we still are. He's gone through a whole bunch of wives, had a whole bunch of kids, and made a whole bunch of money! He's just a pretty decent guy. Never wanted to do anything but make a living acting.

Did McRaney know that Houck re-released *Night of Bloody Horror*?

Oh, yeah.

What was his reaction?

He thought it was funny! Remember, this was before he joined the union. He'd never even heard of the union or Screen Actors Guild. He had no protection. I think we paid him $500 for the whole movie, and he had to sign off rights in perpetuity. It was just a little bit above a homemade movie. We set out to be professional, but we didn't know if we could do it. We'd never done it before. But it came out much better than we thought. It started out with a pretty good script. Joy did a pretty good job directing it. The rest of it, we just did the best we could.

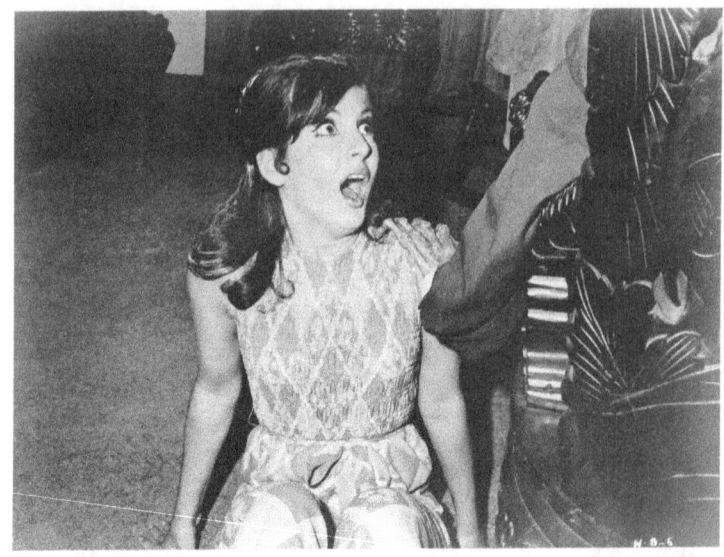

Snoopy reporter Angelle (Gaye Yellen) meets Wesley's dear old dad in *Night of Bloody Horror*.

There was a 16mm print that Joy had, and I don't know what happened to that. He moved away and then he died, and I don't know where his wife is. He was never very well. He was always kind of a sickly guy. He had rheumatoid arthritis and this and that and the other thing. But we kept in touch over the years.

Did you work on *Creature from Black Lake* (1976)?

Yes, I was the production manager. That was Jim McCullough's movie.

Who were the McCulloughs?

Jim McCullough knew Joy, Jr., and knew the old man, too. They all knew each other through that crazy Charlie Pierce who made a fortune with *The Legend of Boggy Creek* (1972).

Did you know Pierce?

Yeah, I knew him. He was the luckiest man alive! He made a lot of money, and blew a lot of money. Then last time I heard he was broke, trying to run a charm school or agency or something. Charlie never had a clue about how to direct a movie. It just all kind of happened. And the movie itself was horrible, but they four-walled it and it had a title and little suspense to it, I guess. It made a fortune. But he was a one-shot deal. He made a few other movies, but none of them did anything.

Creature from Black Lake was like a better version of that, because it was a real movie with a plot and real actors in it. Jack Elam was in it, and some more unusual people.

Dub Taylor was in it, too.

That was the end of the independent stuff for me. I'd already become a location manager for the big movies. I'd already done *The Autobiography of Miss Jane Pittman* (1974), and I had to leave that movie like two days early just doing some pickup shots. I had to leave to get back to Baton Rouge to do another horrible movie called *Mandingo* (1975).

You worked on *Mandingo*?

I was location manager. Then we did *Drum* (1976) after that. Two big slave epics for Dino De Laurentis. That got me going. But *Creature from Black Lake* was the best movie for me in that it came just at the right time. I had enough days that I was able to get into the Guild. I had already pretty much moved to Los Angeles, and that movie gave me just enough days in order to get into the Directors Guild as a production manger. Then I never looked back.

I had a couple of pretty lean years in the 1970s. But then in 1979 I went from the guy trying to get in to the guy doing real well overnight. I got a television series at Warner Brothers. I replaced somebody who had to go off and do something else. They couldn't find anybody to go to Georgia on short notice and do these six episodes of a television series called *The Dukes of Hazzard*.

It became a huge hit. I became production manager and associate producer on it for the first season, and then I stayed on advising the show. I

A Salzer double feature from the early 1970s. *Women and Bloody Terror* and *Night of Bloody Horror* were also packaged on a triple-bill with another Salzer/Joy Houck production, *Night of the Strangler* (1972) (courtesy Fred Adelman).

went on and did other things at Warner Brothers. But *Creature from Black Lake* was the end of my little bitty independent feature career.

Do you remember much about the making of that film? Where was it shot?

It was all shot in Shreveport. That's where McCullough works, and where he lives.

The McCulloughs are still active in the industry, right?

I talked to him a couple of weeks ago. He's still doing little B pictures. Straight-to-video things, I guess. He must be getting on. He's older than me.

The cinematographer on that film was Dean Cundey.

Dean Cundey was the cinematographer, and he went on to be a big star. He went on to work with Spielberg and all kinds of people.

Bill Thurman was also in that film. He worked on a lot of pictures in Louisiana, Texas and Arkansas.

Nice, nice man. He did everything. He'd drive a truck, run transportation and act into between times. He had a nice role in *The Last Picture Show* (1971). That was his claim to fame. He died a few years later. But a really sweet guy. Just like Jack Elam was a really nice guy, too.

What about Dub Taylor?

He was fun. Same with Jack Elam. We had to get them out of there as quickly as we could, so they didn't stay around there a long time.

You were on the set for both *Mandingo* and *Drum*?

I was around the whole time, from day one. I was the first one there in the morning and the last one to leave at night. I handled all the locations and logistics. I did a lot of stuff.

What was the atmosphere like on the set? *Mandingo* is a crazy movie.

We used real plantations, and then they built another plantation, a mock-up back in Lake Sherwood, California, that they burned down. But that was *Mandingo*. I think we did *Drum* all on location.

What did you think of those two films?

They were stupid. I knew they were stupid going in. They were made for a specific audience, I guess. But they made money. I thought they were kind of stupid, but they're making a *lot* of stupid movies today that make money [*laughs*].

What happened to Joy Houck after he made those few films?

He was never well, but he always wrote. He wrote and he wrote and he wrote. He was always trying to get things off the ground. He got paid for a few things. He sold a couple of scripts that never went to production as far as I know. He never really did too much. He did some acting from time to time.

He did do a film called *The Brain Machine* (1977).

I think that was called *The E-Box* originally. They did that in Jackson, Mississippi. I think Jimmy Best was in that, too. Then I went along to work with him on *Dukes of Hazzard*.

I didn't know much about it. I had nothing to do with that movie, except I remember that Joy directed it and it never did much.

How long did you work on *The Dukes of Hazzard*?

I was only technically on the show about a season and a half. But I produced another series. I worked on *Enos*, a spin-off of *Dukes*. And then I worked on *High Performance* (1983). God, that series — high performance, low ratings [*laughs*]! It died after 13 episodes.

What was that about?

I don't remember. I think it was about three people running around solving crimes. It just didn't work. [*Note: This series, which starred Mitch Ryan and Jack Scalia, was about racecar drivers who worked as bodyguards.*] "Dukes" went on and on and on. I just found it kind of boring. I wanted to parlay the credibility that I got from "Dukes" into doing other things, and I moved around town. I worked at Lorimar and Disney, made a lot of friends. I made a lot of movies for television.

Have you always gone back and forth between L.A. and New Orleans?

Not really. From about middle seventies until about middle eighties, I hardly ever came back. In 1983, I did my first movie back here in a while. It was a period piece called *Hobson's Choice* (1983) for CBS. It was directed by Gilbert Cates. Oddly enough, last year I produced a movie called *Deal* (2008) starring Burt Reynolds, directed by Gil Cates, Jr. I'm on the second generation of directors. You've been around for a while when you're on your second generation of directors!

I came back in '87 or '88 and started doing movies back here again. Right on through the 90s I'd come back from time to time doing television movies. Then I did the "Big Easy" television series for USA in 1996. I can't believe it's been ten years ago. Then I produced movies for French television here in '98 and '99. I went up to Montreal and did a few movies there. I seem to kick around.

You have offices in New Orleans now.

I have Crescent City Pictures, which is my permanent production company. I have permanent offices here that I keep open.

Is production picking up down there again since the hurricanes?

It's huge. We're the third largest production center in the country, and didn't miss a beat with Hurricane Katrina. It's devastated the city, but not the movie industry. We're on wheels. "The hurricane's coming, let's go to Shreveport!" I wasn't in production at the time. We went to Shreveport, and when it was over we came back. There are four or five movies going on right now. Plus a huge movie, *The Curious Case of Benjamin Button* (2008) with Brad Pitt, is just winding down. There's plenty of business down here, no question about tit.

Did your offices come through the storms okay?

Yeah. I was uptown near the river. Close to the river is high ground. Also, the whole property where my offices are is owned by the state. I was in California, but the National Guard came in right away and took over all of my offices. They really took care of them pretty well, because they were there for about three months. They just commandeered everything, but they took care of it.

Unfortunately, I live on the lake. My neighborhood was completely devastated, and it still is. I live in a boathouse out at the lake, but I was the first one to move back in.

You live on a boat in L.A., too, right?

I live on a boat in Santa Barbara. I'm a boat guy. I also have my 50-ton captain's license. I'm a captain in the U.S. Merchant Marine. I have a charter business in Santa Barbara when I feel like doing it. But that's just for fun.

When you were making those first few low-budget films, what were your aspirations? Did you want to be a director or a producer?

I went in wanting to be a director. My deal with Joy was I'd direct the next movie. Then I got into it and started producing, which I realized was really my thing, I kind of lost my ambition for directing. Then I just wanted to be a producer. I wanted to get out of super low-budget crap and break the door down in Hollywood. That's what I really wanted to do, which is what I did.

How did you make that transition?

I went out and hustled. They wanted to shoot *Jane Pittman*, which was written for Louisiana, in Mississippi or Alabama, and I just went there and broke down doors in Hollywood trying to get a job. I knew they wouldn't give me a job if they went to Mississippi. I had a lot to do with *Jane Pittman* coming to Louisiana, although I think the creative people wanted it there, because that's where it was written for. It's a masterpiece. It still is. It still holds up today. It was the first three-hour movie for television ever done, I think. It was a big deal. But that's how I got that job; I just really hustled.

That was nominated for like 15 Emmys and won 12 or something like that. Then people knew that if they were coming to Louisiana, I'd be the guy. Dino's people got in touch with me, and that's how I got on those pictures. But being a location manager will never get you into the Directors Guild. I needed production manager credits, which I had on all those pictures. I was the producer plus the production manager, although I wasn't a producer on *Creature from Black Lake*. But it was the production manger gig that got me into the Guild. That was really important.

Teen Terrors
Larry Stouffer
Texas

The early 1970s were a golden age for low-budget Texas horror films, but one that has gotten largely lost in the shuffle was Larry Stouffer's *Horror High* (1974). Produced and released at the same time as S.F. Brownrigg's *Don't Look in the Basement* (1973) — both films featured actress Rosie Holotik — and Tobe Hooper's *The Texas Chainsaw Massacre* (1974),

Stouffer's film received a fairly limited release from Crown International Pictures. It later became a staple of late-night television under the title *Twisted Brain*, with some extraneous additional footage added to the film by director Donald Hulette.

Stouffer first entered the film industry working for Texas institution The Jamieson Film Company before making his genre debut with *Horror High*. Unlike the rural gothics of his friend and mentor Brownrigg, Stouffer took a more contemporary approach, crafting an ahead-of-its time teen revenge flick using elements from *Dr. Jekyll and Mr. Hyde*. Vernon Potts (played by the believably adolescent Pat Cardi) is put-upon science geek who turns into a homicidal maniac after drinking the results of one of his lab experiments. In addition to Holotik and Cardi, the film also featured a stand-out performance from Austin Stoker as a detective, as well as cameos by John Niland, Mean Joe Greene and a number of other pro football players.

After a stint in the oil industry, Stouffer founded The Screenwriting Conference in Santa Fe, which is held every spring in New Mexico. As of 2008, he had several new directing projects in the works, including a remake of *Horror High*. Stouffer's horror film was also adapted and staged as a musical in 2007 by Mansfield, Ohio, fan Jeff Kilgore.

You said you wound up in Texas because your father's job took him there. He was in the steel industry?

Yes, in Youngstown, Ohio.

When did you move to Texas?

Around 1953 or 1954.

Were you interested in writing and in films from a young age?

No. I did not write *Horror High*, you know. My writing started off at a young age, I guess in grade school. Just some poetry. It's an odd thing, but I never even thought about movies. I went to them, of course, but I never thought about actually getting involved because I was never anywhere near the industry living in East Texas, and there was nothing near Youngstown. I don't want to say too many disparaging things about Youngstown, but I don't have anything good to say about it, either, other than I got the hell out of there — thank God and Lonestar Steel [*laughs*]. Living in a small town in East Texas, we had a population of maybe 4,000 or 5,000. Moving from Youngstown was a remarkable change. I went through a time warp, in a sense. Here I am living in a cesspool called Youngstown, Ohio, and for God's sake, I'm moving to Daingerfield, Texas! I didn't realize the spelling was different. It was named after, I think, a confederate captain or something.

Anyway, I had grown up in the North, and segregation was hardly a memory. I moved to Texas, and the schools were segregated. I mean, even with black and white water fountains. It was just a remarkable thing. Not until I graduated from high school (the year after, I think) did they integrate the schools there. It was really a crazy time.

I had gone to work in a town called Marshall, Texas. Marshall is maybe fifty miles from Daingerfield, and I was working for the *Marshall News Messenger* in advertising. Then I got another job working in a liquor store at night. That's when I got this idea to write a movie script. Now where that came from, I have no idea except it was just a great visual thing. I got excited. If you're gonna write a screenplay, the way to start, if it's got a chance to be any good, it has to come from passion. It's not a pragmatic exercise at all. Quite the contrary, actually, because your chances of making any money from writing a screenplay are so improbable that it's like a distant star.

But that didn't matter to me. I had no idea that I would ever sell anything. That wasn't my motivation. My motivation was I had discovered something from some reading that I had done. I discovered a situation that had taken place historically. I was curious about it, and I did some more investigating. This sounds awfully high-falutin' and intellectual, but I'm not any of the above. I did get this from H.G. Wells' outline of history, and the rise and fall of the Roman Empire. It connected some dots, is what happened. From that was born an idea, a story, that I started writing then, and I was not even remotely connected with the movie business. I was just doing it because I was getting off on it.

Believe it or not, I'm still writing that goddamn thing! I've gotten through the first act, but it's 160 pages long. That's just the first act. The story's in three movements. It takes place in 5th Century Persia. I've done an enormous amount of research, and I guess it's the love of my life — my writing life — this one particular story. Maybe now that I'm looking at my calculator, I realize I'm probably not going to live long enough to do it!

But at least I did as much as I did, or have done. Life interferes with things that we want to do. I'm sure that you've got creative endeavors that, if you didn't have to work for a living, you would pursue. You might still do it, but not as vigorously as you would like to. But sometimes that's an excuse. Writers always tend to look for anything to keep from writing. We claim that we love to do it. It's really a crazy thing, because I love to write, but I do know that I can't do it and sit down at the computer or my tablet to start writing until I go get the mail, or I've got to clean out the refrigerator first. We do everything we can to keep from doing it. When we finally look around, and we've got all of this stuff done, then we start writing and we just love it. I don't know what that's all about. Actually, I do know what that's all about, and I do know why we do that, but that's not why you're calling me.

That was how I started getting involved in movies. Then I got a job in 1969 in Dallas, and I had a friend, two friends actually, who had come from that little town that had ended up in the movie business in Dallas. And they couldn't spell movies, you know, when they left Daingerfield. It wasn't that they had gone to school for it or anything like that. The film industry is something that you really don't need to go to school for. It's not a bad thing to do if you've got the time or the money, but the trick is to go to work. You can graduate from UCLA, but that doesn't mean you know the difference between a light meter and a Miller Lite. I'm not disparaging that, but I'm just saying that it's not the only way to get it done.

I got involved in the film industry in Dallas because I was looking for a job. I wanted to get in the advertising business up there and couldn't get a job in advertising, and this opportunity came up to go work for this film company.

Who were the two friends?

You wouldn't know who they are. Dallas in the late sixties, and probably all through the seventies, was the third most prolific film city in the nation. I worked for several film companies in Dallas. I got a job with Jamieson Film Company, the largest film company in the South. At the time, we had five producer-directors on staff, we had two soundstages, we had two complete camera crews, we had five editing suites, but we called them editing rooms. We also had an animation department with artists, animators, we had a sound department for mixing. We also owned our own laboratory. It was just an enormous operation that has its own wonderful history, but I was fortunate enough to go to work there in what they called producer services. One of the functions that kept Jamieson Film Company going was there were a lot of independent producers that needed to come there to get titles done, or do editing and so forth. So it was a producer service facility as well as a facility capable of originating product.

Texas is and was a right-to-work state, which meant that we didn't have to put up with the dictates of the unions, which are, in my opinion, anti–American and anti–free enterprise system. I can't tell you anything that I can say that would be positive about them.

A lot of studios like American-International and Fox would send productions to Texas for that reason.

Yeah. One reason the industry did so well in Texas was — I'm not going to say there are more creative people in Texas than there are in Idaho, but the opportunities were there if you had the talent and the desire and so forth. You could actually dip your toe in the water, rather than just thinking, "Wouldn't it be nice if I could do this?"

We had soundstages all over the city in Dallas. The New York advertising agencies, just like you were talking about, and the Chicago advertising agencies would come to Dallas to get their TV commercials shot because we could do it for less money, because we didn't have the constraints of the unions. We could run a shoot with anybody in the nation. There was talent, there was speed, we could do it on a budget, and could do it well. And did do it well. One year I was shooting TV commercials for After Six and Levis and all those fashion things we were doing in Dallas, among other things, but that was the big deal. That's why the industry survived, and probably is a big factor in why it survives even today

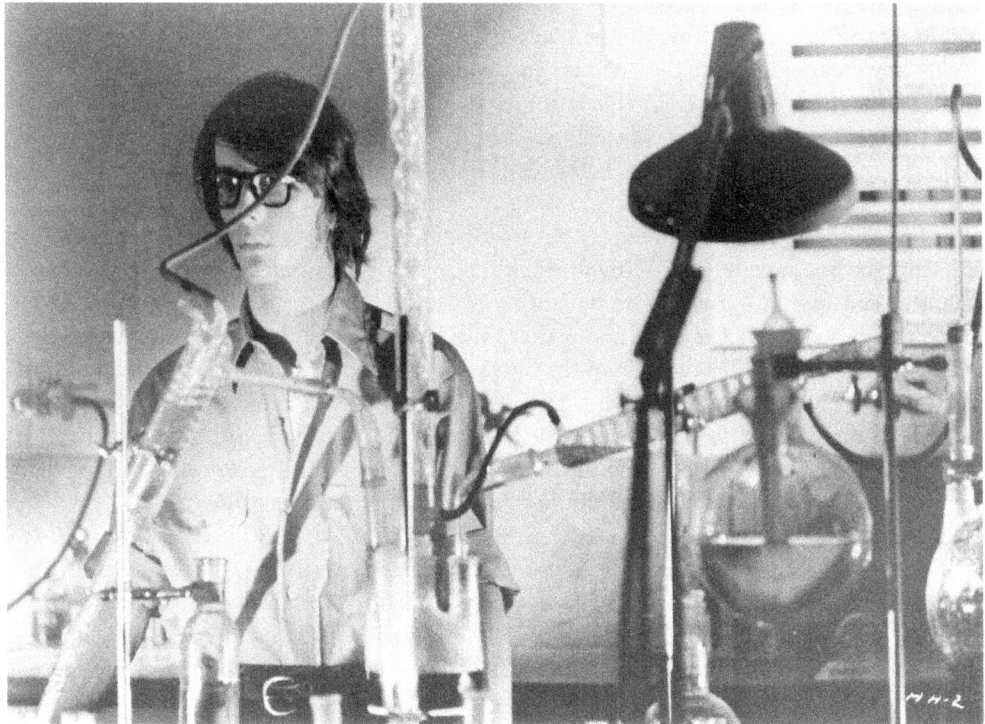

Vernon (Pat Cardi) in his laboratory in *Horror High* (1974).

in Texas. The only thing that's holding Texas back from doing more is their political thing, the legislature. I have to tell you, hopefully there will be some big breakthroughs there, but New Mexico has been leading the charge to stimulate motion picture production. Everybody is now looking over there and saying, what the hell is going on in New Mexico?

If Texas could get the kinds of incentives that New Mexico has, it would be unstoppable. The infrastructure is already in place there. Louisiana is doing the same thing. As a result, we're hoping to do *Horror High*, the remake, as you know. I'm already developing plans and talking with people, and creating the foundation to where we're going to be shooting the picture. I'm not shooting in New Mexico; I'm going to Texas to shoot it. I'm not planning on working with anybody I've worked with in the past, because almost everybody I ever worked with is dead. If I could get 'em back, I'd use them. I don't think that's going to happen. That's movie magic beyond our control! But that's where I'm going to go. I'm going to shoot it non-union, I'm going to shoot it digital. All those people are there, they're great filmmakers, and they just love to make films.

It doesn't mean you can take unfair advantage of them, because they're too smart for that. But they're not going to stand on ceremony. They're going to say, "Let's make this movie, let's get it done, let's do something really great." That's how they work. There's a vibrancy there, where here it's more of a job. There's no passion here, it seems to me. And that's what unions will do to you; they will suck the passion right out of you. But that's another story.

How did *Horror High* get started? Were you still at Jamieson when you made it?

Exactly. What happened there was that I was on staff as a producer/director at that time. I went to work in producer services. I was only in that job about six weeks, and then there was an opening in the editing department.

I knew enough about the business just from that little bit of time to realize — and I was 27 when I got in it, I wasn't this kid. I had a wife and we had a baby. I realized, against the advice of the guy who got me the job to begin with, that I wanted to get into the editing department. He kept telling me, "Larry, you don't want to do that." I said, "No, I *do* want to do that. I want that job."

So I pushed for it and got it. The reason I did that was — and this is what I teach in my seminars on screenwriting — if you want to be a really great screenwriter, one thing you ought to consider doing is take some editing classes. The students all look at me like I'm crazy, and probably they're right about that, but that particular point is not crazy. It's the center of production. The fulcrum of the business, so to speak. On one hand you have production, and on the other hand you have the laboratory. You can learn a hell of a lot. I learned to direct from the editing bench. I found that I was having to save the directors who didn't know that much about editing. They were just good talkers and a lot of them were hustlers. They convinced people they could go out and direct films.

The reality hits when you get to editing. Oh my god, what did I do, or what didn't I do! Then the editor has to figure out ways to get around the oversights made in production. That how I learned, and from editing I went into directing, and from directing I went into producing. In Dallas in those days, if you wanted to survive, you had to wear as many hats as you possibly could. I was a writer/producer/director/editor, and I could stay busy. I was more valuable to companies because of the fact that I could do all of those things, and for the most part do them pretty well.

At Jamieson one day, we looked around and business was maybe slow or something.

I said, "We've got all this stuff here. We can write a film, we can produce a film, we can direct a film, we can edit a film, we can have our own sound department, we can do our titles, we can do laboratory. We can take it all the way from script to screen. Why don't we do that?" Well, of course the company wasn't going to put up the money. I found Jim Graham, who is the executive producer and the general partner, and we created Horror High Limited.

How did you know him?

I knew Jim through his wife, Rosie Holotik. Rosie Holotik was my favorite model. Rosie was just cute, sweet and wonderful as she could possibly be. I decided that if we could put this movie deal together, that I wanted Rosie to play the role of Robin. Out of that came an introduction to Jim, but it was not for the purpose of raising the money. It's been a long time, but Jim and I got together and decided that we would put this deal together.

I worked with him and helped him, but Jim was successful in the oil business as an entrepreneur, and he had done very well. The oil business was thriving then. He knew a lot of people who'd done real well. It was just a matter of putting together a limited partnership and getting it out there. Potential investors would come over to Jamieson Film Company and we would go to the screening room and have meetings and talk about the project. Jim would run with the ball and introduce some of the key players that were going to be involved in the movie. We did the fancy footwork and put the partnership together.

How did you know Rosie Holotik?

She was a model in Dallas with the Kim Dawson Agency, and I had met her numerous times because I was working for various film companies in Dallas as a director. She, along with a lot of other models, came over to interview for commercials and films and things like that. We would have a casting call, so to speak, and agents would send people over who were appropriate for the roles.

She's just one of the nicest, sweetest human beings on the planet, completely unaffected by her beauty. She just was a hard worker, and the type of person you don't run into that often with that kind of beauty.

She had already done a few films.

I don't know how much she had done prior to that. This is when it all sort of started. As a matter of fact, [S.F.] Brownie Brownrigg was doing *Don't Look in the Basement* (1973) at the same time I was shooting *Horror High*.

So she was doing double duty?

It probably wasn't that dramatic. He was in pre-production or post when I was doing *Horror High*, so we didn't get a chance to work together on that project. He wasn't with Jamieson. He was independent, but he had worked there. Everybody in Dallas at the time had worked for Jamieson Film Company.

It was at or about the same time. I'm not saying I was shooting when Brownie was shooting. After that is when I went to work with Brownie, and back then we weren't too concerned with credits. I was the first assistant director on a lot of things he did, or second unit director. I worked with Brownie a lot. It got to where Brownie didn't want to do anything unless I was involved because I had his back. Brownie knew that if I was there, I would watch for things. I would see things for him. I was like Jiminy Cricket sitting on his shoulder. Not that he needed that. He was an extraordinary filmmaker, a brilliant man. Brownie will never, ever get the accolades and the respect that he should have gotten when he was in Dallas. That's one of the sad things I carry with me. I loved that man and his family, and he and I were very close pals.

I had a love-hate relationship with Brownie. I hated that son of a bitch, but at the same time I loved him. It was that kind of a friendship. I think he felt the same way about me. I know there were times when he wanted to kill me, and that's okay [*laughs*]. But I learned a lot from him.

What S.F. Brownrigg films did you work on?

If you're looking on Internet Movie Database, I won't be on there. *Don't Open the Door* (1975), that was one of them. I think I did *Keep My Grave Open* (1976), too. I think those were the two that I did with him. I don't even think I'm listed on the crew or anything.

Did you know Larry Buchanan?

I had met Buchanan several times, but I never worked with him or anything like that. I couldn't give you any good stories about him, but there is one that Brownie told me. He worked with him a lot as a sound guy. They were shooting one of his creature movies up in Arkansas, and his girlfriend went up to Buchanan one day and said, "Larry, we are ten days behind in production."

Larry Buchanan was a great salesman, and probably a really good producer. But if he had any weaknesses, it was in directing. Nonetheless, he said, "I can handle that." He took the script and opened it up, ripped 11 pages out of the script, and said, "Now we're back on schedule. Let's go. We'll dissolve or something." Now that's a story I will never forget [*laughs*].

I always thought Brownrigg's films were really great. He had a very distinctive visual style.

Brownie was an innovator. We did this thing—I think it was on *Don't Open the Door*. Susan Bracken was in it. That's Eddie Bracken's daughter. That's the one. Gene Ross or Larry O'Dwyer was the creepy guy in it. He was up in the attic, and she was in the house.

Those movies were shot down in a town called Jefferson, Texas. Jefferson is the oldest town in Texas. It sits right on the bank of Caddo Lake, which the eeriest, weirdest place. It's like the Everglades. If you get a boat and go back in that lake, it separates Texas from Louisiana. If you go back in there about 200 yards and you don't have a guide, you're lost. Some of the most weird, prehistoric sounds you have ever heard come out of that place. All the trees are cypress trees, and they're hanging with Spanish moss. It's horrific. A perfect place. All of the houses have historic plaques on them. This one in particular had a cupola at the top, and a staircase that goes up that was kind of curved.

What Brownie wanted to do was have a boom shot where the camera could follow Susan Bracken as she's walking up the steps, and it's a freaky, weird scene. Of course, we didn't have anything like that. We didn't have a boom. We didn't have much of anything. What he and Bob Alcott, the cinematographer, figured out was they took a pulley and attached it to the top of the ceiling, and they got a flat board that was about a foot wide and two feet long, hooked ropes to it, and screwed a camera on it. It was a silent camera, or a wild camera. No sound. They turned the camera on and gave her the cue to go. She starts up the stairs and they slowly pull that rope and keep the camera with her walking up those steps. It was a magnificent shot. Nobody could ever figure out how that was done. That was the type of stuff that that Brownie would do. He was just a special guy. Everybody that worked with him, we all miss him.

Who came up with the original concept for *Horror High*? The script is credited to Jack Fowler.

I don't know how in the world we found that script. It's really odd. I don't think Jim found it. I think it somehow came to us. How in the world we did that, again, I don't know. I just really don't know. But the guy, that's not his name, Jack Fowler. That's a *nome de plume*. The guy that wrote the original screenplay came to see the interlock. In film, that's where once you've edited the workprint, and you have the sound edited pretty much, you synchronize the two and interlock them, and then you can project them in a room where you have a projection system tied to a sound system. It's a procedure you go through to sit back and look at the whole thing on a big screen. The titles aren't on it, the dissolve effects are not on the screen.

He came to the interlock. We had the music done, we had pretty much everything done in a premix. He came in to the screening and he hated it so much he said, "I'm not putting my name on this son of a bitch," and he didn't. He came up with another name to use, and that's the name that's been on there ever since.

Austin Stoker and a squad of policemen (all portrayed by professional football players) confront Vernon's more monstrous incarnation.

So what was his real name?

I don't guess it's a secret, because the script was registered in his name. His name was J.D. Feigelson. As a matter of fact, I talked to J.D. a year ago. I found him. I didn't tell him what we were planning to do, but in fact I was looking for the original script. What I needed to do was not rewrite it, but pretty much overhaul it. The damn thing is over 30 years old, so the story needs brought up to contemporary times.

[Note: Julius D. Feigelson operated a Houston studio called Feigelson, Giertz & Hall that specialized in commercials and corporate films during the 1960s. He later wrote the excellent television film Dark Night of the Scarecrow (1981), as well as Wes Craven's Chiller (1985), Nightmare on the 13th Floor (1990), and Red Water (2003).]

There were things I wanted to do to it that, in my opinion, make it better. I added more characters. I added some comedy in it for comic relief. The objective was to stay with the original story. It's a remake, not a sequel or anything else. That said, it needed to be loyal to the original because I wanted the people who had seen the film, when they see it again, to recognize it. I wanted to stay true to it. That's what I did in creating the remake screenplay. That's done and ready to shoot now.

In the early 1970s, that idea of teenage revenge film was not that common. It was more popular later, after *Carrie* was released.

Well, I had to credit that to J.D. I'm not taking any credit for that. I wish I could because I've been pretty proud of that film. I mean, for God's sake, the limited partnership was put together for $125,000. At Jamieson, it was looked at like any other client. We looked at it that way. For example, if you brought a TV commercial concept to Jamieson and you wanted a TV spot done, we would figure a budget and bid on it. We would have profit included so that the company could survive. That's how it worked with Jamieson on *Horror High*. It was sort of a strange thing in the sense that we were all very intimately involved in the project. The idea was that it was going to be a Jamieson production, and we were thinking and hoping that perhaps that could be the beginning of another project, if it worked. At best, it would become a real motion picture production company in the sense of doing features.

All of us were sick of working with advertising agencies. But, that said, there was money built in. We had profit built in. A lot of people don't know this, but I brought that movie all the way through answer print, original music and the whole nine yards for $67,000. One of the reasons I was able to do that, it goes back to this thing I was mentioning earlier about editing. If you know editing, then what you do is you shoot for the editing bench. I don't plan to go shoot a movie and turn it over to an editor to direct it. I'm going to direct the movie. Then I'm going to give it to the editor to splice it. I don't depend on editors to make my movie. I know what I want. When I go out and shoot film, I shoot for the editing bench. I know where I'm going to end, and what I need to get out of it. So I just shoot that. That's all I need to do. What's the point in coverage, coverage, coverage out the ass? That's for people that are insecure and don't know a lot about editing, and they are going to depend on editors to save their rear end and make their film better. Editors are wonderful at doing that. That's why a lot of them become directors.

The whole idea was that we would use the movie as a stepping-stone to bigger and better things. It was time that the industry in Dallas turned to doing features. It never did catch on in Dallas, even though there were a number of independent films made. I would be surprised if you could find an independent film that was made in Dallas back in the

1970s that ever made any money — I mean that ever even got its money back. That would be an achievement.

In Dallas, I was saying for years that we have the ability to do everything that can be done in Hollywood. Hollywood could do no more than what we could do. They had some labs and some special effects companies out there that we didn't have, but we didn't need them. It wasn't that we weren't capable of doing them; we just didn't need them for that type of filmmaking.

So why isn't Dallas Hollywood? The reason was simple to me. It just goes back to manufacturing anything. Films are products, and if you don't have marketing, or what we call distribution in the film industry, then you have a low probability of succeeding. Imagine somebody coming up to you who's invented a gadget, and you're rich and famous, and he comes to you saying, I have this great gadget and I need X amount of dollars to manufacture this thing, and I think we can make some real money on this. The question is going to be, what kind of marketing will you set up? Where are you going to sell it? We couldn't answer any of those questions in Dallas, because we didn't have any marketing. To this day, there's not anything that I know of there, distribution-wise, that has the right kind of connections. Again, I haven't been in Dallas for a number of years. I moved to Santa Fe in 1991, and I was out of the business even then.

That's the story I guess of how *Horror High* got started, and once we got it done it was still the same thing. One of the main causes of my divorce was that I took all the money we had in savings. It was something like $3,500, not an enormous amount, but it was to us. I took that money and I didn't tell her about it, and I invested it in the movie. I lost every penny of it, and her, too. That wasn't the only reason we got divorced, but it certainly did contribute to it. That's not the right thing to do. That was a bad thing for me to do, but I did it, and that's that.

That movie, when we got it done, we all had this idea that it was going to be great and wonderful, and the world would beat a path to our door. All the distributors were going to come flocking around and making outrageous bids. We were going to make millions of dollars and live happily ever after and make movies and have a wonderful life.

Sometimes when a person gets real excited about something, they tend to overlook or take for granted that certain things are going to happen. I think we were all guilty of that. We just knew we were going to find distribution, and that the rest would be history. As it turned out, Jim, as a general partner, had to use a bunch of his own money to seek distribution. We finally found it with Crown International in Hollywood.

How did you cast the film?

I went out and to L.A. and cast the picture. There were three of us that went out: myself, Tom Moore, who was listed as the producer of the film, and then Jimmy Graham.

Is that the same Tom Moore who made —

Return to Boggy Creek? Yeah. All of us that did that movie, except for a few set builders that we brought in from outside, were all people who were at Jamieson Film Company. I'd say 95 percent of the crew were all Jamieson people. Tom was vice president of Jamieson in charge of production. I think that's what his title was.

I went out to L.A. and cast it. We had a string of people, maybe three-dozen candidates for Vernon. We had a casting agency that we used, and they did what they could to send us people that matched up to the character. Pat Cardi was the first one in line. But I'll tell you, that's one of the things that just dazzled the heck out of me about Hollywood. The one thing they do have is the talent out there. It's very impressive that there were three-dozen candidates for Vernon. You could have lined those guys up and put a blindfold on, thrown a dart and hit one, and you'd have made a good decision.

I didn't know any of these people, but Pat Cardi was the one that I chose after going through all the rest of them. He was just perfect. He was Vernon as I saw him. It ended up that it was a good decision on many levels, because Pat's a real good guy. He still is. We still communicate. I was in L.A. six months ago, and Pat and I got together. He's one of the good guys.

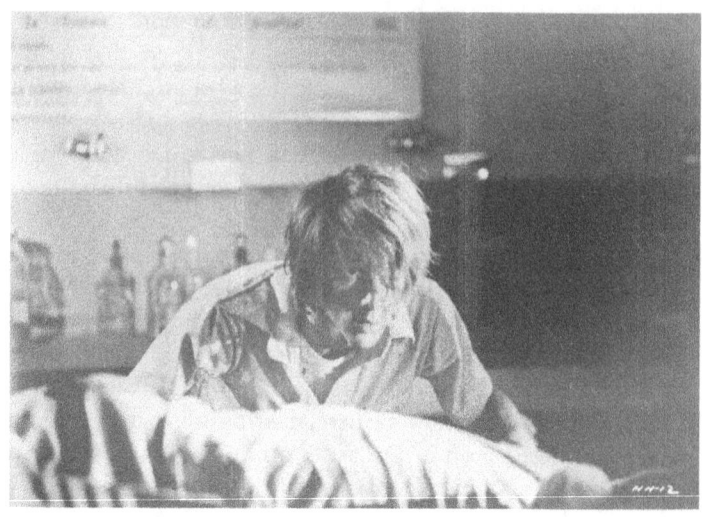

Another shot of Vernon (Pat Cardi), post-transformation.

Is he still working in the film industry?

He's in the business, but not as an actor. He's a producer. He produces non-theatrical projects. He does television things, industrial kinds of business films. He's thrived. He's got a family and kids in college, and he just does real well. I'm proud of him.

I went out to L.A. and cast Pat, and then also from L.A. came the guy that played Roger, Mike McHenry. Good guy, too. I got him from L.A.

Is that where you met Austin Stoker?

I didn't have to have a casting call for Bozeman, because I had worked with Austin on another project earlier. He had come and done a film that Brownie shot. I was not really involved in it for some reason, but he was shooting an industrial film, a fun kind of thing. So Austin came in and did it. He came in and shot the picture with us, and was a great guy. In fact, it was in November when were shooting. I remember we had Thanksgiving dinner in my house, and Austin was here away from his family, so Jane and I invited him to come over and have dinner with us. He's somebody you'd invite home for dinner. He was more than just an actor; a sweetheart of a guy.

In fact, Austin and Pat Cardi worked together in *Battle for the Planet of the Apes* (1973). Austin was a human in that thing, but Pat was one of the primates.

How long did it take to shoot the picture?

Two weeks.

Did it go fairly smoothly?

Are you kidding me [*laughs*]? Sixteen hours a day. It was a lesson to be learned. Did it go smoothly? No, it didn't. We weren't planning to shoot sixteen hours a day. Then it turned out to be that. We were always running behind.

John [Janis] Valtenberg, the guy who was the director of photography, was a brilliant lighting man. John was from Germany, and he'd come over and somehow or other Jamieson was able to find him and hire him. He was just a genius lighting guy. But he was a perfectionist, so John wouldn't let us shoot until he was ready. It would just take him so long because everything had to be perfect. If you look at that picture and look at the lighting, it's not typical lighting for a low-budget horror movie. It's just really wonderful, but at the same time John would say, "Give me five more minutes." We're all waiting, and everybody is pacing and ready to go, and John is fucking around putting barn doors on this one, and having the gaffers get up on a ladder and tilt that light here and put a gel on. It just went on and on until we were screaming and pulling our hair out. But the footage was just beautiful. The objective was not to just get it done on time; the objective was to get it done well. Of course, getting it done on time was important for the budget, but I had that covered. We did okay from that perspective.

I remember we were shooting the last scene in the movie, where Vernon was killed, shot outside the school. I had assigned Mean Joe Green to that job. Here I had all these Dallas Cowboys sequestered in a room in the school where they could just sit around. They were getting anxious and they were coming out, and Craig Morton would come out and say, "Larry, these guys are really getting nervous. They want to go." They were all wearing cop uniforms, and I finally had to talk to Craig. I said, "Look, I need your help on this. Here's the deal. You need to control those guys back there. You're the quarterback. There are things that I cannot control here. There's just so much I can do, but there are other elements out of my hands. You have to keep those guys under control back there." He said he'd handle it, and he did.

Except for Joe Green. Here I am standing out there on the outside, and we're freezing our asses off. I feel this tug at my sleeve. It's Joe. He said, "Larry, Larry, when am I gonna get to shoot Vernon?" "Joe, you go back in that room and sit down until I call you." Fifteen minutes later he'd come running out with his shotgun and grab me. I'd just point back there and he'd turn around. "Okay, just call me when you're ready." It was a running gag we had. You need a little levity in situations like that, and he provided it.

Had you done any work with the football team before?

No. How did that work? I don't remember. I think the first thing we did was we got John Niland in the deal. He played the football coach. John Niland was the right guard on the Dallas Cowboys, all pro. John, in fact, invested in the film. I can't say how much it was, but John was one of the significant investors in the movie. I told him, "If you don't put money in this, I still want you to play the role. One does not have anything to do with the other." He didn't buy his way in. I think, through some of his connections, I was able to meet more players and so forth.

We're talking about John Niland and Mean Joe Green. I'm sitting in my office, and Joe Green came in with his manager or whoever, and sat down across the desk from me. I said, "Joe, I've been thinking about adding a new role in the story where you would be a radio announcer who also did news. So I want to do this scene where you and John Niland, or you and Coach McCall, are talking about what's been going on at the school, and something causes you guys to get into an arm wrestling match. I'm going to cover this with three cameras. I want you two guys to go at it. It doesn't make any difference which one of you wins."

He just leaned back, crossed his arms and kind of smiled. He looked at me and said, "You're kidding me, aren't you? There's no way, baby. Niland would tear my arm off. I'm not about to do that." That wasn't what I was expecting to hear, so I dropped it right there. That was the end of that idea! There was an arm wrestling scene in there, but it wasn't with Joe Green.

How did Graham connect with Crown International?

They offered him a distribution deal that he took really out of desperation. There was an interesting issue on the ratings, too. I went out to L.A. and screened the answer print for the MPAA people. They rated it X for violence. If you remember, it had two hells and maybe one damn, and one little tiny kiss between Vernon and Robin. There was no language. But they gave it an X rating for violence. We had go back and edit some of the violence out of the original picture to get an R rating, and then when Crown International picked it up, we were able to take the original thing back and get that reinstated, and got the X lifted to an R. Politics, power, bullshit. That's how that worked.

In this new version, I'm not holding back. I'm going to get all the good out of this movie that's written into it.

Once Crown got a hold of the film, I imagine you didn't see much money afterward.

Can I be perfectly candid with you and tell you that we've never seen one penny? Especially if you know [Mark] Tenser's history and Crown International. This seems to be what is normal with them, from what I hear. We didn't see a dime. Nothing.

Was Jim able to get any of his money back?

No. But I made a deal with Jim for the remake. I bought an option on *Horror High*, and my part of that exercise is to give Horror High Limited a check for X amount of dollars, which will cover all the cost, and all the investors will be made whole by this exercise. And then I'll be able to make the film.

In the version of the film that Crown released to DVD a few years back, there's a sequence added with Vernon talking on the phone with his father. Did you put that in there? A guy named Donald Hulette, who re-edited a lot of stuff for Crown's TV packages, has a credit on that version, and I thought it might be his work.

It wasn't mine, I can promise you that. Crown did that. They stuck that in there. It was just God-awful atrocious. It didn't make any sense. But apparently, from what I was told, they had to do that to get it to a certain length for TV. They never consulted me on the damn thing. They did it all on their own. They may have talked to Jim Graham about it, but Jimmy never said anything to me about it. It was just an absolute embarrassment. I'm not going to tell you right now that the picture was brilliant or that sort of thing. I'm not implying that at all. You've heard the old saying about fucking up a wet dream? They did that. I mean, you can take something bad and make it worse. They did not improve that film at all by putting that stuff in there. People still shake their heads and wonder what the hell that was about.

Did they come up with the *Twisted Brain* title?

Yeah. Not only that, before *Twisted Brain* they had it as *Kiss the Teacher Goodbye*.

What about the theme song?

We did all the music. That was Jerry Coward that did that. He sang it, and he and his girlfriend wrote it. We used that in the beginning and the ending. We bookended the film with that tune.

What did you do after you left the film industry?

I was involved in the oil business, actually. I had the great idea that I was going to go off in the oil business and meet a bunch of rich oil people. I said, "Now if you think this is making money, let me show you the movie business. And here's what we can do together." But everybody I met in the oil business was broke or got broke real fast! So that experiment failed. That was my idea to go in the oil business, and I had great connections to get in the oil business. I was involved in like 100 wells being produced in Texas and Louisiana, and I owned Stouffer Oil Corporation, which at one time was Stouffer Energy. We all went broke, so that didn't work at all.

Book, Lyrics and Music by J.M. Kilgore
Adapted from a screenplay by Jake Fowler
Directed by J.M. Kilgore

At The Mansfield Playhouse
JULY 20-21 & 27-28

The playbill for a 2008 musical based on *Horror High* that was produced in Mansfield, Ohio.

You've been running the screenwriter's conference for several years now. What spurred your interest in doing a *Horror High* remake?

I don't know. It's just all of a sudden occurred to me. I'm involved on the edge of a deal that has been developing now for three years. I got connected to it because the fellow who is the mastermind and the head of it contacted me three years ago, not because of *Horror High*, but because of the screenwriting conference in Santa Fe. He wanted to know how to be a sponsor of the conference. He told me what it was that he was planning to do. He said when he got the funding that he would like to be a sponsor, so we set it up so he would be the title sponsor for the conference.

I've co-written a script with my oldest and dearest friend who lives in Oklahoma City. We met in Dallas years ago, and the script is about the ballroom dance business. It was ready to go, so I told him about that, and he said he'd like to look at it. Then I found out they were setting up a low-budget division for pictures that could be set up for $2.5 million or less, any genre except porn. There was my opportunity to establish Larry Stouffer Productions, which I will do. What's the fastest thing I can put together? I thought, "Oh my God, what if we did a remake of *Horror High*?" The more I thought about, the more I realized that this was good idea because of the cult following and everything. So that's ready. In the delays of getting that money, I've been pursuing other avenues of funding.

I called Jim. We made that deal, and I told him I wanted to get all the investors whole. That was the important thing for me to do. And I said I'd throw in some points on the movie, too. If the movie makes money, then the investors will see a little profit. Nobody will get rich, but it might be kind of fun to get a check here and there.

It Could Only Happen in Milpitas!

ROBERT BURRILL
Milpitas, California

In 1973, in what may be one of the strangest manifestations of civic unity on record, the citizens of Milpitas, California, rallied their combined economic and artistic resources to make a monster movie. And not just any old monster movie, but a cautionary tale centered on the town's notoriously noxious garbage dump — *The Milpitas Monster* (1976).

In the 1970s, Milpitas was the frequent butt of jokes in the Bay Area. Due to an unfortunate confluence of rampant development in San Jose and an accident of geography, odors from the local landfills would waft through Milpitas, which gave the town a smelly reputation.

It was into this odiferous environment that a young teacher named Robert Burrill arrived in 1969 to coach baseball and teach the photography course at Samuel Ayer High School. When an opportunity arose for Burrill and his students to make a short film, they turned to the local garbage dump for inspiration, and came up with a 10-minute piece about a giant, gas-masked mutant fly that attacks the town.

Encouraged by the quality of the short, Burrill and his kids began expanding the concept, and like the creature itself, the film got bigger and bigger. By the time it was over, nearly the entire town — including the mayor, the local printer, the police and fire departments, hundreds of Milpitas citizens and most of the high school — was involved in the production. Help even appeared from outside the community, and the film's credits soon boasted a well-known horror host, the self-proclaimed "world's most famous cheerleader," a sound effects editor who would later work on *Star Wars*, and Tennessee Ernie Ford.

Shot over a period of four years, the film finally made its theatrical debut in Milpitas in 1976. While Burrill had hoped it would gain a wider release, technical difficulties, additional editing and the film's unusual production structure prevented it. *The Milpitas Monster* was eventually released on video in the 1980s, and built a small cult following.

Several bootleg videos and DVDs of the film have been released (sometimes under the title *The Mutant Beast*), but Burrill himself has continued to make authorized copies available (www.milpitasmonster.com) in partnership with the film's owner, George Loughborough of Huntford Printing & Graphics in Milpitas. Most recently, the Niles Essanay Silent Film Museum added *The Milpitas Monster* to its Halloween fundraising program.

Retired since 2003, Burrill has made several documentaries and published a number of books (including a volume of Milpitas photographs), and served (2003–2006) as president of the Milpitas Historical Society. In March 2007, he was named Milpitas Citizen of the Year for his work in the school system and the community ... and for making *The Milpitas Monster*.

Were you raised in Milpitas?

No, I was raised in the South San Francisco Bay, in the town of Menlo Park, which is right next to Palo Alto and Stanford.

Robert Burrill poses with local horror movie host Bob Wilkins on the set of *Creature Features* while promoting *The Milpitas Monster* (1976) (courtesy Robert Burrill).

Believe it or not, they needed a baseball coach at the high school, and I had played professionally. I played semi-pro and in college. My hobby had always been filmmaking, and they needed to have somebody to teach a photography class. That all fell into the right place for me, and I went ahead and worked toward my master's degree when I got hired as a teacher in photography and film. After about four or five years I was starting to make educational films for teaching photography. Beginning in 1973, within my filmmaking class, we began calling Samuel Ayer High School "Samuel Golden Ayer Production," after Metro-Goldwyn-Mayer.

Who did you play baseball for?

I grew up in Menlo Park, and did a little semi-pro in what is called the winter league in the Menlo Park area, the South Bay. Professional baseball players that lived in the Bay Area would get together in the winter and just stay in shape by playing weekends. That would provide an opportunity for younger ball players to be looked at by the birddogs and the scouts, and I was lucky enough to play with them for a couple of years. I went and I could see how God had given them a gift to throw and run. I was a fast runner, but I didn't have a throwing arm like those guys did. Some football injuries kind of set me back a bit in those days. I thought I would have been good, but my knee was pretty well shattered, and I didn't have a way to really fix it. That was my cop-out. My love has always been there. But that was an opportunity for me.

I look back now upon how everything kind of fell into the right place. I was young and energetic and always interested in pleasing the administrators at the school. I did a little reflection upon that recently because we're celebrating the 30th anniversary of our film. I looked at it, and Milpitas was a smaller town then, and the vice principal of the school at the time [Joseph House] happened to be the mayor of the whole city. It was a little city of 25,000 people. We're about 70,000 now. But at the time, Milpitas was right at the edge where we'd formed a new school district, and there was some interest in new curriculums that could be developed.

When we wanted to do the film, because he was the mayor, I asked him, "Well, who should I talk to?" Because he was mayor of the town, he literally had the keys to the city. I went over and talked to the chamber of commerce, then I talked to the city council, the board of education and everybody gave us letters of recommendation. The fire department, the police department, the public works department — we were all endorsed to go ahead and get support on the project.

Because of the size of the town, it was kind of a magical time. We were coming up to the end of the Vietnam War, and because the country was coming into the Bicentennial era, the politicians wanted everything to be kind of mellow. We had the film scheduled to be finished in '75, but it just seemed that for a little bit more work and a little bit more time, we could do a feature film and premiere it in 1976.

How did it get started? Who came up with idea to make a monster movie?

There was one gentleman named David Kottas, who was quite an interesting artist, and who loved to draw comic books. It was actually a commercial art class. I was teaching art and photography. During the commercial arts class in October, everybody could develop a poster design, so we asked them please design your own movie poster for Halloween. Somewhere in the conversation, this just came out of my mouth without thinking about it, I said, "Somebody ought to do a poster called *The Milpitas Monster.*" That just came to be what it was. David's sketches were very good, and we developed what it could be. He continued to draw and we kept critiquing it. Pretty soon it was a gas-masked monster/half-fly that came out, and it was sort of an homage to Godzilla and King Kong.

Our filmmaking class, the advanced photography class, thought, "Let's do something short and see what this is like." I'd just finished my master's degree in filmmaking and had my 16mm camera. We'd seen this film called *Bambi Meets Godzilla* (1969), a classic short. It was a short little animated thing, where Bambi would come out with nice music, and this horrendous foot just comes down and smashes her.

We looked around, and in our little town and we had a little restaurant called the Kozy Kitchen. We went over to them and asked if they wanted to help us film a little short where the monster comes for a bite to eat at the restaurant.

I knew the kids would enjoy smashing up a restaurant, so we went ahead and built the model as best we could. There was another person who was a model builder [Duane Walz, who also appears in the film as the Director of Civil Emergency], a parent, and he got involved. He said, "Let's build it seriously and do it to scale." Then we had a really nice model, and the footage came out looking amazingly realistic.

Patty Thorpe's mother [Anna Thorpe] was a professional seamstress. We had another kid who didn't have a whole lot to do in terms of participating in school, but he was big: Scott Parker. He was like six-four or something. We all looked at him and said, "Could you be the monster?" Before we knew it, Patty Thorpe's mom had made a body suit to fit this kid. I went over to take a look at it, and all of a sudden I thought, "My God, this is a serious prop!" The footage came out so good, we sent it up to [TV horror host] Bob Wilkins on Channel 2 and showed him a little bit of the footage. He thought it was cute.

He went ahead and let his editors get involved. There was a film called *Earthquake* (1974) that was coming out at the time, and he intercut the footage and made it look really good, and they ran it on Channel 2. All of a sudden I had these phone calls from all over the Bay Area from people saying they wanted to help with the film. It just kept going. It was all based on community involvement, and being in the position of a school teacher, it really became a model of cooperation — civic cooperation between the city and the community. I had an adult education photography class that was working in the evenings, and they became a booster club. What was going to be a 10-minute short ended up to be a 30-minute movie. The local newspaper, *Milpitas Post*, thought it was cute, and they started running it as a regular part of their weekly newspaper. We had this fantastic coverage in our town and it started to expand. They wanted to know when we were having the premiere. We told them it would be in October.

Then more production value started showing up. We had this guy that did the music, Bob Berry [credited as Robert R. Berry], who is a professional musician. He was willing to do the entire theatrical score, 24 sound-on-sound recordings, for credit only. Later, George Loughborough would pay him and Tiki Sound (owned by Gradie O'Neal) $1,000 for permanent music rights. I have a 45rpm record, "Dining on the City Dump" and "The Milpitas Monster," that was issued by Janelle Records. I'm sure they are collectible, as are our "miniature garbage cans" made from Gerber apple juice cans.

The other contact I had was a person I met at San Jose State named David Boston, who went off to USC to become a screenwriter. He wrote screenplays for Disney [including episodes of "The Wonderful World of Disney"], and he was an intern for Robert Wise on *The Hindenburg* (1975) at the time. David invited me to join him on set. I remember being there for a couple of days. David has become a lifelong friend, and kept helping me with ideas. He produced the initial script during the Christmas holidays in 1974.

He kept helping me with ideas. He became my contact with the Hollywood scene. He wasn't interested in documentary filmmaking as much as I was, but he liked the feature film potential, so this had a chance of becoming something bigger. I kept him alert of what was happening.

And the community support kept building, right?

Don Edwards, our congressman, wrote us into the Congressional Record, and we were published in the Congressional Record in October of 1976. That was probably the highest record of acknowledgement that we had. We buried it in the time capsule. A little booklet was prepared and publicity was out. We had our world premiere and that was pretty magical because we had the band there, and the limousines, and the searchlights. We had a 30-foot red carpet installed, which I later used in my classroom for years. Everybody showed up at this new theater that had just opened up, the Serra Theater. We brought our local creature feature guy from Channel 2, Bob Wilkins, who was in the film, and it was quite a festive night. All the news teams came in with their cameras, and it was just unbelievable. A magical day. They ran us on the front page of most papers all the way across the United States. We almost got on the Johnny Carson show. That's when a guy from Texas, William Thrush, walked up and said, "Mr. Burrill, I like your motion picture. I'm gonna buy your motion picture and we're gonna put it out nationally, and you're gonna be a star!" I'll never forget that.

We had a local printer in town, George Loughborough at Huntford Printing. He thought the project was worthy, and because of the printing business he used it as a write-off, and did a lot of the advertising for us. He really made us look good, because he printed this poster up, originally on some old card stock that he didn't know what to do with. It was pink. The title *Milpitas Monster* on pink cardboard was kind of a comical thing, but looked great with our graphic candlestick-drip lettering. We had a great title. *The Milpitas Monster* is fun to say, especially when spoken by Paul Frees, who may best be remembered as the voice of the Haunted Mansion at Disneyland.

That's another thing that's really special about the movie is the title itself, MM, *Milpitas Monster*. Word spread from one person to another, and then people would say, "I know somebody." It was endorsed by the Browning-Ferris Garbage Company, so it really starred the entire town, literally. We had one semi-professional actor come in and join us from the stage. Doug Hagdohl had been doing local theater gigs in South San Jose, and had his costume in hand to volunteer his talents. Hence, Doug's "George Keester" character was the only player that changed his natural demeanor. Everybody else pretty much played themselves. In that way, I did not have to direct them to be someone they were not.

The fire department got in an argument as to which firehouse was going to be used the most. The policemen didn't know what to think of it, but the firemen just had a ball. However, the police did come up with a great scene when Officer Don Pavack slipped on a pig mask for a joke. At first, I reshot the scene of the police leaving City Hall because I didn't want to offend anyone. But after the second cut of the film I thought, well, they did come up with the idea, and everybody — including the police — *did* laugh. So watch closely and look for the third cop out of the door. It's quick, but he is wearing a pig mask, and it's the type of thing you love to have in a film such as this.

I had the city cherry pickers they used for changing the light bulbs to film from up above. The production value wound up being pretty good for what we had to work with. You put that all together and it kind of fell into place.

The most unique thing is the fact that everybody was in the right place. We not only had the mayor, but the mayor's daughter [Priscilla House] was already doing television commercials. She was a very attractive young lady. Her boyfriend Mike Pegg was an interesting gentleman, too, and had done a little acting in theater. Fans may be pleased to know that Mike married Priscilla, and they are still married. The kids in my class were really responsive to it. The student body president of the school got on the phone, and we had the cooperation of our school that we could teach photography and filmmaking and develop that during the day.

I looked at the high school and realized that a high school facility, if you have access to all the teachers, is literally a Hollywood studio in miniature. You've got a wood shop, a metal shop and auto shop; you've a got an English department and all types of facilities; you've got free labor with the kids that love to be in a movie. That was a pretty unique position to be in as a young teacher, about my third year teaching. I had the energy and things kind of took off.

The big garbage trucks were kind of a monstrous thing, and the thought in the back of everybody's mind was the issue of pollution. We all were thinking about it, and it was a concern in the sixties, and we jumped on that bandwagon somewhat to look for a motif. Besides that, there was a real need to defend Milpitas. If you know the history of the area, we're in the South Bay, and based on the jokes of vaudeville, there was lots of humor to drop on the bottom part of the South Bay and the smells that came out of the area, especially the garbage fill.

I wanted to ask about that—what is the deal with all the jokes about the funny smells?

In the south part of the bay, the wind comes through the Golden Gate and it blows southerly, because it gives us a nice breeze in the afternoon. However, San Jose, a large city, wanted to develop into a larger town. Of course, all of us have the concern about what to do with the garbage.

What happened in our area is that Milpitas is in the northern part of San Jose, Santa Clara County. Historically what would happen is people would come when the gold rush came through, before bridges, they'd walk the southern route to Mission Santa Clara and they'd walk through around Alviso and Milpitas, and make the bottom loop around to the gold country. It developed in that location, and the first cash crops of California were hay and wheat. The Portuguese farmers actually produced quite a bit of vegetation up there in the earliest form of agriculture for the state of California. It's hard to believe that the middle of the state didn't have any agriculture, but all the agriculture for California was right here in the southern part of the bay.

The second poster design for *The Milpitas Monster*, with artwork by Steve Wathen (courtesy Robert Burrill).

It's a little warmer and away from the fog, so it got quite a reputation. As it grew, San Jose, situated about 10 miles to the south, really was becoming quite prosperous. Then they needed someplace to control where the garbage was going to be. They went ahead and ran this pipeline out halfway between Alviso and Milpitas. A landfill was put out there as well. The wind blows through the Golden Gate, picks up the odor of the sewage treatment plant and the landfills, and it blows towards Milpitas. Alviso really didn't smell it as much as Milpitas.

You'd be driving along Highway 17 from Oakland to San Jose, and that was the big joke. "What's that smell? Hmm, we must be in Milpitas." During the Civil War there was a time that there was a thought we should vote for the Union during the war, and one of the farmers put up a big marker that said, "As goes Milpitas, so goes the state." And people laughed. That became another icon. People think the name Milpitas means "little cornfield." It means garden, land of a thousand gardens. But after the 1920s it became corn. People smiled and picked up on the name that Milpitas means little cornfield. That was a chance to say Milpitas was known as a corny little town.

I became kind of defensive as a young teacher, because you get all these jokes and you hear it on the news a lot. When the movie theater finally opened up in town, I remember

Another later poster design for *The Milpitas Monster* **(courtesy Robert Burrill).**

Bob Wilkins on Channel 2 made some jokes about it. He kind of lifted his nose a couple of times and said, "Yeah, in Milpitas they've got a movie theater, believe it or not."

I said, "I really am tired of hearing that," so when this film idea started taking off, it was going to be a ten-minute short, but it just seemed to keep going. We made little bumper stickers and buttons, and people started to take on the buttons to celebrate the pride of our town. I got involved in the historical society somewhat, saying that Milpitas had all these Portuguese people that worked up on the sides of the hills that were really proud farmers, but they didn't understand the jokes. They just went back to the plow and continued to provide for early agriculture.

I wanted to get the kids to develop some avenue of community pride. In the film, we have a 50-foot monster that came into town and they had to unite to overcome the beast.

Did you hope, once you got started, that you could get theatrical distribution for the film?

Yeah. I wanted to know how synchronous sound would work and everything else, and see if we could really make a film. It was a real learning experience for everybody involved — including myself, probably more than anybody else!

So the first portion of this was done in 1973?

The film test started in '73.

How long did it take to complete the film?

We postponed the premiere, and by the time we finished the film it was four years before it was really put into the theater. The premiere was in 1976, and then there was another year of cutting the film to another length. It was cut down to 80 minutes, and we just about sent it out through the local printer, who had paid the bill for the lawyer. A local named George Loughborough helped get it out. He paid the initial bills. We went even further with another cut. The second cut was a 70-minute version. We had some technical problems with sound, which had to be redone. Finally, we had a 70-minute cut, which is pretty much the film today. That was four years of work, plus a couple more, so by the time it got released it was eight years later when it was distributed internationally, on the East Coast and through television packaging.

The whole thing was shot in 16mm?

Yeah, 16mm in what was called ECO, which is commercial slide film. It wasn't even shot in a negative. But it was clean. The original was professionally separated. Usually you shoot the camera original, put that away and then you take a work print for editing. It was done the old way. Computers weren't in the scene at that point. This was also just before the "goo" application of monsters had come in, too, if you think about *Alien* and some of that technology. This was shot just before that came out. Our biggest homage turned out to be — be sure you don't quote me on this. Ben Burtt, who did the *Star Wars* film, he did give us some of his sound effects early on and did the sound of the sloshing monster for us. He was a classmate of David Boston down at USC, and they had made a series of successful student films together. It turned out that year, 1976, *Star Wars* hit the scene and there was a complete revolution in filmmaking, as you know.

David Boston is another person that knows the genre. He's a good friend of mine, too. I met him at San Jose State when I started making films. He went to USC and worked with a lot of the Hollywood people. He's been an integral part of making me look good. It was good to have good networking. Luckily, he'd been making films with Ben Burtt at USC. Ben was a projectionist, and he would put alligator clips on the projectors and started collecting these sounds. George Lucas found out he had this collection, so he said, "Here, why don't you try some stuff?"

I was down there the month he was doing this. He had this big bulletin board with pins all over it, and he was going all over Hollywood making these recordings. For fifty dollars he lifted me about 30 sound effects that I put on a reel-to-reel. I still have it.

Did you have much interest in sci-fi or horror films?

Walt Disney was always my hero. *20,000 Leagues Under the Sea* (1954) was the film that did it for me as a kid. Whatever it was that was making a person's eyes open up and go, "Oh wow!" I was really interested in that as an artist myself. That's what I told everybody: you want to make a picture that makes the audience go, "Oh wow!" How do you do that? It has to do with composition, lighting, and all the parts of cinematography that you actually see, probably best presented in television commercials.

There's a good chunk of stop motion work in the film. How did you pull that off?

His name was Stephen Wathen. That was another magical part of everybody being in the right place at the right time. Steve worked as a graphic artist for the printer friend, Mr. Loughborough. He was really a cinematography expert. He's pretty well known in the local area as a stage coordinator, does a lot of stage work, illustration, has written a couple of nice screenplays and plays for theater. [Wathen also worked on the film *Planet of Dinosaurs* and the TV series "Gumby Adventures."] He is really one of the top sci-fi guys, and he hap-

Robert Burrill in his classroom in 1975 (courtesy Robert Burrill).

pens to be right here in Milpitas. He took the original artwork, added his ink pen to it, did a couple of layouts, incorporated some nice touches on the drip, the candlestick lettering, and he really presented the posters that came out of Huntford Printing with this extra little bit of expertise. His hobby was that he loved Ray Harryhausen and animation, so he said, "I'll work up some animation sequences with the stop motion." Some of the local pros that I knew helped us technically get the right film stock and get it processed the right way. I grew into understanding how films were made the old fashioned way.

By the time you had the premiere, were a lot of kids in the film out of school?

Yeah, a couple of them came back for the premiere. The kid who actually played the monster did a wonderful job in the parades, and did pick up photography. There's another person who stayed with me, Scot Henderson, and he ended up being in the costume even more than Scott Parker. He lives in Denver now. He was here last weekend. He's one of my adopted kids. The bunch of us that made this film really bonded when we were working together. Scot was there from the first day all the way through it. One of my best friends to this day.

That was what happened. They still come back and I get phone calls. When some of them found out the film was on DVD I got quite a few orders from kids who were part of it. A lot of them didn't even know it was available

How did you get Paul Frees for the opening narration?

Steve Wathen knew that the local recording studio, Coast Recording Studio in San Francisco, did commercials. Steve was always a serious film collector and author, and encouraged me to pursue him for the film.

Actually, to go back a little bit, we actually had Tennessee Ernie Ford as the original narrator of the film. We knew that he lived in Portola Valley near Palo Alto, knocked on his door many times, found his agent. About 18 phone calls later, Tennessee Ernie Ford actually did the original narration.

But when it was about to go for theatrical release, his agent didn't want his name tied to a horror film. In that case, Stephen Wathen looked at me and said, "We ought to go down and get Paul Frees." We found out that he does local recordings in the San Francisco area. He would do a lot of recordings. So it was just a matter of a couple of phone calls. When he got the word that we were a high school, boy you ought to hear the recording. The recording I've got with him, he sent me the whole thing. He said, "I'm really honored to be able to do this for you. This is very well written. I'm going to do a couple of different versions. If you need any more help, you be sure to let me know. *Milpitas Monster*, take one."

Then he did this delivery that anybody who takes a radio class, this really needs to be available to people. He said, "Now let me give you another version. I'll go a little bit faster." He talks about tempo. It's something on the DVD version that'd really like to put together.

Horror host Bob Wilkins, who you mentioned had been making fun of Milpitas, also made an appearance in the film.

He thought the film was cute. I was just listening to him for years, but boy when he started making jokes and using the name Milpitas, and joking about our movie theater, I got on the phone and said, "You know, we're proud of this little town." I thought if there was a chance to put him in the movie, I would. I knew he'd play the monster expert. After the feedback, and I had been on the show a couple of times talking about it, I just knew he'd be great. We went up there to Channel 2 with the kids, and within 10 minutes we had him sitting at his desk going, "What you need, Mayor House, is the Odorolla." He was just comically perfect for all that.

I got on a few times with the film when John Stanley was the host. It must have been on Channel 2 at least three times. It turns out that was the only film we knew that Bob Wilkins was in. If you go on the Web site, he's got a DVD coming out. Last Halloween they did a special and showed a lot of the things he did. He really had a great following.

You explained about the mayor being the vice principal. Once you started talking to rest of town about this, what was the initial response?

I walked in as a local teacher with this poster in my hand, which was graphically laid out, and it said, *Milpitas Monster*. Everyone would smile. They thought it was kind of cute. I just said, "You know, we'd like to put you in the movie. We'd like to get $50 from you, and we'll put your name in the title credits. If the movie ever makes it big, we'll turn the money over to the school district." It was pretty easy to get $50 from there. Then it became a challenge to the town. People would say, "Why don't you go over and talk to my friend over at the other gas station? He knows somebody."

One more thing I wanted to mention to you: Looking back on this 30-year anniversary, I found out historically that Milpitas had really been defending itself before I came into town. They fought off the big giant of San Jose, which was trying to annex all the town areas. Milpitas was offended by San Jose coming in and saying they wanted to buy up the town and make it part of San Jose. On Casper Street there were several military people that lived on that street. They looked at each other and said, "They want to pull us into San Jose? I don't think so." They literally formed the minutemen, and fought off this giant monster of San Jose. That was eight years before I came to town. I didn't realize how unified this city was because they had this history. I looked into all this history and how I happened to come in at the right time. Everything fell into place. The town was already a unified town with a strong spirit and good leadership.

You eventually got the film distributed nationally on video.

If you remember, about 1980 the video store thing started to happen. Anything that might be out on video had real potential. The distribution went out, and we got a contact from a guy in New York City. That was the key. He started booking sales. They would package the film with *Attack of the Killer Tomatoes*, just to see if anyone wanted it. They put all of these films together as a joke. Ours was one of the better bad films [*laughs*]!

The artwork came back with a different poster in Australia. Canada had a different version. They did put it out quite a bit. Recently I got one that was distributed in Japan. I've been having a lot of fun collecting the new designs and posters.

What was the actual budget?

We probably spent $5,000 or $6,000 by the time we paid for the original cut and shooting it. We had to be careful with the actual script because the film started with the model of the Kozy Kitchen being destroyed by the monster. Then we needed something before that to explain why that happened. Then we needed a scene to put before that scene. Then we needed a conclusion of what the result of that was. The film literally grew from the inside out, and we had to make it up as we were going along. It would be a great double feature with *Ed Wood* (1994). *Dark Star* (1974) was another film that was compared to our movie in some of the reviews.

Everybody really would love to be in a movie, and this was their chance to do it. They were actually asked to play themselves, which was my best direction [*laughs*]. We stayed back and tried not to get too close. We probably should have had more close ups to make it work, but I was coached that we need it to be out so wide to make it a 35mm release blow-up.

Did you actually get to appear on "The Tonight Show"?

The principal of our school grew up in the same area of Nebraska as Johnny Carson, so we wrote a nice long letter to Johnny Carson thinking we could get on the show. We had some correspondence going, and then the lawyers got involved and the whole film got held up. For one year I had to go around the town and talk to everyone who had been in it to ask if they'd sign a release. We couldn't make any commitments because the film got put in the closet for a couple of years.

The school district was kind of scared because you can take a film like this and make a porno out of it very easily by adding footage, and they were really nervous that there'd even be more jokes, so they were really concerned about that. I didn't want it to be taken advantage of, so I kind of defended it, too. We had a local printer in town who was going to pay the $10,000 bill that we owed the lawyer, so he made a bid to see if they would take it. There was no other bid that came in except for $85,000 from somebody in San Francisco.

Actress Priscilla House (daughter of Milpitas mayor Joe House, who also appeared in the film) waits as the crew prepares for the giant claw sequence (courtesy Robert Burrill).

We didn't know who they were or what they were going to do with it. We felt pretty confident, because Mr. Loughborough had been in the town as long as I had, that he would be a good person to have it.

As a result, George and I have a pretty good friendship. If I ever need anything printed, he lets me come over and print it.

I didn't realize that he'd done quite as much as he had. Recently, he came over to me and said, "We've made some money with this movie. I've pretty much made my money back." George put probably another $10,000 after that into recutting the other version. He was really a close part of it and real proud to say that he owned the movie.

It would have been nice to have kept ownership, in some ways. It could have paid for my son's education; that would have been nice to have done that. Everybody looks at me and says, "I wish you would have kept the movie to yourself." I owed it to my reputation, though. I said if we ever made any money, I'd give it to the school district, and I needed to live with that. I said what I said, and I really need to stand away from it.

Who was this Texas distributor?

A guy named William Thrush. He was a big, classical tycoon guy that had done another film. He did a film with somebody in Utah that was a Native American Indian. He had a 35mm film that was talking about somebody that looked like a drug dealer, but he was really a Native American making health supplies. He wanted to take this film, which ends with a big barbeque and American flags, and thought it would be a good film to run with it, because it was a cooperative, proud-to-be-an-American type of movie. He felt that would be a good double billing.

I got involved with watching that film come together, and hoping that ours could be released. The film really became a monster. It kind of changed my life when all that happened.

But that gets into the red tape. We brought it back to the principal the next day and said, "Hey, we sold this thing, and he offered us $100,000 dollars," and the school district didn't know what to do with the $100,000 except to give it to the council. The lawyers got involved, you know, and then it *really* became a monster. He needed it right away, and we didn't have the legal paperwork and the proper releases available. It took some time for the lawyers to do that. The guy needed the film right away and then he said, "You've got to give it to me right away. I'm gonna pay for the first cut." He wanted to cut from 120 minutes to something a little tighter that would play better in other cities. We couldn't give it to him within the time and he had to withdraw his bid to buy the film. It sat there for a couple of years in a closet, and it was just really frustrating. We really wanted to have this happen and it didn't happen.

Tell me about the DVD.

We had a trailer with Paul Frees, two-and-a-half minutes, as well as a 30-second lift, and a 15-second lift. That's what we've got presented. I've been thinking I'd love to put together a director's commentary and everything. Now that we've got access to things like Apple's iMovie, that can happen.

I was approached by Celestial Arts at one point. They did a bunch of books on Bruce Jenner, the decathlon winner. There was a book that his wife wrote. So they took on the film and got me a ghostwriter, and put together a book called *The Making of The Milpitas Monster: Feature Films at the Community Level*. We worked on it quite a bit. Then when the film didn't go out, they decided not to go with this. They gave me the covers and that was the end of that.

I've always thought that would be an interesting thing. I did chapter curriculum on how you could go into any community, look at the physical environment of the location, and come up with some motifs so you could make a film in your own town. That was a curriculum that I always wanted to finish. I thought, with all these pictures I've got, I've got some that would make a nice spread.

There is another film that's out now, Al Gore's *An Inconvenient Truth* (2006), that has a similar theme [*laughs*]. As silly as *The Milpitas Monster* is, there was a message here: We're all gonna see pollution in the end, my friend. So I'm thinking about doing a Charlie Rose-type thing where you get some of the more influential people together, and doing another version where you might even have some commentary. It's a great tool for getting younger people involved with it, although younger kids will look at this movie and compare it to *Star Wars*. "Boy, this film sure is slow!" But then you get the other audience that looks back, and it has a little bit of *American Graffiti* to it.

Of course, we were trying to make an homage, and I think it's a good B-movie. People that watch it don't get up and walk away. It's got parallel editing, and it seems to build. The first cut was done in the 1950s style, where the monster doesn't even show up until the end of the movie, so we turned it around where the monster comes out about a minute into the movie. It's been structured pretty well.

There were a couple of scenes that were deleted that I'd like to put in, but everyone involved thought it was better paced as the 70-minute version.

There was talk of a sequel at one point, correct?

There was a thought to do *Milpitas 2*, and I spent a couple of years of my life putting that screenplay together. I think that was even better that the original. It was interesting to try it 20 years later: "The city of Milpitas is all grown up, but it's not alone. *Milpitas Monster 2*—it's back, and this time we're not kidding!"

I don't know if you remember Krazy George. He was the big cheerleader that appeared for the Kansas City Chiefs and San Jose State. Right in the beginning of the movie, this guy growls like a lion. That's him. He was another person that helped me a lot with the film.

Krazy George was also at San Jose State, one year ahead of me, and was also assigned to do his student teaching at Samuel Ayer High School in 1968. I remember meeting him physically when we collided during a student-faculty softball game in 1969. At that time, George was really beginning his manic cheerleading exhibitions as a classic Spartan. He was and still is amazing. We stayed in touch, and it was convenient in 1974 to have him come and growl like a lion for our logo. He always appeared as the San Jose Spartan, which was practically the same as our Trojans mascot.

He's the guy that invented the wave. A lot of people don't know that. Ten years ago we did this pick-up where he came in and did a cheer with the kids, and it's a really nice piece. I put that into a presentation and we just showed it on local television. We showed *The Milpitas Monster* with that scene in Japanese with subtitles. It was the footage we did as a promo for *Milpitas Monster 2*.

[*NOTE: Krazy George Henderson, the self-proclaimed World's Most Famous Cheerleader, began cheering as a student at San Jose State in 1968, and later worked for the San Jose Earthquakes, Oakland Seals, and Kansas City Chiefs. He claims to have invented "the wave" in 1981 at an Oakland Athletics' game against the New York Yankees. His Web site is www.krazy george.com.]*

Some of the people that were involved with me before thought, "Boy, if we'd have known we were actually going to make a feature, we would have approached it differently." But I found the town had grown up. We had a different school district, and there was a lot of education to reorient people to know how much community effort we had. They closed the high school I was at. They moved us to a newer high school. That was another whole communication thing. The school was laid out differently. The campus was spread out. On the first campus, we had 45 teachers; now we had 150 teachers. I found that communication was almost impossible.

Then we had a new administrator that ran the district. They were impressed with what they saw, but didn't realize how involved it was. I was all ready to talk to Sun Microsystems, which had just moved some of its new offices to Milpitas. Spielberg had worked with some of their computers for *Jurassic Park* in 1993, and we needed their technology. I thought we could get some sponsorship, and the administrator said, "Oh, you want to ask for money from Sun Microsystems? I've already asked them for money and I don't want you talking to them." It was just the wrong person, wrong place. The local newspaper had been purchased by a different person, too. It was so frustrating.

I finally got to a point that I raised so much money, and people had their hand out and said, "If you want to do this, pay me and we'll do it." It was a different group of people. The Silicon Valley started moving in here. That was one of the reasons I wanted to try it, because of the technology. I thought I had a good chance to do it. But the newspaper and the superintendent didn't quite follow through. The lawyers were another thing, too. They were really worried about lawsuits. You should have seen the paperwork I had to go through, and the insurance. It got to be crazy.

You have to go back and say 1973 and 1974 was a real magical time. I think when you look back on it,

Student Scott Parker gets suited up as The Milpitas Monster with some help from Patti Thorpe, whose mother created the costume (courtesy Robert Burrill).

that's really how it happened. The story of the *Milpitas Monster* is really a story of how everything was in the right place and in the right town. I watched these big garbage trucks come up to my street, and just really took advantage of what was happening right in front of me. That was the magic.

Is the film still screened around Milpitas?

Every Halloween it was a natural for a fundraiser, so various groups would take it on. I've been so involved in this Milpitas Historical Society, we've been using it as a historical vehicle.

They've got this new technology with Apple Computer called iMovie, which I'm just getting into. Now I can really go ahead and make the same films I would do on 16mm, and I'm kind of glad I waited awhile. I'm right in the middle of doing a piece for the Alviso book I just wrote for Arcadia Publishing. We're getting into movie making indirectly that way. This is a whole other genre potential. It's really an amazing thing to see.

I've also got a film with Ruth Bernhard, which is probably my masterpiece as far as documentary filmmaking. She's 101, and was friends with Ansel Adams. I've gone on to do films about photographers. Everybody remembers me as the guy who did *The Milpitas Monster*. Well, I've done other films beyond that. Twenty years later we tried *Milpitas Monster 2*, and I thought I just about overdid it. So I said, "No more filmmaking for me. It's too political." Now I'm kind of inspired by this iMovie stuff. My juices are starting to move again. The DVD presentation can really look like 35mm. I took my Bernhard movie, went to the Balboa Theater and ran it at 100 feet. I came in as a guest speaker and said, "My God, that looks like 35mm."

It seems like the technology might make it possible for more people to make these types of movies.

Even this film, somebody could take this and redo some of the animation scenes, add just a few things and a little more dialogue, and it could be another movie. Somebody down in Los Angeles ripped us off and called it *The Mutant Beast*. You can probably order it on Amazon. The guy actually took our movie, and right when our title comes up, he fades to black and puts up *Mutant Beast*! Loughborough took him to court or gave him some serious letters about him ripping us off.

When we did the first release of the movie, we did cut one and cut two. When Monaco Labs released the film, I thought they released cut three, but they released cut two, which still had some sound bugs in it that I'd spent a year fixing. I don't know how many tapes they sent out, probably 1,000 tapes. That's the one *Variety* saw in Los Angeles. They just wrote, "Unviewable." They somehow got the wrong version. Monaco said, "You should have taken the original out. We don't know one from the other." That's a classical horror story in its own right [*laughs*]. Now everyone's getting a copy of *The Milpitas Monster*, and it's a copy of a copy. I was real concerned about quality. That's why I did the re-release.

What are you doing now? Are you still teaching?

Well, after 35 years of teaching I got this retirement thing, and they had a buy out. They actually paid me to leave! I don't miss the bells ringing all the time and putting up with the administrators. You have to realize that high school is a time when kids are learning to grow up, and they cannot be quite accountable because they're not 18 years old yet. There's this game that goes on in public education where the kids say, "Well, I didn't understand, so you just didn't say it right." The way education changed, because of the lawyers, they would say, "Mr. Burrill, you have to give this student a chance to take the test again. He didn't quite get it." After so many years you realize the game that you're playing is not quite the real world. You're teaching the real world, but it's frustrating. When most of us get to retirement age, we're finally ready to retire [*laughs*]. It's not because of the kids. It's because of the red tape and the confinement that is going on. We really could teach if they would just let us teach.

Nobody really knows how to teach well, and that was the thing about this curriculum when it took off. It had wide-open potential. Talk about an educational experience! We had everyone, even the math department, involved with it, and it was just learning by doing. Not teaching to the test. The kids involved with it really had something special. It was so unique. After that experience, the years after that were always downhill compared to what happened during that particular year. I'll never forget seeing all these TV people coming in for the premiere. There were five or six networks with their cameras. It was magical.

Part II • The Films

State-by-State Listing of Regional Horror Films, 1958 to 1990

The following is a state-by-state listing of regional, independent horror films produced between 1958 and 1990. Alternate titles are listed in parentheses, along with release dates. For films currently available on legitimate DVD, distributor names have been listed at the end of each entry, again in parentheses.

Key to Abbreviations: *D—Director; W—Writer; P—Producer; EP—Executive Producer; AP—Associate Producer; C—Cast*

ALABAMA

Valley of Blood (*Legend of Valley of Blood*, 1973)

D: Dean Turner; W: Wayne Forsythe; P: John Daly; C: Penny DeHaven, Ernie Ashworth, Zeke Clements, Wayne Forsythe, Herman Floyd

Lost film allegedly produced by the prolific John Daly, who would go on to produce *Platoon* and *The Last Emperor*. It was filmed some time before 1971, and it may or may not be about an alchemist who turns into a monster.

Writer and actor Wayne Forsythe wrote a number of western novels. DeHaven, Clements, and Ashworth were country singers.

ALASKA

Claws (1977)

D: Richard Bansbach, R.E. Pierson; W: Chuck D. Keen, Brian Russell; P: Chuck D. Keen; C: Jason Evers, Leon Ames, Anthony Caruso, Carla Layton, Myron Healey

Often confused with Williams Girdler's *Grizzly* (1976) or its unreleased sequel, this hunters-versus-bear film was the brainchild of Alaska Pictures head Chuck D. Keen. A notoriously cantankerous figure in his hometown of Juneau, Arkansas-born Keen began making films as a civilian cameraman during the Vietnam War (logging 3,300 combat flight hours) and later shot documentary footage for Disney. After making the children's film *Joniko and the Kush Ta Ta* (a.k.a. *Wilderness Journey*, 1969), he produced the pro-war documentary *No Substitute for Victory* (1970), narrated by John Wayne and directed by Robert Slatzer, who would later become a preeminent Marilyn Monroe conspiracy theorist. Wayne later provided accommodations on his yacht for the all-star cast of Keen's *The Timber Tramps* (1975), which included Claude Akins, Leon Ames, Stanley Clements, Joseph Cotten, Rosey Grier, Tab Hunter, Stubby Kaye and Cesar Romero. Keen also wrote and produced *Challenge to Be Free* (1975), starring Mike Mazurki.

When he wasn't making films or hobnobbing with over-the-hill actors, Keen operated a gift shop, ran unsuccessfully for the Juneau Assembly (four times), and pursued his (some would say quixotic) dream of building a tramway on Mount Juneau, a project that made little headway despite significant investments on Keen's part (another developer eventually built a tram on Mt. Roberts). He died in 2003.

The director of *Claws*, Richard Bansbach, produced the obscure slasher film *Bits and Pieces* (1985). Star Jason Evers was in *The Brain that Wouldn't Die* (1962) and *Basket Case 2* (1990), both made in New York.

ARIZONA

The Haunted (1979)

D: Michael A. DeGaetano; W: Michael A. DeGaetano; P: Michael A. DeGaetano, Nicholas P. Nizich; C: Aldo Ray, Virginia Mayo, Ann Michelle, Carl B. Belfor, Linda Best, Robert Bickston

In the 1860s, a Native American girl is accused of witchcraft and left in the desert to die. A century later, the arrival of her possible reincarnation (Michelle, in a dual role) at a run-down movie ranch sparks a series of murders. Filmed at the Apacheland Movie Ranch in Arizona.

This was DeGaetano's second genre film after *UFO: Target Earth* (1974), which he made in Georgia. He later made the women's basketball film *Dribble* (*Scoring*, 1979) in Iowa. (Code Red)

Natas: The Reflection (1983)

D: Jack Dunlap; W: Jack Dunlap; P: Jack Dunlap (EP), Peggy Dunlap (EP); C: Randy Mulkey, Pat Bolt, Craig Hensley, Kelli Kuhn, Fred Perry

A reporter investigates the Native American legend of Natas, a demon that is holding the souls of the dead prisoner so he can take them down to hell, in this slow-moving (and weird) film that also features an Indian mystic and a ghost town filled with zombie cowboys.

The Indian mystic Smohalla in this film was based on a Native American prophet from the Pacific Northwest. The Dunlaps also worked on the Arizona-lensed *Fleshburn* (1984).

ARKANSAS

The Barbaric Beast of Boggy Creek Part II (*Boggy Creek II: The Legend Continues*, 1983)

D: Charles B. Pierce; W: Charles B. Pierce; P: Charles B. Pierce, Joy N. Houck Jr.; C: Charles B. Pierce, Cindy Butler, Chuck Pierce, Jimmy Clem, Serene Hedin, Don Adkins

Pierce returns to his bigfoot roots with this fictional sequel from Howco about a college professor (Pierce himself) and a group of students out hunting for the monster in the familiar Fouke swamps. Clem plays a cranky hermit who kidnaps a young Sasquatch and raises the ire of its rampaging mother. Much of the cast (including Pierce) wear frighteningly short cut-off blue jeans.

This film was later lampooned on *Mystery Science Theater*. Pierce finished off the 1980s with *Hawken's Breed* (1987), a western with Peter Fonda that was distributed by New World. (Elite Entertainment)

The Day It Came to Earth (1979)

D: Harry Thomason; W: Paul Fisk; C: Wink Roberts, Roger Manning, Robert Ginnaven, Rita Wilson, George Gobel; P: John Braden, Harry Thomason (EP), Vernon Williams (AP), Bill Blackburn (AP)

A meteor falls into a lake and reanimates the corpse of a man who was killed by gangsters. This was one of Thomason's final horror efforts before he married Linda Bloodworth and segued into TV production. Paul Fisk also wrote *The Evictors* (1979) for Charles B. Pierce. Manning appeared in *The Shadow of Chikara* (1977). (Image)

Encounter with the Unknown (1973)

D: Harry Thomason; W: Jack Anderson, Joe Glass, Hillman Taylor, Harry Thomason; P: Joe Glass; C: Rod Serling, Gene Ross, Rosie Holotik, Mark F. Barnes, Charlie Dell, Bill Thurman, Annabelle Weenick

Debut effort from Harry Thomason, an Arkansas native and former high school football coach who later produced the TV series "Designing Women" and "Evening Shade" with his wife, Linda Bloodworth-Thomason.

Rod Serling hosts this anthology film about paranormal events, featuring several Larry Buchanan and S.F. Brownrigg regulars. In the first story, a woman puts a curse on the three men who inadvertently caused her son's death. The second, and most well remembered by viewers who saw the film when they were young, is about a boy who finds a mysterious hole in the ground. The third retells the familiar "Girl on the Bridge" urban legend about a ghostly hitchhiker.

Holotik was in *Playboy* and was married to *Horror High* (1974) producer James Graham. Co-scripter Hillman Taylor also wrote *Zontar: the Thing from Venus* (1966) and appeared in *The Eye Creatures* (1965).

A childhood friend of Charles B. Pierce, Thomason ran the Arkansas–based film company Centronics International in the 1970s. He was a close friend of former President Bill Clinton, and produced the biographic film *The Man from Hope* (1992) for his campaign. Thomason was also involved in the "Travelgate" controversy, served as co-chair of the 1992 Presidential Inauguration Committee, and testified before the grand jury investigating the Monica Lewinsky scandal. He later produced *The Hunting of the President* (2004). (Code Red)

www.mozarkproductions.com

It's Alive! (1969)

D: Larry Buchanan; W: Larry Buchanan; P: Larry Buchanan, Edwin Tobolowsky (AP); C: Tommy Kirk, Shirley Bonne, Bill Thurman, Annabelle Weenick, Corveth Ousterhouse

Another of Buchanan's AIP-TV projects, this one about the crazy owner of an out-of-the-way tourist trap/reptile farm (Thurman) feeding people to a giant prehistoric monster (actually, the same critter from the earlier *Creature of Destruction*, 1967). Former Disney star Kirk plays a paleontologist held captive in the subterranean monster's lair.

This was mostly filmed in Eureka Springs, Arkansas The opening sequences were filmed at Dinosaur World, an old tourist attraction in nearby Beaver, Arkansas, that was at one time called John Agar's Land of Kong. According to 1991 article in Psychotronic magazine, Agar (who appeared in a number of other Buchanan films) lent his name to the park as a favor to owner Ken Chilles, who added a King Kong statue to the park (which Agar never visited) to capitalize on the 1976 Dino De Laurentis remake. *It's Alive!* Was allegedly based on a short story ("Being") by Richard Matheson. (RetroMedia)

The Legend of Boggy Creek (1972)

D: *Charles B. Pierce;* W: *Earl E. Smith;* P: *Charles B. Pierce, L.W. Ledwell (EP), Earl E. Smith (AP);* C: *Vern Stierman, Chuck Pierce Jr., William Stumpp, Will E. Smith, Lloyd Bowen, J.E. "Smokey" Crabtree*

    This documentary-style film is based on the legend of the Bigfoot-like Fouke Monster, which made headlines around Fouke, Arkansas, in 1971 when a local family claimed they were attacked by the creature. Although the film partly inspired the makers of *The Blair Witch Project* (1999), anyone who saw this when they were younger will probably remember it as being much scarier than it actually is.

    Pierce, who had worked in advertising and TV production, borrowed money from a local trucking company (Ledwell & Son Enterprises) to finance *Boggy Creek*. He initially four-walled the film himself before teaming up with Howco owner Joy Houck for a wider release. The film was a surprise hit, grossing nearly $20 million in 1973, and not only kick-started the bigfoot craze of the 1970s, but put Pierce in a position to produce and direct another nine films over the next decade. He followed up with *Bootleggers* (1974), a moonshine film starring Paul Koslo, Dennis Fimple, Slim Pickens, Jaclyn Smith and Joy Houck, Jr., and *Winterhawk* (1975), with Leif Erickson, Woody Strode, L.Q. Jones, and Dawn Wells.

    In 2008, Pierce was honored by the Little Rock Film Festival with a lifetime achievement award and the establishment of the Charles B. Pierce Filming Arkansas award for local filmmakers. He died in 2010.

    You can learn more about Smokey Crabtree and the Fouke Monster at *www.smokeyandthefoukemonster.com*. (Sterling)

Psycho from Texas (*Wheeler/The Mama's Boy/The Hurting/The Butcher/Evil + Hate = Killer*, 1974)

D: *Jim Feazell;* W: *Jim Feazell;* P: *Jim Feazell, Jack Collins, Sherry Feazell (AP);* C: *John King III, Herschell Mays, Tommy Lamey, Candy Dee, Janel King, Joanne Bruno, Jack Collins, Christian Feazell, Linnea Quigley*

    A crazy drifter (King) is hired to kidnap a wealthy oil man, then terrorizes the man's daughter.

    Details vary as to exactly when and where this film was shot. A review in *Variety* in 1982 claimed it was filmed in Louisiana in 1974, but it was actually made in El Dorado, Arkansas, and briefly released as *Wheeler*. New footage was filmed in California later in the 1970s, including an uncomfortable scene in which King forces a waitress (Linnea Quigley) to strip naked, then dumps a beer over her head. Feazell later sold the film to a different distributor, who re-edited and released it as *Psycho from Texas*.

    Feazell worked in Hollywood as a stuntman (including on *The Wild Bunch* and *Butch Cassidy and the Sundance Kid*), cinematographer and singer, and headed his own film companies in Arkansas and Arizona. He also worked on *Kingdom of the Spiders* (1977).

    Cinematographer Paul Hipp had credits on several Sunn Classics productions in Utah, and he and Feazell worked together on *Blood and Lace* (1971). Feazell later made some short films, a horror anthology called *Horror Showcase* (1985), and wrote several novels, including one called *Come the Swine* about possessed wild hogs.

Return to Boggy Creek (1977)

D: *Tom Moore;* W: *John David Woody;* P: *Bob Gates, Robert Buford (EP), Jamie Coulter (EP), Robert A. Geist (EP), Joe Hathoot (EP), Clyde H. Jones (EP), L.W. Ledwell Jr.(EP), Stephen H. Ledwell (EP), Ken Wagnon (EP);* C: *Dawn Wells, Dana Plato, David Sobiesk, Marcus Claudel, Jim Wilson*

    Mark of the Witch director Moore made this unofficial *Boggy Creek* sequel using cast and crew members who had worked on other Charles B. Pierce productions. This one is more of a family film, with the monster coming to the aid of two children lost in the swamps.

    The Ledwells, who also financed the original *Boggy Creek*, operate a Texarkana-based truck manufacturing company.

Revenge of Bigfoot (*Rufus J. Pickle and the Indian*, 1979)

D: Harry Thomason; W: Dwayne; P: Joe Glass, Harry Thomason; C: Rory Calhoun, Mike Hackworth, T. Dan Hopkins, Patricia Kane, Jeffrey L. Cox

One of the last of Thomason's indie features before he switched to television productions, this one concerns a bigot (Hackworth) harassing an Indian and running afoul of a sasquatch. Hackworth also appeared in *The Town that Dreaded Sundown* (1976).

So Sad About Gloria (*Visions of Evil*, 1973)

D: Harry Thomason; W: Marshall Riggan; P: Harry Thomason, Douglas Jackson (AP); C: Lori Saunders, Dean Jagger, Robert Ginnaven, Lou Hoffman, Seymour Trietman, Linda Wyse

A recently released mental patient may be committing a series of axe murders.

Saunders had been one of the stars of *Petticoat Junction* and was also in Jack Hill's *Blood Bath* (1966). Several of the cast members were also in Thomason's *The Great Lester Boggs* (1975). (Code Red)

The Town that Dreaded Sundown (1977)

D: Charles B. Pierce; W: Earl E. Smith; C: Ben Johnson, Andrew Prine, Dawn Wells, Jimmy Clem, Charles B. Pierce, Robert Aquino, Earl E. Smith; P: Charles B. Pierce, Tom Moore (AP), Samuel Z. Akroff (EP)

Jim Feazell's *Psycho from Texas* (1974) was actually filmed in Arkansas, severely re-edited and released under at least three different titles, including *Wheeler* and *Evil + Hate = Killer*.

This was Pierce's first non–Howco release, and the first of several for American International Pictures. Like *Boggy Creek*, the film takes a pseudo-documentary approach to another true story, the unsolved "Texarkana Moonlight Murders" that occurred in 1946. A hooded man (dubbed "The Phantom" by the local press) murdered between four and six people over the space of several months before disappearing. Only one major suspect ever emerged, a car thief named Youell Swinney, who was sentenced to life in prison on unrelated charges. He died in 1994.

In the film, the killer wears what appears to be a pillowcase on his head, both recalling the similarly attired Zodiac Killer, and foreshadowing the hooded Jason Voorhees of *Friday the 13th, Part 2*

Lori Saunders is terrorized by an axe-wielding maniac (Robert Ginnaven) in *So Sad About Gloria* (1973), an early production by Arkansas director/producer Harry Thomason.

(1981). Pierce took his usual creative license with the story, even concocting a scene in which a woman (Pierce's then-wife, Cindy Butler) is stabbed with a trombone that has a knife attached to it.

In 1977, the Texarkana, Arkansas, city council voted to file a lawsuit against Pierce for advertising that the killer was still roaming free there. According to an Associated Press article, the council's lawsuit was filed after Texarkana officials visiting Washington, D.C., were "kidded about the advertisement."

The script supervisor on this film was Barbara Pryor, wife of Arkansas governor (and future Senator) David Pryor, who worked with Pierce on a number of other films and served as executive producer on *Shadow of Chikara* (1977). The Pryors' son, Mark Pryor, is the current Senator for Arkansas.

The director followed this film with the western *The Winds of Autumn* (1976), with Jack Elam, Prine, Dub Taylor and Jeanette Nolan; *Grayeagle* (1977), with Ben Johnson and Iron Eyes Cody; and *The Norseman* (1978), his ill-conceived Viking epic (shot in Florida and North Carolina) starring Lee Majors, Mel Ferrer, Jack Elam, and Cornel Wilde.

CALIFORNIA
(See Introduction)

COLORADO

The Jar (1984)

D: Bruce Toscano; W: George Bradley; P: Charles MacLeod; C: Gary Wallace, Karin Sjöberg, Robert Gerald Witt, Dean Schoepter, Les Miller

Here's an odd one: A man named Paul (Wallace) is in an auto accident involving another car, then takes the elderly driver of the vehicle back to his apartment. The old man vanishes, but leaves behind a mason jar containing a nasty-looking fetus. Paul then hallucinates and has nightmares while trying to romance his neighbor (Sjöberg).

This Denver production was Toscano's only film.

CONNECTICUT

Attack of the Beast Creatures (*Hell Island*, 1985)

D: Michael Stanley; W: Robert A. Hutton; P: William R. Szlinsky, Michael Stanley, Robert Haborak (AP), Robert W. Sherwood (AP); C: Robert Nolfi, Julia Rust, Robert Lengyel, Lisa Pak, Frank Murgalo, Robert A. Hutton, Joanne Stanley

Survivors of a shipwreck face furry, fanged trolls (which look suspiciously like the nasty doll from *Trilogy of Terror*, 1975) on a deserted island (which looks suspiciously like the backwoods of Connecticut). Although out of print on video for many years, you can order a DVD from director Stanley himself at *www.beastcreatures.com*, and learn more about his new(er) comedy *Doing Agatha* (2006) at *www.doingagatha.com*.

Cannibal Campout (1988)

D: Tom Fisher, Jon McBride; W: John Rayl; P: Tom Fisher, Jon McBride, Marshall Peck (AP), Joseph Salheb (AP); C: Jon McBride, Amy Chludzinski, Christopher A. Granger, Richard Marcus, Gene Robbins, Carrie Lindell, Joseph Salheb

College kids on a campout are attacked by three backwoods hillbillies (one of whom wears a jet pilot helmet) with a taste for human flesh and gratuitous profanity. Includes tons of over-the-top gore combined with mostly awkward acting — except for a stand-out performance by Marcus, who is hilarious as the most talkative of the three killers.

This was the debut shot-on-video feature of actor/director McBride, who also made *Woodchipper Massacre* (1989) and *Feeders* (1996). He's directed another eight films since, the last being *Black Mass* (2005). He also frequently collaborates with the like-minded Polonia brothers, and appeared in *Blades* (1989). Associate producer Peck is a casting director. Shot in New York and Connecticut. (Camp)

The Curse of the Living Corpse (1964)

D: Del Tenney; W: Del Tenney; P: Del Tenney, Alan V. Iselin (AP); C: Roy Scheider, Helen Warren, Robert Milli, Margot Hartman, Hugh Franklin, Candace Hilligoss

A dead man with a fear of being buried alive appears to be terrorizing his relatives from beyond the grave after they fail to meet the conditions of his will. This was the film debut of Roy Scheider, and also features *Carnival of Souls* (1962) star Candace Hilligoss. (Dark Sky)

Deadtime Stories (1986)

D: Jeffrey Delman; W: Jeffrey Delman, J. Edward Kiernan; P: Jeffrey Delman, William Paul, William J. Links (EP), Steve D. Mackler (EP); C: Scott Valentine, Nicole Picard, Matt Mitler, Cathryn de Prume, Melissa Leo

Scott Valentine made two horror films at the height of his brief run as Justine Bateman's dimwitted boyfriend Nick on "Family Ties": this film and the goofy *My Demon Lover* (1987). This anthology horror/comedy had a theatrical run and a very successful video release.

A man babysitting his nephew tells the boy three scary stories: a variation on Little Red Riding Hood featuring a werewolf; a story about psycho killer Goldi Lox and the three equally deranged members of the Baer family; and Valentine's segment about a trio of evil witches.

Delman had previously written *Stuck on You!* (1983) for Troma, and co-wrote the script for *Voodoo Dawn* (1990), based on a John Russo novel. He has since served as a writer on several kids shows (including "Dexter's Laboratory"). His only other directing credit is *Random Shooting in L.A.* (2002). Executive producer William J. Links also produced *Deep Throat* (1972). (Image/Mill Creek)

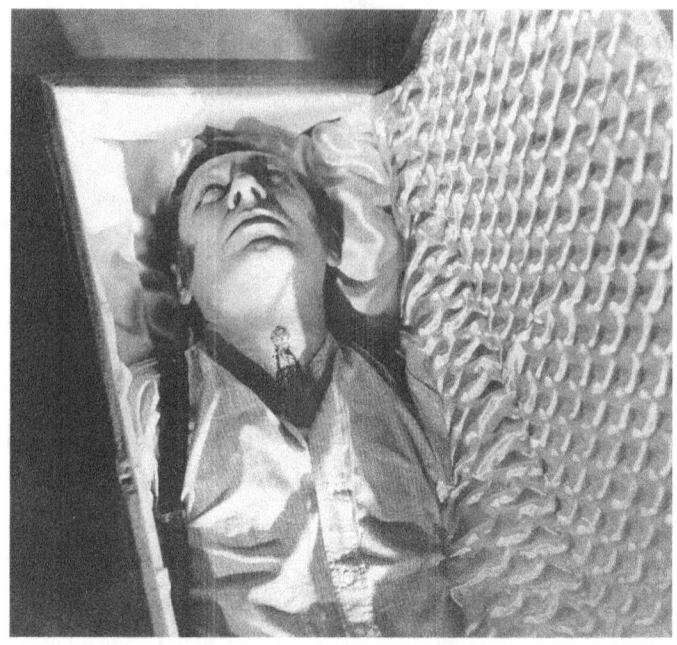

J. Frank Lucas as a decidedly dead corpse in Del Tenney's *Curse of the Living Corpse* (1964).

Death Collector (1988)

D: Tom Garrett; W: John McLaughlin; P: Jean Bodon, Paul Falcone, Tom Garrett, Leonard Wurm; C: Daniel Chapman, Ruth Collins, Loren Blackwell, John Pierce, Karen Rizzo, Phil Nutman

A post-apocalyptic western from bottom-of-the-barrel distributor Raedon Home Video. This is the only directing credit for Garrett, who otherwise has worked in production, distribution, advertising and public relations. Actor Phil Nutman wrote for *Fangoria*, and recently penned a film called *Shiver* (2007) that reunited several cast and crew members from *Death Collector* and *The Shaman* (1987). (Synergy)

Disconnected (1983)

D: Gorman Bechard; W: Gorman Bechard, Virginia Gilroy; P: Gorman Bechard; C: Frances Raines, Mark Walker, Carl Koch, Professor Morono, William A. Roberts, Bechard

Artsy debut effort from Bechard about a pair of twin sisters (one of whom works in a video store) and a sex killer called "The Slasher." Bechard followed this with *Psychos in Love* (1987), and several films for Charles Band's company. He continues to make films and write novels in Connecticut. www.gormanbechard.com

The Horror of Party Beach (1964)

D: Del Tenney; W: Richard Hilliard, Ronald Gianettino, Lou Binder; P: Del Tenney, Alan V. Iselin (AP); C: John Scott, Alice Lyon, Allan Laurel, Eulabelle Moore, Marilyn Clarke

   The second and most famous of Tenney's New England schlock films is about radioactive sea

The promotional filmbook published for Del Tenney's *The Horror of Party Beach* (1964).

monsters attacking teeny boppers. With bikers, frenetic dancing, music by the Del-Aires (including the outstanding "Zombie Stomp"), and an unforgettable monster attack on a slumber party.

The film was released on a double feature with *The Curse of the Living Corpse* (1964), and was the subject of a photo book from Warren Publishing.

Tenney was a stage actor who had previously worked as an assistant director on *Satan in High Heels* (1962) and *Orgy at Lil's Place* (1963) before making a series of low-budget horror films that included *Psychomania* (*Violent Midnight*, 1963) and *I Eat Your Skin* (*Zombies*, 1964). He and his wife Margot Hartman also made *Clean and Narrow* (1999), along with the horror films *Do You Wanna Know a Secret?* (2001) and *Descendant* (2003). Associate producer Iselin, who owned a chain of movie theaters, also made *Frankenstein Meets the Space Monster* (1965). (Dark Sky)

The House That Cried Murder (*No Way Out/The Bride*, 1973)

D: Jean-Marie Pelissie; W: John Grissmer, Jean-Marie Pelissie; P: John Grissmer; C: Robin Strasser, John Beal, Arthur Roberts, Iva Jean Saraceni

This weird little Bryanston release is an uneven but occasionally fascinating bit of murderous melodrama from one-shot director Pelissie. A jilted bride uses her wealthy father's resources to trap and torture her philandering fiancé and his lover in their new house. A print of this film has also turned up bearing the title *Last House on Massacre Street*.

Grissmer directed *Blood Rage* (1987) in Jacksonville, Florida, and wrote the Georgia-based film *Scalpel* (1977). (BCI/Brentwood)

I Spit on Your Grave (*Day of the Woman*, 1978)

D: Meir Zarchi; W: Meir Zarchi; P: Meir Zarchi, Joseph Zbeda; C: Camille Keaton, Eron Tabor, Richard Pace, Anthony Nichols, Gunter Kleemann

Originally made as *Day of the Woman*, distributor Jerry Gross gave the film its more exploitive title when he re-released it in 1980. Keaton (allegedly a grand-niece of Buster Keaton) plays a writer who retreats to the countryside in search of seclusion, but is attacked and raped by a gang of local goons in an unbearably lengthy sequence. Left for dead, she returns to seek gruesome revenge.

Zarchi (who was married to Keaton at the time) has said he was inspired to write this film after he tried to assist a rape victim in New York City. Gene Siskel and Roger Ebert singled it out for scorn in their newspaper columns and on "Sneak Previews," and the video was banned in several countries.

Camille Keaton was later married to producer Sidney Luft, an ex-husband of Judy Garland. In 1993, she appeared (using a pseudonym) in Donald Farmer's *Savage Vengeance*, which was presented on a video as a sort-of sequel to *I Spit on Your Grave*. Zarchi later directed *Don't Mess with My Sister* (1985). A remake was released in 2010. (Elite)

The Last House on the Left (1972)

D: Wes Craven; W: Wes Craven; P: Sean S. Cunningham; C: Sandra Cassel, Lucy Grantham, David Hess, Fred J. Lincoln, Jeramie Rain, Marc Sheffler, Richard Towers, Cynthia Carr

Grim thriller about a trio of sick criminals who kidnap, torture and kill two young girls, then inadvertently wind up spending the night in the home of one of the girls' parents. Inspired by Ingmar Bergman's *The Virgin Spring* (1960).

This controversial film launched the careers of both Craven and Cunningham, and was popularized through Hallmark Releasing's memorable slogan "To avoid fainting, keep repeating: 'It's only a movie ... it's only a movie ... it's only a movie,'" which the company also used for S.F. Brownrigg's *Don't Look in the Basement* (1973). Roger Ebert, who a few years later would spearhead a campaign against violent films, gave *Last House* a surprisingly good review when it was released.

Ohio native Wes Craven was a college professor and taxi driver who had co-directed *Together* (1971) with Cunningham, and worked on a number of adult films in the early 1970s. Hess was a songwriter (penning tunes for Elvis and Pat Boone) and a Mercury Records A&R executive before he started acting in the early 1970s. He later directed *To All a Good Night* (1980). Actress Jeramie Rain was married to Richard Dreyfuss, and Sheffler (who plays Junior) became a sitcom wrier.

Fred Lincoln was a prolific porno actor and director before and after he appeared in *Last House*. He also had roles in Andy Milligan's *Fleshpot on 42nd Street* (1973) and Cunningham's *Case of the Full Moon Murders* (1973), and directed and appeared in *The Last Whore House on the Left* (2004). At one time he owned the notorious New York sex club Plato's Retreat.

Cunningham and Craven produced the 2009 *Last House* remake. (MGM)

Let's Scare Jessica to Death (1971)

D: John D. Hancock; W: John D. Hancock, Lee Kalcheim; P: Bill Badalato, Charles B. Moss, Jr.; C: Zohra Lampert, Barton Heyman, Mariclare Costello, Kevin O'Connor, Gretchen Corbett, Alan Manson

Well-regarded thriller about a woman (recently released from a mental institution) who moves to a remote apple farm with her husband and a friend, where she is tormented by mysterious voices and a strange female squatter (Costello) who may or may not be the ghost of a woman drowned in a nearby lake in the 1800s. It was originally conceived as a comedy by screenwriter Kalcheim, who replaced his own name with a pseudonym (Norman Jonas) after his script was altered.

The memorable advertising campaign for one of cinema's most shocking exploitation films, *The Last House on the Left* (1972) (courtesy Fred Adelman).

Hancock had primarily worked in theater prior to this film. He later directed *Bang the Drum Slowly* (1973), *Prancer* (1989) and *Suspended Animation* (2001). He was also the first director of *Jaws 2* (1978), before being replaced by Jeannot Szwarc.

Badalato went on to produce *Nighthawks* (1981), *Top Gun* (1986) and other big-budget films. Charles Moss and his father (Charles Moss, Sr.) owned a chain of East Coast movie theaters, including the Criterion in New York. Filmed in Old Saybrook and East Haddon, Connecticut (Paramount)
www.letsscarejessicatodeath.net

Psychomania (*Violent Midnight*, 1963)

D: Richard Hilliard, Del Tenney; W: Richard Hilliard, Robin Miller; P: Del Tenney, Art Wolff (AP); C: Lee Philips, Shepperd Strudwick, James Farentino, Sylvia Miles, Jean Hale, Lorraine Rogers, Margot Hartman, Dick Van Patten

A knife-wielding murderer terrorizes a Connecticut town in Del Tenney's first feature, which was based on a murder that occurred at Bennington College while his wife was attending school there.

Tenney co-directed and wrote the film (without credit), and his father-in-law provided most of the budget. (Dark Sky)

Psychos in Love (1987)

D: Gorman Bechard; W: Gorman Bechard, Carmine Capobianco; P: Gorman Bechard, Charles Band; C: Carmine Capobianco, Angela Nicholas, Debi Thibeault, Patti Chambers, Carla Bragoli, Carrie Gordon

Actor Kevin O'Connor meets his end in *Let's Scare Jessica to Death* (1971).

A manicurist and a strip club owner, who also happen to be psycho killers, fall in love after they discover their mutual hatred of grapes. A cannibal plumber tries to blackmail them. The film was adapted for the stage in 2003 and performed at the Broom Street Theater.

Bechard followed with *Galactic Gigolo* (1988), *Twenty Questions* (1989), and *Cemetery High* (1989), also filmed in Connecticut. As of this writing, his most recent project is *Color Me Obsessed: A Film About The Replacements* (2011). (Media Blasters)

www.psychosinlove.com

Woodchipper Massacre (1989)

D: Jon McBride; W: Jon McBride; P: Jon McBride; C: Kim Bailey, Tom Casiello, Denice Edeal, Jon McBride, Patricia McBride, Robert C. Moseley Jr.

Second shot-on-video horror film from *Cannibal Campout* (1988) director McBride. After their babysitting aunt dies, three children dispose of her body using the titular machine. McBride based this on an actual murder where a husband had chopped up his wife, stored her body parts in a freezer, and then dropped them into a woodchipper. (Camp)

DELAWARE

Redneck Zombies (1987)

D: Pericles Lewnes; W: Zoofeet, P. Floyd Piranha, Fester Smellman; P: Pericles Lewnes, George Scott, Edward Bishop (EP), William E. Benson (AP); C: Stan Morrow, Brent Thurston-Rogers, Zoofeet, Alex Lewnes, William-Livingston Dekker, P. Floyd Piranha, Lisa M. DeHaven, Steve Sooy

Redneck moonshiners put radioactive waste in their hooch and turn into flesh-eating zombies in this shot-on-video horror-comedy that was distributed by Troma. It was shot for approximately $8,000 in Delaware and Maryland.

Pericles Lewnes (his real name) is a former wrestler who worked on a number of other Troma films and several documentaries about mixed martial arts fighting. His most recent film is *Loop* (2007). (Troma)

FLORIDA

Alien Dead (1980)

D: *Fred Olen Ray;* W: *Martin Alan Nicholas, Fred Olen Ray;* P: *Fred Olen Ray, Chuck Sumner, Henry Kaplan (EP), Shelley Youngren (AP);* C: *Buster Crabbe, Raymond Roberts, Linda Lewis, George Kelsey, Mike Bonavia, Dennis Underwood, John Leirier, Rich Vogan*

A meteor crashes into the Florida swamps and turns some tourists into man-eating zombies in this ultra-cheap second feature from Wellston, Ohio's own Fred Olen Ray.

Ray made this film (the second-to-last for Crabbe) in Florida for $12,000 before relocating to California, where he made a much bigger splash with *Scalps* (1983). Executive producer Kaplan was a former executive at Cinemation (the Jerry Gross company), and had worked on *I Drink Your Blood* (1970). (RetroMedia)

Barracuda (*The Lucifer Project*, 1978)

D: *Harry Kerwin;* W: *Harry Kerwin, Wayne Crawford;* P: *Harry Kerwin, Wayne Crawford;* C: *Wayne Crawford, Jason Evers, Roberta Leighton, Bert Freed, William Kerwin, Cliff Emmich*

Waste from a chemical plant causes local marine life to become both homicidal and hypoglycemic (!). A marine biologist (Crawford) and the local sheriff investigate in this *Jaws/China Syndrome* hybrid. Filmed in Ft. Lauderdale.

Crawford had appeared in and produced *God's Bloody Acre* (1975) and *Deadbeat* (1976) with Kerwin, and acted in *Sometimes Aunt Martha Does Dreadful Things* (1971). He continues to work as an actor and director. Harry Kerwin, brother of frequent H.G. Lewis actor William Kerwin, died in 1979. (Dark Sky)

The Beast That Killed Women (1965)

D: *Barry Mahon;* W: *Clelle Mahon;* P: *Barry Mahon, Bob Gordon (EP);* C: *Juliet Anderson, Janet Banzet, Byron Mabe, Darlene Bennett, Dolores Carlos, Gigi Darlene*

Horror-themed nudie with a gorilla terrorizing a nudist camp.

WWII vet Barry Mahon, who died in 1999, worked as the personal pilot and later manager of Errol Flynn. Byron Mabe was a busy TV actor who also worked as a producer and director, often with David F. Friedman. He directed *She Freak* (1967), *The Acid Eaters* (1968), *Space-Thing* (1968) and *The Adult Version of Jekyll & Hyde* (1972), among others. (Something Weird)

Blood Feast (1963)

D: *Herschell Gordon Lewis;* W: *Allison Louise Downe (story by H.G. Lewis and David F. Friedman);* P: *Herschell Gordon Lewis, David F. Friedman, Stanford S. Kohlberg (uncredited);* C: *William Kerwin, Mal Arnold, Connie Mason, Lyn Bolton, Scott H. Hall, Astrid Olson*

Inaugural gore film from H.G. Lewis about a mad Egyptian caterer (Arnold) who dismembers women in Miami as part of an offering to the Egyptian goddess Ishtar.

Lewis was a former English literature professor, radio station manager and advertising executive who entered Chicago's thriving commercial/industrial film industry in the 1950s. He moved into features with *The Prime Time* (1960), and after teaming with producer David F. Friedman, directed a series of nudie cuties (mostly filmed in Florida) until he made the move into horror films. *Blood Feast* was banned in several parts of the country, and many newspapers refused to run the film's advertisements, but this notoriety only helped fuel its success. Lewis and Friedman followed up with *Two Thousand Maniacs!* (1964) and *Color Me Blood Red* (1965).

Lewis directed another two-dozen films in Florida, Chicago and California before retiring from the industry in 1972, and at one point operated a Grand Guignol-style theater in Chicago called The Blood Shed Theatre. He has since written a number of books about advertising, direct marketing, public relations and plate collecting, and conducts direct marketing seminars. He and Friedman reunited for *Blood Feast 2: All U Can Eat* (2002). (Something Weird)
www.herschellgordonlewis.com

Blood Freak (1972)

D: Brad F. Grinter, Steve Hawkes; W: Brad F. Grinter, Steve Hawkes; P: Brad F. Grinter, Steve Hawkes; C: Steve Hawkes, Brad Grinter, Dana Cullivan, Heather Hughes, Bob Currier, Linda Past

This may be one of the most bizarre, confusing, and inexplicable films ever made. Hawkes plays Herschell, a muscle-bound biker who is torn between sexy Jesus freak Angel and her slutty, pot-smoking sister Ann. Herschell gets hooked (?) on marijuana, and takes a job at a poultry ranch where he eats some drugged drumsticks and turns into a bloodthirsty turkey monster. Brad Grinter, who worked on films with William Grefé and Bill Kerwin, occasionally interrupts the action as a chain-smoking narrator who rambles on about the dangers of drug abuse while obviously reading from a script.

The muscle-bound Hawkes (nee Steve Sipek), who was born in Croatia and has a fabulous head of hair, had previously appeared in a couple of Spanish Tarzan films, *Tarzan in the Golden Grotto* (1969) and *Tarzan and the Brown Prince* (1972). During the making of one of those films, he was severely burned and claimed in an interview that he had to take over directing and producing *Blood Freak* so that he could pay off his medical bills. Hawkes still lives in Florida, where he operates a small game preserve for exotic animals (formerly open to the public as an attraction called Jungle World). He made the national news in 2004 when one of his tigers escaped and was shot by Florida wildlife officials. He also made a film called *Stevie, Samson and Delilah* (1975) starring his son and some of his animals. (Something Weird)

Blood Rage (*Nightmare at Shadow Woods*, 1983)

D: John Grissmer; W: Bruce Rubin; P: Marianne Kanter, J.W. Stanley (EP), Stanley Westreich (EP), William C. Brakefield (EP), Jared M. Drescher (EP); C: Louise Lasser, Mark Soper, Marianne Kanter, Julie Gordon, Jayne Bentzen, Ted Raimi

A homicidal ten-year-old pins a murder on his twin brother, who is committed to a mental instution. Years later, their mother's impending marriage and the innocent twin's escape prompt another murder spree.

The film was released as *Blood Rage* in 1983, then cut and retitled *Nightmare at Shadow Woods* for a 1987 release. Kanter produced *Dark August* (1976) in Vermont, while Grissmer directed *False Face* (1977) in Georgia and wrote the Connecticut-lensed *The House That Cried Murder* (1973), which is playing at the drive-in in the opening sequence of this film. Both Grissmer and Kanter went on to write novels. *Mary Hartman* star Louise Lasser was also in Sam Raimi's *Crimewave* (1985). Filmed in Jacksonville, Florida (Legacy Entertainment)

Blood Stalkers (*The Night Daniel Died*, 1976)

D: Robert W. Morgan; W: Robert W. Morgan; P: Ben Morse; C: Ken Miller, Toni Crabtree, Jerry Albert, Celea Ann Cole, Robert W. Morgan

Middle-aged couples head out to the boonies around Ft. Lauderdale to "blood stalker country," where nasty hillbillies and a furry monster harass them until the film's over-the-top climax.

Robert Morgan is a well-known bigfoot researcher who founded the American Anthropological Research Foundation (he hosts the group's Internet radio program) and appeared in the documentaries *Monsters! Mysteries or Myths?* (1974) and *The Mysterious Monsters* (1976). *In Search of Bigfoot* (*The Search for Bigfoot*, 1976) was a documentary about one of Morgan's expeditions that was later re-edited into *Bigfoot: Man or Beast?*. He also worked on Williams Grefé's *Impulse* (1974) and *Mako: the Jaws of Death* (1976), and the Burt Reynolds film *Lucky Lady* (1975). In 2008, Morgan announced that two sequels to *Blood Stalkers* were in the works.

Miller was in *I Was a Teenage Werewolf* (1957) and other 1950s horror and rock and roll flicks. Albert was in *Little Laura and Big John* (1973) and *Mako*. Doug Hobart did the make-up. Shot in 1975 in the Everglades. (RetroMedia)

Blood Stalkers (1976) was originally released as *The Night Daniel Died* (courtesy Robert W. Morgan).

www.trueseekers.org   www.blogtalkradio.com/theaarfshow

The Brain Leeches (1977)

D: Fred Olen Ray; W: Brad Linaweaver, Fred Ray, Jim Kennedy; P: Fred Olen Ray; C: Paul Jones, Fred Olen Ray, Brian Wolfe, Ray Starr, Marcia Scott, Brad Linaweaver, Wild Bill Cooksey

Alien bugs turn Earthlings into mindless zombies in a bid to take over the planet. This was the first feature from director/pro-wrestler Fred Olen Ray, who would revisit the zombie concept in *The Alien Dead* (1980) a few years later. Sinister Cinema released the film on VHS.

Brad Linaweaver has continued to work in the film industry (occasionally with Ray), has written a number of science fiction novels, publishes *Mondo Cult* magazine, and is a prolific libertarian columnist and blogger. Cooksey was a local TV personality who held the world record for continuous playing as a one-man band.

The Brides Wore Blood (1972)

D: Robert R. Favorite; W: Liz Blanda, Bob Favorite, Dorothy Favorite, Tom Rahner, Bob Smith; P: Robert R. Favorite, Tom Rahner (AP), Rick Voight (AP); C: Rita Ballard, Chuck Faulkner, Dolores Heiser, Paul Everett, Bob Letizia, Jan Sherman

This odd, confusing and often dull film was shot by Robert Favorite, who ran a commercial film company and sometimes made movies for the Florida Department of Transportation. The patriarch of the DeLorca family wants to save his nephew from the centuries-old vampiric curse that has been visited on his family, so he kidnaps some female tourists and offers them as potential mates to the paunchy, caped bloodsucker.

Filmed in 16mm on the campus of Flagler College in St. Augustine, Florida, this movie never received a wide theatrical release. Fred Olen Ray purchased the film from Robert Favorite's widow and began distributing it on video in the 1980s.

Actor Paul Everett was the dean of Flagler College. In addition to *The Brides Wore Blood*, Favorite (who died in 1978) also directed *Riverboat Mama* (1969) and *Indian Raid, Indian Made* (1969), two nudies starring Morganna, the "Kissing Bandit" who notoriously interrupted professional sporting events to lip-lock athletes in the 1970s. (RetroMedia)

Case of the Full Moon Murders (*Case of the Smiling Stiffs*/*Sex on the Groove Tube*, 1973)

D: Sean S. Cunningham, Brad Talbot; W: Jerry Hayling; P: Sean S. Cunningham; C: Fred J. Lincoln, Ron Browne, Ron Millke, Ken Abston, Cathy Walker, Harry Reems, Jean Jennings

A female vampire drains male victims of their blood via fellatio in this early film from *Friday the 13th* (1980) director Cunningham.

Porn actor Fred Lincoln was also in the Cunningham/Wes Craven production *The Last House on the Left* (1972). Actress Jean Jennings began working in adult films as a teenager, and was later married to actor Joe Spinell. (Something Weird)

Children Shouldn't Play with Dead Things (1972)

D: Bob Clark; W: Bob Clark, Alan Ormsby; P: Bob Clark, Gary Goch, Peter James (EP); C: Alan Ormsby, Valerie Mamches, Jeff Gillen, Anya Ormsby, Paul Cronin, Jane Daly, Robert Phillip, Seth Sklarey

Members of an aggravating theater troupe in outlandish 1970s clothing trek to a burial island to conduct a Satanic ceremony at the behest of their arrogant leader (Ormsby), and wind up raising a gaggle of crusty-faced zombies.

Zombies invaded Florida in Bob Clark's *Children Shouldn't Play with Dead Things* (1972) (courtesy Fred Adelman).

This was Clark's first straight feature after making a couple of softcore cross-dressing films in the 1960s (*She-Man*, 1967, and *The Emperor's New Clothes*, 1966), and he intended it as a rip-off of *Night of the Living Dead* (1968). He followed it up with *Deranged* (1974), *Black Christmas* (1974) and *Dead of Night* (1974) before achieving mainstream success with *Porky's* (1981) and *A Christmas Story* (1983). He and Ormsby later collaborated on *Popcorn* (1991), although Ormsby was replaced as director early in the production. Clark and his son were killed in a car crash in 2007.

Ormsby also worked as a make-up artist on *Shock Waves* (1977), wrote *My Bodyguard* (1980) and the *Cat People* (1982) remake, published a how-to monster makeup book for children called *Movie Monsters* (1975), and (according to some sources) created Kenner's "Hugo: Man of a Thousand Faces" disguise puppet, one of the most disturbing toys released in the 1970s. Not long after *Children*, Ormsby directed an unreleased comedy called *The Great Masquerade* in Miami, produced by cinematographer Jack McGowan.

Executive producer Peter James has credits on *The Corpse Grinders* (1972), *Blood Orgy of the She Devils* (1972) and *I Dismember Mama* (1974). He and producer Peter Goch also worked on other Clark/Ormsby productions, and *Corpse Grinders* director Ted V. Mikels helped out behind the camera on this film. (VCI/Diamond)

Color Me Blood Red (1965)

D: Herschell Gordon Lewis; W: Herschell Gordon Lewis; P: David F. Friedman; C: Don Joseph (Gordon Oas-Heim), Scott H. Hall, Candi Conder, Elyn Wanrer, Pat Lee, Jerome Eden, James Jaekel

The third and final film in the H.G. Lewis/Dave Friedman "Blood Trilogy" is probably the lesser of the three. A crazed artist discovers that his paintings are much more interesting when he uses human blood instead of acrylics. Listen for the immortal line, "Holy bananas, it's a girls' leg!"

Friedman split with Lewis after this film was completed because of a dispute involving producer Stanford Kohlberg, and headed to California to make adults-only features. Gordon Oas-Heim, who had a lengthy career as a stage actor, was also in the Lewis film *Moonshine Mountain* (1964), and later turned up playing the butler on the short-lived "New Monkees" series. (Something Weird)

Day of the Reaper (1984)

D: Tim Ritter; W: Tim Ritter, Joe Preuth; P: Tim Ritter; C: Cathy O'Hanlon, Patrick Foster, Todd Nolf

Cheap, gory Super 8 film about a group of vacationing women being terrorized by a hooded, cannibalistic killer.

Ritter made this film while still in high school, and self-distributed it to video wholesalers. He directed a number of other direct-to-video horror films in the 1980s and 1990s, including *Twisted Illusions* (1985), the notorious *Truth or Dare? A Critical Madness* (1986) and *Killing Spree* (1987), and also worked with Donald Farmer. In addition to directing and producing, he has written two novels.

www.timritter.com

Dead of Night (*Deathdream*, 1974)

D: Bob Clark; W: Alan Ormsby; P: Bob Clark, Peter James, John Trent, Geoffrey Nethercott (EP), Gerald Flint-Shipman (EP); C: John Marley, Lynn Carlin, Richard Backus, Henderson Forsythe, Anya Ormsby, Jane Daly

The Ormsby/Clark team took a major creative leap forward in this creepy take on "The Monkey's Paw," about a Vietnam vet returning home as a bloodthirsty zombie. They followed this with the even better *Deranged* (1974).

The film was financed by Canadian company Quadrant Films. John Marley is best known as the producer who finds a horse's head in his bed in *The Godfather* (1972). Backus went on to be a soap opera actor and writer. Tom Savini provided the special effects. (Blue Underground)

Death Curse of Tartu (1966)

D: William Grefé; W: William Grefé; P: Joseph Fink, Juan Hidalgo-Gato; C: Fred Pinero, Babette Sherrill, Mayra Gomez Kemp, Bill Marcus, Gary Holtz, Doug Hobart

This was Grefé's South Florida version of a mummy film, with a Seminole witch doctor who can transform himself into a variety of animals hunting down the archaeology students who desecrated his tomb.

This played on a double feature with the lesser-known but far more ridiculous *Sting of Death* (1965). The two leads in this film were also in Grefé's *The Devil's Sisters* (1966). (Something Weird)

The Devil's Sisters (1966)

D: William Grefé; W: William Grefé, John Nicholas; P: Joseph Fink, Juan Hidalgo-Gato; C: Sharon Saxon, Fred Pinero, Velia Martinez, Anita Crystal, William Marcos, Babette Sherrill

This crime/sexploitation film is a previously lost Grefé production about a woman who is kidnapped by a white slavery ring, then tortured and humiliated.

The movie was based on the real case of the Gonzales sisters who ran a prostitution ring in Mexico. They were convicted of killing several dozen women and men in 1964.

K. Gordon Murray re-released this film in 1968 as *Sisters of the Devil*. The Gonzales sisters' story also inspired the novel *Las Muertas* by Jorge Ibargüengoitia and the Mexican film *Las Poquianchis* (1976). Although never available on video, in 2011 Grefé announced he had located a print in Germany and planned to release the film on DVD.

The Disturbance (1989)

D: Cliff Guest, Trent Meeks; W: Laura Radford; P: Ron Cerasuolo, Cliff Guest, Tom House, Peter Diebele; C: Timothy Greeson, Lisa Geoffrion, Ken Ceresne, Carole Garlin, Jerry Disson, Nina Mazey

A mentally ill young man (Greeson) slowly loses his grasp on reality in this slow-moving character study that ends with a bloody killing spree.

Newspaper accounts indicate the film was shot in 1985 as an educational docudrama about schizophrenia called *What's Wrong with the Neighbor's Son?*. That version was directed by Trent Meeks. Four years later, Guest added new footage to expand the film to feature length.

Producer Cerasuolo (who has primarily worked in the night club and restaurant industry) ran a movie-themed club called Flix that he claims was the inspiration for Planet Hollywood. Actress Carole Garlin is the mother of actor and producer Jeff Garlin (*Curb Your Enthusiasm*). Guest directed music videos (among them, Madonna's "True Blue" video) and commercials, and currently operates Knee Deep Films in Florida. (Media Blasters)

www.kneedeepfilms.com   www.cerasuolo.com

The Evil Below (1989)

D: Jean-Claude Dubois; W: Arthur Payne; P: Barrie Saint Clair; C: Wayne Crawford, June Chadwick, Paul Siebert, Sheri Able, Graham Clarke, Ted Le Plat

Crawford stars as the captain of a boat-for-hire who helps search for an allegedly cursed Spanish treasure. Like Crawford's *Barracuda* (1978), this is more of an action film than a horror film, but there are some weird nightmare sequences interspersed between the lengthy diving scenes.

Flesh Feast (1970)

D: Brad F. Grinter; W: Thomas Casey, Brad F. Grinter; P: Brad F. Grinter, V.L. Grinter, Veronica Lake (EP); C: Veronica Lake, Phil Philbin, Doug Foster, Harry Kerwin, Brad Townes

First horror film from director/actor/nudist Brad F. Grinter (who died in 1993), which was touted as the "Winner of the Golden Maggot Award for Boxoffice Excellence." Former starlet Veronica Lake headlines as a scientist who has discovered how to reverse the aging process for former Nazis using maggots, all at the behest of Adolf Hitler.

Lake had been a budding star at Paramount in the 1940s. By 1967, when this film was originally made, she was living in Hollywood, Florida, surviving on alimony payments and drinking heavily. She had already made a cheap film about dug trafficking called *Footsteps in the Snow* (1966) when Grinter approached her to work on *Flesh Feast*.

Screenwriter Thomas Casey later directed *Sometimes Aunt Martha Does Dreadful Things* (1971). Harry Kerwin served as production designer, and Doug Hobart handled the special effects.

God's Bloody Acre (1975)

D: Harry Kerwin; W: Wayne Crawford, Harry Kerwin, Robert Boodburn; P: Wayne Crawford, Andrew Lane; C: Wayne Crawford (as Scott Lawrence), Jennifer Stock (Jennifer Gregory), Kayelynne, Sam Moree, Robert Rosano, Daniel Schweitzer, William Kerwin

The Kerwin Brothers' entry in the killer hick genre is a misogynistic tale about three homicidal hillbilly brothers who menace a construction crew and some unlucky tourists.

Lane and Crawford (a Florida Atlantic University graduate) made this film for $22,500 over 16 days. Lane also worked on other Kerwin/Crawford projects, and went on to direct the Crawford-produced *Jake Speed* (1986), *Mortal Passions* (1989), and several TV movies. He and Crawford also worked together on the recent horror film *South of Hell* (2005). Jennifer Gregory is allegedly Jennifer Stock, who appeared in *Blood Sucking Freaks* (1976) and *Shriek of the Mutilated* (1974). (Code Red)

The Gruesome Twosome (1967)

D: Herschell Gordon Lewis; W: Allison Louise Downe; P: Herschell Gordon Lewis, Fred M. Sandy (EP); C: Elizabeth Davis, Gretchen Wells, Christ Martell, Rodney Bedell, Barbara Kerwin, Ronnie Cass

After a few forays into both skin

Killer hillbillies targeted construction workers and tourists in Wayne Crawford's *God's Bloody Acre* (1975).

and kiddie flicks following his split with Dave Friedman, Lewis returned to form with this tale of a crazy old lady and her retarded son who scalp coeds to supply their wig shop. To stretch the running time, Lewis opened the film with a surreal sequence featuring two head-shaped wig stands talking to each other.

Screenwriter and former probation officer Allison Downe (a.k.a. Bunny Downe, Vickie Miles, etc.) appeared in a number of nudie cuties, and also scripted and directed second-unit on some of Lewis' later films. J.G. "Pat" Patterson, who made *The Body Shop* (1973) and *The Electric Chair* (1977), provided the gore effects. (Something Weird)

Honeymoon of Horror (*Orgy of the Golden Nudes*, 1964)

D: Irwin Meyer; W: Alexander Panas; P: Herb Meyer, Lucille Cohen (AP), Martin Fried (AP); C: Robert Parsons, Abbey Heller, Alexander Panas, Vincenzo Petti, Beverly Lane, Snuffy Miller

The new bride of an eccentric sculptor may be the target of a murder plot hatched by one of her new husband's strange artist friends in this nudie film with horror overtones.

Irwin and Herb Meyer also produced *Passion Holiday* (1963), one of nine features planned for the Meyers' company, Flamingo Productions. Irwin Meyer later produced several TV movies. (Alpha)

I Eat Your Skin (*Zombies/Voodoo Blood Bath*, 1964)

D: Del Tenney; W: Del Tenney; P: Del Tenney, Dan Stapleton (AP), Jesse Hartman (AP); C: William Joyce, Heather Hewitt, Betty Hyatt Linton, Dan Stapleton, Walter Coy, Robert Stanton

A jet-setting writer (Joyce) is sent by his publisher to Voodoo Island to gather material for his next book. Instead, he encounters bug-eyed zombies who are trying to kidnap Heather Hewitt (from *Mission Mars*, 1968).

This sat unreleased for several years until Jerry Gross retitled it and added it to a notorious Cinemation double-bill with *I Drink Your Blood* (1970). Although it's somewhat obscure, it seems to have had at least some influence on latter-day Italian zombie flicks, with its jungle locale, delusional scientist and (especially) the oatmeal-faced, machete-wielding zombies. William Grefé was the second-unit director. Shot in Key Biscayne. (Something Weird/Mill Creek/Alpha/RetroMedia)

Impulse (*Want a Ride, Little Girl?*, 1974)

D: William Grefé; W: Tony Crechales; P: Socrates Ballis; C: William Shatner, Jenifer Bishop, Ruth Roman, Kim Nicholas, Harold Sakata, William Kerwin, Marcy Lafferty

Notoriously whacked-out Florida flick with a tour-de-force performance by Shatner as a sweaty, preening, homocidal gigolo out to separate wealthy women from their cash. After strangling his latest sugar mama, Shatner turns his attention to bedding Jenifer Bishop and swindling her best friend (Roman), but winds up in a war of wits with Bishop's bratty daughter, who knows he's not playing with a full deck. Notable primarily for Shatner's crazed, scenery-chewing performance as the infantile killer—decked out in a paisley pimp wardrobe, he rants, raves, cries, bites his fingernails, strangles Harold "Odd Job" Sakata, and tries to drown Bishop in a fish tank.

Shatner and Lafferty were married. Producer Socrates Ballis frequently appeared on "Rat Patrol" and "Mission Impossible," and was also in Grefe's *The Hooked Generation* (1968) and *The Godmothers* (1973). He and Bishop announced their engagement during the making of this film in 1972, although they were never actually married. He died in 1998. Screenwriter Tony Crechales wrote a number of much better psychological thrillers, including *The Killing Kind* (1973) and *House of Terror* (1973), and acted under the name Tony Kent in the 1950s. Filmed in Tampa Bay.

Island Claws (1980)

D: Hernan Cardenas; W: Jack Cowden, Ricou Browning, Colby Cardenas, Hernan Cardenas; P: Ted Swanson, Hernan Cardenas (EP), Dario Cardenas (EP); C: Robert Lansing, Steve Hanks, Nita

Talbot, Jo McDonnell, Barry Nelson, Martina Deignan

Pollution causes the local crab population (along with one giant crustacean) to turn hostile and attack people in this 1950s throwback eco-horror that resembles *Kingdom of the Spiders* (1977) and several other similar films.

Shot in Key Biscayne, *Island Claws* was the first and last film from Hernan Cardenas, described in newspaper accounts as a Colombian "abstract expressionist painter." Producer Dario was Hernan's brother. According to a 1987 article in the *Lakeland Ledger*, a third Cardenas brother, Gabriel, was connected to the Medellin drug cartel, and it was speculated that this film's alleged $3.5 million budget was a Medellin "investment." Hernan Cardenas came up with the idea for the movie while bicycling with his wife in Miami's Crandon Park.

In their effort to wrangle 2,000 crabs for the film, the producers offered $1 for every live land crab the locals could deliver to them. The 9,000-pound giant mechanical crab (dubbed "Mandy") allegedly cost $500,000 and was created by special effects artist Glen Robinson, whose credits stretched from *The Wizard of Oz* (1939) to the 1976 *King Kong* remake (which garnered him an Oscar). The news coverage of the production indicated that cinematographer Jimmy Pergola, editor Ron Sinclair and TV director David Whorf would "direct and edit" the film.

Swanson was a producer on *Hot Stuff* (1979), *Cool as Ice* (1991) and several TV movies, and worked regularly as a production manager and second-unit director. He also operated a marine survey company in Key Largo. He died in 2009.

Island Claws (1980) was touted as a $3.5 million potential blockbuster, but didn't even receive a theatrical release.

Killing Spree (1987)

D: *Tim Ritter;* W: *Tim Ritter;* P: *Al Nicolosi, Joel D. Wynkoop, Tim Ritter (EP);* C: *Asbestos Felt, Courtney Lercara, Raymond Carbone, Bruce Paquette, Joel D. Wynkoop*

A mechanic (the wild-eyed, bushy-bearded Asbestos Felt) who thinks his wife is cheating on him (her "diary" turns out to be a collection of trashy romance stories she hopes to sell) hunts down and kills her suspected lovers in a variety of gory and imaginative ways using a lawnmower, a hammer, a screwdriver, a chainsaw and a machete-equipped ceiling fan.

Ritter made this 16mm film for $75,000, and released it on his own video label in 1990 (Magnum Entertainment released it again in 1992). He has continued making direct-to-video horror flicks, including *Wicked Games: Truth or Dare 2* (1994), *Creep* (1995), and *Screaming for Sanity: Truth or Dare 3* (1998). Now a born-again Christian, he also directed *Reconciled Through the Christ* (2004), a religious horror film about another man in a troubled marriage who plans to go on a ... killing spree. (Camp)

Love Goddesses of Blood Island (*Six Shes and a He*, 1964)

D: Richard S. Flink; W: William Kerwin; P: Richard S. Flink, Frank Malagon, Hank Rifkin; C: Launa Hodges, Bill Rogers, Carol Wintress, Dawn Meredith, Liz Burton

An astronaut (Bill Rogers, star of *A Taste of Blood*, 1967) is stranded on an island with a tribe of violent women who torture and mutilate men. Also known as *Six Shes and a He*, this was probably the very first *Blood Feast* (1963) knock-off, and featured the special effects work of H.G. Lewis collaborator Harry Kerwin as well as a script by *Blood Feast* star William Kerwin.

Flink, a building contractor who also operated a drive-in, produced William Grefé's *Sting of Death* (1965). *Love Goddesses* was to be the first release from his Thunderbird International company, but only played a few theaters. Something Weird released a truncated, 28-minute version of the film on its *Sting of Death/Death Curse of Tartu* DVD, then issued a near-complete print a few years later. (Something Weird)

Mako: The Jaws of Death (1976)

D: William Grefé; W: William Grefé, Robert W. Morgan (as Robert Madaris); P: William Grefé, Bob Bagley (AP), Doro Vlado Hreljanovic (EP), Paul Joseph (EP), Robert Plumb (AP); C: Richard Jaeckel, Jenifer Bishop, Buffy Dee, Harold Sakata, John Davis Chandler

Although marketed as a *Jaws* knock-off, *Mako* is more in the vein of *Willard* (1971) and Grefe's own *Stanley* (1972), with Richard Jaeckel as a man with a mystical connection to sharks who kills anyone who threatens his aquatic friends.

Grefé had previously worked with sharks while shooting second unit on *Live and Let Die* (1973). This was his last horror film, as well as the last film appearance for Jenifer Bishop. Associate producer Bagley was also responsible for *Battle of the Network Stars*. Co-writer Robert Morgan worked on Grefé's *Impulse* (1974) and directed *Blood Stalkers* (1978).

The Nest of the Cuckoo Bird (1965)

D: Bert Williams; W: Bert Williams; P: Bert Williams; C: Bert Williams, Ann Long, Chuck Frankle, Jackie Scelza, Larry Wright

A detective on the trail of some moonshiners discovers an inn in the Everglades run by wacky showgirl Ann Long, a taxidermist who has created a gallery of stuffed humans.

This lost Miami-area film was made by a company called Experimental Camera Workshop in 1964. According to *BoxOffice*, the title song was written by Fulford Methodist Church organist Peggy Williams and performed by The Four Bits, a group that performed regularly at the Skyways Hotel.

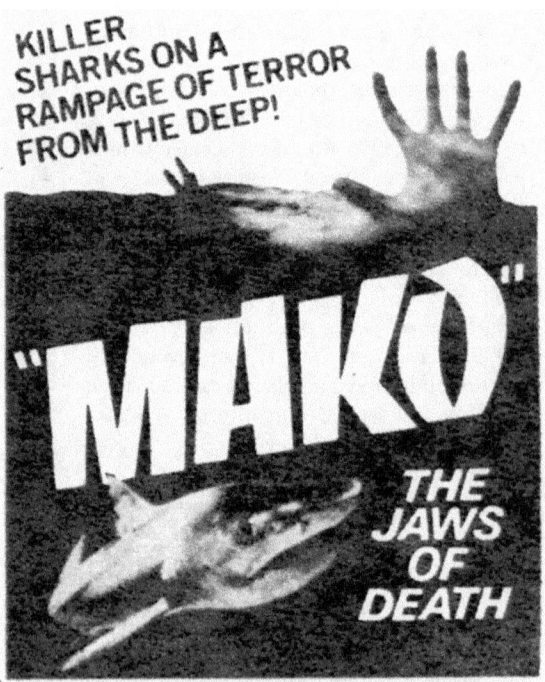

Richard Jaeckel used sharks to enact his revenge in William Grefé's *Mako: The Jaws of Death* (1976) (courtesy Fred Adelman).

Nude on the Moon (1961)

D: *Doris Wishman, Raymond Phelan*; W: *Doris Wishman, Raymond Phelan*; P: *Martin Caplan, Doris Wishman*; C: *Marietta, William Mayer, Lester Brown, Pat Reilly, Ira Magee, Lacey Kelly*

Two astronauts land on the moon and encounter topless, telepathic women with pipe-cleaner antennae on their heads.

Wishman was a housewife until the unexpected death of her husband. She found a job working for a sexploitation film distributor before striking out on her own as a filmmaker. This was her second film after *Hideout in the Sun* (1960), and helped establish her reputation for producing memorable (if idiosyncratic) sex films, most of them shot in New York. Music by Daniel Hart and Doc Severinsen. Shot at the Coral Castle in Coral Gables, Florida (Something Weird)

Satan Place: A Soap Opera from Hell (1990)

D: *Alfred Ramirez, Scott Aschbrenner*; W: *Mel Johnson, Alfred Ramirez, Scott Aschbrenner, Jeff Stogner*; C: *Warren Andrews, Lisa Hatter, Stephanie Spencer, Mark Rackstraw, Jeffrey Stogner*

Nude on the Moon (1961) was filmed at the Coral Castle in Coral Gables, Florida.

Rare, Miami-lensed horror anthology. According to the Joe Bob Briggs' review, the stories include a woman who uses zombies to kill sexist men, and a girl who gets ideas about how to killer her mother by watching slasher movies on cable TV.

Alfred Ramirez is a comic book artist, and the film was evidently adapted as a comic (released by Thunderhill Comics in 1992).

Satan's Children (1975)

D: *Joe Wiezycki*; W: *Gary Garrett, Ron Levitt*; P: *Joe Wiezycki*; C: *Stephen White, Eldon Mecham, Joyce Molloy, Kathleen Marie Archer, Rosemary Orlando, Harry Williams*

This Satanic oddity, made by the staff of WTVT-TV in Tampa, was rescued by Something Weird Video after decades of obscurity. Stephen White is Bobby, a troubled teenager with an abusive stepfather and a bratty stepsister who goes off for a night on the town and winds up being kidnapped and raped by a gang of burly hillbillies, dumped in a field, and then taken in by a cult of bickering, homophobic, Satanic hippies.

In May 1975, in a fairly crass stab at publicity, Wiezycki was quoted in *BoxOffice* as claiming that his film did not in any way inspire the murder of Kenneth Robert Houston in Tampa not long after the film was completed. Houston was killed by a young couple that claimed they were members of a cult.

Most of the cast came from the University of South Florida's theater department. Wiezycki, who died in 1994, also made a blaxploitation film called *Willy's Gone* (1972). (Something Weird)

Scarecrows (1988)

D: *William Wesley;* W: *Richard Jefferies, William Wesley, Marcus Crowder, Stephen Gerard;* P: *Ted Vernon (EP), Cami Winikoff, William Wesley;* C: *Ted Vernon, Michael David Simms, Richard Vidan, Victoria Christian, Kristina Sanborn, B.J. Turner, David James Campbell*

One of the last of the great Florida horror films (although, oddly, it's set in Southern California). A group of paramilitary bank robbers make off with $3 million from Camp Pendleton and hijack a cargo plane, the pilot and his daughter. When one of the gang members parachutes out of the plane with the loot, the others track him down to an abandoned farmhouse where they encounter murderous, scythe-wielding scarecrows.

This was the first film for director Wesley, producer Winikoff (who went on to work on the *Leprechaun* and *Warlock* franchises), cameraman Peter Deming, effects artist Norman Cabrera (who went to work for Rick Baker, and is a member of the band The Ghastly Ones), and production manager Barry Waldman (who went on to make bombastic action films like *The Rock*, 1996, and *National Treasure*, 2004). Top-billed producer/actor Ted Vernon, who provided the bulk of the financing, operates an auto restoration business in Miami, and has also worked as a boxer, professional wrestler and demolition derby driver.

Richard Vidan and Michael Simms had both been in *Hard Rock Zombies* (1985), and several members of the crew also worked on *Shallow Grave* (1987).

Cuban-born Wesley later directed *Route 666* (2001), and started a film school called the L.A. Feature Film Academy. He and Winikoff were briefly married. (MGM)

www.tedvernon.com   *www.lafeaturefilmacademy.com*

William Wesley's *Scarecrows* (1988) boasted impressive special effects from then-teenage artist Norman Cabrera, who went on to work with the legendary Rick Baker.

Scared Stiff (*The Masterson Curse*, 1987)

D: Richard Friedman; W: Daniel F. Bacaner, Richard Friedman, Mark Frost; P: Daniel F. Bacaner, Charles S. Carroll (AP); C: Andrew Stevens, Nicole Fortier, Mary Page Keller, Jack McDermott, Josh Segal

A family moves into the former home of an abusive slave owner, and the father is gradually possessed by the spirit of an African demon.

Director Friedman previously made the New York–lensed *Deathmask* (1984) as his Master's thesis while a student at NYU, and followed with the New Jersey film *Doom Asylum* (1987) before working in television ("Tales from the Darkside," "Friday the 13th," "Monsters"). His most recent films were *Dark Wolf* (2003) and *Born* (2007), and he is the co-founder of Lucky Butterfly Productions.

Sound editor Thomas Rondinella directed *Blades* (1989), and worked on *Girls School Screamers* (1986).

www.luckybutterflyproductions.com

Scream, Baby, Scream (1969)

D: Joseph Adler; W: Laurence Robert Cohen; P: Joseph Adler, Boris Pritcher (AP); C: Ross Harris, Eugenie Wingate, Chris Martell, Naomi Fink, Brad F. Grinter

A mad artist uses his zombie henchman to kidnap models so he can disfigure their faces in this rambling psychedelic horror film.

Adler also directed *Revenge is My Destiny* (1971) with Chris Robinson and *Convention Girls* (1978). He had made commercials and industrial films in New York before making this film, and has since become an award-winning director in the Florida theater community. He is currently the producing artistic director at the GableStage in Coral Gables. Chris Martell was in movies for H.G. Lewis, William Grefe, and the Kerwin brothers, and appeared in *Flesh Feast* (1970). Harry Kerwin was the production manager, Doug Hobart provided the makeup, and Brad Grinter appears in a small role. (Troma)

Scream Bloody Murder (*My Brother Has Bad Dreams*, 1972)

D: Robert J. Emery; W: Robert J. Emery; P: Robert J. Emery, Sam Hyman (EP), Paul Ecenia (EP); C: Paul Vincent, Marlena Lustik, Paul Ecenia, Nick Kleinholz III, Frank Logan

Not to be confused with that other *Scream Bloody Murder* (1973) movie, which was shot in California, this obscurity is about a disturbed young man who sleeps with mannequins, fantasizes about his sister, and goes on a killing spree.

Emery had previously made a number of independent films, including *Ghetto Freaks* (1970). He later made *The Florida Connection* (1974) with Massey Cramer (of *Legend of Blood Mountain* fame), *Ride in a Pink Car* (1974) with William Kerwin, and a bunch of documentaries. Most recently, he made a film called *Swimming Upstream* (2002) for the Lifetime Television Movie Channel, and helmed the cable series "The Directors."

www.robertjemery.com

Shallow Grave (1987)

D: Richard Styles; W: George Fernandez; P: Ralph Clemente (AP), Ed Fernandez (EP), George Fernandez (EP), Barry H. Waldman; C: Tony March, Lisa Stahl, Tom Law, Carol Cadby, Donna Baltron, Just Kelly, Kevin Quigley

Four girls on a road trip are terrorized by a rural sheriff after they see him murder a woman in the woods.

Producer Waldman and special effects artists Clifford Guest and Gary Roberts also worked on *Scarecrows* (1989). Ralph Clemente was a stand-in on "Flipper," and later became head of the film program at Valencia Community College in Orlando. He continues to make movies in Florida. Waldman went on to work with Jerry Bruckheimer.

Shock Waves (1977)

D: Ken Wiederhorn; W: John Kent Harrison, Ken Pare, Ken Wiederhorn; P: Reuben Trane; C: Peter Cushing, Brooke Adams, John Carradine, Fred Buch, Jack Davidson, Luke Halpin, D.J. Sidney

Tourists on a wrecked cruise ship seek shelter at an abandoned hotel on a small island where they encounter exiled Nazi commander Peter Cushing and his army of amphibious zombies. By far, the best of the then-popular Nazi zombie films, and much more entertaining than its aquatic Nazi zombie counterpart, *Zombie Lake* (1981).

Shot in 1975, partly at a vacant Biltmore Hotel, this was the first feature for Wiederhorn, who had previously worked at CBS in New York. He and producer Reuben Trane later made the obnoxious *King Frat* (1979) before Wiederhorn moved on to *Eyes of a Stranger* (1981) and a lengthy career in television. Trane, whose family owned the Trane air conditioning company, later became a boat designer.

Actor Luke Halpin had starred on "Flipper." Alan Ormsby did the makeup, and Fred Olen Ray was the still photographer. (Blue Underground)

Sometimes Aunt Martha Does Dreadful Things (1971)

D: Thomas Casey; W: Thomas Casey; P: Thomas Casey, Eva Barnett (EP), Paul Moore (AP), Ronald Sinclair (AP); C: Abe Zwick, Wayne Crawford, Marty Cordova, Yanka Mann, Robin Hughes, Don Craig, Brad F. Grinter, William Kerwin

Deranged story of two gay jewel thieves who go into hiding, with Zwick dressing in drag and impersonating his partner's aunt. The more submissive, younger thief Stanley (Crawford) brings home hippie girls who are promptly dispatched by the increasingly deranged "Martha."

Thomas Casey also co-wrote *Flesh Feast* (1970) and edited *Monster a Go-Go* (1965). Actor Wayne Crawford appeared in *God's Bloody Acre* (1975, which he wrote and produced), Harry Kerwin's *Deadbeat* (1976) and *Cheering Section* (1977), and *Barracuda* (1978). He later had producing and acting credits in *Valley Girl* (1983), *Night of the Comet* (1984), *Jake Speed* (1986), and *Servants of Twilight* (1991). He is currently on the faculty at the North Carolina School of the Arts in Winston-Salem.

Stanley (1972)

D: William Grefé; W: William Grefé, Gary Crutcher; P: John H. Burrows, William Grefé; C: Chris Robinson, Alex Rocco, Steve Alaimo, Susan Carroll, Mark Harris, Gary Crutcher

Robinson is a Seminole Indian and Vietnam vet who uses his collection of pet snakes to take revenge on his enemies — primarily a gang of snake poachers led by Alex Rocco.

Grefé developed and pitched this film (one of his most successful horror projects) to Crown International head Red Jacobs after the success of *Willard* (1971). Robinson also appeared in other shot-in-Florida films, including *Charcoal Black* (1972) and *Thunder County* (1974), and was later a regular on "General Hospital." He recently appeared in the film *Rez Bomb* (2008), set on the Pine Ridge Indian Reservation. (Rhino/BCI/Code Red)

Sting of Death (1965)

D: William Grefé; W: Al Dempsey, William Kerwin; P: Richard S. Flink, Joseph Fink, Juan Hidalgo-Gato, Hank Rifkin (AP); C: Joe Morrison, Valerie Hawkins, John Vella, Jack Nagle, Deanna Lund, Doug Hobart

The companion feature to Grefé's *Death Curse of Tartu* (1966) is about a marine biologist who can transform himself into a walking jellyfish monster (actually, special effects artist Doug Hobart in a diving suit with what appears to be a plastic sack over his head).

Vella was a former professional football player (for the Oakland Raiders) who also appeared in Grefé's *The Wild Rebels* (1966). The film features the Neil Sedaka song "Do the Jellyfish." (Something Weird)

A Taste of Blood (1967)

D: Herschell Gordon Lewis; W: Donald Stanford; P: Herschell Gordon Lewis, Sidney J. Reich; C: Bill Rogers, Elizabeth Wilkinson, William Kerwin, Lawrence Tobin, Ted Schell

This was Lewis' most elaborate horror feature. A descendent of Count Dracula slowly turns into a vampire and kills the relatives of those responsible for his ancestor's death.

Bill Rogers (who died in 2004) was a voice actor for K. Gordon Murray, and also appeared in *Love Goddesses of Blood Island* (1964), Murray's *Shanty Tramp* (1967), Lewis' *The Girl, the Body and the Pill* (1967), and the notorious *Flesh Feast* (1970). Lewis himself appears as a cockney sailor. Shot in Miami. (Something Weird)

Truth or Dare? A Critical Madness (1986)

D: Tim Ritter, Yale Wilson; W: Tim Ritter; P: Tim Ritter, Geoffrey Miller (EP); C: John Brace, Mary Fanaro, Terence Andreucci, Bruce Gold, A.J. McLean, Raymond Carbone

A man (Brace) finds his wife cheating on him with his best friend and has a breakdown. He begins playing truth or dare with imaginary people in a mental hospital, mutilating his own face in the process. He escapes (wearing a copper mask) and starts killing random strangers (using guns, knives and a chainsaw) while on his way to kill his ex-wife.

Future Backstreet Boy A.J. McLean appears in a small role. Carbone, who plays one of the detectives, was actually a retired police officer. The theme song was performed by Kay Reed and the Church of Our Savior Choir.

Ritter made this 16mm film on a budget of more than $200,000, just six months after he finished high school. It was financed by a group of investors from Chicago (who ran a company called Video Swap International/Peerless Films) that later tried to fire him from the film. A *Palm Beach Post* article from 1986 indicates that production manager Yale Wilson directed part of the film. An unofficial sequel, *Writer's Block: Truth or Dare 2* (1995) was directed by Chris LaMont, while Ritter himself helmed two official sequels, *Wicked Games: Truth or Dare 2* (1994) and *Screaming for Sanity: Truth or Dare 3* (1998). Filmed in Palm Beach, Florida (Sub Rosa)

www.timritter.com

Twisted Illusions (1985)

D: Tim Ritter, Joel D. Wynkoop; W: Tim Ritter, Joel D. Wynkoop; P: Al Nicolosi, Tim Ritter, Joel D. Wynkoop; C: Joel D. Wynkoop, Jerry Zel, Colleen Foley, Anthony T. Townes

A seven-part (!) horror anthology from Ritter and collaborator Joel Wynkoop, who would go on to work as an actor or producer on several subsequent Ritter projects. One segment of this film served as the basis for Ritter's *Truth or Dare?* (1986). He released a sequel in 2004.

Ritter had made one film prior to this, a $1,000 Super 8 production called *Day of the Reaper* (1984), which he self-distributed on home video.

Twisted Issues (1988)

D: Charles Pinion; W: Steve Antczak; P: Charles Pinion; C: Steve Antczak, Charles Pinion, Lisa Soto, Paul Soto, Chuck Speta, Sam Gough, Michelle Gould, Pam Gauthier

A skateboarding teenager is murdered, then brought back to life by a scientist. The resurrected kid (whose skateboard is now permanently attached to his foot) then takes revenge on his killers in this surreal experiment that also includes drugs, karate, medieval weaponry, and an all-knowing television set.

This shot-on-video movie (which received good notices in *Film Threat* and other magazines) was made in Gainesville, Florida, and features music by a number of local punk bands. Pinion, who also performed in the band Psychic Violents, later directed *Red Spirit Lake* (1993) and *We Await* (1996).

Antczak was the front man for the punk band Officer Friendly, and is now a writer. (Inferential Pictures)

www.charlespinion.com

Two Thousand Maniacs! (1964)

D: Herschell Gordon Lewis; W: Herschell Gordon Lewis; P: David F. Friedman; C: William Kerwin, Connie Mason, Jeffrey Allen, Ben Moore, Gary Bakeman, Jerome Eden

One of H.G. Lewis' best films is what the director once called a "bloody *Brigadoon*," with the victims of a Union Army slaughter returning to life and luring a group Yankee tourists into creative death traps. Lewis himself sang the bluegrass theme song. Shot in St. Cloud, Florida (Something Weird)

Wild Women of Wongo (1958)

D: James L. Wolcott; W: Cedric Rutherford; P: George R. Black, James L. Wolcott (EP); C: Jean Hawkshaw, Mary Ann Webb, Johnny Walsh, Cande Gerrard, Adrienne Bourbeau, Marie Goodhart, Michelle Lamarck

Odd picture about warring tribes of prehistoric cave dwellers (attractive women paired with brutish men in Wongo; and the citizens of Goona, who have the opposite problem) being invaded by a group of ape men. Filmed at the Coral Castle in Homestead, Florida, a tourist attraction built by Edward Leedskalnin, an eccentric who went to great lengths to conceal his construction methods. Doris Wishman's *Nude on the Moon* (1961) was also filmed there.

The Tubes recorded a song about this film on their album *Outside Inside* in 1983. In 2008, filmmaker Bruce Merwin announced a remake that was later canceled after a group of *Mystery Science Theater 3000* alums known as The Film Crew copyrighted their "riffed" version of the film. (Alpha)

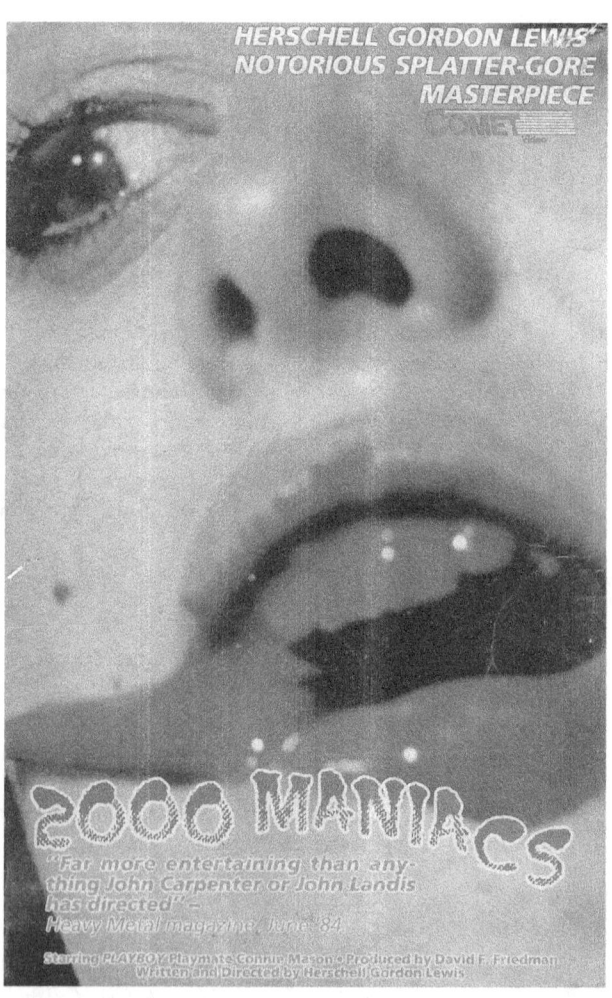

The striking video box cover for H.G. Lewis' *Two Thousand Maniacs!* (1964).

Zaat (*The Blood Waters of Dr. Z/Hydra/Attack of the Swamp Creature*, 1973)

D: Don Barton; W: Ron Kivett, Lee O. Larew, Don Barton, Arnold Stevens; P: Don Barton, Robert M. Smith Jr. (AP), Dick Stratton (AP); C: Marshall Grauer, Wade Popwell, Paul Galloway, Gerald Cruse, Sanna Ringhaver, Dave Dickerson

The mad Dr. Leopold (Grauer) attempts to create a race of fish people by injecting himself with a substance called Zaat and transforming into a weird looking killer catfish monster in this slow-moving but fun oddity.

Director Don Barton ran an industrial and commercial film company in Florida, and made this in an attempt to movie into feature filmmaking. The film wound up being released by a number of distributors (including Aquarius Releasing), with the film's title and opening credits altered. It was still playing theaters as late as 1982.

Barton had earlier optioned the novel *Surrounded on Three Sides* by John Keasler, but that project was never filmed.

In recent years, Florida fan Ed Tucker arranged for a 2001 theatrical screening of *Zaat* in Jacksonville and a VHS release of the original cut of the film.

Cinematographer Jack McGowan worked on Bob Clark movies, as well as *Mardi Gras Massacre* (1978). Filmed in Crystal Springs, Greencove Springs, and Marine Land of Florida. (Film Chest) *www.zaatmovie.com*

GEORGIA

Grizzly (1976)

D: William Girdler; W: Harvey Flaxman, David Sheldon; P: Harvey Flaxman, David Sheldon, Lee Jones (AP), Edward L. Montoro (EP); C: Christopher George, Andrew Prine, Richard Jaeckel, Joan McCall, Charles Kissinger, Joe Dorsey

Girdler left the comfy confines of Kentucky and headed to Georgia, armed with a better cast, an actual grizzly bear, and financing from low-budget distributor Edward L. Montoro of Film Ventures International (FVI). In this *Jaws* knock-off (inspired by screenwriter's Flaxman's youthful encounter with a bear), ranger Christopher George and wacky bear expert Richard Jaeckel have to stop a giant, killer grizzly from munching on national park visitors.

Although FVI would later move its operations to California, at the time *Grizzly* was filmed the company was based in Atlanta. Girdler and Montoro reteamed for *Day of the Animals* (1977), although Girdler eventually sued Montoro over the revenue (estimated at nearly $39 million) that *Grizzly* brought in to Film Ventures. Sheldon later wrote *Grizzly 2: The Predator* (1983), an unfinished film shot in Hungary that boasted among its cast a young Charlie Sheen, Laura Dern, John Rhys-Davies, and Kentucky's own George Clooney.

Kiss of the Tarantula (1976)

D: Chris Munger; W: Daniel Cady, Warren Hamilton Jr.; P: Curt Drady, Daniel Cady, John H. Burrows; C: Suzanna Ling, Eric Mason, Herman Wallner, Linda Spatz, Everly Eddins, Patricia Landon

A peculiar girl (Ling) can psychically control her pet spiders, using them to kill her philandering stepmother, as well as a gang of tormenting teenage hoods.

Filmed in 1974 in Columbus, Ga., *Kiss* was the brainchild of local resident Curt Drady, who had initially planned to make the film using only local talent. California-based producers Burrows and Cady, however, convinced Drady to import lead actors Ling and Mason. According to a 2002 interview with his daughter, Drady (who died in 1997) nearly bankrupted his family and almost lost his house when the film failed to turn a profit.

The house used in the film also served as a location for John Wayne's *The Green Berets* (1968). (VCI)

Legend of Blood Mountain (*Legend of McCullough's Mountain/ Blood Beast of Monster Mountain*, 1965)

D: Massey Cramer; W: Bob Corley; P: Don Hadley, Frank Winecoff (EP); C: George Ellis, Marianne Gordon, Erin Fleming, Bob Corley, Toni Taylor

Reporter Bestoink Dooley (Ellis) investigates the legend of a mountain-dwelling monster (a furbottomed, scaly-faced critter with tentacles on his hips) in this low-budget comedy shot on Stone Mountain.

Despite being both extremely cheap and extremely obscure, *Legend of Blood Mountain* had quite an active afterlife once its initial run through regional theaters was complete. Years later, producer and spook show magician Donn Davison added bigfoot footage to the film, creating a movie called *Legend of McCullough's Mountain* (1976) during the 1970s sasquatch craze. Davison himself appears as a bigfoot expert. The film was later acquired by Jeffrey C. Hogue, who retitled it *Blood Beast of Monster Mountain*. An edited version without Davison's footage was also released on video as *Demon Hunter*.

Bestoink Dooley/George Ellis was an Atlanta-area TV horror host who later managed the Ansley Mall Film Forum, where he programmed cult and arthouse films. He also played "Jake" in Gy Waldron's *Moonrunners* (1975), the character that served as the basis for Boss Hogg when Waldron recycled the premise as *The Dukes of Hazzard* several years later. Ellis died in 1983.

Director Cramer wrote and produced *The Florida Connection* (1974) with *Scream Bloody Murder* (1972) director Robert J. Emery. He also worked for Universal and Disney, and produced a Mexican film called *The Rage Within* (1963). (Something Weird)

The Offspring (*From a Whisper to a Scream*, 1987)

D: Jeff Burr; W: C. Courtney Joyner, Darin Scott, Jeff Burr; P: William Burr, Darin Scott, David Shaheen (EP), Bubba Truckadoro (EP), Ron Arnold (AP), Craig Greene (AP), Mark Hannah (AP), Mike Malone (AP), Allen Posten (AP); C: Martine Beswick, Lawrence Tierney, Susan Tyrrell, Vincent Price, Clu Gulager, Terence Knox, Terry Kiser, Rosalind Cash, Cameron Mitchell, Angelo Rossitto

After the execution of a female serial killer in Oldfield, Tennessee, a reporter (Tyrrell) visits local historian/librarian Vincent Price, who shares four stories about the town's horrifying history. The stories are about a con man double-crossing a voodoo practitioner; a glass eater at a 1930s carnival trying to escape his sideshow cohorts; and Union soldiers encountering a group of crazy orphans during the Civil War. An almost unrecognizable Gulager appears in the opening segment about a nerdy, repressed necrophiliac.

While the four main stories were filmed in Georgia, Price's linking segment was shot in California several months later after Burr secured additional financing. Since this was billed as his final genre appearance, he was visited on set by Roger Corman and Hazel Court.

Ohio-born Jeff Burr grew up in Dalton, Georgia (where this was partially filmed), and it was his first feature after leaving USC and directing the Civil War drama *Divided We Fall* (1982). He's gone on to direct a number of horror sequels including *Stepfather II* (1989), *Leatherface: Texas Chainsaw Massacre III* (1990), and *Pumpkinhead II* (1994), as well as *Eddie Presley* (1992) and *Straight Into Darkness* (2005). Darin Scott produced *Menace II Society* (1993) and *Tales from the Hood* (1995). Film journalist David Del Valle served as the casting director for this film, and Rob Burman provided the special effects. (MGM)

Scalpel (*False Face*, 1977)

D: *John Grissmer;* W: *Joseph Weintraub, John Grissmer;* P: *John Grissmer, Jospeh Weintraub, Lester Berman (AP);* C: *Robert Lansing, Judith Chapman, Arlen Dean Snyder, David Scarroll, Sandy Martin*

Lansing plays a surgeon who murders his wife and his daughter's boyfriend, then schemes to collect an inheritance from the missing daughter (left to her by a suspicious grandfather) by performing plastic surgery on a stripper to create a look-alike. Filmed in Covington, Ga. Grissmer wrote the Connecticut film *The House that Cried Murder* (1973), and directed *Blood Rage* (1987) in Florida. He also wrote the book *The Ghosts of Antietam* (1999).

The Slayer (*Nightmare Island*, 1982)

D: *J.S. Cardone;* W: *J.S. Cardone, William R. Ewing;* P: *William R. Ewing, Gerald T. Olson (AP), Anne Kimmel (AP), Lloyd N. Adams, Jr. (EP);* C: *Sarah Kendall, Frederick Flynn, Carol Kottenbrook, Alan McRae, Carl Kraines, Sandy Simpson*

Kendall is a painter troubled by nightmares about being stalked by the mysterious "Slayer." When her husband drags her and some friends to a remote island for a vacation, she realizes that the island has figured in her dreams. When she falls asleep, the monster in her nightmares begins killing her traveling companions.

Shot on Tybee Island in Georgia, *The Slayer* was the debut feature of director Cardone, and was shot with a mostly experienced cast and crew from Hollywood. Cardone has continued to work as a writer and director, and most recently co-wrote and produced the remakes of *Prom Night* (2008) and *The Stepfather* (2009). *The Slayer* was released by Continental Video on a tape that also included Fred Olen Ray's *Scalps*.

Squirm (1976)

D: *Jeff Lieberman;* W: *Jeff Lieberman;* P: *George Manasse, Edgar Lansbury (EP), Joseph Beruh (EP);* C: *Don Scardino, Patricia Pearcy, R.A. Dow, Jean Sullivan, Peter MacLean*

City boy Don Scardino, on a visit to see his girlfriend's family in rural Georgia, finds himself trapped after a downed power line electrifies the ground and unleashes a horde of blood-sucking worms on an isolated town. With special effects by Rick Baker.

New York–based filmmaker Lieberman also directed the excellent *Blue Sunshine* (1978) and *Just Before Dawn* (1981), as well as the more recent *Satan's Little Helper* (2004). Manasse also produced *Blade* (1973) and *He Knows You're Alone* (1980). Producers Lansbury and Beruh produced *Godspell*, in which Scardino appeared as Jesus. Filmed in Port Wentworth, Ga. (MGM)

UFO: Target Earth (1974)

D: *Michael A. DeGaetano;* W: *Michael A. DeGaetano;* P: *Michael A. DeGaetano, Thomas H. Talbert (AP);* C: *Nick Plakias, Cynthia Cline, LaVerne Light, Tom Arcuragi, Phil Erickson*

An electronics expert and a psychic investigate a UFO that may be submerged in a local lake. The film, shot around Atlanta, includes some early computer-generated special effects. It premiered in Albuquerque in May 1974.

Benton Harbor, Michigan, native DeGaetano made this film for less than $100,000 (some books claim $70,000) under the aegis of his Atlanta-based advertising firm, Centrum International Marketing Research/Centrum International Film Corp. A University of Michigan graduate, he had originally worked in theater, serving as general manager of the Ann Arbor Shakespeare Festival and the Michigan Professional Theater. According to a 1968 article in the Benton Harbor *News-Palladium*, DeGaetano also managed the Chicago garage band The Faded Blue, who appeared in H.G. Lewis' *Blast-Off Girls* (1967). He claimed in the article to have directed portions of that film, and to have worked behind the scenes on *The Killing of Sister George* (1968) and *They Shoot Horses, Don't They?* (1969). DeGaetano later helped write and direct infomercials, including spots for Scott Madsen's SoloFlex aerobics workout video.

He made *The Haunted* (1979) in Arizona, and as "Alessandro DeGaetano" (sometimes listed as Alessandro di Gaetano) directed *Bloodbath in Psycho Town* (1989), *Project: Metalbeast* (1995), and *Butch Camp* (1996). (RetroMedia)

Vampire Cop (1990)

D: Donald Farmer; W: Donald Farmer; C: Ed Cannon, Melissa Moore, Mal Arnold, Joey Thrower, Don Tilley, Morrow Faye, Donald Farmer

Farmer ventured out of Tennessee and into the wilds of Atlanta (and Florida) for this film about an undead policeman who kills other vampires.

Moore (who plays a reporter here) was in *Evil Spawn* (1987), on which Farmer had an early credit as a production assistant, and also appeared in *Samurai Cop* (1989), *Sorority House Massacre II* (1990), *Repossessed* (1990), and other low-budget action and horror films. Farmer, meanwhile, has continued making films in Tennessee (and elsewhere), the most recent being *Dorm of the Dead* (2006). He also made a documentary about the invasion of Iraq called *Whose War?* (2006) featuring "M.A.S.H." star Mike Farrell and former Dead Kennedy's frontman Jello Biafra, and appeared on the reality show "Megan Wants a Millionaire" in 2009.

HAWAII
(None)

IDAHO
(None)

ILLINOIS

555 (1988)

D: Wally Koz; W: Roy Koz; P: Wally Koz, Roy Koz (AP), Linda Koz (AP); C: Mara Lynn Bastian, Charles Fuller, Bob Grabill, Scott Hermes, Greg Kerouac

Wally Koz made this movie with the help of his family after seeing how successful cheap horror films were on video at the time. A necrophiliac slasher kills and dismembers teenagers (five couples in five nights, every five years) in this gory, shot-on-video horror film made in Chicago's Ukrainian Village and released by Koz's own King Video Distributors label. Koz, who was also a gold prospector, died of cancer in 2006 and his wife Linda was killed not long afterward in a fire. Special effects artist Jeff Segal also worked on *Re-Animator* (1985) and *Henry: Portrait of a Serial Killer* (1986). (Massacre Video)

Black Devil Doll from Hell (1984)

D: Chester Novell Turner; W: Chester Novell Turner; P: Chester Novell Turner; C: Shirley L. Jones, Rev. Obie Dunson, Keefe Turner, Chester Tankersley, Ricky Roach, Mari Sainvilvs

This is one of the earliest, and crudest, shot-on-video horror films. It's also one of the craziest black-cast films ever made. A deeply religious woman buys a blackface Jerry Mahoney puppet with dreadlocks. The possessed doll swears a lot and has sex with the woman, who (in what may be an homage to William Girdler's *Abby*, 1974) turns into a slutty sex fiend.

The film was shot with an off-the-rack camcorder, and the (not bad) synthesizer score was obviously played on a Casio keyboard held close to the built-in microphone on the camera during production. Turner later made the anthology film *Tales from the Quadead Zone* (1987).

Who is Chester N. Turner, and what demons drove him to create these freakish cinematic experiments? Nobody seems to know. A Turner imposter briefly emerged on MySpace a few years ago, and some sources now claim that Turner died in a car accident in the 1990s. (Massacre Video)

The Gore Gore Girls (1972)

D: Herschell Gordon Lewis; W: Alan J. Dachman; P: Herschell Gordon Lewis; C: Frank Kress, Amy Farrell, Hedda Lubin, Henny Youngman, Russ Badger

Lewis's final gore film before vanishing from the film industry for nearly two decades. A private detective investigates the gruesome murders of a several strippers in this wildly offensive mix of violence, gore, angry feminists, ugly naked people, and Henny Youngman.

This was Lewis' last film as a director until he made *Blood Feast 2: All U Can Eat* (2002). Lewis later declared bankruptcy after being sued by franchisees who had taken part in a failed auto rental franchise business. He and business partner Irving Kaufman were arrested in 1974 for their part in what was described as a "bogus" abortion referral franchise business; Lewis was eventually convicted of mail fraud charges related to the auto rental service. In an interview with John Waters in the book *Shock Value*, Lewis said he had simply acted as the advertising agency in the abortion referral business, and did not actually serve any jail time. By the early 1980s, he had reinvented himself as a direct marketing consultant, and he continues to write books and conduct marketing seminars. (Something Weird)

Monster a Go-Go (1965)

D: Bill Rebane, Herschell Gordon Lewis; W: Jeff Smith, Dok Stanford, Bill Rebane; P: Herschell Gordon Lewis (as Sheldon S. Seymour), Henry Marsh (AP), Bill Rebane; C: Phil Morton, June Travis, George Perry, Lois Brooks, Henry Hite

This Chicago-lensed monster movie was started by Bill Rebane (as *Terror at Halfday*), but completed by H.G. Lewis, and both directors' voices can be heard at various points throughout the film.

An astronaut returns from space as a giant, crusty-faced monster who can turn people's blood to powder. The star, Henry Hite, was actually over seven feet tall.

Rebane had worked part time for Lewis's commercial studio in the 1950s. In an interview with Bijouflix, he claimed he pitched this film to Ronald Reagan, whom he encountered on the street in Chicago one night. (Something Weird)

The Psychic (1968)

D: James F. Hurley; W: James F. Hurley, Herschell Gordon Lewis; P: James F. Hurley; C: Dick Genola, Robyn Guest, Arlene Banas, Elaine Blake

After being let down by H.G. Lewis' treatment of his script for *Something Weird* (1967), Hurley helmed this lackluster attempt to bring the world of psychic phenomenon to the screen. An ad executive (Genola) falls off a ladder and develops psychic powers, which he uses to launch a show business career. He eventually abandons his family and abuses everyone he comes in contact with.

Lewis acted as cinematographer on the film, and also added some softcore sex scenes when Hurley was unable to sell the film (it was released as *Copenhagen's Psychic Loves*). The trailer is a hoot. (Something Weird)

The Psychotronic Man (1978)

D: Jack M. Sell; W: Jack M. Sell, Peter Spelson; P: Peter Spelson; C: Peter Spelson, Chris Cargbis, Curt Colbert, Robin Newton, Jeff Cliendo

This obscure, Chicago-lensed sci-fi flick received a new lease on life when its title became synonymous with all that is weird and wild in cinema, thanks to writer Michael Weldon's late, lamented *Psychotronic* magazine.

Spelson was an insurance salesman who wanted to be an actor, and decided to produce this film as a starring vehicle for himself. He appears as Rocky Foscoe, a barber who can kill people with his mind. The film was shot guerrilla-style (without permits) as then–Mayor Richard Daley had actively discouraged film production in the city. That means all of the gun battles, car chases and explosions were staged without notifying the police (or anyone else).

The film also has a marvelous Web site (*www.psychotronicman.com*) where, among other things, you can buy *Psychotronic Man* underpants (and a DVD of the film). Director Jack Sell later made *Outtakes* (1987) and *Spygames* (1989), and also has a Web site at *www.sellcommunications.net*. Spelson died in 2006.

Something Weird (1967)

D: Herschell Gordon Lewis; W: James F. Hurley; P: James F. Hurley, Fred M. Sandy (AP); C: Tony McCabe, Elizabeth Lee, William Brooker, Mudite Arums, Ted Heil

An accident victim has his face restored by a hideous witch in exchange for becoming her lover, and develops psychic powers. He later helps the police find a serial killer. There's no gore, but McCabe is attacked by an evil blanket, and there's an LSD freak-out sequence.

This was Lewis' first film after moving his operation back to Chicago. He followed up with *The Girl, the Body and the Pill* (1967), *Blast-Off Girls* (1967), and *The Magic Land of Mother Goose* (1967), before heading back to Florida for the biker film *She-Devils on Wheels* (1968). He continued making sexploitation pics in Chicago and California until returning to horror again in 1970 with *The Wizard of Gore*.

Screenwriter/producer Hurley was a friend of TV psychic Peter Hurkos, and intended this as a serious study of psychic phenomenon. Disappointed by the results, he made his own film, *The Psychic* (1968). Hurley was also a college professor and a karate buff (which at least partly explains the awkward martial arts sequences). (Something Weird)

Tales from the Quadead Zone (1987)

D: Chester Novell Turner; W: Chester Novell Turner; P: Chester Novell Turner; C: W.J. Rider, Doug Davenport, Keefe L. Turner, Larry Jones, Shirley Latanya Jones, Tommy L. Miller

Second and final (?) camcorder epic from Turner, with actress Shirley Jones returning from *Black Devil Doll from Hell* (1984). Here, she stars as the mother of a dead boy who returns from the grave with a book called *Tales from the Quadead Zone*. She reads the stories in the book to him, which are then played out omnibus style. This is a step up technically, but still has the same goofy Casio keyboard music in the background. Turner himself composed and sang the crazy theme song. Filmed in Chicago. (Massacre Video)

The Wizard of Gore (1970)

D: Herschell Gordon Lewis; W: Allen Kahn; P: Herschell Gordon Lewis, Fred M. Sandy (EP); C: Ray Sager, Judy Cler, Wayne Ratay, Phil Laurenson, Jim Rau

Although this latter-day Lewis film is painfully boring, it is a favorite of many of the director's fans, in part because it is a literal expression of the type of grand guignol effects Lewis tired to approximate in his films and at a short-lived live venue he operated in Chicago called the Blood Shed

Theatre. Sager plays a nightclub magician whose grisly illusions (sawing the lady in half with a chainsaw, etc.) come to life hours after his show, leaving his victims awash in the usual Lewis stew of fake blood and spoiled meat. It was shot in 1968 but not released until 1970. The film was remade in 2008 with Crispin Glover in the titular role.

Screenwriter Allen Kahn also wrote Lewis' *Year of the Yahoo* (1972). Sager went on to be a successful film and television producer. (Something Weird)

INDIANA

Backwoods (*The Geek*, 1986)

D: Dean Crow; W: Dean Crow, Charles Joseph; P: Maureen Sweeney; C: Christina Noonan, Jack O'Hara, Brad Armacost, Dick Kreusser, Leslie Denise

A camping couple are terrorized by the brain damaged, chicken-head-biting son of a backwoods moonshiner.

Texas native Dean Crow began his career in local television before relocating to Indianapolis in the mid 1960s. In 1971 he formed Dean Crow Productions, which specialized in making TV commercials for companies like Red Roof Inn and Hardees.

Twice Under (1987)

D: Dean Crow; W: Charles Joseph; P: Maureen Sweeney, Lisa Dashiell (AP); C: Ian Borger, Ron Spencer, Amy Lacy, Jack O'Hara, Jack Williams, Charles Cooper

Tales from the Quadead Zone (1987), another shot-on-video oddity from the mysterious Chester Novell Turner (courtesy Fred Adelman).

A crazed veteran, left for dead in Vietnam, returns to kill the members of the unit who abandoned him. Crow followed this with one more direct-to-video thriller, *Father's Day* (1988).

IOWA

Luther the Geek (1990)

D: Carlton J. Albright; W: Carlton J. Albright; P: David Platt, Ernest Shapiro (AP); C: Edward Terry, Joan Rother, Stacy Haiduk, Thomas Mills, Jerry Clarke, Carlton Williams, Gil Rogers

Ten years after *The Children* (1980), Carlton Albright returns (this time as director) with this tale of a demented, metal-fanged killer who (inspired by a carnival geek) clucks like a chicken. Although the plot sounds almost like a comedy (it was distributed by Troma), the bulk of the film actually plays out as a gruesome home invasion, with Luther capturing a woman, her daughter, and the daughter's boyfriend in a remote farmhouse.

Star Edward Terry (who helped write and produce *The Children*, and had a bit part in the film) makes for a compelling (if very odd) psycho. Albright's son plays young Luther in the film. Filmed in Iowa and Illinois. (Troma)

KANSAS

The Beast from the Beginning of Time (1965)

D: Tom Leahy; W: Tom Leahy; P: Tom Leahy; C: Tom Leahy, Dick Welsbacher, Webb Smith, Henry Harvey, Chuck Kneisler, Ralph Seeley, John Froome, Dusty Herring

Two archaeologists uncover the preserved remains of a prehistoric man who awakens and goes on a murderous rampage every time he hears thunder.

This 58-minute film, almost completely unheard of and undocumented outside of Kansas, was financed by KARD Channel 3 in Wichita as a made-for-TV movie, and cost just $10,000. It sat unreleased for 16 years until making its debut on Channel 3 just before Halloween in 1981.

Prior to making this film, Leahy had been Wichita's local horror movie host on a show called "The Host and Rodney" off and on from 1958 until the early 1970s.

Welsbacher was director of the theater department at Wichita State, and has had small roles in other Kansas-set films (including *The Attic*, 1980). Harvey was better known as kiddie show host Freddy Fudd, and other members of the cast were local broadcasters. According to an article in the *Wichita Eagle-Beacon*, Leahy (who died in 2010) also shot 20 minutes worth of footage for a color film called *Green Hell from the Void* that was never completed. He also appeared in *King Kung Fu* (1976).

Carnival of Souls (1962)

D: Herk Harvey; W: John Clifford; C: Candace Hilligoss, Frances Feist, Sidney Berger, Art Ellison, Stan Levitt, Herk Harvey

Shot in Lawrence, Kansas, and Salt Lake City, Utah, *Carnival of Souls* is one of the earliest successful regional horror movies. The dream-like film, about an icy church organist (Hilligoss) caught in a sort-of limbo between life and death and pursued by pasty-faced zombies that may or may not be hallucinations, was a staple of late-night television and built a sizable cult following over the years. Some of the most effective sequences take place at the eerie Saltair Amusement Park in Utah.

Harvey (who also plays the lead ghoul) and screenwriter John Clifford worked for Centron Studios, an industrial film company based in Lawrence, where Harvey directed such educational classics as *Pork: The Meal with a Squeal* and *Exchanging Greetings and Introductions*. He also shot some footage for an unfinished horror film called *The Reluctant Witch*, based on a story by novelist James Gunn. Harvey died in 1996. Hilligoss appeared in Del Tenney's *The Curse of the Living Corpse* (1964). A sort-of remake of *Carnival of Souls* released in 1998 included a cameo by Berger. (Criterion/Image/Rhino)

King Kung Fu (1976)

D: Lance D. Hayes; W: Lance D. Hayes; P: Bob Walterscheid; C: Lance D. Hayes, Allan Baker, John Ballee, Dan Campbell, Maxine Gray, Tim McGill, Tom Leahy

Dumb-but-fun absurdist comedy that combines elements of *King Kong* and the David Carradine "Kung Fu" series. A sentient Chinese gorilla trained in the martial arts is sent on a goodwill tour of the United States. While on display in Wichita, he is freed by two bumbling, would-be filmmakers who want to break into the local TV news business, then hunted relentlessly by a police captain (horror host Tom Leahy) who looks and acts suspiciously like John Wayne. He eventually climbs to the top of the tallest building in Wichita (the Holiday Inn) for a final stand-off with authorities. Shot in "SimianScope."

Ballee, who plays the gorilla, was a tae kwon do instructor in Salina and Wichita. Bob Walterscheid owned a commercial production company in Wichita, and most of the cast and crew came from Wichita State University. According to Walterscheid's comments on the Internet Movie Database, the film began production in 1974 and played in 11 theaters. (Retromedia)

Herk Harvey's eerie *Carnival of Souls* (1962) was a staple of late-night TV (courtesy Fred Adelman).

Night Screams (1987)

D: Allen Plone; W: Mitch Brian, Dillis L. Hart II; P: Dillis L. Hart II, Dillis L. Hart Sr. (EP), Richard Caliendo, Jack Isgro (AP); C: Joseph Paul Manno, Ron Thomas, Randy Lundsford, Megan Wyss

"Tonight, their cries will fall on dead ears!" Two escaped convicts invade a high school graduation party, where someone is picking off party guests one by one. The opening sequence features a couple watching *Graduation Day* (1981) on television, and other characters watch porn videos throughout the film.

Executive producer Richard Caliendo (a stockholder and director with a local bank) pleaded guilty in 1992 to making false statements in order to obtain $280,000 in bank loans in order for Dillis Hart II to finance *Night Screams* via a shady real estate transaction. Dillis Hart, Sr. was a physician in Wichita.

Director Plone went on to helm several television specials and designed video games. He also directed *Sweet Justice* (1992), with Kathleen Kinmont, Marc Singer and Frank Gorshin, and *Phantom of the Ritz* (1992). Actor Ron Thomas was in *The Karate Kid* (1984). (Image)

KENTUCKY

Abby (1974)

D: *William Girdler;* W: *William Girdler, Gordon Cornell Layne;* P: *William Girdler, Mike Henry, Gordon Cornell Layne, David Sheldon, Samuel Z. Arkoff (EP);* C: *William Marshall, Terry Carter, Austin Stoker, Carol Speed, Juanita Moore, Charles Kissinger*

When minister/professor/archeologist Marshall accidentally unleashes an African demon while on a dig, the malign spirit immediately heads for Louisville, Kentucky, and possesses his daughter-in-law (Speed). The devout, well-mannered minister's wife turns into a foul-mouthed, promiscuous tramp who is prone kicking her pious husband in the groin.

This was Girdler's blaxploitation version of *The Exorcist* (1973), and was financed primarily by American International Pictures. Warner Brothers sued AIP for copyright infringement and had the film pulled from theaters. Speed sings a gospel song on the soundtrack. (Televista)

Asylum of Satan (1972)

D: *William Girdler;* W: *William Girdler, J. Patrick Kelly;* P: *J. Patrick Kelly;* C: *Charles Kissinger, Nick Jolley, Carla Borelli, Louis Bandy, Lila Boden*

William Girdler's first film is an awkward, bizarre debut riddled with bad dialogue, clumsy compositions and cheap special effects.

AIP hired William Girdler to direct the company's *Exorcist* knock-off, *Abby* (1974), starring Carol Speed and Terry Carter.

Concert pianist Borelli awakens in the mysterious asylum of a diabolical doctor and his mannish female adjunct Martine (both played by local horror host Charles Kissinger). Patients at the asylum are being sacrificed to the devil in order for the doctor to achieve immortality, while Borelli's paunchy plaid-clad boyfriend (Jolley) races around trying to save her.

Girdler was a film nut from a well-heeled Louisville, Kentucky, family who began his career making commercials with partner and brother-in-law J. Patrick Kelly. He shot six of his nine films in Kentucky, including the blaxploitaiton films *The Zebra Killer* (1973) and *Abby* (1974), an Exorcist rip-off made for American International Pictures; *Sheba Baby* (1975), another AIP film, this time with Pam Grier; and *Project Kill* (1976) with Leslie Nielsen. He made *Grizzly* (1976) and *Day of the Animals* (1977) for Film Ventures, then hit the big time with the all-star opus *The Manitou* (1978). Girdler died in a helicopter crash while scouting locations in the Philippines in 1978.

This was shot at Girdler's Studio One facility in Louisville for around $50,000. The asylum sequences were filmed at a decrepit local mansion that was

Asylum of Satan (1972) was one of the first films made by Kentucky director William Girdler.

covered in poodle poop, courtesy of the owner's untrained gaggle of pets. Michael Aquino, a Spock-haired Satanist once associated with Anton LaVey's Church of Satan, served as technical advisor on the film, and contributed to the miscellaneous Satanic chants heard throughout. Watch for the devil costume from *Rosemary's Baby* during the climax. (Something Weird)

Three on a Meathook (1972)

D: William Girdler; W: William Girdler; P: John Asman, Lee S. Jones Jr., Joseph Shulten (EP); C: Charles Kissinger, James Pickett, Sherry Steiner, Madelyn Buzzard, John Shaw, Marsha Tarbis

Girdler's second film was a take on the Ed Gein story, which also inspired the much better *Deranged* (1974) and *The Texas Chain Saw Massacre* (1974). Pickett plays the troubled Billy, who may or may not be killing the girls he brings to the family farm where he lives with his demented pa (Charles Kissinger). Includes the usual Girdler trademarks: splashy gore (courtesy of Pat Patterson), endless padding, and mind-numbingly bad rock music.

Once again, Girdler relied on the Asman brothers on the technical side (John Asman on sound, William Asman behind the camera, and editor Henry Asman), and received funding from a local realtor named Joe Schulten (augmented with some cash from Girdler's trust fund).

LOUISIANA

Creature from Black Lake (1976)

D: Joy N. Houck Jr.; W: Jim McCullough Jr.; P: Jim McCullough Jr., Jim McCullough Sr., William Lewis Ryder Jr. (EP); C: Jack Elam, Dub Taylor, Dennis Fimple, John David Carson, Bill Thurman, Jim McCullough Jr., Chase Tatum, Joy N. Houck Jr.

This was Houck and McCullough's answer to occasional collaborator Charles B. Pierce's *Legend of Boggy Creek* (1972). Fimple and Carson are bigfoot researchers who arrive in the Louisiana swamps to study a particularly violent and dangerous sasquatch that's been attacking the locals.

Dean Cundey was cinematographer on this film, and Albert Salzer was on hand as production manager. Jim McCullough, Jr., wrote and sang the title song "Exits and Truck Stops." (United American)

Crypt of Dark Secrets (1976)

D: Jack Weis; W: Irwin Blache, Jack Weis; P: Jack Weis; C: Ronald Tanet, Maureen Ridley, Herbert G. Jahncke, Wayne Mack, Butch Benit

After a group of backwoods thieves rob and kill a paunchy Vietnam vet (Tanet) who lives alone in the swamp, a naked swamp witch (who can also turn into a snake) resurrects the murdered man to take revenge. The plot is a bit confusing, but the glistening Damballa (Ridley) drops her clothes and does enough sexy witch dances to make up for it.

Weis and Donn Davison originally made this film as a straight exploitation flick, and extra nudity was added later.

Weis also made *Mardi Gras Massacre* (1978), as well as the earlier *Storyville* (1974) and the plantation melodrama *Quadroon* (1972) with frequent S.F. Brownrigg player Bill McGhee. Writer Irwin Blache was part of the crew on the made-in-Georgia mess *Legend of Blood Mountain* (1965). Tanet went on to produce several TV movies. (Something Weird)

The Dead One (*Blood of the Zombie*, 1961)

D: Barry Mahon; W: Barry Mahon; P: Barry Mahon, Brandon Chase (EP); C: John MacKay, Linda Ormond, Monica Davis, Clyde Kelly, Darlene Myrick

A man inherits an old plantation, but his voodoo priestess cousin conjures up a zombie (her dead brother) to kill him so she can keep their ancestral home. The plot of this film is basically lifted from the old black-cast exploitation quickie *The Devil's Daughter* (1939), but with zombies. It eventually became part of the Independent-International Pictures catalog.

The DVD of this film also includes a creditless movie called *Voodoo Swamp*, an unfinished film from Mardi Gras Productions. In *Voodoo Swamp*, a woman and a private detective head into the swamps to search for the woman's missing twin sister, but wind up tangling with a voodoo priestess. Bodybuilder Bill Pearl appears as a zombie. (Media Blasters/Shriek Show)

John David Carson, Becky Smiser, Michelle Willingham, and Dennis Fimple take a break from Bigfoot hunting in Joy Houck, Jr.'s *Creature from Black Lake* (1976).

The Evictors (1979)

D: *Charles B. Pierce;* W: *Charles B. Pierce, Garry Rusoff, Paul Fisk;* P: *Charles B. Pierce, Steve Lyons (AP);* C: *Vic Morrow, Michael Parks, Jessica Harper, Dennis Fimple, Bill Thurman, Sue Ane Langdon*

A couple moves into a house in Louisiana in the 1940s that turns out to have a violent past, and are terrorized by a mysterious killer. It was distributed by AIP.

After this film, Pierce teamed with *The Wilderness Family* (1975) producer Arthur R. Dubs on the western *Sacred Ground* (1983) before returning to more familiar territory with *Boggy Creek II* (1985). He also wrote the original story for *Sudden Impact* (1983).

Mardi Gras Massacre (1978)

D: *Jack Weis;* W: *Jack Weis;* P: *Jack Weis, John Stimac (AP);* C: *Curt Dawson, Gwen Arment, William Metzo, Wayne Mack, Ronald Tanet, Laura Misch Owens*

Jack Weis and Ronald Tanet, the director/actor duo who brought us *Crypt of Dark Secrets* (1976), return with this film about a devil worshipping priest who kills prostitutes and sacrifices them to an Aztec deity. The film has an interesting (to say the least) soundtrack of R&B and disco tunes from producers Dennis Coffey and Mike Theodore of Westbound Records.

Mountaintop Motel Massacre (1986)

D: *Jim McCullough Sr.;* W: *Jim McCullough Jr.;* C: *Bill Thurman, Anna Chappell, Will Mitchel, Virginia Loridans, Major Brock, James Bradford, Amy Hill*

Surprisingly fun and creepy backwoods flick, probably best known for its video box art and tag line: "Please do not disturb Evelyn. She ALREADY is." Evelyn (Anna Chappel) is the crazy proprietor of an out-of-the-way motel where she lives with her daughter, who appears to have some kind of psychic link to the large menagerie of pets she keeps in the house. Evelyn, a former mental patient, kills her daughter and makes it look like an accident, then starts killing her guests after sneaking into their cabins through a network of underground tunnels.

While it was marketed as a slasher film, *Mountaintop Motel Massacre* is actually a pseudo-supernatural thriller with some good scares and gore effects. This was Bill Thurman's last horror film (he died in 1995). The film was shot in 1983, but not released until 1986 through New World. (Anchor Bay)

Night of Bloody Horror (1969)

D: Joy N. Houck Jr.; W: Joy N. Houck Jr., Robert A. Weaver; P: Joy N. Houck Jr., Albert J. Salzer (EP); C: Gerald McRaney, Gaye Yellen, Michael Anthony, Gerald C. Amato, John Barber

Houck, son of Howco head Joy Houck, Sr., made this film independently, hoping to cash in on the success of *Night of the Living Dead* (1968). McRaney stars as a disturbed young man who lives with his mother. He occasionally breaks down in screaming fits, and has a habit of turning up near the mutilated bodies of dead women.

Weird, wild, and featuring a stand-out performance by McRaney, who can shriek hysterically with the best of them.

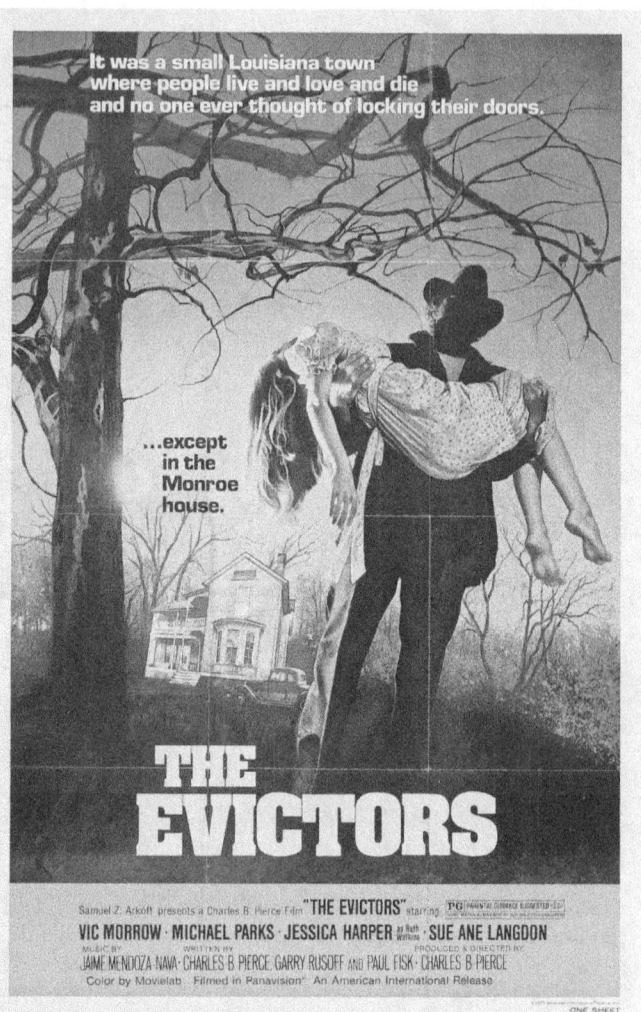

The Evictors (1979) was one of a handful of films made by Charles B. Pierce for American-International Pictures (courtesy Fred Adelman).

Filmed in "Violent Vision," with psychedelic light effects, and an acid rock band called The Bored.

This was McRaney's first film role, and he followed it up by appearing in Houck's *Women and Bloody Terror* (*His Wife's Habit*, 1969), which was paired with this film and Houck's *Night of the Strangler* (1975) on double- and triple-bills for years. (Something Weird/Brentwood)

Night of the Strangler (*The Ace of Spades/Is the Father Black Enough?/Dirty Dan's Women*, 1975)

D: Joy N. Houck, Jr.; W: J.J. Milane; P: Albert J. Salzer; C: Mickey Dolenz, Ann Barrett, Susan McCullough, Chuck Patterson, Harold Sylvester

A white woman and her black lover are murdered in Louisiana. While her racist brother fumes in the background, a black priest and the woman's more sensitive sibling (Dolenz) investigate.

Dolenz was also in *Keep Off My Grass!* (1975) for Salzer, a comedy directed by Shelley Berman that was distributed by Gamalex Associates.

Screams of a Winter Night (1979)

D: James L. Wilson; W: Richard H. Wadsack; P: S. Mark Lovell (EP), Richard H. Wadsack, James L. Wilson; C: Matt Borel, Gil Glasgow, Patrick Byers, Mary Agen Cox, Robin Bradley, William Ragsdale

This cheap anthology film has a small but enthusiastic following among the few people who actually got to see it during its theatrical run. A group of college students spend the night in a remote cabin and tell each other scary stories. One is about a couple being terrorized by a Bigfoot-like creature; another has a bunch of fraternity brothers spending the night in an abandoned hospital; and the third is about a girl who loses her mind after an attempted rape. The wraparound segment, with the kids talking about a wind spirit who haunts a local lake, is more effective than the rest of the stories. Filmed in Natchitoches, La.

Video box art for the Jack Weis film *Mardi Gras Massacre* (1978) (courtesy Fred Adelman).

Wilson and Wadsack both had backgrounds in theatrical production, and were inspired to try their hand at filmmaking by the success of Charles B. Pierce, Joy Houck and others in the region. Producer Mark Lovell was a real estate developer. William Ragsdale, who plays one of the service station attendants, starred in *Fright Night* (1985) and the TV series *Herman's Head*.

Teen Vamp (1988)

D: Samuel Bradford; W: Samuel Bradford; P: Jim McCullough, Jr.; C: Clu Gulager, Karen Carlson, Beau Bishop, Angie Brown, Evans Dietz, Edd Anderson

Teen Wolf (1985) knock-off set in the 1950s about a teenage boy who gets bitten by a vampire while he's looking for a prostitute. His new powers help him impress women and beat up the school bully.

Terror in the Swamp (1985)

D: Joe Catalanotto, Joy N. Houck Jr. (uncredited); W: Henry Brien, Martin Folse, Terry Hebb, Billy Holiday; P: Martin Folse; C: Billy Holiday, Keith Barker, Chuck Bush, Gerald Daigal, Albert Dyket

Scientists breeding nutria (massive, ugly rodents) for the fur industry accidentally create a murderous "Nutriaman" who escapes into the swamps.

Filmed in 1983 as *Nutria Man: Terror in the Swamp* in Houma, La., by 22-year-old producer Martin Folse. Folse owns Houma's only TV station, KFOL/KJUN HTV 10, and is also a singer and songwriter. In 2005, he spearheaded an effort to have a levee built in Terrebonne Parish after Hurricanes Katrina and Rita devastated the Gulf Coast.

Catalanotto also worked on *The Town That Dreaded Sundown* (1976), *The Shadow of Chikara* (1977), *Grayeagle* (1977), and *Pretty Baby* (1978), and directed *French Quarter Undercover* (1986).

Actor Chuck Bush (who plays the taller of the two massive poachers in the film) is a consultant to the local film industry, and has worked with the film commissions in Louisiana and Mississippi to draw more productions to the region. He also appeared in *Fandango* (1985).

Video Murders (1987)

D: Jim McCullough Sr.; W: Jim McCullough Jr.; P: Jim McCullough Sr.; C: Eric Brown, Virginia Loridans, John P. Fertitta, Frank Baggett, Jan Huber, Deborah Dreher

A serial killer videotapes himself strangling hookers in his hotel room, while the local police try to track him down.

Brown appeared as the grandson on *Mama's Family*, and later became the communications director for the Center for a New American Dream, a nonprofit group dedicated to reducing high levels of consumerism. He now holds a similar position for the William and Flora Hewlett Foundation, a major donor to National Public Radio.

This was the last horror film for the McCulloughs, who went on to produce *Where the Red Fern Grows: Part 2* (1992) and *The St. Tammany Miracle* (1994).

The Wacky World of Dr. Morgus (1962)

D: Roul Haig; W: Noel Haig, Roul Haig; P: Eugene T. Calongne, Jules Sevin; C: Sid Noel, Dan Barton, Jeanne Teslof, David Kleinberger

Dr. Morgus (Sid Noel) was a New Orleans-based horror host. Here, he plays an inventor who creates a machine that can turn people into sand. Director Roul Haig also made the obscure *Okefenokee* (1959).

In addition to starring in this feature film, Morgus recorded a song called "Morgus the Magnificent" with a backing band (called The Ghouls) that included Dr. John and Frankie Ford.

www.morgus.com

Women and Bloody Terror (*His Wife's Habit*, 1969)

D: Joy N. Houck Jr.; W: Joy N. Houck Jr., J.J. Milane, Albert Salzer, Robert A. Weaver; P: Albert J. Salzer; C: Georgine Darcy, Marcus J. Grapes, Christina Hart, David Gelpi, Michael Anthony, Gerald McCraney

This non-horror melodrama was originally titled *His Wife's Habit*, then retitled by Howco so it could be paired with *Night of Bloody Horror*, a double bill with a memorable poster and turgid trailer. Darcy stars as a promiscuous woman who sleeps with almost every man she meets (including her daughter's boyfriend). Eventually, she's stalked by a crazy parking attendant who rides a motorcycle. A soundtrack was released on Capitol.

Darcy was also in *Rear Window* (1954), playing "Miss Torso." Christina Hart was in Salzer's counter-culture film *Keep Off My Grass!* (1975). She had a long career on television, and played Patricia Krenwinkle in *Helter Skelter* (1976).

MAINE
(None)

MARYLAND

The Alien Factor (1978)

D: Don Dohler; W: Don Dohler; P: Don Dohler; C: Don Leifert, Tom Griffith, Richard Dyszel, Mary Mertens, Richard Geiwitz, George Stover

This was the first feature film from Dohler, who was also the creator/editor of *Cinemagic* magazine (which he sold to the Starlog group), as well as managing editor (and one-time owner) of a local newspaper, *The Times-Herald*. A spaceship containing a freakish collection of alien monsters (specimens destined for an intergalactic research lab) crashes near a small town. The escaped monsters slaughter the locals until another alien, disguised as a human, arrives to hunt them down.

Richard Dyszel, who plays the mayor, is better known as horror host Count Gore de Vol. Actor George Stover was the editor of two magazines, *Black Oracle* and *Cinemacabre*. Special effects artist Ernest D. Farino went on to work on *The Abyss* (1989) and *Terminator 2: Judgment Day* (1991).

Dohler, who died in 2006, directed a sequel called *Alien Factor 2: The Alien Rampage* (2001). In 2007, director John Paul Kinhart released a documentary titled *Blood, Boobs & Beast* about Dohler's life and films. (RetroMedia)

www.bloodboobsandbeast.com

Blood Circus (1985)

D: John Corso, Joseph Ryan Zwick; P: Joseph Ryan Zwick; C: Santo Gold (Santo Victor Rigatuso), John Harris III, Jerry Reese (Voodoo Malumba), Vinnie Valentino

The most notorious lost film ever made in Baltimore. Rigatuso (a.k.a. Bob Harris) was an obnoxious infomercial star who hawked cheap jewelry (Santo Gold) on late-night television. He produced this aliens-versus-wrestlers film that was screened once and then vanished, although he endlessly promoted it during his TV spots. Viewers who attended the premiere were given a "scream bag," which included a coupon for a free diamond ring.

Blood Circus was filmed at the Baltimore Civic Center, where extras paid $10 for the privilege of sitting around for hours and watching Rigatuso and his hapless crew floundering under the klieg lights. It allegedly cost more than $2 million to make, and was financed by proceeds from Rigatuso's Credit Card Authorization Center business. This enterprise rooked customers with bad credit histories into paying $50 for a fake credit card with which they could only purchase Santo Gold merchandise. Rigatuso was eventually convicted of mail fraud in 1989, and served 10 months in prison.

New York native Corso was a cinematographer who filmed TV spots for Howard Stern's pay-per-view special, and also worked on Joe Dante's *Matinee* (1993). Wrestler John Harris was better known as Silo Sam.

For more information on Santo Gold, visit the glorious Santo Gold Museum at *www.geocities.com/santogoldmuseum*. You can also order a one-hour "making-of" documentary about

Blood Circus at *www.santogold.com*, if you feel like giving the illustrious Santo your credit card number.

According to Santo's Web site, the original 35mm elements of *Blood Circus* were located in 2008 and "Limited License Rights are now available for Executive Producers to come forward and contact us!" The busy Santo also recorded a novelty CD titled *I Am the Real Santo Gold* (with tracks like "Obama Stomp"), and then threatened to sue Brooklyn hip-hop star Santogold over rights to the name. The singer eventually gave in and changed her name to "Santigold" in 2009.

The Boogeyman (1980)

D: Ulli Lommel; W: David Herschel, Ulli Lommel; P: Ulli Lommel, Wolf Schmidt (EP), Terrell Tannen (AP); C: Suzanna Love, John Carradine, Ron James, Nicholas Love

In an opening flashback, an abusive drunk is murdered by his girlfriend's son while the boy's sister watches in a mirror. Years later when the mirror is shattered, the boyfriend's evil spirit is unleashed.

German-born Lommel previously worked with Rainer Werner Fassbinder (as an actor) and Andy Warhol, and directed cult items like *Tenderness of the Wolves* (1973) and *Cocaine Cowboys* (1980) prior to his horror breakthrough. He followed *The Boogeyman* with a series of horror films, including *BrainWaves* (1983) and *The Devonsville Terror* (1983). He later dabbled in several other genres, and has spent the past decade churning out a series of uneven (some would call them unwatchable), direct-to-video horror films, many of them based on the exploits of real serial killers.

Love, who was married to

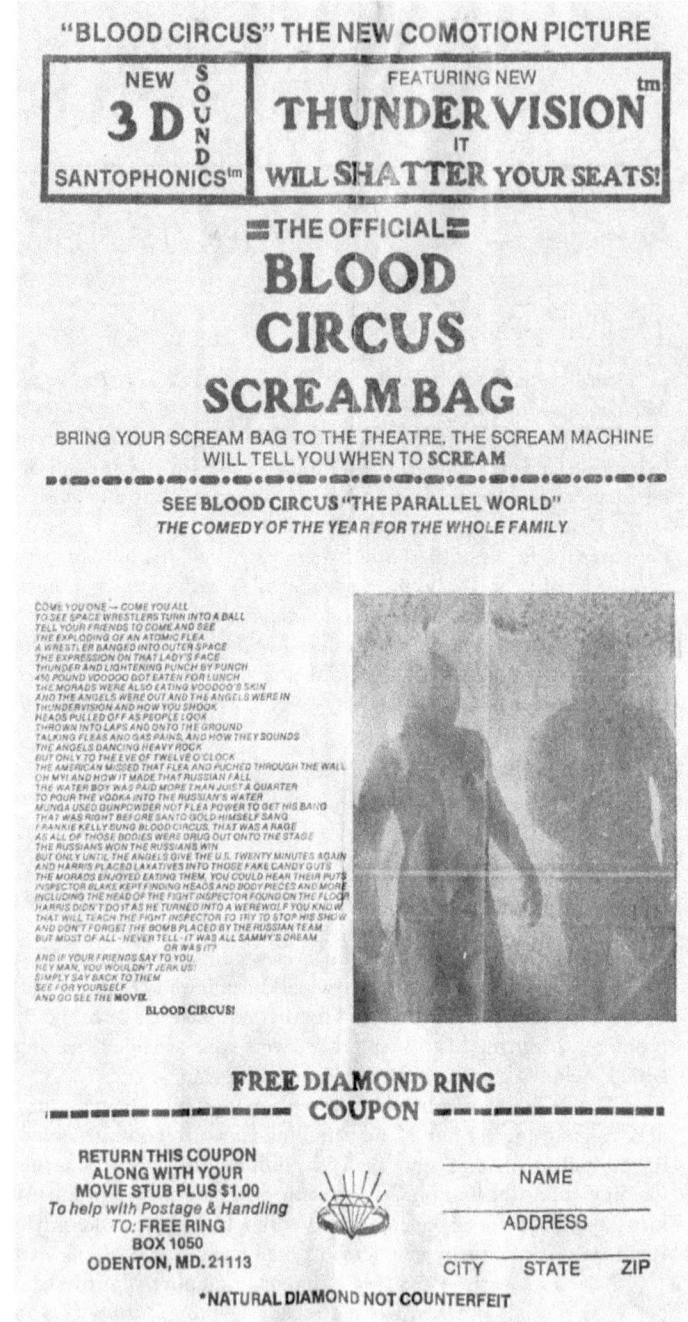

A "Scream Bag" was issued to viewers of the horror-wrestling opus *Blood Circus* (1985).

Lommel at the time, is a Dupont heiress who had a small part in *Hair* (1979) and appeared in a number of other Lommel productions (many of which she personally financed). *The Boogeyman* was partly shot at Love's aunt's farm in Maryland.

Curse of the Screaming Dead (*Curse of the Cannibal Confederates*, 1982)

D: *Tony Malanowski*; W: *Lon Huber, Tony Malanowski*; P: *Tony Malanowski*; C: *Steve Sandkuhler, Christopher Gummer, Rebecca Bach, Judy Dixon, Jim Ball, Mark Redfield, Richard Ruxton*

A bunch of kids on a hunting trip are attacked by the zombified corpses of some Confederate soldiers in this sort-of remake of Malanowski's earlier *Night of Horror* (1978). When Troma picked up the film for distribution, they lifted a zombie resurrection scene from later in the film and stuck it in the opening credits. This film and Armand Mastroianni's *The Supernaturals* (1986) comprised almost the entirety of the short-lived Confederate zombie sub-genre. (Troma)

Fiend (1980)

D: *Don Dohler*; W: *Don Dohler*; P: *Don Dohler, Ted A. Bohus (AP), George Stover (AP), Anne Frith (AP)*; C: *Don Leifert, Richard Nelson, Elaine White, George Stover, Greg Dohler, Kim Dohler*

A reanimated corpse (Leifert) who gains energy by killing people moves into a suburban Baltimore neighborhood, where he poses as a violin instructor and drains the life out of his neighbors. This was Dohler's second film, and like *The Alien Factor* (1978) was promoted heavily in *Famous Monsters of Filmland*.

Bohus went on to produce *Return of the Aliens: The Deadly Spawn* (1983) in New Jersey. (Retro-Media)

The Galaxy Invader (1985)

D: *Don Dohler*; W: *Don Dohler, David W. Donoho, Anne Frith*; P: *Anne Frith (AP), George Stover (AP)*; C: *Richard Ruxton, Faye Tilles, George Stover, Greg Dohler, Anne Frith, Richard Dyszel*

This was Dohler's last film of the 1980s. Yet another alien lands near Baltimore and begins killing people. An abusive, alcoholic redneck decides he wants to hunt him down, while some local college students try to save the visitor from another planet.

Dohler followed this with *Blood Massacre* (1991) and *Alien Factor 2: The Alien Rampage* (2001). (Mill Creek/Alpha)

Multiple Maniacs (1970)

D: *John Waters*; W: *John Waters*; P: *John Waters*; C: *Divine, Mink Stole, David Lochary, Cookie Mueller, Mary Vivian Pearce, Edith Massey*

The first sync-sound effort from Baltimore's resident miscreant Waters, and the closest thing he made to an actual horror film until *Serial Mom* (1994). Divine (nee Glen Milstead) and her brain-washed boyfriend (Lochary) operate Lady Divine's Cavalcade of Perversions, a traveling variety show (actually a front for a robbery/murder operation) that allows square suburbanites to see such "perversions" as a gay couple kissing and a man that eats vomit. After being raped in the street, Divine is led into a church by the Infant of Prague, has a religious epiphany, is further sexually assaulted by a giant lobster and (spoiler alert) finally gunned down by the National Guard.

Waters followed this with *Pink Flamingos* (1972), which established his reputation on the Midnight movie circuit. He appeared in *Blood Feast 2: All U Can Eat* (2002), and was last seen as a flasher in the 2007 big studio version of the Broadway adaptation of his original film *Hairspray* (1988).

Night of Horror (1978)

D: *Tony Malanowski*; W: *Rebecca Bach, Tony Malanowski, Gae Schmitt*; P: *Tony Malanowski*; C: *Rebecca Bach, Jeff Canfield, Phil Davis, Tony Malanowski, Steve Sandkuhler, Gae Schmitt*

This was Malanowski's first film as a director. A group of campers encounter a gaggle of Confederate ghosts at an old battlefield in Virginia. Most of the cast and crew returned for Malanowski's similarly-themed *Curse of the Screaming Dead* (1982).

Malanowski was part of the lively East Coast fan/filmmaker subculture in the 1970s, and was an investor and crew member on Don Dohler's *The Alien Factor* (1978). He went on to work with David DeCoteau, Donald F. Glut, Ewing "Lucky" Brown and Fred Olen Ray as an editor and production manager. He later worked for Disney. More recently, Malanowski started Light a Candle Films in California to produce a series of historical DVDs called "America: Her People, Her Stories."

www.bunkerhilldvd.com

Nightbeast (1982)

D: *Don Dohler*; W: *Don Dohler*; P: *Don Dohler, Ted A. Bohus*; C: *Tom Griffith, Jamie Zemarel, Karin Kardian, George Stover, Don Leifert, Anne Frith, Richard Dyszel*

An alien monster in a tuxedo kills another batch of Baltimore residents in Dohler's third film. This includes the usual crazed Dohler special effects, but with more gore, some nudity, and a ridiculous sex scene. (Troma)

MASSACHUSETTS

Attack of the Killer Refrigerator/The Hook of Woodland Heights (1985)

D: *Michael Savino, Mark Veau*; W: *Michael Savino, Mark Veau*; P: *Michael Savino, Mark Veau*; C: *Christine McNamara, Robert W. Allen, Michael Elyanow (Hook); Lori Regonini, Christina Murphy, Lori Carson (Refrigerator)*

In *Attack of the Killer Refrigerator*, a menacing refrigerator takes revenge on the people who have abused it. *Hook* is based on the classic campfire story, but this time with an escaped mental patient killing people with the barbeque fork he has jammed into the stump where his hand used to be.

Savino and Veau made these two short films (which were released together on video by Donna Michelle Productions in 1990) while students at Worcester State College. *Refrigerator* was made for $25 on half-inch video with no script. Savino went on to direct more than 400 commercials, and Veau is now a DJ at an oldies station. (Media House Films)

www.mediahousefilms.com

The Children (1980)

D: *Max Kalmanowicz*; W: *Carlton J. Albright, Edward Terry*; P: *Carlton J. Albright, Max Kalmanowicz, Edward Terry (AP)*; C: *Martin Shakar, Gil Rogers, Gale Garnett, Shannon Bolin, Tracy Griswold, Joy Glaccum, Jeptha Evans, Sarah Albright, Nathanael Albright, Edward Terry*

A busload of children (actually just four or five kids) are exposed to a cloud of radiation and turn into murderous zombies who can burn adults alive by "hugging" them to death. A cheap but fun take on the killer kids genre, with the producer's children cast as some of the zombie kids.

Gil Rogers (who plays the sheriff) will be familiar to soap opera fans from his roles on "All My

Children" and "The Guiding Light." He also appeared briefly in Albright's *Luther the Geek* (1990), which starred *Children* co-writer and producer Edward Terry.

Several crew members went on to work on the *Friday the 13th* films, including composer Harry Manfredini, who modified his music cues from this film for the memorable score of the Sean Cunningham movie. (Troma)

Sasqua (1975)

D: *Channon J. Scott;* W: *Channon J. Scott;* P: *Channon J. Scott, Linda Diefendorf (AP), Joseph T. Scarlata (AP), Marland Proctor (AP);* C: *James Whitworth, Tom Johnigarn, Camilla Gallien, Nate White, Jim McKenna*

Presumed lost Bigfoot film (made in Lowell, Massachusetts) about the conflict between locals and a commune full of hippies after a pack of man-eating sasquatch commit a series of murders.

Scott was a native of Lowell who returned there from Los Angeles to make this film. He also had a small role in *The Black Angels* (1970), which featured several other members of the *Sasqua* cast, and is credited as associate producer on *Dolly Dearest* (1991). He later worked as an agent. Scott's cousin, Tom Lannan, provided the music.

According to an interview with Scott on the Web site Cult Reviews, he briefly distributed the film himself before turning it over to distributor Lou Peralta. Actor James Whitworth was the lead mutant in *The Hills Have Eyes* (1977).

Winterbeast (1986/1992)

D: *Christopher Thies;* W: *Christopher Thies;* P: *Mark Frizzell;* C: *Tim R. Morgan, Mike Magri, Charles Majika, Bob Harlow, Dori May Kelly, Chris Lenge*

Sloppy-but-charming 16mm production about an ancient demon killing revelers at the Wild Goose Lodge with the help of a gaggle of stop-motion monsters. Lead actor Tim R. Morgan sports a variety of fake mustaches throughout the film to compensate for the fact that he shaved off his real one mid-way through production.

Made in 1986, but not released until 1992 through J.R. Bookwalter's Tempe Video. A special edition DVD was released in 2008. Filmed primarily Waltham, Massachusetts, with some footage shot in New Hampshire. (Winterbeast Entertainment Group) *www.winterbeast.com*

A sell sheet for the original video release of *Winterbeast* (1986) (courtesy J.R. Bookwalter).

MICHIGAN

The Carrier (1988)

D: Nathan J. White; W: Nathan J. White; P: Michael Jarema, Jeff Dougherty; C: Gregory Fortescue, Stevie Lee, Steve Dixon, Paul Silverman, Paul Urbanski, DeLaney Provencher

Ambitiously weird social horror film about a young outcast who is infected with a strange disease by a monster in the woods. If he touches an inanimate object, the disease causes the next person who touches the object to dissolve into a pile of goo. The townspeople wrap themselves in plastic bags for protection, and hoard cats to use them as test subjects before they touch anything. Eventually, they divide into competing camps (wearing either white or black garbage bags) and ransack each other's cat stockpiles.

White and producer Michael Jarema also produced *Hellmaster* (1992), another Michigan film, and Jarema produced *Dark Heaven* (2002), another film by *Hellmaster* director Douglas Schulze. Cinematographer Peter Deming worked on this film just after the excellent Florida flick *Scarecrows* (1988), and then moved on to Sam Raimi's *Evil Dead II* (1987), along with several other crew members. Bruce Campbell is credited as sound effects recordist. (Code Red)

The Carrier (1988), a peculiar meditation on disease and societal breakdown ... and cat hoarding (courtesy Fred Adelman).

Death Bed: The Bed That Eats (1977)

D: George Barry; W: George Barry; P: George Barry, Maureen Petrucci, Jim Williams (AP); C: Demene Hall, William Russ, Julie Ritter, Linda Bond

A Death Bed, actually an evil spirit locked forever in the form a four-post bed, waits in a cave where it consumes unwary souls while spewing yellow, foamy, acidic goop.

Film school student George

Barry shot this $30,000 movie (based on a dream he had) between 1972 and 1977 near Detroit. Unable to find a distributor, he put the film into storage, where it remained unknown and unknowable, locked away with the other bricabrac of his youth. But somehow, some way, copies of the movie began turning up on muddy, European bootlegs, and years later Barry discovered that his strange little film had a bit of a following. He finally got the film released in the U.S. on DVD in 2003. It had a theatrical premiere at the San Francisco Independent Film Festival the same year.

This was Barry's only feature-length film. He eventually went into the used book business. The waspish, dead narrator in the film is played by *CREEM* magazine scribe and rock critic Dave Marsh. Actor William Russ was later a regular on *Boy Meets World*. Comedian Patton Oswald used this film as the premise of a bit in some of his standup performances in 2006. (Cult Epics)

The Demon Lover (*The Devil Master*, 1977)

D: Donald Jackson, Jerry Younkins; W: Donald G. Jackson, Jerry Younkins; P: Donald G. Jackson, Jerry Younkins, Bob Russell (EP), Jean Morris (AP), Les Morris (AP); C: Christmas Robbins (Jerry Younkins), Val Mayerik, Gunnar Hansen, Tom Hutton, David J. Howard

This low-budget movie was the debut feature of prolific filmmaker Donald G. Jackson, but its reputation is based largely on the behind-the-scenes drama that nearly engulfed the film. A disaffected cult of backwoods hippies, led by a karate-kicking guru with enormous hair (co-director Younkins), raises a demon. Said demon then spends the rest of the film killing off the guru's former followers.

Jackson met Younkins when he was selling his comic book collection in order to raise money for a planned film project called *The Adventures of Lincoln Green*. *The Demon Lover* was financed partly with insurance money Younkins received after losing a finger to a punch press at the factory where he worked.

The film might have slipped into complete obscurity were it not for the machinations of for-hire cinematographer

The making of Donald Jackson's *The Demon Lover* (1977) was captured in the unflattering *Demon Lover Diary* (1980), a documentary by Joel DeMott (courtesy Steve Puchalski).

Jeff Kreines, his along-for-the-ride girlfriend Joel DeMott and their friend, soundman Mark Rance, who were brought in by Younkins and Jackson to shoot the film. Kreines and DeMott were film students who shot a behind-the-scenes documentary about the experience called *Demon Lover Diary* (1980) that focuses largely on Jackson and Younkins squabbling and acting like incompetent jerks while the film collapses around them.

According to Jackson and others involved in the film, though, Kreines and DeMott deliberately made the filmmakers look bad so that their documentary would be more interesting.

Jackson eventually went to California at the behest of the award-winning special effects artists Robert and Dennis Skotak (who also helped out on *Demon Lover*) to work on Roger Corman's *Galaxy of Terror* (1981), but it was several years before he directed another film, the wrestling movie *I Like to Hurt People* (1985). He followed that with *Roller Blade* (1986), about roller skating, post-apocalyptic nuns, and *Hell Comes to Frogtown* (1987). He directed another 26 films before his death in 2003.

Rance now directs and produces supplements for DVDs. Actor Val Mayerik was a Marvel Comics artist who worked on *Man-Thing* and created *Howard the Duck*.

Jerry Younkins later wrote the book *Combat and Survival Knives: A User's Guide* (1991). Kreines runs the Kinetta Camera Company (*www.kinetta.com*). He and DeMott now live in Alabama, where they continue to make documentaries.

The Hackers (1987)
D: John Duncan; W: John Duncan; P: John Duncan; C: Howard Coburn, Dale Caughel, Steve Prichard, Michelle Rank, Bruce Phillips, James Larsen

Crazy handymen (one wearing an aluminum foil mask) terrorize and kill people in this obscure and mysterious shot-on-video horror film from Croswell and Lexington, Michigan. According to the Bleeding Skull Web site, the film was only distributed in the Midwest. It was made by a corporate and commercial video company called Camelot Studios, which is still in business in North Street, Michigan (Camelot Studios).

www.camelotstudios.net

Night of the Bloody Transplant (*Transplant*, 1970)
D: David W. Hanson; W: Paula McKinney, D.W. Hanson, A.J. Schramke; P: David W. Hanson; C: Dick Grimm, Elizabeth Rawlings, Cal Seeley

A late-entry in the H.G. Lewis Look-Alike Sweepstakes, this one from Flint, Michigan. A renegade doctor hopes to perform the first heart transplant on a wealthy old woman, but the medical establishment won't let him. When his dopey brother accidentally injures a girl outside of a bar, he decides to use her as a unwitting donor. With real heart surgery footage and some lame strippers.

Hanson also made the serial killer film *Judy* (1970) with co-director George Meadows.

MINNESOTA
(None)

MISSISSIPPI

The Brain Machine (1977)
D: Joy N. Houck Jr.; W: Christian Garrison, Joy N. Houck Jr., Thomas Hal Phillips; P: Stephen C. Burn-

ham, Gilles de Turenne, Christian Garrison (AP), Thomas Hal Phillips (EP); C: James Best, Barbara Burgess, Gil Peterson, Gerald McRaney, Marcus J. Grapes, Doug Collins, Ann Latham

Four volunteers take part in a government experiment to test a machine that can read their minds in this boring sci-fi flick, which seems to consist primarily of establishing shots of various buildings. This Howco release was Joy Houck, Jr.'s final genre film, and his last film as a director until *The St. Tammany Miracle* (1994) with Jim McCullough. Filmed in 1972, but not released until 1977. (Alpha)

The Premonition (1976)

D: Robert Allen Schnitzer; W: Anthony Mahon, Louis Pastore, Robert Allen Schnitzer; P: M. Wayne Fuller (EP), Laurie Silver (AP), Dale Trevillion (AP); C: Sharon Farrell, Edward Bell, Danielle Brisebois, Richard Lynch, Jeff Corey, Ellen Barber

An odd psychological thriller about a woman (Barber) trying to kidnap the daughter she gave up for adoption from the girl's foster parents (Farrell and Bell) with the help of her clown/mime boyfriend (the creepy Lynch). Once the child vanishes, Bell and Farrell enlist the aid of a parapsychologist to help interpret the foster mother's frightening premonitions.

Farrell is married to associate producer Trevillion. New York–born Schnitzer, who previously made a number of short films and documentaries, also directed *No Place to Hide* (1970), an early Sylvester Stallone film that was later redubbed with comedic dialogue by David Casci and released as *A Man Called ... Rainbo* (1990). He shot *The Premonition* in Mississippi primarily because, as a right-to-work state, it was cheaper than filming in New York. His last credit as director was *Kandyland* (1987). Currently, he serves as CEO of Oasis TV, a New Age cable network based in California. (Media Blasters)

www.oasistv.com

Southern Shockers (*Spirit of the Zombie*, 1985)

D: David Coleman; P: Mike Gordon, David Hopper; C: Eric Shusterman, Mike Gordon, Robert Harrell, Tom Hatcher, Tammy King, John Sorrels, Thomas Shinn, Ronald Demerit, Vicki Stevens

A true rarity, this shot-on-video horror anthology was only released on tape in Spain via Robert G. Hussong's International Film

Special effects artist Christopher Witherspoon (center) with hillbilly ghouls Ken Sanders, Ronald Demerit, Don Smith and Jerry Sanders on the set of *Southern Shockers* (1985).

Enterprises under the title *Spirit of the Zombie*. Three men enter a church where a maniacal preacher foretells their doom via tales of the supernatural (I'm guessing here, since as of this writing I've only seen the film dubbed in Spanish): A small town doctor discovers he can heal the sick (and raise the dead) with his touch; a frumpy scofflaw is chased by a hearse-driving, scythe-wielding demon from hell; and (in the best segment) a moonshiner sells some tainted hooch to a group of hillbillies, who transform into gooey-faced zombies.

Director Coleman was a USC film student when he returned to his hometown of West Point, Mississippi, to make this with producer David Hopper (then the general manager at a local TV station). Special effects artist Chris Witherspoon also worked with John Buechler on *Re-Animator*, *Ghoulies*, and *From Beyond*. He went on to direct his own horror film called *Rage* (2010). Hopper now operates Hopper Media Group. Coleman worked as a screenwriter and helped start the Bijou Café website and BijouFlix Releasing. He recently published a book about Bigfoot movies.

authordavecoleman.wordpress.com   *www.hoppermediagroup.com*

MISSOURI

Copperhead (1983/1984)

D: Leland Payton; W: Leland Payton; P: Crystal Payton, Leland Payton; C: Jack Renner, Gretta Ratliff, David Fritts, Cheryl Nickerson, Marianne Blaine

This obscure shot-on-video project is about a crazy family in the Ozarks, a Peruvian treasure, and a horde of nasty copperheads. Leland Payton (a photographer) and his wife Crystal run Lens & Pen Press in Springfield, Mo., and have published several books, including *The Beautiful and Enduring Ozarks*, *Space Toys*, and *The Insiders' Guide to Branson & the Ozark Mountains*.

www.beautifulozarks.com

Zombie Rampage (1989)

D: Todd Sheets; W: Erin Kehr, Todd Sheets, Roger Williams; P: Lanzo Boles, Louis Garrett, David DeCoteau (EP); C: Dave Byerly, Erin Kehr, Stanna Bippus, Beth Belanti, Brian Everad, Deric Bernier, Lisa Cottoner

Shot-on-video full-length debut (I think) from the prolific Sheets about a street gang fighting a horde of flesh-eating zombies. The plot is a bit muddled, but it does have Sheets' signature over-the-top gore, including a sequence in which a baby is ripped in half.

Sheets followed this film with *Sorority Babes in the Dance-A-Thon of Death* (1991, also backed by DeCoteau), *Madhouse* (1991), *Zombie Rampage 2* (1992), and about a dozen other low-budget gore films (released through his Extreme Entertainment imprint), shot around his hometown of Kansas City, Mo. He also hosts an Internet radio show about the supernatural called "NightWatch" (*www.nightwatchshow.com*).

www.zombiebloodbath.com

MONTANA

(None)

NEBRASKA
(None)

NEVADA

Las Vegas Bloodbath (1989)

D: *David Schwartz;* W: *David Schwartz;* P: *David Schwartz;* C: *Ari Levin, Rebecca Gandara, Barbara Bell, Susanne Ciddio, Tiffany Heisler, Leah Luchette*

A man kills his cheating wife and her lover, then goes on what may be the slowest killing spree ever filmed in this shot-on-video cheapie that thematically resembles the work of Florida's Tim Ritter. There's also oil wrestling, gratuitous donut eating, a fetus thrown against a wall, and a gore-filled toilet. Special effects artist David Royal Dalton (who designed haunted house attractions in the Vegas area) also wrote and performed the goofy theme song. Schwartz later managed a discount movie theater in Las Vegas, directed *American Revenge* (1988) with James Van Patten, and produced *Kindergarten Ninja* (1994).

Las Vegas Serial Killer (1986)

D: *Ray Dennis Steckler;* W: *Ray Dennis Steckler;* P: *Ray Dennis Steckler, James Golff (EP), Salvatore Richichi (EP);* C: *Pierre Agostino, Kathryn Downey, Ron Jason, Suzee Slater*

A latter-day Steckler effort, from the period after he moved from California to Nevada and worked in adult films. This one features Pierre Agostino (Pierre D'Agostino) as a serial killer in Vegas. Agostino was also in Steckler's previous *Hollywood Strangler Meets the Skid Row Slasher* (1979) as the same character, and the Vegas-lensed *The Ravager* (1970) as Pierre Gaston.

Executive producers Richichi and Golff also produced the *Video Violence* films, as well as *Death Row Diner* (1988) and *Hollywood Chainsaw Hookers* (1988). The two producers owned Camp Video, which was a subsidiary of their primary business, an adult label called LA Video.

Richichi was the son of Natale "Big Chris" Richichi, an associate of mob boss John Gotti, who was highly active in the pornography industry in the 1970s and 1980s. (Media Blasters)

Loch Ness Horror (1981)

D: *Larry Buchanan;* W: *Larry Buchanan, Lynn Shubert;* P: *Larry Buchanan, John F. Rickert, Jane Buchanan (EP), Irv Berwick (AP);* C: *Sandy Kenyon, Miki McKenzie, Barry Buchanan, Eric Scott, Karey-Louis Scott, Doc Livingston, Stuart Lancaster*

Family-affair production for the Buchanan clan filmed around Lake Tahoe. The famous Loch Ness Monster (a rubbery creature that belches smoke) emerges from the water and begins biting the heads off tourists after some researchers steal its egg.

Producer Berwick directed *The Monster of Piedras Blancas* (1959) and *Hitch Hike to Hell* (1977). His son Wayne (who did the sound on *Loch Ness Horror*) directed *Microwave Massacre* (1983).

Voodoo Heartbeat (1972)

D: *Charles Nizet;* W: *Charles Nizet;* P: *Ray Molina;* C: *Ray Molina, Philip Ahn, Ern Dugo, Forrest Duke, Stan Mason*

This is one of a handful of films from the mysterious Nizet, who worked in Nevada and California in the 1960s and 1970s. According to a synopsis in *TV Guide*, Ray Molina plays a spy who takes an experimental serum that transforms him into a bloodsucking vampire. The Chinese are also after the serum, because they believe it will keep Mao Tse Tung in power forever.

Released overseas as *Sex Serum of Dr. Blake* (the film's original production title). Nizet directed *Mission: Africa* (1968), a war film starring Chuck Alford (who had previously appeared in *The Hollywood Strangler Meets the Skid Row Slasher*, 1979, and *Ride a Wild Stud*, 1969); *Slaves of Love* (1969); the heist film *Three-Way Split* (1970); and the appalling *The Ravager* (1970). The latter stars Pierre Agostino (who also worked for Ray Dennis Steckler) as a psychotic Vietnam vet who becomes a dynamite-wielding serial killer and rapist. Nizet later made *Help Me ... I'm Possessed* (1976) in California and *Rescue Force* (1989), a film that was originally announced as *Target Gaddafi*. According to the Internet Movie Database, Nizet (who was born either in Belgium or France) was murdered in 2003 while in Brazil.

Forrest Duke was also in the aforementioned *Hollywood Strangler Meets the Skid Row Slasher*.

NEW HAMPSHIRE

Battle for the Lost Planet (*Galaxy Destroyer*, 1986)

D: Brett Piper; W: Brett Piper; P: Charles H. Baldwin; C: Matt Mitler, Denise Coward, Joe Gentissi, Bill MacGlaughlin

A man returns to Earth in a stolen spaceship, only to find that the world has been destroyed by alien invaders.

Piper followed this with a sequel, *Mutant War* (1988). He has gone on to write and direct a number of low-budget films (mostly in New Hampshire), including *A Nymphoid Barbarian in Dinosaur Hell* (1991), *Drainiac!* (2000), *Screaming Dead* (2003) and *Bacterium* (2006).

Lead actor Mitler was also in *The Mutilator* (1985), *Deadtime Stories* (1986) and *Basket Case 2* (1990). Coward was Miss Australia 1978.

Mutant War (*Mutant Men Want Pretty Women*, 1988)

D: Brett Piper; W: Brett Piper; P: Charles H. Baldwin, Arthur Schweitzer (EP); C: Matt Mitler, Kristine Waterman, Deborah Quayle, Cameron Mitchell

Mitler returns as Harry Trent (his character from *Battle for the Lost Planet*, 1986), this time enlisted by a woman to save her sister from Cameron Mitchell and his gang of mutants.

Mysterious Planet (1982)

D: Brett Piper; W: Brett Piper; P: Brett Piper, Charles Baldwin (AP); C: Paula Taupier, Boydd Piper, Michael Quigley, Bruce E. Nadeau, Jr.

Escaped convicts meet up with monsters and a scantily-clad woman in this sci-fi update of Jules Verne's *Mysterious Island*, shot on Super 8 for $5,000 and featuring Piper's impressive stop-motion animation.

New Hampshire–born Brett Piper began making movies and experimenting with stop-motion animation as a child. His debut feature is marred by atrocious sound — at various points you can hear the voices of both the original actors and voices that were dubbed over them — but is still a lot of fun.

www.brettpiper.com

Raiders of the Living Dead (1986)

D: Samuel M. Sherman, Brett Piper; W: Brett Piper, Samuel M. Sherman; P: Samuel M. Sherman, Dan Q. Kennis, Charles Baldwin (EP), David Weisman (AP); C: Scott Schwartz, Robert Deveau, Robert Allen, Donna Asali, Corri Burt, Leonard Corman, Zita Johann

"They're back from the dead, and they don't eat potato salad!" A mad doctor raises an army of zombies, while a reporter and precocious kid (who makes a weapon out of his laser disc player) try to stop him.

As with many Independent-International Pictures (IIP) productions, this disjointed film was created in several stages. It began life as a low-budget Piper project called *Dying Day*, which Sam Sherman re-cut and expanded into *Dark Night*. Sherman then shot a substantial amount of new material (using the original actors) to create the *Raiders* version, which he ultimately sold to cable and released on the Super Video label. The film was released on DVD in an unbelievable two-disc set that includes all three (!) versions.

While Sherman is best known for his work with Al Adamson, he also had a hand in several other

Brett Piper's *Dying Day* was repurposed by distributor Samuel M. Sherman as *Raiders of the Living Dead* (1986) (courtesy Fred Adelman).

East Coast productions. He produced John Russo's *Midnight* (1982), oversaw additional footage shot in the New York/New Jersey area for *Dracula vs. Frankenstein* (1971), *The Bloody Dead* (*Creature with the Blue Hand*, 1967), and *Exorcism at Midnight* (*Naked Evil*, 1966). In 2008, Sherman and John Russo announced a new film project called *Escape of the Living Dead*, set to star Tony Todd and Gunnar Hansen.

Frequent *Fangoria* contributor Tim Ferrante served as music coordinator, and George Edward Ott provided the snappy, synth-heavy title song. Robert Allen was a cowboy actor with credits stretching back to the 1930s. Johann was the lead actress in *The Mummy* (1932). Schwartz was in *The Toy* (1982) and played Flick in *A Christmas Story* (1983). He later worked in the adult film industry. (Image)

NEW JERSEY

Alice, Sweet Alice (*Communion*, 1976)

D: Alfred Sole; W: Rosemary Ritvo, Alfred Sole; P: Richard K. Rosenberg, Alfred Sole (EP), Marc G. Greenberg (AP); C: Linda Miller, Mildred Clinton, Paula E. Sheppard, Niles McMaster, Jane Lowry, Rudolph Willrich, Brooke Shields

This well-regarded and unjustly obscure shocker from Alfred Sole may be one of the most unsettling films of the 1970s. Sheppard (who plays a 12-year-old here, but who was actually 19) is Alice, a withdrawn girl who becomes the prime suspect in the murder of her spoiled, screechy sister (Shields), who was killed just before her first communion.

New Jersey native Sole, who was trained as an architect, had previously directed *Deep Sleep* (1972), an adult film that got him excommunicated from the Catholic Church and brought up on obscenity charges in New Jersey and Oklahoma. *Alice, Sweet Alice* (originally called *Communion*) was supposed to be a fairly big release from Columbia, and was even adapted as a book, but instead had a lackluster theatrical run via Allied Artists. It was re-released after Brooke Shields became famous. Sole later directed *Tanya's Island* (1980) and the slasher spoof *Pandemonium* (1982). He has since become a successful production designer.

Brooke Shields made her feature debut in Alfred Sole's excellent *Alice, Sweet Alice* (1976).

The most memorably grotesque character in the film is Alphonso DeNoble as the obese, perverted landlord who lives in a filth-strewn apartment with dozens of cats. DeNoble was a bouncer at a Paterson gay bar who (according to Sole's commentary track on the DVD) would often hang out in local cemeteries dressed as a priest, pocketing "donations" given to him by mourners to say a blessing for their deceased relatives. He was also in *Blood Sucking Freaks* (1976) and *Night of the Zombies* for Joel M. Reed.

Linda Miller is Jackie Gleason's daughter and *Exorcist* star Jason Miller's ex-wife. McMaster, who is now a painter, also appeared in *Blood Sucking Freaks*. The funeral director was played by professional wrestler Antonino Rocca, and the pathologist by singer Lillian Roth. (Henstooth)

The Basement (1989)

D: Tim O'Rawe; W: Tim O'Rawe; P: Tim O'Rawe, Michael Raso, Kathleen Heidinger; C: Dennis Driscoll, Kathleen Heidinger, David Webber, Pamela Kramer, J.R. Bookwalter, Scott Hart

This Super 8 flick was shot just before O'Rawe made *Ghoul School*, but was never actually completed until producer Michael Raso pulled the footage together, re-dubbed the sound and released it on DVD (and VHS!) in 2011. It's an anthology film in which four people get stuck in a basement. A monster/Crypt Keeper knock-off tells them about the horrible "future sins" they will commit, involving a demon in a swimming pool, a teacher who refuses to hand out candy at Halloween, a haunted house, and zombies running rampant on the set of a low-budget horror movie.

Raso now operates Camp Motion Pictures and its affiliated labels (Retro Seduction, Shock-O-Rama, Alternative Cinema, etc.). He and O'Rawe attended William Paterson University together in the 1980s. (Camp)

Beware: Children at Play (1989)

D: Mik Cribben; W: Fred Scharkey; P: Ellen Wedner, Michael Koslow, Lawrence Littler (EP), Linda Sanford (EP); C: Michael Robertson, Rich Hamilton, Robin Lilly, Lori Tirgrath, Jamie Krause, Sunshine Barrett, Mark Diekman

Children in a remote town go missing, then return as brainwashed, cannibal killers in Troma's take on the "killer kid" genre. As you would expect from a Troma release, there is plenty of over-the-top violence committed by and against children, including a grotesque finale/massacre.

This is the only directing credit for Mik Cribben, who primarily works as a cinematographer and sound mixer. (Troma)

www.mikcribben.com

Blades (1989)

D: Thomas R. Rondinella; W: John P. Finegan, William R. Pace, Thomas R. Rondinella; P: John P. Finegan, William R. Pace (AP); C: David Aldrich, Hank Berkheimer, Ron Butko, Kara Callahan, Peter Cosimano

Troma presents another low-budget horror spoof, this one about a massive killer lawnmower terrorizing a country club.

Director Rondinella, a graduate of NYU's film school, had been assistant director on *Girls School Screamers* (1986, directed by *Blades* co-writer John Finegan), and a sound editor or editor on *The Shaman* (1987), *Scared Stiff* (1987) and *Severance* (1988). He directed one other feature, *A Girl's Guide to Sex* (1993), and produced the shorts *A Relaxing Day* (2007) and *Unholy* (2007). In 2010, he co-directed *Scrappers*, a documentary about the 1942 Nebraska scrap metal drive.

Rondinella is also an associate professor at Seton Hall University, and operates a corporate video and feature film production company called Catfish Studios along with William Pace and Douglas Huebner. (Troma)

www.catfishstudios.com

The Chair (1989)

D: *Waldemar Korzeniowsky;* W: *Montieth Illingworth, Carolyn Swartz;* P: *Anthony Jones, Jerry Lott, Angelika Saleh (EP), Joseph Saleh (EP);* C: *James Coco, Trini Alvarado, Paul Benedict, Gary McCleery, Stephen Geoffreys, Brad Greenquist*

The ghost of a prison warden, killed in his own electric chair during a riot, returns to torment inmates and staff.

This film, which was shot in 1986 and 1987, was released around the same time as Renny Harlin's *Prison* (1988), which had a very similar plot. The production was shut down for several months after the film went overschedule, and star James Coco died in the interim (his scenes were already completed). Korzeniowsky (a documentary filmmaker originally from Poland) and Swartz, who are married, operated a company called B-Pictures in New York. Paul Benedict played Mr. Bentley on "The Jeffersons." Filmed at the Essex County Jail in Newark, New Jersey

Christmas Evil (*You Better Watch Out*, 1980)

D: *Lewis Jackson;* W: *Lewis Jackson;* P: *Pete Kameron, Burt Kleiner, Michael A. Levine (AP);* C: *Brandon Maggart, Jeffrey DeMunn, Dianne Hull, Andy Fenwick, Brian Neville, Joe Jamrog*

Santa-obsessed toy factory employee Harry Stadling (Maggart) keeps a running list of who's been naughty and nice in his neighborhood, and spends Christmas Eve rewarding the good and punishing the bad, with sometimes fatal consequences. Equal parts funny, absurd and depressing, *Christmas Evil* is an amalgam of arty, East Coast indie cinema and exploitation, with an unexpectedly whimsical climax.

This was Lewis Jackson's third film as director after making The *Deviators* (1970) and *The Transformation (A Sandwich of Nightmares)* (1974) in New York, and he has been highly active in making sure the film was released and restored to his original vision on DVD. Maggart, who gives an outstanding performance, was nominated for a Tony in 1970 for his work in "Applause," and is the father of actor Garrett Maggart and singer Fiona Apple. He also appeared on the first few seasons of "Sesame Street."

Levine executive produced *Murder By Phone* (1982) and *Santa Baby* (2006). Pete Kameron managed The Weavers, co-founded The Who's record label, and started the *L.A. Weekly*. Kleiner was a Hollywood stockbroker. (Synapse)

Class of Nuke 'Em High (1986)

D: *Richard W. Haines, Lloyd Kaufman;* W: *Richard W. Haines, Lloyd Kaufman, Mark Rudnitsky, Stuart Strutin;* P: *Lloyd Kaufman, Michael Herz, Stuart Strutin (AP), James Treadwell (EP);* C: *Janelle Brady, Gil Brenton, Robert Prichard, Pat Ryan, James Nugent Vernon, Brad Dunker*

Radioactive marijuana has an odd effect on the student body at Tromaville High. The honor society mutates into anti-social punk rockers, and pregnant teen Brady's baby transforms into a rampaging monster that lives in the septic system. This was Troma's second hit after *The Toxic Avenger* (1985).

Troma used the Annunciation Church School in Paramus, New Jersey, for exteriors, and Rye Neck High School in Mamaroneck, New York, for interiors. Haines also directed *Splatter University* (1984) and *Alien Space Avenger* (1989).

There were two sequels, *Class of Nuke 'Em High II: Subhumanoid Meltdown* (1991) and *Class of Nuke 'Em High III: the Good, the Bad and the Subhumanoid* (1994). (Troma)

The Devil Inside Her (1977)

D: *Zebedy Colt;* W: *Zebedy Colt;* P: *Jason West, Leon DeLeon (Leonard Kirtman), Howard North;* C: *Jody Maxell, Terri Hall, Dean Tait, Zebedy Colt, Rod Dumont, Chad Lambert, Annie Sprinkle*

Period porn set in 19th century New England about members of a farm family being possessed by Satan (a mustached actor in KISS-style makeup).

The late Colt (nee: Edward Earle Marsh) was a child actor and singer who began using the stage name "Zebedy Colt" when he recorded a gay-themed record (*I'll Sing For You*) with the London Philharmonic Orchestra. He worked on Broadway under his real name, while directing porn using his alias. This movie was made in Colt's home in Lambertville, New Jersey

Doom Asylum (1987)

D: Richard Friedman; W: Richard Friedman, Rick Marx, Steven G. Menkin; P: Steven G. Menkin, Barry Tucker (EP), Alexander W. Kogan, Jr. (EP); C: Patty Mullen, Ruth Collins, Kristin Davis, William Hay, Kenny L. Price

A hideously mutilated car crash survivor (an attorney who for some reason is referred to as The Coroner) takes refuge in the basement of an abandoned asylum. When an all-girl punk band and a group of obnoxious kids enter the building, he kills them off one by one.

This was shot at the Essex Mountain Asylum in New Jersey, which is allegedly haunted. Friedman also directed *Scared Stiff* (1987) in Florida and the similarly themed *Phantom of the Mall: Eric's Revenge* (1989).

Patty Mullen was in *Frankenhooker* (1990), and Kristin Davis went on to star in "Sex and the City." Executive producers Tucker and Kogan also produced Andy Milligan's *Monstrosity* (1989). (Code Red)

www.doomasylum.com

Dungeon of Death (1989)

D: Gary Whitson; P: Gary Whitson; C: Launa Kane, Clancy McCauley, Chris Stonage

This was an early, shot-on-video film from Gary Whitson, who also released *Sleepover Massacre* the same year (with the same cast), and has gone on to direct dozens of other cheap horror films through his company, Deerfield, New Jersey–based W.A.V.E. Productions.

A former school teacher, Whitson began making shot-on-video horror films in 1987. In addition to his own productions, he also makes custom videos. Customers can send an original script or story idea to Whitson, who (for a fee) will turn it into a movie. Most of these projects feature topless actresses in jeopardy. He made a sequel to *Dungeon of Death* with actress Tina Krause in 1998.

www.wavemovies.com

Forced Entry (*The Last Victim*, 1975)

D: Jim Sotos; W: Henry Scarpelli; P: Henry Scarpelli, Jim Sotos; C: Tanya Roberts, Ron Max, Nancy Allen, Brian Freilino, Vasco Valladeres, Robin Leslie, Bill Longo, Michael Tucci

Roberts is the obsession of a depraved serial rapist and murderer (Max). Shot in New York and New Jersey by the director of *Sweet 16* (1983) and *Hot Moves* (1985).

Producer Scarpelli was an artist for Archie Comics, and is the father of actor Glenn Scarpelli, who appeared in this film as well as on *One Day at a Time*. This was the first film appearance of *Charlie's Angels* star Roberts, who was also in *Tourist Trap* (1979). Allen was in *Carrie* (1976) and *Dressed to Kill* (1980), and later married director Brian De Palma. Michael Tucci was in *Grease* (1978).

Friday the 13th (1980)

D: Sean S. Cunningham; W: Victor Miller, Ron Kurz (uncredited); P: Sean S. Cunningham, Steve Miner (AP), Alvin Geiler (EP); C: Betsy Palmer, Harry Crosby, Adrienne King, Jeannine Taylor, Robbi Morgan, Peter Brouwer, Kevin Bacon, Ari Lehman, Walt Gorney, Mark Nelson

Shot independently but distributed by Paramount, *Friday the 13th* served as the template for most of the slasher films released afterward. Camp Crystal Lake has been closed for 20 years, ever since a couple of copulating teens were found slaughtered in one of the cabins. The new owner (Brouwer) decides to re-open and, despite the warnings of Crazy Ralph (Gorney) — "You're all doomed!" — recruits a new group of sex-crazed counselors to fix up the cursed camp.

Cunningham had previously produced *Last House on the Left* (1972) and directed *Case of the Full Moon Murders* (1973). Harry Manfredini's distinctive score sounds suspiciously like the one he wrote for Carlton Albright's *The Children* (1980), which was also shot by cinematographer Barry Abrams. Tom Savini provided the special effects. Bacon was in the midst of his transition from soap star (on *The Guiding Light*) to movie star when this came out.

The film spawned ten sequels (ending with *Freddy vs. Jason* in 2003), and a 2009 remake. Filmed at Camp No-Be-Bo-Sco in Blairstown, New Jersey (Paramount)

Ghoul School (1990)

D: Timothy O'Rawe; W: Timothy O'Rawe; P: Timothy O'Rawe, David DeCoteau (EP), John Paul Fedele (AP); C: Nancy Sirianni, Anthony Scavone, Richard Bright, Carl Burrows, Ed Burrows, Lorna Courtney, Joe Franklin

Toxic contamination turns the swim team at a New Jersey high school into blue-skinned, flesh-eating zombies. With cameos by former Howard Stern sidekick Jackie "The Joke Man" Martling and TV host Joe Franklin, along with gore, bad jokes, lots of swearing, and a band called Blood Sucking Ghouls.

Producer DeCoteau is a prolific California-based director who also financed several cheap, shot-on-video films for Ohio director J.R. Bookwalter (who has a cameo in this film). Associate producer Fedele is an actor and writer who specializes in softcore sexploitation films. (Camp)

Girls Nite Out (*The Scaremaker*, 1984)

D: Robert Deubel; W: Joe Bolster, Anthony N. Gurvis, Kevin Kurgis, Gil Spencer, Jr.; P: Anthony N. Gurvis, Arthur Ginsberg (AP), Richard Barclay (EP), Kevin Kurgis (EP); C: Julia Montgomery, Hal Holbrook, David Holbrook, James Carroll, Suzanne Barnes, Rutanya Alda, Al McGuire

A killer wearing a cartoonish bear mascot costume outfitted with a claw fashioned from serrated steak knives slashes his way through the students at a fictional Ohio college during the annual scavenger hunt.

A sell sheet for Tim O'Rawe's *Ghoul School* (1990), about a zombified swim team (courtesy J.R. Bookwalter).

An obnoxious DJ spins pop records by The Lovin' Spoonful and The Ohio Express, while security guard Hal Holbrook (whose son David also appears in the film) tries to stop the killer, who he thinks is the escaped lunatic that killed his daughter years earlier. Filmed at Upsala College in East Orange, New Jersey

Montgomery was also in *Revenge of the Nerds* (1984). Producers Anthony Gurvis and Kevin Kurgis are well known attorneys in Columbus, Ohio. Director Deubel previously made documentaries. (Media Blasters)

Last Rights (*Dracula's Last Rites*, 1980)

D: Domonic Paris; W: Ben Donnelly, Domonic Paris; P: Kelly Van Horn; C: Patricia Hammond, Gerald Fielding, Mimi Weddell, Victor Jorge

Funeral director/vampire Mr. A. Lucard uses his business as a front for supplying his undead cronies with blood from not-quite-dead accident victims (who get a stake through the heart before they turn into vampires themselves). When he denies Hammond's request for an open casket funeral for her granny (Weddell), her interference causes Lucard to accidentally let the geriatric bloodsucker loose. Filmed in Vineland, New Jersey

Paris is best known for helming a series of trailer and film clip compilation tapes for a variety of labels in the 1980s and 1990s, including *Bad Girls in the Movies* (1986), *Afros, Macks and Zodiacs* (1995) for Something Weird, and *Film House Fever* (1986), which features a young Steve Buscemi and Mark Boone Jr. attending an all-night movie marathon that consists primarily of clips from Al Adamson and H.G. Lewis films. He directed *Splitz* (1984) and *The Sleepless* (1997), which Paris also published as a novel in 2000. More recently, he wrote the animated 3D films *Fly Me to the Moon* (2008) and *Around the World in 50 Years 3D* (2009), produced by his company Illuminata Pictures.

Weddell also appeared in *Student Bodies* (1981).

Girls Nite Out (1984) was made in New Jersey by two Ohio attorneys (courtesy Fred Adelman).

Metamorphosis: The Alien Factor (1990)

D: Glenn Takakjian; W: Glenn Takakjian; P: Ted A. Bohus, Scott Morette, Ron Giannotto (AP), Tony Grazia (AP); C: Matt Kulis, Patrick Barnes, George C. Colucci (as George Gerard), Tara Leigh, Dianna Flaherty, Katherine Romaine

A scientist is bitten by an alien creature, then mutates into a monster. This was intended as a sequel to *Return of the Aliens: The Deadly Spawn* (1983), which Bohus also produced. By all accounts it has excellent stop-motion effects.

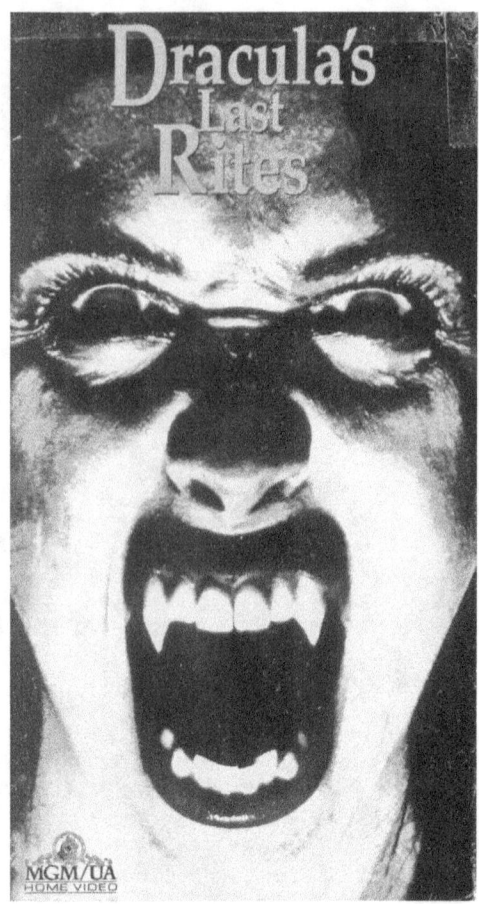 

Left: The intriguing vampire film *Last Rites* (1980) was filmed in Vineland, New Jersey (courtesy Fred Adelman). *Right: Metamorphosis: The Alien Factor* (1990) was a sequel to *Return of the Aliens: The Deadly Spawn* (1983) (courtesy Fred Adelman).

Takakjian is an actor who worked in community and regional theater in New York, and who still appears in TV and films. (Lions Gate)
www.takactor.com

Mother's Day (1980)

D: Charles Kaufman; W: Charles Kaufman, Warren Leight; P: Charles Kaufman, Michael Kravits, Michael Herz (AP), Lloyd Kaufman (AP), Alexander Beck (EP); C: Nancy Hendrickson, Deborah Luce, Tiana Pierce, Frederick Coffin (Holden McGuire), Michael McCleery (Billy Ray McQuade), Beatrice Pons (Rose Ross)

Three college roommates reunite for a camping trip and wind up prisoners of a nutty matriarch (Ross) and her perverted sons (McGuire and McQuade), who spend most of their time watching cartoons, eating buckets of cereal and arguing about music (their "punk sucks–disco's stupid" monologue is a highlight). The boys torture and kill one girl, but the other two escape. After some impromptu commando training, they return to the house and kill the psychos with a can of Draino, a TV set, an electric knife and a pair of inflatable breasts.

This was an early Troma effort, directed by company founder Lloyd Kaufman's brother, Charles. The brothers had previously made a porno called *Secret Dreams of Mona Q* (1977). This was allegedly shot at the same time as *Friday the 13th* (1980), in roughly the same area of New Jersey.

Charles Kaufman later directed the overdubbed spoof *Ferocious Female Freedom Fighters* (1982), *When Nature Calls* (1985) and *Jakarta* (1988). Darren Lynn Bousman directed a (sort of) remake in 2010 starring Rebecca De Mornay. (Troma)

The Naked Witch (*The Naked Temptress*, 1967)

D: Andy Milligan; W: Clay Guss; P: Andy Milligan; C: Beth Porter, Robert Burgos, Bryarly Lee, Maggie Rogers, Hal Borske

Milligan's first period horror film, about a woman burned at the stake for being promiscuous who passes on a "witch's curse" to her daughter. The film is lost, but is often confused with Larry Buchanan's *The Naked Witch* (1964). Shot in Manasquan, New Jersey, and financed by William Mishkin.

The Orphan (*Friday the 13th: The Orphan*, 1979)

D: John Ballard; W: John Ballard; P: John Ballard, Peter Muller, Sondra Gilman, Sidney Ann MacKenzie, Louise Westergaard, Lance Bird (AP), Rita Fredricks (AP), Anne Murphy (AP); C: Peggy Feury, Donn Whyte, Mark Owens, Afolabi Ajayi, Stanley Church, Joanna Miles, David Foreman

Low-key story set in the 1930s about an orphaned boy (Owens) taken in by his well-meaning, but overly strict aunt who systematically isolates him from his few friends. The boy begins practicing a weird mixture of Christianity and African voodoo (partly learned from his late father and a friend from Africa), centered around a stuffed monkey he has enshrined in an old chicken coop, and through which he attempts to channel his rage at his aunt. Based on Saki's "Sredni Vashtar."

Ballard started shooting this film in 1968 and continued adding to it over the next ten years until two additional producers (Gilman and Westergaard) helped get the movie completed and distributed. Ballard has since written a series of books based on his travels to India and Africa, including *Monsoon: A Novel to End World Hunger* (1985) and *The Soul Guide to African-American Consciousness: Reclaiming Your History* (1993). He is currently married to jazz singer Jackie Ryan

Feury was a well-known drama teacher who worked with Lee Strasberg and operated her own L.A.–based acting school. Janis Ian sang the theme song.

The Prowler (1981)

D: Joseph Zito; W: Neal F. Barbera, Glenn Leopold; P: Joseph Zito, David Streit, James Bochis; C: Vicky Dawson, Christopher Goutman, Lawrence Tierney, Farley Granger, Cindy Weintraub, Lisa Dunsheath, Thom Bray

Early slasher film notable for its special effects (by Tom Savini) and the fact that it has almost the exact same plot as *My Bloody Valentine* (also 1981). The film opens in 1945, with a soldier being spurned by his girlfriend after he comes home from the war. Said wayward girlfriend is then murdered (along with her new beau) during a graduation dance. When the town resurrects the dance years later, a mysterious helmet-wearing killer appears and makes short work of the local teens using a bayonet and a pitchfork.

Goutman worked primarily in soap operas. Thom Bray played the geeky Boz on *Riptide* and wrote for a number of TV series in the 1990s. (Blue Underground)

Return of the Aliens: The Deadly Spawn (1983)

D: Douglas McKeown; W: Ted A. Bohus, John Dods; P: Ted A. Bohus, John Dods (AP), Tim Hildebrandt (EP); C: Charles George Hildebrandt, Tom DeFranco, Richard Lee Porter, Jean Tafler, Karen Tighe

Toothy alien parasites arrive in the New Jersey woods via meteorite, then take up residence in the basement of an old house where they eat people and prepare to reproduce. Although cheap, the film is fast-paced, fun, and features some incredible creature effects by John Dods, who directed portions of the film after Bohus fired McKeown from the production.

McKeown was a teacher and stage actor prior to making this film. Writer/producer Bohus had worked on Don Dohler's *Fiend* (1980) and *Nightbeast* (1982), and later produced a pseudo-sequel to this film called *Metamorphasis: The Alien Factor* (1990). Dods also worked on *The Alien Factor* (1978) and *Nightbeast*, as well as *Spookies* (1987), *My Demon Lover* (1987), *Black Roses* (1988), *Ghostbusters II* (1989), *Alien: Resurrection* (1997), and "The X-Files." Co-writer Tim Sullivan later directed *2001 Maniacs* (2005), a remake of the H.G. Lewis film. Producer Tim Hildebrandt (father of the child actor in this film, Charles Hildebrandt) was a well-known fantasy and sci-fi illustrator who, along with his brother Greg, worked on the original *Star Wars* (1977) poster. He died in 2006. (Synapse)

The Shaman (1987)

D: Michael Yakub; W: Michael Yakub, Robert Yakub; P: Roberto Munoz (EP); C: Avind Harum, Michael Conforti, James Farkas, Mike Hodge, Mark Folger, Ilene Kristen

Norwegian actor Harum is The Shaman, a mysterious figure who stalks a suburban neighborhood looking for a successor. Thomas R. Rondinella (director of *Blades*, 1989, and editor of *Girls School Screamers*, 1986) acted as the sound editor on this film, which was shot near the Tappan Zee Bridge on the border of New York and New Jersey.

Conforti wrote for and acted in soap operas, as did several other members of the cast.

Silent Death (1983)

D: Vaughn Christion; P: Joe Sollazzo, Chuck Geiger, Doyle Taylor (EP), Chris Christion (EP); C: Freddy James, Doyle Taylor, David Arts, Natalie Carter

According to *Gore Gazette* (the only publication to review this film, as far as I can tell), *Silent Death* is a 69-minute film with a predominantly black cast about a masked killer who stalks criminals. Filmed in May and June of 1982 in Freehold, Union, and Elizabeth, New Jersey, it played for one week in February 1983 at the Paramount Theater in Newark, New Jersey, on a triple bill with *Maniac* (1980) and *An Eye for an Eye* (1981). A Reina production filmed in "T.C." (Total Color). According to Doyle Taylor's IMDB biography, it was shot on 16mm and blown up to 35mm.

Christion later made the films *The Wrong Disciple* (1991) and *Heaven* (1997), both featuring Taylor, who

Silent Death (1983) had only one theatrical showing before vanishing into obscurity (courtesy Chris Poggiali).

operates Down Right Talented Entertainment (a management/film company) in Los Angeles. In 2009, Christion debuted a Web series called *Wildflower*, and in 2011 announced a new feature called *Key of Brown*

The Toxic Avenger (1985)

D: Michael Herz, Lloyd Kaufman; W: Lloyd Kaufman, Joe Ritter, Stuart Strutin, Gay Partington Terry; P: Michael Herz, Lloyd Kaufman, Stuart Strutin (AP); C: Andree Maranda, Mitch Cohen, Jennifer Prichard, Cindy Manion, Robert Prichard, Gary Schneider, Mark Rorgl

More than any other property, this was the film that made Lloyd Kaufman's Troma a household name (well, at least in *some* households). A nerdy janitor is dumped in a vat of toxic waste and emerges as a muscular, mop-wielding mutant superhero. Marisa Tomei appears in a bit part.

It was followed by *The Toxic Avenger, Part II* (1989), *The Toxic Avenger Part III: The Last Temptation of Toxie* (1989), *Citizen Toxie: The Toxic Avenger IV* (2000) the short-lived *Toxic Crusaders* animated series, and a comic book. (Troma)

Video Violence ... When Renting Is Not Enough (1987)

D: Gary Cohen; W: Gary Cohen, Paul Kaye; P: Ray Clark, James Golff (EP), Salvatore Richichi (EP); C: Gary Schwartz, Chick Kaplan, Jackie Neill, Art Neill, Robin Leeds, Kevin Haver, Bart Summer, William Toddie

Married New Yorkers move to a small town and open a video store, but discover that the locals only want to rent horror films and pornography. When one of their customers mistakenly returns a snuff film to the store, they decide to investigate.

Shot on video by director Gary Cohen, who had previously operated a video store in New Jersey, this became one of the most widely distributed SOV horror films of the era. Cohen later wrote a book about community theater, and serves as Producing Director for the Plays in the Park program in Middlesex County, New Jersey (Camp)

New Jersey's favorite homegrown superhero, *The Toxic Avenger* (1985) (courtesy Fred Adelman).

Video Violence 2 ... The Exploitation (1987)

D: Gary Cohen; W: Gary Cohen; P: Ray Clark, James Golff (EP), Salvatore Richichi (EP); C: Uke, Bart Summer, David Christopher, Neil Cerbone, Art Neill, Jackie Neill, Lisa Cohen

The killers from the first *Video Violence* host a snuff film pirate cable program in this over-the-top comic sequel. In between the two VV films, Cohen also made the home-invasion flick *Captives* (a.k.a. *Mama's Home*, 1988), which was released by Majestic Video. Richichi, whose family had ties to John Gotti, also had a hand in several other low-budget horror films (see the entry for *Las Vegas Serial Killer*). (Camp)

NEW MEXICO

The Devil's Mistress (1965)

D: Orville Wanzer; W: Orville Wanzer; P: Wes Moreland; C: Joan Stapleton, Robert Gregory, Forrest Westmoreland, Douglas Warren, Oren Williams

This weird horror western is about four outlaws escaping to the mountains of New Mexico. Two of them murder a man, then rape and kidnap his half-Indian mistress. She kills her captors one by one before reuniting with her undead lover.

This film premiered in Las Cruces, New Mexico, on November 3, 1965. Orville Wanzer is a professor emeritus of journalism and mass communication at New Mexico State University, where he was teaching when he made *The Devil's Mistress*. He shot one other feature, *George Andrews*, in 1972. He also appears to have written a novel called *The Elfin Brood* (1996).

In 1967 Wanzer was hired to make a promotional, behind-the-scenes documentary about the filming of *Hang'Em High* (1968), which was also made in New Mexico. Wes Moreland and Forrest Westmoreland (a local land developer) are probably the same person. Actress Joan Stapleton was actually Mrs. Wanzer.

Track of the Moonbeast (1976)

D: Richard Ashe; W: Bill Finger, Charles Sinclair; P: Frank J. Desiderio (EP), Ralph T. Desiderio; C: Chase Cordell, Leigh Drake, Gregorio Sala, Patrick M. Wright, Francine Kessler

Cordell is a mineralogist who gets hit in the head by a moon rock during a meteor shower, which causes him to transform into a lizard-man at night. The film includes a lengthy cooking scene with the Native American anthropology professor, a folk rock band singing "California Lady," and special effects by Joe Blasco and Rick Baker.

Ashe primarily worked as an assistant director throughout most of his career. Producers Frank and Ralph Desiderio operated car dealerships in New Jersey and bankrolled the *Ginger* films starring Cheri Caffaro. Ashe worked on at least one of those films, *Girls are for Loving* (1973). Screenwriters Bill Finger (a comic book writer who was the uncredited co-creator of Batman) and Charles Sinclair also penned *The Green Slime* (1968) and a number of television episodes together. This was filmed in New Mexico in 1972. (Mill Creek)

NEW YORK

Alien Space Avenger (*Space Avenger*, 1989)

D: Richard W. Haines; W: Leslie Delano, Brad Dunker, Richard W. Haines, Kay Gelfman, Clyde Lynwood Sawyer; P: Robert A. Harris, Richard W. Harris, Ray Sundlin, Richard Albert (EP), Timothy McGinn

(EP), David Smith (EP), Frank Calo (AP); C: Robert Prichard, Michael McCleery, Charity Staley, Gina Mastrogiacomo, Angela Nicholas, Kirk Fogg, Jamie Gillis

A group of aliens take over the bodies of some teenagers in the 1930s, then go into hibernation for 50 years. When they awaken and begin killing people, an interstellar bounty hunter tracks them down using the body of a comic book artist's girlfriend.

Haines also directed *Splatter University* (1984) and *Class of Nuke 'Em High* (1986). He works in film restoration (he had a hand in restoring *Carnival of Souls*, 1962), and also wrote the book *Technicolor Movies* (1993). *Space Avenger* was one of the last American films printed using the old Technicolor system, and Haines had to go to China in 1989 to make 3-strip Technicolor prints of the film.

The Amazing Transplant (1970)

D: Doris Wishman (as Louis Silverman); W: Doris Wishman; P: Doris Wishman; C: Juan Fernandez, Linda Southern, Larry Hunter, Olive Denneccio, Bernard Marcel, Janet Banzet

Wishman's kinky take on *The Hands of Orlac* concerns mild mannered Arthur (Fernandez) who turns into a sex-crazed rapist/killer after having the penis of his late (and more virile) friend Felix transplanted on to his body. The film is presented in flashback, with Arthur's police detective uncle (Hunter) interviewing the victims.

Fernandez also served as cinematographer on several other Wishman films. (Something Weird)

The Astrologer (*Suicide Cult*, 1977)

D: James Glickenhaus; W: John Cameron (novel); P: Mark Buntzman; C: Bob Byrd, Monica Tidwell, Mark Buntzman, James Glickenhaus, Alison McCarthy, Al Narcisse

An astrologer uses advanced computers to foretell the second coming of Christ, and crosses paths with an evil cult leader.

Glickenhaus made this for $65,000 and self-distributed the film, literally carrying the prints across the South himself. It was later distributed by 21st Century Distribution under the *Suicide Cult* title.

Glickenhaus and Buntzman re-teamed for the successful action film *The Exterminator* (1980). Glickenhaus later produced *Maniac Cop* (1988) and several Frank Henenlotter films, and directed *The Protector* (1985), *McBain* (1991) and *Slaughter of the Innocents* (1994). Glickenhaus is also a car collector and a partner at the investment firm Glickenhaus & Co.

Based on a John Cameron novel, which was reprinted in 1981 as a movie tie-in by Sphere.

Banned (1989)

D: Roberta Findlay; W: Jim Cirile; P: Jim Cirile, Gary Levinson, Walter E. Sear; C: Amy Brentano, Fred Cabral, Roger Coleman, Dan Erickson, T.J. Glenn, Cheryl Hendricks, Debbie Rochon

Findlay's final feature as a director is a horror comedy about a jazz guitarist who is possessed by a punk rocker. This was the only Sear/Findlay production that failed to find distribution, and remains unavailable on video.

Screenwriter and producer Jim Cirile now runs a "professional screenplay analysis, development and editing" service called Coverage, Ink. He originally worked as an assistant for Sear and Findlay at Reeltime Distributing Corp., and served as co-writer or associate producer on some of the company's titles. This was also an early credit for prolific genre actress Debbie Rochon.

www.coverageink.com

Basket Case (1982)

D: Frank Henenlotter; W: Frank Henenlotter; P: Edgar Ievins, Arnold H. Bruck (EP); C: Kevin Van Hentenryck, Terri Susan Smith, Beverly Bonner, Robert Vogel, Diana Browne, Lloyd Pace

Van Hentenryck is Duane, a troubled young man who keeps his deformed, murderous Siamese twin in a wicker basket. Together, they hunt down and kill the doctors that surgically separated them.

Native New Yorker Henenlotter was a commercial artist, graphic designer and lifelong fan of trashy horror films who made his feature film debut with *Basket Case* (shot in 16mm). He made two more-polished sequels in 1990 and 1992, as well as *Brain Damage* (1988) and *Frankenhooker* (1990). More than a decade passed before he returned to filmmaking with *Bad Biology* (2008). (Something Weird)

Basket Case 2 (1990)

D: Frank Henenlotter; W: Frank Henenlotter; P: James Glickenhaus (EP), Edgar Ievins; C: Kevin Van Hentenryck, Annie Ross, Kathryn Meisle, Heather Rattray, Beverly Bonner, Jason Evers, Ted Sorel, David Emge

After surviving their fall from the fire escape at the end of the first film, the Bradley brothers escape the hospital and are taken in by Granny Ruth (Ross) who shelters a houseful of human oddities on Staten Island. When reporters start snooping around looking for the still-wanted twins, the freaks fight back to protect their sanctuary.

Producer Glickenhaus directed *The Astrologer* (1975), and also produced *Maniac Cop* (1988) and *Frankenhooker* (1990). Actor Jason Evers starred in *The Brain that Wouldn't Die* (1962), and one of the freaks in this film was modeled on the giant mutant in that film. Emge was in *Dawn of the Dead* (1978). (Synapse)

The Beautiful, the Bloody and the Bare (1964)

D: Sande N. Johnsen; W: Sande N. Johnsen; P: Al Ruban; C: Jack Jowe, Marlene Denes, Mai Dey, Debra Page, Tom Signorelli

A photographer of nude models goes into murderous rages whenever he sees red lipstick or nail polish.

Frank Henenlotter's *Basket Case* (1982) was one of the most inventive films to emerge from New York in the 1980s (courtesy Fred Adelman).

Tom Signorelli was in *Alice, Sweet Alice*. Producer/cinematographer Al Ruban also worked with John Cassavetes, and directed *The Sexploiters* (1965). (Something Weird)

Behind Locked Doors (*Any Body Any Way*, 1968)

D: Charles Romine; W: Stanley H. Brassloff, Charles Romine; P: Stanley H. Brassloff, Harry Novak (EP); C: Eve Reeves, Joyce Danner, Daniel Garth, Ivan Agar, Irene Lawrence

Two female swingers are kidnapped by a creepy scientist (Garth) and taken to his mansion, where they become the subjects of his perverse experiments. This off-kilter adults-only feature includes lesbianism, necrophilia, reanimated corpses and rampant go-go dancing, as well as *Shriek of the Mutilated* star Ivan Agar as another weird handyman. (Something Weird)

Blade (1973)

D: Ernest Pintoff; W: Jeff Lieberman, Ernest Pintoff; P: George Manasse; C: John Marley, Jon Cypher, Kathryn Walker, William Prince, Michael McGuire, Joe Santos, Ted Lange, Morgan Freeman, Julius Harris, Rue McClanahan

Low-budget detective-versus-psycho flick starring Marley as a private investigator alongside a high-profile cast of character actors.

Director Pintoff won an Oscar for his animated short *The Critic* (1963), and later directed *Dynamite Chicken* (1971), *St. Helens* (1981) and a lot of TV episodes. George Manasse also produced Lieberman's *Blue Sunshine* (1976) and *Squirm* (1976), as well as *He Knows You're Alone* (1980). *Blade* was distributed by Joseph Green, director of *The Brain that Wouldn't Die* (1962). New scenes were added in 1979 for the television version of the film. (Code Red)

Blood (1974)

D: Andy Milligan; W: Andy Milligan; P: Walter Kent; C: Allan Berendt, Hope Stansbury, Patricia Gaul, Michael Fischetti, Eve Crosby

Dracula's daughter and the Wolf Man's son get married in one of the few Milligan films that wasn't distributed by William Mishkin. There is also a carnivorous plant, along with the typical Milligan period costumes and crude gore.

Producer Walter Kent was part owner of the Continental Baths (a men's bathhouse in Manhattan), and had worked with Milligan on *Dragula* (1973). *Blood* was distributed by Bryanston Distributing, owned by alleged mobster Lou "Butchie" Peraino.

Blood Bath (1976)

D: Joel M. Reed; W: Joel M. Reed; P: Philip Dearborn (EP), Anthony Fingleton; C: Harve Presnell, Jack Somack, Curt Dawson, Doris Roberts, Jerry Lacy, P.J. Soles, Neil Flanagan

Early PG-rated omnibus film from the director of *Bloodsucking Freaks* about a horror film director who holds a dinner party at his apartment. His guests tell spooky stories with ironic twist endings about a hit man who gets blown up by his own bomb, a magic coin, a loan shark locked inside his bank vault with a ghost, and a greedy martial arts instructor.

Reed, a former combat photographer in Korea, had worked in theater (Broadway and off-Broadway) and in publicity for MGM. He directed two softcore sex films in the late 1960s, then made *G.I. Executioner* (1975) in the Philippines. He followed *Blood Bath* with *Blood Sucking Freaks* (1976) and *Night of the Zombies* (1981). He later wrote novels and a book about Donald Trump.

Roberts was a regular on "Remington Steele" and "Everybody Loves Raymond." Lacy was on "Dark Shadows" and played Humphrey Bogart in *Play it Again Sam* (1972). Flanagan was in Andy Milligan movies.

Australian producer (and champion swimmer) Anthony Fingleton later wrote and produced *Drop Dead Fred* (1991) and *Swimming Upstream* (2003), the latter based on his own life. Ron Sullivan (a.k.a. Henri Pachard) was the art director. (Subversive Cinema)

Blood Sisters (1987)

D: *Roberta Findlay; W: Roberta Findlay; P: Walter E. Sear; C: Amy Brentano, Shannon McMahon, Dan Erickson, Marla Machart, Elizabeth Rose*

Ditzy sorority sisters spend the night in a haunted whorehouse during a university scavenger hunt. Their boyfriends have rigged the house to frighten them, but real ghosts make the girls have flashbacks while staring into mirrors. The transvestite son of one of the dead hookers — who looks sort of like Bea Arthur from the back — kills the girls one by one. Writer Maitland McDonagh appears as one of the pledges. (Shriek Show)

Blood Sucking Freaks (*The Incredible Torture Show*, 1976)

D: *Joel M. Reed; W: Joel M. Reed; P: Joel M. Reed, Alan G. Margolin; C: Seamus O'Brien, Viju Krem, Niles McMaster, Dan Fauci, Ernie Pysher, Luis De Jesus, Alphonso DeNoble*

Master Sardu and his dwarf assistant Ralphus kidnap and torture people at their Grand Guignol theater in this graphic, tasteless, goofy gore flick. Although designed as a satire (director Reed claims he was inspired by an actual Soho S&M club), the film's unrelenting parade of perversity gained it a well-deserved reputation as one of the sickest things put on screen in the 1970s. When Troma acquired the film, it had to significantly cut the movie to acquire an R rating, then released the original unrated version to theaters and on video (via Vestron).

Both McMaster and DeNoble were in *Alice, Sweet Alice* (1976). Luis De Jesus was in the equally infamous porn loop *The Anal Dwarf* (1971), and also appeared in *Under the Rainbow* (1981) and as an Ewok in *Return of the Jedi* (1983). He died in 1988. (Troma)

Bloodrage (1979)

D: *Joseph Zito (as Joseph Bigwood); W: Robert Jahn; P: Joseph Zito, Alan M. Braveman, Tom Gioulos (AP), Claire Liberman (AP), William Tasgal (AP), Milton Wolosky (AP),*

Blood Sisters (1987), one of a series of horror films made by former adult film director Roberta Findlay (courtesy Fred Adelman).

Teddy Kariofilis (EP); C: Ian Scott, James Johnson, Judith-Marie Bergan, Irwin Keyes, Patrick Hines, Lawrence Tierney

A small-town boy flees home after killing a hooker, then heads to New York where he continues to kill even more hookers. Zito also produced and directed *The Prowler* (1981) and *Friday the 13th: The Final Chapter* (1984) before moving on to *Missing in Action* (1984) and *Invasion U.S.A.* (1985).

Brain Damage (1988)

D: Frank Henenlotter; W: Frank Henenlotter; P: Edgar Ievins, Ray Sundlin (AP), Al Eicher (EP), Andre Blay (EP); C: Rick Hearst, Gordon MacDonald, Jennifer Lowry, Theo Barnes, Lucille Saint-Peter

Henenlotter's second horror-comedy is about a man (Hearst) who becomes dependent on an evil, phallic slug that shoots him up with a hallucinogenic substance in exchange for his help in obtaining victims whose brains the alien critter sucks out.

Horror host John Zacherle provided the voice of Aylmer the slug. Former *Fangoria* editor Bob Martin wrote a novelization of the screenplay. (Synapse/Image)

The Brain That Wouldn't Die (1962)

D: Joseph Green; W: Rex Carlton, Joseph Green; P: Rex Carlton, Mort Landberg (AP); C: Jason Evers, Virginia Leith, Leslie Daniel, Adele Lamont, Eddie Carmel

The VHS artwork for the notoriously depraved *Blood Sucking Freaks* (1976) (courtesy Fred Adelman).

Notoriously wacky flick about a doctor who salvages his girlfriend's severed head after a car accident, then spends the rest of the film trying to find a stripper's body onto which he can attach it. The head, wrapped in bandages and sitting in a shallow pan in Evers' lab, kvetches to a giant mutant (Carmel) locked in a nearby closet.

This film, shot independently in 1959, was Rex Carlton's last film in New York before he relocated to L.A. Carlton probably knew Carmel (sometimes billed as "The Jewish Giant") from his days as a wrestling promoter in Delaware. Racy topless footage of some of the actresses was filmed for the European release. Carlton committed suicide in 1968. (Synapse/Alpha)

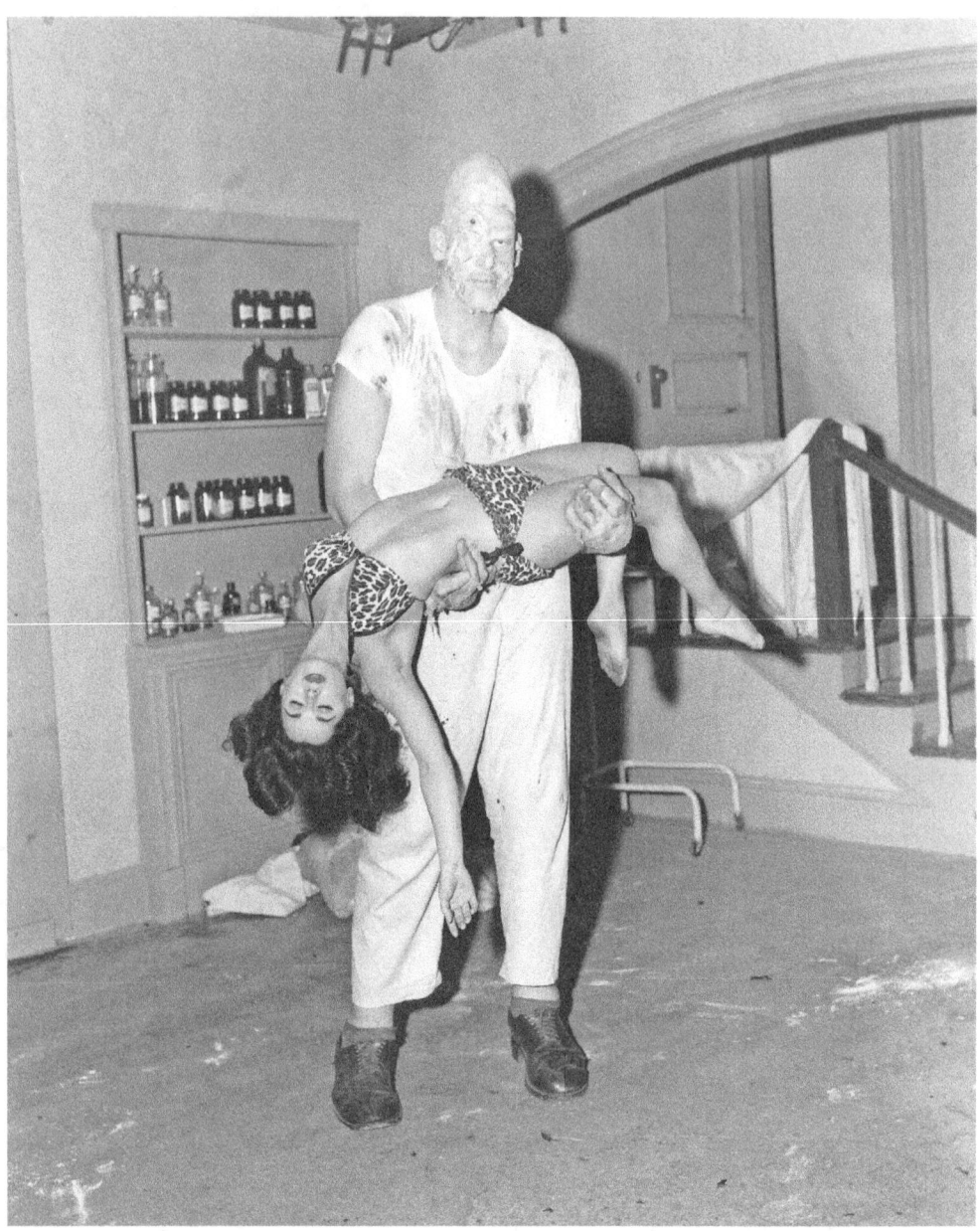

The "Jewish Giant" Ed Carmel holds actress Adele Lamont in a posed still for Rex Carlton's *The Brain That Wouldn't Die* (1962) (courtesy Tom Weaver).

The Brother from Another Planet (1984)

D: John Sayles; W: John Sayles; P: Maggie Renzi, Peggy Rajski; C: Joe Morton, Steve James, Daryl Edwards, Maggie Renzi, Leonard Jackson, Tom Wright

Mute, black alien Morton lands in New York where he fights crime, tries to avoid capture by the Men in Black, and is generally perplexed at the response people give his silent passivity. Sayles has contributed screenplays to a number of horror and science fiction films (including *Alligator*, 1980), but this is his only pseudo-genre film as director. (MGM)

The Burning (1981)

D: Tony Maylam; W: Peter Lawrence, Tony Maylam, Brad Grey, Bob Weinstein; P: Harvey Weinstein, Michael Cohl (EP), Andre Djauoi (EP), Dany Ubaud (AP), Jean Ubaud (AP); C: Brian Matthews, Fisher Stevens, Brian Backer, Leah Ayres, Jason Alexander, Lou David, Holly Hunter

One of two slasher films based on the local "Cropsey/Cropsy Maniac" urban legend that were shot simultaneously in New York (the other was Joe Giannone's *Madman*). Cranky caretaker Cropsy is accidentally set on fire in his bed during a summer camp prank gone wrong. Five years later, after being kicked out of his home at the state hospital, he heads out to the woods and starts hacking up campers using oversized gardening shears.

This was one of the first films produced by Miramax, an independent distribution company founded by Harvey and Bob Weinstein, who had previously made their fortunes as concert promoters. Tom Savini handled the special effects, and Rick Wakeman provided the score (which was released as a soundtrack album).

Carnage (1984)

D: Andy Milligan; W: Andy Milligan; P: Lew Mishkin; C: Leslie Den Dooven, Michael Chiodo, John Garitt, Deeann Veeder, Jack Poggi, Dennis Malvasi (as Albert Alfano)

This was Milligan's last New York horror film, and was produced by Lew Mishkin, son of Milligan's longtime producer/nemesis William Mishkin. A couple moves into a house haunted by the previous tenants — a bride and groom who committed suicide while wearing their wedding regalia. There are some good kill scenes, but most of the "scares" involve the bloody apparition of the bride (Veeder) making a mess in the kitchen or destroying stemware. In place of Milligan's usual manic camera work, he pads the film with long takes of people walking to cars and filling up bathtubs, and at one point lingers on Dooven very slowly making a pot of tea.

Actor Dennis Malvasi and his wife, Loretta Marra, later gained notoriety when they helped James Kopp (who had killed an abortion clinic doctor) flee the country. Malvasi was associated with the militant anti-abortion group The Army of God, and was arrested in 1987 for bombing several New York City abortion clinics. He was actually on the run from federal authorities as he drove Milligan (who never had a driver's license) to California when the aging director finally left New York in the 1980s. Malvasi was arrested in 2001 for assisting Kopp, then released in 2003.

Milligan made three horror films in Los Angeles: *The Weirdo* (1989), *Monstrosity* (1989), and *Surgikill* (1990). He died in 1991. Lew Mishkin died in 2001. (Mill Creek)

Carnival of Blood (1970)

D: Leonard Kirtman; W: Leonard Kirtman; P: Leonard Kirtman; C: Earle Edgerton, Judith Resnick, Martin Barolsky, Burt Young, Kaly Mills

A psycho kills women on Coney Island in this weird, amateurish film from New York–based Kirtman. Soon-to-be-famous character actor Burt Young (as "John Harris") is Gimpy the hunchback, assistant to carny barker Earle Edgerton. Full of awkward, improvised dialogue, erratic zooms, and shoddy photography, this ran on a double bill with Kirtman's California-lensed *Curse of the Headless Horseman* (1972).

Kirtman also produced and directed a number of adult films using the name Leon Gucci. (Something Weird)

The Dead Come Home (*Dead Dudes in the House/The House on Tombstone Hill*, 1989)

D: James Riffel; W: James Riffel; P: Mark Bladis, Melisse Lewis, James Riffel; C: J.D. Cerna, Douglas Gibson, Victor Verhaeghe, James Griffin, Naomi Kooker, Sarah Newhouse

Gore-comedy about youngsters trying to rehab a haunted house and falling victim to the ghost of the murderous old lady (actually Gibson) who haunts the place, then being reanimated as zombies. Filmed on 16mm in Cherry Valley, New York

NYU film school grad Riffel distributed this film himself, and it played at the Fabian Theater in Paterson, New Jersey, as well as having a run as a Midnight movie. It was originally released on AIP video as *House on Tombstone Hill*, then picked by the folks at Troma (who saddled it with the dopey *Dead Dudes* title). He has since directed *Black-Eyed Susan* (2004) and *Mass of Angels* (2004), and created re-dubbed versions of older cult movies (like *Night of the Living Dead* and *The Brain that Wouldn't Die*) with new comedy soundtracks and some additional footage. Riffel also wrote *The Video Detectives Guide to the Top 1,000 Films of All Time*.

The Degenerates (1967)

D: Andy Milligan; W: Gerald Jacuzzo, Andy Milligan; P: Andy Milligan; C: Bryarly Lee, Marcia Howard, Anne Linden, Susan Howard, Laura Weiss, Hope Stansbury, Robert Burgos, Vernon Newman, David Haine

In the aftermath of a nuclear holocaust, three men searching for other survivors stumble across five crazy sisters living in an old house. After the men take liberties with them, the oldest, craziest sister goes on a murderous rampage.

Shot in an abandoned mansion in Woodstock, New York, this was one of three Milligan pictures released by ASA Productions, along with *The Ghastly Ones* (1968) and *Depraved!* (1967).

Deranged (1987)

D: Chuck Vincent; W: Craig Horrall; P: Chuck Vincent, Bill Slobodian (AP); C: Veronica Hart, Jerry Butler, Jennifer Delora, Jamie Gillis, Jill Cumer

Low-rent take on Polanski's *Repulsion*, with Hart as an unbalanced pregnant woman who kills a burglar in self defense, and is then plagued by hallucinations.

Chuck Vincent was a prolific adult film director who moved into more mainstream features in the 1980s. Most of the cast also worked in porn.

Devil's Due (1973)

D: Ernest Danna; W: Gerry Pound; P: Nino De Roma; C: Cindy West, Andrea True, Darby Lloyd Rains, Gus Thomas, Davey Jones

One of several Satanic-themed porno films, this one is about a girl who leaves her abusive home and joins a Satanic cult. (Alpha Blue Archives)

Deranged (1987) was a mainstream horror outing from adult film director Chuck Vincent (courtesy Fred Adelman).

Don't Go in the House (1979)

D: *Joseph Ellison;* W: *Joseph Ellison, Ellen Hammill, Joseph R. Masefield;* P: *Ellen Hammill;* C: *Dan Grimaldi, Robert Osth, Ruth Dardick, Charles Bonet, Bill Ricci, Dennis Hunt*

Intriguing proto-slasher film and *Psycho* (1960) knock-off about a disturbed man who starts killing women after his mother dies. His modus operandi: he binds the women inside a fireproof room in his house, burns them alive with a flame thrower, then dresses and arranges their charred corpses in his home.

Ellison had previously worked in post-production, re-dubbing exploitation films like *The Bodyguard* (1976) and *Revenge of the Streetfighter* (1974). His only other film as a director was *Joey* (1986), about a fictitious doo-wop group. Grimaldi is better known for his role as Patsy on "The Sopranos." Filmed in New York and New Jersey. (Media Blasters)

Dracula Exotica (1980)

D: *Shaun Costello (as Warren Evans);* W: *Shaun Costello;* P: *Shaun Costello, Zora Coast (EP), Bill Millings (AP);* C: *Jamie Gillis, Vanessa Del Rio, Samantha Fox, Eric Edwards, Denise Sloan, Ron Jeremy*

Another erotic version of Dracula. This was Gillis' second turn as the Count (he had previously appeared in *Dracula Sucks*, 1979).

Dragula (1973)

D: *Jim Moss, Andy Milligan;* P: *Calvin Holt;* C: *Calvin Culver, Calvin Holt, Walter Kent, Hal Borske, Jacques Brower*

Homoerotic take on the vampire mythos shot on Fire Island, featuring a hairdresser who turns people into drag queens by biting them. Walter Kent later produced Milligan's *Blood* (1974).

The Driller Killer (1979)

D: *Abel Ferrara;* W: *Nicholas St. John;* P: *Rochelle Weisberg (EP), Douglas Anthony Metrov (AP);* C: *Abel Ferrara, Carolyn Marz, Baybi Day, Harry Schultz, Alan Wynroth*

Like many other underground films made in New York during the 1970s, *Driller Killer* takes advantage of the city's seedy locations, but populates them with whiney, self-absorbed, annoying characters. A cranky artist (Ferrara) is slowly driven nuts by his nagging roommates, bill collectors, a condescending art dealer, and the punk band that just moved into his apartment building. He snaps and starts killing derelicts using a portable electric power drill.

New York native Ferrara shot this on weekends over a period of two years. After the

The Driller Killer (1979), arthouse horror from Abel Ferrara (courtesy Fred Adelman).

much better *Ms. 45* (1981), he moved on to higher-profile studio and TV projects. Prior to *Driller Killer*, he directed the porn film *9 Lives of a Wet Pussy* (1976) using the alias "Jimmy Laine." Associate producer Metrov wrote most of the music in the film, and provided much of the artwork. (Cult Epics)

Echoes (Living Nightmare, 1983)

D: Arthur Allan Seidelman; W: Richard Alfieri, Richard J. Anthony; P: George R. Nice, Valerie Y. Belsky, Marilyn R. Atlas; C: Richard Alfieri, Gale Sondergaard, Ruth Roman, Nathalie Nell, Mercedes McCambridge, Mike Kellin

An artist in New York has nightmares about being chased by an evil man with a mustache in this talky sort-of horror film that includes reincarnation, a dead twin, and ballet dancing.

Director Seidelman also helmed *Hercules in New York* (1970), innumerable TV movies, stage musicals and episodes of *Murder, She Wrote*. (Peter Pan Industries)

Fear No Evil (1981)

D: Frank LaLoggia; W: Frank LaLoggia; P: Frank LaLoggia, Charles M. LaLoggia, Becky Morrison, Donald P. Borchers (AP), Carl Reynolds (AP); C: Stefan Arngrim, Elizabeth Hoffman, Kathleen Rowe McAllen, Frank Birney, Daniel Eden, Jack Holland

One of the better post–*Carrie* supernatural teen revenge flicks, with Arngrim as a teenage antichrist who smites his enemies in creative fashion (one male thug sprouts a pair of female breasts), raises the dead and causes the audience at a seaside performance of the Passion Play to develop stigmata. The soundtrack includes songs from The Ramones, Talking Heads, Sex Pistols and Boomtown Rats.

This was LaLoggia's first film (actually shot in 1979), and it would be another seven years before his follow-up, *Lady in White* (1988). Born in Rochester, New York, LaLoggia worked as a stage and TV actor, and attended USC. Richard Jay Silverthorn published a novelization of the film called *Satan's Spawn* in 1988.

The VHS cover for Frank LaLoggia's *Fear No Evil* (1981).

Arngrim was on *Land of the Giants* and at one point had a band called The Knights of the Living Dead. (Anchor Bay)
www.stefanarngrim.com

The Flesh Eaters (1964)

D: Jack Curtis; W: Arnold Drake; P: Jack Curtis, Arnold Drake, Terry Curtis, Bernard Cherin (AP); C: Martin Kosleck, Byron Sanders, Barbara Wilkin, Rita Morley, Ray Tudor

A pilot, an alcoholic actress, her secretary and a loopy beatnik crash land on a remote island where they discover ex–Nazi marine biologist Martin Kosleck and a pack of flesh-eating sea creatures. The film includes some impressively gooey monsters and unusually graphic (for the time) gore effects.

The film began production in 1960 but was not completed until 1961 because a hurricane destroyed the sets and equipment. Some of the money used to complete the film came from Terry Curtis, wife of director Jack Curtis, who won $70,000 on the TV quiz show "High Low." When it was released, plastic packets of "instant blood" were handed out at theaters.

Arnold Drake (who died in 2007) had worked in radio and TV for Milton Berle and Xavier Cugat, and later became a well-respected comic book scribe on titles like *Deadman* and *The Doom Patrol*. He wrote *Who Killed Teddy Bear?* (1965) and *50,000 B.C. (Before Clothing)* (1963), and also wrote and performed the song "Pete's Beat" for this film. Jack Curtis was a one-handed actor and voiceover performer. He died in 1970.

Distributor Mike Ripps (of *Poor White Trash* fame) added the Nazi flashback sequence. Filmed in Montauk, New York (Dark Sky)

Flesh Eating Mothers (1989)

D: James Aviles Martin; W: James Aviles Martin, Zev Shlasinger; P: James Aviles Martin, Miljan Peter Ilich, Fred Martin (EP), Peter Lewnes (EP), Michael Helman (AP), Harry Eisenstein (AP); C: Robert Lee Oliver, Terry Hayes, Grace Gawthrop, Donatella Hecht, Neal Rosen, Valorie Hubbard

The wife of director Jack Curtis helped partially finance *The Flesh Eaters* (1964) with money she won on a quiz show (courtesy Fred Adelman).

A strange sexually transmitted disease spread by a small-town lothario turns lonely housewives into flesh-eating cannibals.

Martin, who was in film school when he made *Flesh Eating Mothers*, co-wrote *I Was a Teenage Zombie* (1987). Producer Miljan Ilich also worked on that film, as well as *Splatter University* (1984). He and Martin reteamed for the documentary *Artwatch* (2003) and *!DIEGA!* (2007). (Elite Entertainment)

Frankenhooker (1990)

D: Frank Henenlotter; W: Frank Henenlotter, Robert Martin; P: James Glickenhaus, Edgar Ievins; C: James Lorinz, Joanne Ritchie, Patty Mullen, J.J. Clark, Carissa Channing, Louise Lasser, John Zacherle

Lorinz is an electrician/mad doctor whose girlfriend (Mullen) is killed in a lawnmower accident. He saves her severed head in his freezer and plots to bring her back to life using replacement body parts from hookers that he kills with his specially designed "Super Crack."

Henenlotter shot this simultaneously with *Basket Case 2* (1990). Co-scripter Martin was the original editor of *Fangoria* magazine. Lead actor Lorinz had appeared in *Street Trash* (1987), and Mullen (a former Penhouse Pet) was in *Doom Asylum* (1987). Henenlotter followed this up with *Basket Case 3* (1992) and *Bad Biology* (2008). (Unearthed/Synapse)

Frankenstein Meets the Space Monster (1965)

D: Robert Gaffney; W: R.H.W. Dillard, George Garrett, John Rodenbeck; P: Robert McCarty, Alan V. Iselin (EP), Stanley P. Darer (AP); C: James Karen, Robert Reilly, Marilyn Hanold, Lou Cutell, Bruce Glover, Nancy Marshall

Cheap, black-and-white sci-fi film about an android astronaut who takes on a group of pointy-eared space invaders and their hulking, freaky-looking space monster.

Producer Alan Iselin also had a hand in Del Tenney's *The Horror of Party Beach* (1964) and *The Curse of the Living Corpse* (1964). Screenwriter Dillard is an author, poet and professor at Hollins University in Virginia. George Garrett is also a novelist, poet and professor, and was named the poet laureate of Virginia in 2002. Bruce Glover plays one of the aliens and the space monster. Hanold was also in *The Brain that Wouldn't Die* (1962), and Karen had prominent roles in *Poltergeist* (1982) and *The Return of the Living Dead* (1985). Filmed in Long Island and Puerto Rico. (Dark Sky)

A Super 8 "digest" version of *Frankenstein Meets the Space Monster* (1965).

Ganja & Hess (*Blood Couple/Black Evil/Black Vampire/Double Possession*, 1973)

D: Bill Gunn; W: Bill Gunn; P: Chiz Schultz, Jack Jordan (EP), Quentin Kelly (EP), Joan Shigekawa (AP); C: Marlene Clark, Duane Jones, Bill Gunn, Sam Waymon, Leonard Jackson, Mabel King

Languid, surreal tale of vampirism and addiction, with *Night of the Living Dead* (1968) star Duane Jones as an anthropologist who develops a taste for human blood after being stabbed with a ceremonial dagger by his assistant (Gunn).

Although well-received at Cannes (where it was the only American film screened during Critic's Week), the film tanked on its initial release in the U.S. It was re-edited by distributor Heritage Enterprises into *Blood Couple* (shorn of 33 minutes total running time, but including 15 minutes of footage not used in the original) and marketed as a blaxploitation film. Kelly-Jordan Enterprises then re-issued this shorter version as *Double Possession*. The film was released on video under even more titles.

Gunn was a playwright, actor and novelist who had written *The Angel Levine* and *The Landlord* (both 1970). He directed two other films: the unreleased Warner Brothers production *Stop* (1970) with Clark and *Personal Problems* (1981). He continued to direct and act for both the stage and television, and had a recurring role on "The Cosby Show" as one of Bill Cosby's poker buddies. Gunn died of encephalitis in 1989, the day before the opening of his final stage production, "The Forbidden City."

Kelly-Jordan Enterprises had previously released *Georgia, Georgia* (1972), written by Maya Angelou, and at one point optioned James Baldwin's novels for the screen. Filmed in Croton-on-Hudson, New York (All-Day Entertainment)

Geek Maggot Bingo (1983)

D: Nick Zedd; W: Robert Kirkpatrick, Nick Zedd; P: Nick Zedd, Donna Death (EP); C: Robert Andrews, Richard Hell, Brenda Bergman, Donna Death, Bruno Zeus, Gumby Sangler, John Zacherle

Underground filmmaker Zedd takes on the Frankenstein story, tossing in a cowboy and some vampires for good measure in this cheap, shoddy New York flick that also features horror host Zacherley and a cameo by former *Fangoria* editor Bob Martin.

Zedd, who describes himself on his Web site as a "crypto-insurrectionary mastermind of underground film," is also a musician and author, and coined the term "cinema of transgression" in the 1980s to describe the work of fellow filmmakers like Richard Kern and Lydia Lunch. He had previously made the feature *They Eat Scum* (1979), in addition to numerous short films. Hell was the front man for the punk bands Television and The Voidoids. Ed French worked on the special effects. (Eclectic DVD)

www.nickzedd.com

The Ghastly Ones (1968)

D: Andy Milligan; W: Andy Milligan, Hal Sherwood; P: Jerome Frederick; C: Veronica Radburn, Maggie Rogers, Hal Borske, Anne Linden, Fib LaBlaque, Hal Sherwood

Milligan's first color horror film is about a trio of sisters and their husbands who must spend the night in the family mansion in a state of "sexual harmony" to collect their inheritance. However, a mad killer is picking off the heirs one at a time. Sam Sherman created the advertising campaign, and distributor Jerry Balsam booked the film with *The Headless Eyes* (1971) at drive-ins.

Milligan briefly relocated to London in the late 1960s at the behest of the owner of the Compton Cinema Club. He made several horror films there, including *Bloodthirsty Butchers* (1970), *The Body Beneath* (1970), *The Rats Are Coming! The Werewolves are Here!* (1972), and *The Man with Two Heads* (1972), before returning to New York. (Something Weird)

Graverobbers (*Dead Mate*, 1988)

D: Straw Weisman; W: Straw Weisman; P: Lew Mishkin; C: Elizabeth Mannino, David Gregory, Larry Bockius, Judith Mayes, Adam Wahl, Kevin Scullin

A waitress is hypnotized into abruptly marrying an undertaker, and finds herself trapped in a small town full of necrophiliacs and zombies. It's much more technically competent than most of the Mishkin filmography and includes some decent gore effects, but is marred by bad jokes and horrible synth pop. Filmed in Red Hook and Rhinebeck, New York

Producer Lew Mishkin was William Mishkin's son. Lew continued his father's volatile relationship with low-budget director Andy Milligan on two of Milligan's last features, *Carnage* (1984) and the Hollywood-lensed *Monstrosity* (1989). He died in 2001.

Weisman (who worked for the Mishkins as a film booker) wrote and produced *Fight for Your Life* (1977), and later directed the John Ritter film *Man of the Year* (2002) and *Trunk* (2008). (Video Kart)

Guru the Mad Monk (1970)

D: Andy Milligan; W: Andy Milligan, M.A. Isaacs; P: M.A. Isaacs; C: Neil Flanagan, Jaqueline Webb, Judith Israel, Jack Spencer, Gerald Jacuzzo

Sadistic priest Guru ("Lust was his religion!") terrorizes the residents of Mortavia with the help of a female vampire and his hunchback assistant in what Milligan (who designed the outlandish period costumes) sometimes said was his worst film. Shot at St. Peter's Church in Manhattan. (Retro-Media)

The Headless Eyes (1971)

D: Kent Bateman; W: Kent Bateman; P: Henri Pachard (as Ronald Sullivan), David Bowman (EP), Bayard Stevens (AP), Chandler Warren (EP); C: Bo Brundin, Gordon Ramon, Kelley Swartz, Mary Jane Early

After having his eye gouged out with a spoon during a botched burglary, a crazy artist kills people and scoops out their eyes so he can use them to create sculptures.

This gory oddity (released on a memorable double-bill with Andy Milligan's *The Ghastly Ones*) was directed by Kent Bateman, father of Jason and Justine Bateman. He directed episodes of his children's respective TV series, and even produced *Teen Wolf, Too* (1987). Henri Pachard, a.k.a. Ron Sullivan, produced *Putney Swope* (1969), made roughies in the 1960s, and became a prolific porn director in later years. The video box artwork for this film was re-used for *The Killer Eye* (1999).

Hell High (1989)

D: Douglas Grossman; W: Leo Evans, Douglas Grossman; P: Douglas Grossman, David Steinman; C: Christopher Stryker, Maureen Mooney, Christopher Cousins, Millie Prezioso, Jason Brill

A group of teens torment their biology teacher using fright masks, nearly killing her in the process. She becomes unhinged and begins killing her former students. Shot in 1986 (in Westchester, New York) but not released until several years after lead actor Christopher Stryker died. (Shriek Show)

I Drink Your Blood (1970)

D: David E. Durston; W: David E. Durston; P: Jerry Gross, Henry Kaplan (AP); C: Bhaskar Roy Chowdhury, Jadine Wong, Rhonda Fultz, Lynn Lowry, Jack Damon, Richard Bowler, George Patterson

Infamous drive-in classic that mixes elements of *Night of the Living Dead* (1968), the Manson

Family and Sweeney Todd. After a group of Satanic hippies rape a young girl, her young brother contaminates their meat pies with rabies, turning them into frothy-mouthed, homicidal zombies.

One of the first films to be rated X for violence, this was distributed on a double bill with Del Tenney's black-and-white zombie flick *I Eat Your Skin* (1964) by Cinemation founder Jerry Gross.

Chowdhury was a dancer and artist who in later years was confined to a wheelchair after he fell from a stage. He died in 2003. Durston (who died in 2010) had worked in television in the 1950s, most notably on *Your Hit Parade* and *Kraft Television Theatre.* He later made *Stigma* (1972) and *Boy-napped* (1975). Filmed near Sharon Springs, New York (Grindhouse Releasing/Something Weird)

I Was a Teenage Zombie (1987)

D: *John Elias Michalakis;* W: *James Aviles Martin, Steve McKoy, George Seminara;* P: *Richard Hirsh, John Elias Michalakis, Miljan Peter Ilich (EP), Sam Lumetta (AP);* C: *Michael Rubin, Steve McCoy, George Seminara, Robert C. Sabin, Allen Lewis Rickman*

Teenagers kill a brutal drug dealer named Mussolini and dump his body in a contaminated river. He returns to life as a super-strong, bloodthirsty zombie in this dopey horror-comedy that was filmed in New York and New Jersey.

Michalakis also wrote and appeared in *Splatter University* (1984). A number of Web sites claim that he later became a monk, but I have been unable to confirm this. Allen Lewis Rickman was also in *Shock! Shock! Shock!* (1987) and *Slime City* (1988).

Although the film isn't that great, the excellent soundtrack includes songs by The Fleshtones (who appear in the film), Dream Syndicate, The Violent Femmes, The Waitresses, and Alex Chilton. (Image)

Igor and the Lunatics (*Bloodshed*, 1985)

D: *Billy Parolini;* W: *Jocelyn Beard, Billy Parolini;* P: *Jocelyn Beard, Billy Parolini, Lloyd Kaufman (EP), Michael Herz (EP);* C: *Joseph Eero, Mary Ann Schacht, Joe Niola, T.J. Glenn, Joan Ellen Delaney, Peter Dain*

Manson-inspired story about a murderous hippie cult. When the leader of the cult is released from prison, he sets out to take revenge on the people who helped put him there.

Producer/writer Jocelyn Beard is an NYU film school grad, and an award-winning playwright. (Troma)

Invasion of the Blood Farmers (1972)

D: *Ed Kelleher;* W: *Ed Adlum, Ed Kelleher;* P: *Ed Adlum, Milton S. Greenman;* C: *Norman Kelley, Tanna Hunter, Bruce Detrick, Paul Craig Jennings, Jack Neubeck*

"The plant the LIVING and harvest the DEAD!" Evil druids disguised as farmers arrive in a small town and begin draining the citizens of blood in an effort to revive their dead queen in this compellingly ridiculous feature from the folks who also gave us *Shriek of the Mutilated* (1974).

Adlum (who appears as the man in the shower) and Kelleher both worked at *CashBox* magazine, and raised the money for the film through their contacts in the jukebox industry. Michael and Roberta Findlay also worked on this film and *Shriek of the Mutilated.*

Kelleher went on to write for *Creem*, was a publicist for singer/songwriter Melanie, penned a biography of Wendy O. Williams and the Plasmatics (*Your Heart in Your Mouth*, 1982) in addition to a number of plays and horror novels, and served as associate editor of *Film Journal International.* He worked with Roberta Findlay again on *Prime Evil* (1988) and *Lurkers* (1988). He died in 2005 from a degenerative brain disorder. (RetroMedia)

Janie (1970)

D: *Jack Bravman;* W: *James Foley;* P: *Jack Bravman;* C: *Mary Jane Carpenter, William Dunnett, Michael Findlay, Roberta Findlay, Tina Grasco*

Meandering, freaky exploitation oddity about a young girl who murders pretty much everyone she encounters while traveling to see her father. Bravman produced Ed Adlum's first film, *Blonde on a Bum Trip* (1968), and helped him develop *Invasion of the Blood Farmers* (1972). He primarily worked in nudies and adult films, frequently collaborating with Mike and Roberta Findlay, and also served as producer of *Snuff* (1976).

Bravman's last credits were as producer of *The Carpenter* (1989) and *Voodoo Dolls* (1990), which was written by Ed Kelleher. He also produced and co-directed *Zombie Nightmare* (1986) with John Fasano. (Something Weird)

The Kirlian Witness (*The Plants are Watching*, 1979)

D: *Jonathan Sarno;* W: *Lamar Sanders, Jonathan Sarno;* P: *Jonathan Sarno, Graham Place (AP);* C: *Nancy Snyder, Nancy Boykin, Joel Colodner, Ted Laplat, Lawrence Tierney*

The original *Invasion of the Blood Farmers* (1972) poster. Actor Jack Neubeck was featured prominently in the promotional art, stabbing producer Ed Adlum's wife Tippy with a pitchfork.

Murder mystery about a woman investigating her sister's death, spiced up with some hokum about the psychic abilities of plants and Kirlian photography.

Director/producer Sarno (a Yale School of Drama grad) is also a playwright.

The Lady in White (1988)

D: *Frank LaLoggia;* W: *Frank LaLoggia;* P: *Frank LaLoggia, Andrew G. La Marca, Cliff Payne (EP), Carl Reynolds (AP), Charles M. LaLoggia (EP), Peter Kolokouris (AP);* C: *Lukas Haas, Len Cariou, Alex Rocco, Katherine Helmond, Jason Presson, Sydney Lassick*

Low-key ghost story from the director of *Fear No Evil* (1981) about a boy (Haas) who has visions of a ghostly girl and winds up the target of the man who killed her many years before.

The film was loosely based on an urban legend from LaLoggia's hometown of Rochester, New York Producer Charles LaLoggia (Frank's cousin) is an investment analyst, and helped finance the film through a public penny stock offering. (MGM)

Last House on Dead End Street (*The Fun House*, 1977)

D: Roger Michael Watkins; W: Roger Michael Watkins; P: Roger Michael Watkins (as Norman F. Kaiser); C: Roger Michael Watkins, Ken Fisher, Bill Schlageter, Kathy Curtin, Paul M. Jensen

A drug-fueled production partially inspired by legends of the Manson Family making snuff films. A drug-dealing filmmaker, fresh out of prison, decides to take vengeance on the lame pornographers he has to work for. He and his miscreant film crew kidnap, torture and kill their enemies in a large, decaying house, all with the cameras running.

This was originally made as a 175-minute movie called *The Cuckoo Clocks of Hell*, but was cut down and redubbed by the distributor, who also attached a set of fake credits. Made in 1973, it wasn't released until several years later because one of the actresses sued Watkins over the use of her sex scenes. It gained a significant reputation in the ensuing years because of both of its obscurity and its brutality.

The origins of the film remained mysterious until 2000, when Watkins finally stepped forward and claimed it. Watkins later worked in the porn industry, appeared on NBC's "The Doctors," and made the films *Shadows of the Mind* (1980) and *Spittoon* (1981), sometimes working under the aliases Bernard Travis and Richard Mahler. He died in 2007.

Paul M. Jensen was Watkins' teacher, and is a professor of film at State University of New York at Oneonta. (Barrel Entertainment)

Legacy of Horror (*Legacy of Blood*, 1978)

D: Andy Milligan; W: Andy Milligan; P: Andy Milligan; C: Pete Barcia, Elaine Boies, Chris Broderick, Julia Curry, Jeannie Cusick

This is, believe it or not, a slightly more polished remake of Milligan's *The Ghastly Ones* (1968). Once again, three sisters and their husbands arrive at the family mansion for a reading of their nasty father's will, and discover that they have to spend three nights in the house to collect their inheritance. A mysterious figure then starts murdering the husbands.

The controversial *Last House on Dead End Street* (1977) was originally called *The Cuckoo Clocks of Hell* (courtesy Fred Adelman)

After completing this film and shooting part of a Civil War horror film called *The House of Seven Belles*, Milligan left Staten Island and operated a run-down theater in Times Square that he called The Troupe. He would make only one more film in New York, *Carnage* (1984). (Synergy)

Legacy of Satan (1974)

D: Gerard Damiano; W: Gerard Damiano; P: Gerard Damiano, Louis Peraino; C: John Francis, Lisa Christian, Paul Barry, Jarrar Ramze, Ann Paul, James Procter, Christa Helm

Satanic soap opera about a vampire cult trying to recruit a woman in order to fulfill an ancient prophecy. This 68-minute film appears to be cut, and may have contained additional gore and/or nudity when it was originally filmed.

Damiano (who died in 2008) was a porn director who helmed the groundbreaking adult films *Deep Throat* (1972) and *The Devil in Miss Jones* (1973). He owned a beauty parlor in New York before making his first sex documentaries in the late 1960s. *Legacy* was distributed by Bryanston, a company formed by alleged mobster Louis "Butchie" Peraino, which also handled *Deep Throat*, *The Texas Chain Saw Massacre* (1974), *The House the Cried Murder* (1973), Andy Milligan's *Blood* (1974), *Lord Shango* (1975) and *The Devil's Rain* (1975).

Peraino was indicted in 1980 for transporting pornographic material across state lines during the FBI's MIPORN investigation and sentenced to three years in prison. He died in 1999.

Actress and fashion model (and former girlfriend of Joe Namath) Christa Helm also appeared in *Let's Go for Broke* (1974) and was an original investor in the play *Godspell*. She was murdered in 1977, and that crime (which remains unsolved) was the subject of a *48 Hours* episode in 2008. (BCI)

Liquid Sky (1982)

D: Slava Tsukerman; W: Anne Carlisle, Nina V. Kerova, Slava Tsukerman; P: Nina V. Kerova, Slava Tsukerman; C: Anne Carlisle, Paula E. Sheppard, Susan Doukas, Otto von Wernherr, Bob Brady

Surreal cult item, made by a Russian production team, about a drug-addled fashion model (Carlisle) whose lovers are killed by the tiny aliens that have taken up residence on the roof of her loft. This is the only other film appearance of *Alice, Sweet Alice* (1976) star Paula Sheppard, who plays Carlisle's roommate. (MTI Home Video)

Long Island Cannibal Massacre (1980)

D: Nathan Schiff; W: Nathan Schiff; P: Nathan Schiff; C: John Smihula, Fred Borges, Michael Siegal, Paul Smihula, Nancy Canberg, Judy Guerevich

A renegade cop goes on the hunt for a pair of serial killers (one wearing a pillowcase and goggles on his head) who supply bodies to feed the leprous, cannibal father of their boss (Borges, sporting and incredible afro and mustache) in another ultra-gory, Super 8 Schiff flick. Made for $900. (Image)

Love After Death (*Unsatisfied Love*, 1968)

D: Glauco del Mar; W: Antonio Velázquez; P: Charles Abrams; C: Guillermo de Cordova, Roberto Maurano, Carmin O'Neal, Angel Mario Ramirez

Obscure and bizarre skin flick by Puerto Rican director del Mar about a wealthy cataleptic man who is accidentally buried alive. He digs his way out of the grave and has a series of voyeuristic softcore encounters before taking revenge on his cheating wife and her lover.

Glauco del Mar made at least five films in New York and Puerto Rico in the 1960s and 1970s, and may be the same Glauco del Mar who recorded spoken word poetry albums in the 1950s and 1960s. Producer Abrams made several other sexploitation films during the same period. This one was filmed in Spanish and poorly dubbed into English. (Something Weird)

Lurkers (1988)

D: Roberta Findlay; W: Ed Kelleher, Hariette Vidal; P: Walter E. Sear; C: Christine Moore, Gary Warner, Marina Taylor, Roy MacArthur, Nancy Goff, Tom Billett

A woman has eerie visions and sees ghoulish looking spirits that seem to emanate from the apartment building where she grew up. This is Findlay's most effective horror film, and had a much higher budget than her previous efforts. Author Maitland McDonagh and actress Debbie Rochon make uncredited cameos. (Rhino/BCI)

Madame Zenobia (1973)

D: Eduardo Cemano; W: Eduardo Cemano; P: Ed Seeman, Patrick Malloy (EP), Alexander Beck (AP); C: Tina Russell, Jamie Gillis, Elizabeth O'Donovan, Levi Richards

A widow is unable to be satisfied sexually by her fiancé because she is still in love with her deceased husband. Medium Madame Zenobia (O'Donovan) intervenes, channeling the spirit of the dead husband through the new boyfriend.

Levi Richards was in Doris Wishman's *A Night to Dismember* (1983). Cemano (Ed Seeman) was an artist, painter, and cartoon cell animator in addition to being an experimental filmmaker. This film was the third in a trio of odd porno flicks (the others being *The Healers* and *Fongaluli*) he directed under the Cemano pseudonym. He and his wife later operated a cartoon t-shirt company in Florida. Associate producer Alexander Beck also produced *Mother's Day*. (After Hours)

www.edseeman.com

Liquid Sky (1982) was the second and final film of *Alice, Sweet Alice* star Paula Sheppard (courtesy Fred Adelman).

Madman (1982)

D: Joe Giannone; W: Joe Giannone, Gary Sales; P: Sam Marion, Gary Sales; C: Gaylen Ross, Seth Jones, Tony Fish, Alex Murphy, Paul Ehlers

Filmed in Long Island, the original script for *Madman* was based on the "Cropsey Maniac" story (a New York urban legend about a maniac who kills campers). Unfortunately, the makers of *The Burning* (1981) had already begun their own slasher film based on the same story (also filmed in New York), so Sales and Giannone quickly rewrote the film to center on the exploits of "Madman Marz."

Marz was a crazy farmer who killed his wife and children with an axe, and was then hung from a tree and left to die. When some kids at a nearby summer camp call out his name, Marz returns and starts slaughtering campers.

Giannone was also an assistant director on *The Clonus Horror* (1979). He died in 2006. (Anchor Bay/Code Red)

Maniac (1980)

D: William Lustig; W: C.A. Rosenberg, Joe Spinell; P: William Lustig, Andrew W. Garroni, Judd Hamilton (EP), John Packard (AP), Joe Spinell (EP); C: Joe Spinell, Caroline Munro, Abigail Clayton, Kelly Piper, Rita Montone, Tom Savini

Spinell is a sweaty psychopath who kills women and attaches their scalps to the mannequins he keeps in his apartment. The controversial release was banned in the UK during the "Video Nasties" era.

Character actor Spinell had worked on Broadway and appeared in *The Godfather* (1972) and *Rocky* (1976). He and Munro also appeared in the thematically similar *The Last Horror Film* (1982), and Spinell was trying to raise money for a *Maniac* sequel when he died in 1989.

Lustig started his career working as a production assistant on pornos and mainstream films like *Death Wish* (1974). Using the alias Billy Bagg, he directed *Hot Honey* (1977) and *The Violation of Claudia* (1977) before his controversial horror debut. He later made *Maniac Cop* (1988) and its two sequels, and several other action and horror films. He currently runs the DVD company Blue Underground. (Anchor Bay/Blue Underground)

Monster of Camp Sunshine (or, How I Learned to Stop Worrying and Love Nature) (1964)

D: Ferenc Leroget; W: Ferenc Leroget; P: Gene R. Kearney; C: Harrison Pebbles, Deborah Spray, Sally Parfait, James Gatsby, Ron Cheney Jr.

The gardener at a nudist camp ingests some chemicals (discarded by a scientist after they make lab rats go insane) and turns into an axe-wielding "monster" that attacks topless models in this ridiculous, tossed-off nudie.

Gene Kearney was a prolific writer, director and producer of TV cop shows like *Kojack*. "Photographed and Edited by Motley Crue," and with a Monty Python-style credit sequence. The film was never released theatrically. (Something Weird)

The Nesting (*Phobia/Massacre Mansion*, 1981)

D: Armand Weston; W: Dana Price, Armand Weston; P: Armand Weston, Don Walters (AP), Sam Lake (EP), Robert Sumner (EP); C: Robin Groves, Christopher Loomis, Michael David Lally, John Carradine, Gloria Grahame, Bill Rowley

An agoraphobic author (Groves) takes a trip to the country to cure a bout of writer's block, and is haunted by the ghosts of dead prostitutes who inhabit her rented house (a rambling former brothel).

Weston, who died in 1988, worked primarily in adult films. This was the final film appearance of Oscar winner Gloria Grahame. (Blue Underground)

Night of the Zombies (1981)

D: Joel M. Reed; W: Joel M. Reed; P: Lorin E. Price; C: Jamie Gillis, Samantha Grey, Ryan Hilliard, Ron Armstrong, Joel M. Reed, Shoshana Ascher, Alphonso DeNoble

A rare U.S. entry in the short-lived Nazi zombie movie sub-genre, Reed's film has undead German soldiers who were exposed to a secret chemical weapon eating interlopers in the Bavarian

Alps (actually, New York). Porn star Jamie Gillis plays a CIA agent. It was distributed by N.M.D. Film Distributing.

A Night to Dismember (1983)

D: Doris Wishman; W: Judy J. Kushner; P: Doris Wishman, Larry Marinelli (AP); C: Samantha Fox, Diane Cummins, Saul Meth, Miriam Meth, William Szarka

Nudie director Wishman's slasher entry was originally shot in 1979, but several reels were consumed in a fire at Movielab, so she pieced the final film together from outtakes, additional footage and unrelated bits of film from other projects. The result: an incomprehensible, yet compelling, post-modern mish-mash of gore and nudity about a former mental patient (porn star Fox) who may or may not be responsible for a series of murders that occur after her release. Wishman died in 2002. (Elite Entertainment)

The Oracle (1985)

D: Roberta Findlay; W: R. Allen Leider; P: Walter E. Sear; C: Caroline Capers Powers, Roger Neil, Pam La Testa, Victoria Dryden, Chris Maria De Koron, Dan Lutsky

A couple living in the apartment of a dead psychic are haunted by a man who was murdered by his wife. To release the spirit, the wife (Powers) has to solve his murder.

This film and *Tenement* (1985) were Findlay's first two forays into mainstream filmmaking after leaving the adult film industry, and were distributed by Findlay's own company, Reeltime. The DVD from Media Blasters includes highly entertaining interviews and a commentary from Findlay.

Screenwriter R. Allen Leider worked in public relations and now operates Black Cat Media Associates (www.blackcatmedia.com). (Media Blasters)

Phantom Brother (1988)

D: William Szarka; W: Joseph Santi, William Szarka; P: William Szarka, Paul Grossman (EP), David Bronsztein (AP); C: Jon Hammer, Patrick Molloy, John Gigante, Ben DiGregorio, Dallas Monroe

Joel M. Reed's *Night of the Zombies* (1981), starring adult film actor Jamie Gillis.

Shot-on-video slasher film about a strange man and a trio of killers (one of which, the "Phantom Brother" of the title, wears a black-and-white Halloween mask) offing teens and an annoying film crew at an abandoned house.

Szarka directed *South Bronx Heroes* (1985) and parts of *Plutonium Baby* (1987). Filmed partly in Mamaroneck, New York, at a house owned by *Deadtime Stories* (1986) director Jeffrey Delman.

Plutonium Baby (1987)

D: Ray Hirschman, William Szarka (uncredited); W: Wayne Behar; P: Ray Hirschman, Clifford J. Schorer (EP), Dale Cunningham (EP), Richard A. Bunstein (EP); C: Patrick Molloy, Danny Guerra, Mary Beth Pelshaw, David Pike, Joe Viviani, Ciaran Sheehan, Daniel Frye

Scientists try to capture and kill a man who was exposed to massive levels of radiation at birth during illegal experiments that turned his mother into a killer mutant zombie.

Szarka was an editor who also directed *Phantom Brother* (1988).

Prime Evil (1988)

D: Roberta Findlay; W: Ed Kelleher, Harriette Vidal; P: Walter E. Sear; C: William Beckwith, Christine Moore, Mavis Harris, Max Jacobs, Tim Gail, Amy Brentano

A nun goes undercover to infiltrate a group of Satanic monks who are sacrificing women in New York City. This, *Lurkers* (1988) and *Banned* (1989) were Findlay's last three films as a director. She later became the manager at Walter Sear's Sear Sound recording studio. Sear died in 2010. (Rhino/BCI)

www.searsound.com

Rejuvenatrix (1988)

D: Brian Thomas Jones; W: Brian Thomas Jones, Simon Nuchtern; P: Steve D. Mackler, Bernard E. Goldberg (AP), Robert Zimmerman (LP); C: Vivian Lanko, John MacKay, James Hogue, Katell Pleven, Jessica Dublin, Marcus Powell

An aging actress hires a scientist to create a youth serum for her. The serum (made from brain fluids) makes her young again, but she turns into a murderous monster when it wears off.

This was co-written by *Silent Madness* (1984) director Simon Nuchtern. Steve Mackler also produced *Deadtime Stories* (1986), *Neon Maniacs* (1986) and *Voodoo Dawn* (1990). Director Jones has since relocated to California and become an architectural photographer.

www.brianthomasjones.com

Santa Claus Conquers the Martians (1964)

D: Nicholas Webster; W: Paul L. Jacobson, Glenville Mareth; P: Paul L. Jacobson, Arnold Leeds (AP), Joseph E. Levine (EP); C: John Call, Leonard Hicks, Vincent Beck, Bill McCutcheon, Victor Stiles, Pia Zadora, Leila Martin, Ned Wertimer

Martians come to Earth to kidnap the real Santa Claus so that he can bring happiness to the children of Mars. Pia Zadora's debut film was shot in an airplane hangar on Long Island and was targeted at the then-thriving kiddie matinee circuit.

Dell released a comic book based on the movie along with a read-along record (that featured the snappy Milton DeLugg theme song "Hooray for Santy Claus"). In recent years, the film has been the subject of a mock novelization by Lou Harry and a number of theatrical adaptations, including productions by The Maverick Theater in Fullerton, California, and St. Anthony of Padua Parish High School in Effingham, Illinois (Alpha/ Various)

Seeds (*Seeds of Sin*, 1968)

D: *Andy Milligan*; W: *Andy Milligan, John Borske*; P: *Allen Bazzini, Rosily Bazzini*; C: *Maggie Rogers, Candy Hammond, Robert Service, Helena Velos, Neil Flanagan*

Milligan returns to the themes of *The Ghastly Ones* (1968), with the Christmas reunion of a dysfunctional, hateful, incestuous family that ends in a *Ten Little Indians*-style murder spree.

The Bazzinis owned a restaurant called The Grotto, and later had a hand in David Durston's gay 3D porn *The Manhole* (1978). They added hardcore scenes to this film. Milligan married actress Candy Hammond during the making of this movie, but the union was short-lived. (Something Weird)

The Sex Killer (1967)

D: *Barry Mahon*; P: *Barry Mahon*; C: *Rita Bennett, Bob Meyer, Helena Clayton, Uta Erickson, Sharon Kent, Bob Oran*

A man who works in a mannequin warehouse peeps on women, eventually strangling several of them in fits of sexually frustrated rage. Great footage of late-sixties New York, but otherwise it's slow going. (Something Weird)

Shadows of the Mind (*A Heritage of Blood*, 1980)

D: *Roger Michael Watkins (uncredited), Bernard Travis*; W: *Marion Joyce, Roger Michael Watkins (uncredited), Paul Jensen (uncredited)*; P: *Leo Fenton (EP), Steven A. Florin (EP), Jay Marshall*; C: *Marion Joyce, Erik Rolfe, G.E. Barrymore, Bianca Sloane, Anthony Frank, Don Renshaw*

Slow-moving psychodrama about a woman (Joyce) moving back into the family mansion after being released from a mental institution. She may be haunted by the ghosts of her dead parents, or perhaps her greedy relatives are trying to drive her nuts. Made in 1976 as *A Heritage of Blood*. According to Watkins, his credits on this film were removed by Fenton, who was married to lead actress and alleged screenwriter Marion Joyce.

Watkins (better known for *Last House on Dead End Street*, 1973) also directed *Spittoon* (1980) about his experiences making this film. He died in 2007.

Shock! Shock! Shock! (1987)

D: *Arn McConnell, Todd Rutt*; W: *Arn McConnel, Todd Rutt*; P: *Judy Marriott (AP)*; C: *Brad Isaac, Cyndy McCrossen, Brian Fuorry, Allen Lewis Rickman, Kelly Anne Ross, James Gandolfini*

Cheap, black-and-white, 8mm horror/sci-fi spoof that barely runs an hour. It starts out like a slasher film, and ends up as a superhero film. Todd Rutt works as an art director on a number of TV shows (including "Wonder Showzen" and "The Al Franken Show"). McConnell works as a DJ (under the name Craven Lovelace) in Colorado. Actor Brad Isaac (Brad Schwartz) is still active in theater in the St. Louis area. This was the film debut of James Gandolfini, who appears briefly as a hospital orderly (his voice was dubbed by someone else).

Shriek of the Mutilated (1974)

D: *Michael Findlay*; W: *Ed Adlum, Ed Kelleher*; P: *Ed Adlum*; C: *Alan Brock, Jennifer Stock, Tawm Ellis, Michael Harris, Darcy Brown, Jack Neubeck*

The Adlum/Kelleher team followed up *Invasion of the Blood Farmers* (1972) with this film, about a group of college kids who go on a field trip with their kindly professor to search secluded Boot Island for an albino bigfoot (that looks suspiciously like Disney's Shaggy D.A.). Jack Neubeck (who also worked on Broadway) sings a song about the yeti, and "Popcorn" by Hot Butter is played during a party sequence that introduces an outlandish non-sequitur murder scene featuring an electric carving knife and a toaster. (RetroMedia)

Silent Madness (1984)

D: Simon Nuchtern; W: Nelson DeMille, Bill Milling, Simon Nuchtern, Bob Zimmerman; P: Bill Milling, Simon Nuchtern, Bob Gallagher (AP); C: Belinda Montgomery, Viveca Lindfors, Solly Marx, David Greenan, Sydney Lassick, Roderick Cook

A homicidal maniac is accidentally released from an asylum due to a computer glitch and returns to the scene of his previous crimes to murder co-eds, while hospital administrators scramble to cover up their mistake.

This was shot in New York and New Jersey, and originally released in 3D.

Simon Nuchtern had worked on some adults-only films, was a production manager on *Nightmare* (1981), and later directed *Savage Dawn* (1985). Producer Milling, who also worked on a lot of sexploitation films, works for American Movie Company in Manhattan.

www.americanmovieco.com

Silent Madness (1984) was originally released in 3D.

Shriek of the Mutilated (1974), Ed Adlum's follow up to *Invasion of the Blood Farmers.*

Silent Night, Bloody Night (1974)

D: Theodore Gershuny; W: Theodore Gershuny, Jeffrey Konvitz, Ira Teller; P: Jeffrey Konvitz, Ami Artzi,

Lloyd Kaufman (AP), Frank Vitale (AP); C: Patrick O'Neal, James Patterson, Mary Woronov, Astrid Heeren, John Carradine, Walter Abel, Walter Klavun, Ondine, Candy Darling

Surreal and sometimes confusing film (made in 1972) about a maniac killing the elders of a small town who are planning to buy an abandoned mansion/mental hospital from the original owner's possibly insane grandson. Members of Andy Warhol's "Superstars" appear as mental patients in a flashback. Filmed in Oyster Bay, Long Island.

Theodore Gershuny (who died in 2007) was married to Mary Woronov. He also directed and co-wrote *Sugar Cookies* (1973), and helmed several episodes of "Tales from the Darkside" and "Monsters." Jeffrey Konvitz was an attorney (he represented star O'Neal, among others) and later wrote and produced *The Sentinel* (1977). This was also an early credit for Troma founder (and Yale grad) Lloyd Kaufman, who by this point had formed 15th Street Films with Frank Vitale and Oliver Stone. (Alpha/Mill Creek/Diamond)

Sleepaway Camp (1983)

D: Robert Hiltzik; W: Robert Hiltzik; P: Robert Hiltzik (EP), Jerry Silva, Michele Tatosian; C: Felissa Rose, Jonathan Tiersten, Karen Fields, Mike Kellin, Tom Van Dell, Desiree Gould

What might otherwise have been just another summer camp-set slasher film has gained a tremendous cult following over the years thanks in part to its inventive death scenes (including a gruesome bit with a curling iron), but primarily because it has what may be the most shocking ending of any film (horror or otherwise) made during that period.

Silent Night, Bloody Night (1974) was a moody, confusing Christmas-themed horror film written and produced by attorney Jeffrey Konvitz (courtesy Fred Adelman).

Hiltzik was a film school grad who raised money to make *Sleepaway Camp* by selling shares. He was not involved in the film's two sequels (which substituted Pamela Springsteen for original star Felissa Rose). He married producer Michele Tatosian and later became an attorney.

A third sequel, *Sleepaway Camp 4: The Survivor*, was filmed in 1992 but never completed. In 2003, Hiltzik reunited with a number of original cast members and began production on *Return to Sleepaway Camp*, which was finally released in 2008. *Sleepaway Camp Reunion* was slated for 2011. (Anchor Bay)

www.sleepawaycampfilms.com   www.sleepawaycampmovies.com

Slime City (1988)

D: Greg Lamberson; W: Greg Lamberson; P: Mark J. Makowski, Greg Lamberson, Peter Clark, Calvin Chao (AP), Elizabeth Karol (AP), Jeanne T. Keefe (AP), Angel E. Napoleani (AP), Briton J. Petrucelly (AP), Sandy Soloc (AP), Lydia T. Texidor (AP), William Tyler (AP), Jesus Valdes (AP); C: Robert C. Sabin, Mary Huner, T.J. Merrick, Dennis Embry, Dick Biel, Bunny Levine, Jane Doniger Reibel

Energetic, low-budget 16mm gore pic about a guy (Sabin) who becomes addicted to a special "Himalayan Yogurt" given to him by his neighbors, which transforms him into a murderous slime monster.

Lamberson later directed *New York Vampire* (1991) and *Naked Fear* (1999), was a production manager on *I Was a Teenage Zombie* (1987), and an assistant director on *Plutonium Baby* (1987) and *Brain Damage* (1988). He now works as a novelist. (E.I. Independent)
www.slimeguy.com

Splatter University (1984)

D: Richard W. Haines; W: Richard W. Haines, Michael Cunningham, John Elias Michalakis, Miljan

Left: The inventive *Slime City* (1988)—"A Horror Film with Guts" (courtesy Fred Adelman). *Right*: *Splatter University* (1984), another horror/comedy from the team at Troma (courtesy Fred Adelman).

Peter Illich; P: Richard W. Haines, John Michaels, Miljan Peter Illich (AP); C: Forbes Riley, Ric Randig, Dick Biel, Kathy LaCommare, Laura Gold, Ken Gerson

Horror/comedy from Troma about a knife-wielding killer running rampant on the campus of a Catholic college. Brought to you by some of the same folks who made *I Was a Teenage Zombie* (1987) and *Flesh Eating Mothers* (1989).

Haines later directed *Class of Nuke 'Em High* (1986) and *Alien Space Avenger* (1989). (Elite Entertainment)

Spookies (1987)

D: Brendan Faulkner, Thomas Doran, Eugenie Joseph; W: Thomas Doran, Frank M. Farel, Brendan Faulkner, "Joseph Burgund" (Eugenie Joseph, Ann Burgund); P: Thomas Doran, Frank M. Farel, Brendan Faulkner, Eugenie Joseph, Michael Lee (EP); C: Felix Ward, Maria Pechukas, Dan Scott, Alec Nemser, A.J. Lowenthal, Peter Dain

A dead sorcerer in an abandoned mansion unleashes a horde of cartoonish monsters and zombies to kill random characters that wander into his house, all in an effort to revive his dead bride.

If this film seems disjointed to viewers, it is largely due to its troubled production history. The movie began as a project called *Twisted Souls*, directed by Faulkner and Doran in the mid–1980s, about a group of teenagers being tormented by evil spirits in an old mansion. After a falling out with the original directors and crew, producer Michael Lee hired Joseph (who had worked on some Roger Michael Watkins films) to edit and reshoot half the film, adding the footage of the old man and the girl in the coffin, along with some additional monster sequences. As a result, the tone of the film and quality of the special effects vary wildly from scene to scene.

When released, the film was marketed as a *Gremlins/Ghoulies* knock-off, and the video box touted that the film won the 1986 Delirium Award from the International Science Fiction & Film Fantasy Festival. Steadicam operator Jim Muro later directed *Street Trash* (1987) utilizing a number of *Spookies* crew members. Faulkner and Doran also worked on *Igor and the Lunatics* (1985). You can read Joseph's version of the making of this film at her Web site, *hawaiimoviestudios.com*.

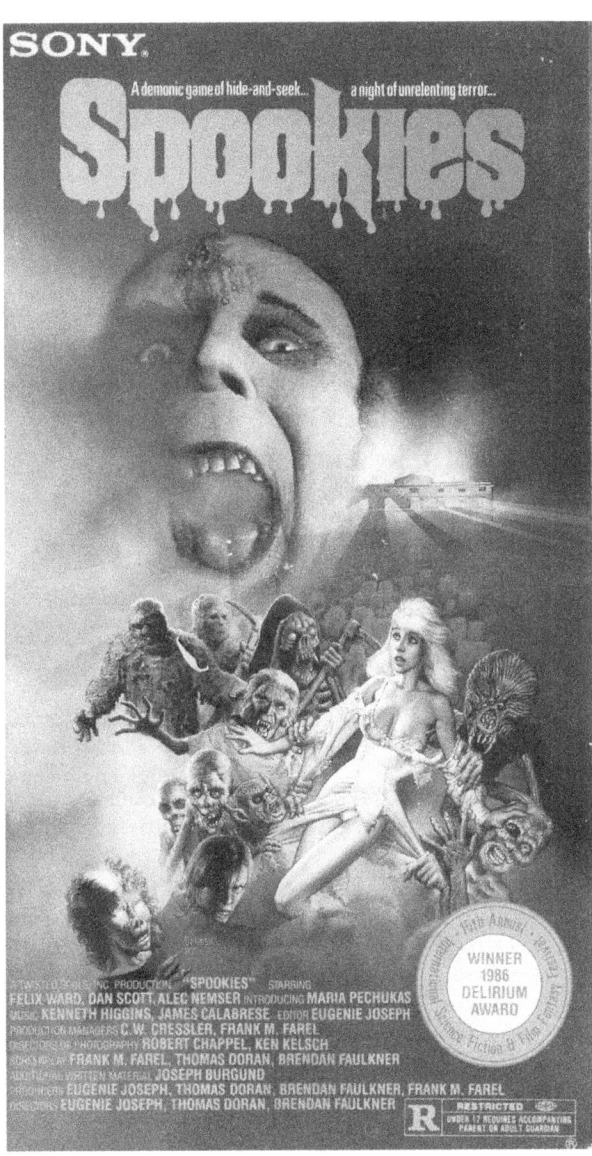

Spookies (1987) was originally called *Twisted Souls*, and includes the work of three different directors (courtesy Fred Adelman).

Street Trash (1987)

D: *James Michael Muro*; W: *Roy Frumkes*; P: *Roy Frumkes, Edward Muro Sr. (EP), James Muro Sr. (EP), Frank M. Farel (AP)*; C: *Mike Lackey, Bill Chepil, Marc Sferazza, Jane Arakawa, Nicole Potter, Pat Ryan, Clarenze Jarmon, Vic Noto, Tony Darrow*

A great, nearly forgotten minor classic about two homeless brothers (Lackey and Sferazza) living in a junkyard with a bunch of crazy winos who are lorded over by a psychotic Vietnam vet (real-life veteran Noto). A liquor store owner starts peddling 60-year-old bottles of Tenafly Viper wine to the local homeless population, which turns them into bubbling piles of acidic, day-glow goop.

While it's full to the brim with the usual cast of shrill characters spouting stream-of-consciousness dialogue that you could find in pretty much every New York indie from the period, *Street Trash* is elevated by great cinematography, excellent steadicam work, and some over-the-top special effects. It's fast-paced, funny, gross and offensive, and features (among other things) necrophilia, an implied gang rape, a game of keep-away with a severed penis, a man melting in a toilet, and characters who puke and piss on each other.

Street Trash (1987) featured the inventive camera work of director/cinematographer James Michael Muro (courtesy Fred Adelman).

The director first conceived this as a short student film for a class he was taking at the School of Visual Arts, where Frumkes was teaching. Muro also worked on *Basket Case* (1982), *Maniac Cop* (1988), *Brain Damage* (1988) and *Slime City* (1988), and became a cinematographer and steadicam operator on films like *The Abyss* (1989), *Dances with Wolves* (1990), and *Terminator 2* (1991). His father owned the junkyard where this was filmed.

Writer/producer Frumkes was the pie-in-face zombie in *Dawn of the Dead* (1978), and made the documentary *Document of the Dead* (1985). He wrote *The Substitute* (1996) and *Meltdown Memoirs* (2006), a documentary about *Street Trash* that was a bonus feature on the DVD. He also provided footage that was added to the film *Make Them Die Slowly* (1981) by Aquarius Releasing. (Synapse)

Sweet Savior (*The Love Thrill Murders*, 1971)

D: *Robert L. Roberts*; W: *Matt Cavanagh, Robert L. Roberts*; P: *Robert L. Roberts*; C: *Troy Donahue, Renay Granville, Francine Middleton, Tallie Cochrane, Matt Greene*

Another Manson-inspired hippie horror flick, with Troy Donahue as cult leader "Moon" who leads his followers on a suburban killing spree.

Director/producer Roberts also made adult films and operated a closed-circuit TV operation that provided adult content to hotels. He later made *Patty* (1976), a pornographic faux documentary about the Patty Hearst kidnapping. Troma re-released *Sweet Savior* in the 1980s (Troma head Lloyd Kaufman was the film's production manager).

Tenement (1985)

D: *Roberta Findlay*; W: *Joel Bender, Rick Marx*; P: *Walter E. Sear*; C: *Joe Lynn, Mina Bern, Walter Bryant, Corinne Chateau, Angel David, Olivia Ward*

Roberta Findlay (mostly) left behind the world of adult films following the release of *Shauna: Every Man's Fantasy* (1985), featuring footage of the late Shauna Grant, a porn star who had killed herself in 1984. One of her first mainstream outings was *Tenement*, probably the best of her 1980s films. A vicious (and unrealistically inter-racial) street gang lays siege to the residents of a run-down tenement, recalling both *Night of the Living Dead* (1968) and John Carpenter's *Assault on Precinct 13* (1976).

Producer Walter Sear, Findlay's partner in Reeltime Distributing Corp. and on many of her porn films, was a sound engineer, musician and tuba designer who operated Sear Sound studio in New York until his death in 2010. He worked with Robert Moog during the development of Moog's popular synthesizers and has music credits on a number of films, including *Midnight Cowboy* (1969), *Let's Scare Jessica to Death* (1971), *Dr. Butcher, M.D.* (1980), and most of Findlay's later films. (Media Blasters)

There's Nothing Out There (1990)

D: *Rolfe Kanefsky*; W: *Rolfe Kanefsky*; P: *Victor Kanefsky*; C: *Craig Peck, Wendy Bednarz, Mark Coliver, Jeff Dachis, Claudia Flores, Bonnie Bowers*

A group of high school students on spring break spend the weekend at a cabin in the woods, where they are attacked by an alien monster that wants to mate with the females.

This 16mm horror/comedy has decent special effects and camerawork, and like the earlier *Final Exam* and later Wes Craven flick *Scream* (1996), includes a horror movie geek (Craig Peck) whose fright film knowledge comes into play. Director Kanefsky went on to direct several softcore skinflicks (like *Sex Files: Alien Erotica*, 1998) and the horror film *Nightmare Man* (2006). His father/producer, Victor Kanefsky, is an editor whose credits include *Ganja & Hess* and *Bloodsucking Freaks*. Shot in Piermont, New York. (Image/Troma)

www.theresnothingoutthere.com

They Don't Cut the Grass Anymore (1985)

D: *Nathan Schiff*; W: *Nathan Schiff*; P: *Nathan Schiff*; C: *Adam Burke, John Smihula, Mary Spadaro, Leanna Mangiarano, Matt Zagon, Maura Del Veccio*

A pair of redneck gardeners from Texas murder their yuppie clients in gory, crude and frequently offensive ways. After this film was made, Schiff started getting attention from magazines like *Gore Gazette*, *Deep Red* and *In the Flesh* and became something of an underground celebrity. He made only one other feature, *Vermillion Eyes* (1991). Since then, he's made a few short films with Smihula and experimental filmmaker Joseph Marzano. (Image)

Torture Dungeon (1970)

D: *Andy Milligan*; W: *John Borske, Andy Milligan*; P: *William Mishkin*; C: *Gerald Jacuzzo, Susan Cassidy, Patricia Dillon, Neil Flanagan, Hal Borske, Maggie Rogers*

Medieval horror from exotic Staten Island concerning various dukes and princes in shoddy wigs jockeying for the throne of England. With more elaborate costumes but slightly less gore than other Milligan features from the same period, and bursting at the seams with ridiculous dialogue.

The Transformation (A Sandwich of Nightmares) (1974)

D: Lewis Jackson; W: Lewis Jackson; P: Elliot Krasnow; C: Dianna Mitchell, Michael Baxter, David Kirk, Les Crook, Elliot Kastner, Lewis Jackson

This was *Christmas Evil* (1980) director Lewis Jackson's second film, after the softcore flick *The Deviators* (1970). Baxter falls in love with an exotic singer, who turns out to be the high priestess of a cult he's investigating. The fictional part of the film is book-ended with behind-the-scenes footage of the production. According to Jackson, this film is lost.

Krasnow (who appeared in this film as "Elliot Kastner") worked in advertising, and later sat on the board of directors of Fanfare Film Corp. He and Jackson also produced the film *Lialeh* (1974), a black-cast porno musical.

www.elliotkrasnow.tv

Two Girls for a Madman (1968)

D: Stanley H. Brassloff; W: Stanley H. Brassloff, Dustin Williams; P: Victor Petrashevic; C: Arlene Farber, Jean Weston, Lucky Kargo, Jerome Heller, Jay Jayson, Naomi Riis

Arlene Farber (wife of Jerry Gross) and Jean Weston star in this roughie as ballet dancers who hope to break into show business in New York City, but wind up stalked by a psychotic rapist. Farber also appeared in *I Drink Your Blood* (1970), and director Brassloff was responsible for the weird sexploitation pic *Toys are Not for Children* (1972). (Something Weird)

The Undertaker (*Death Merchant*, 1988)

D: Franco de Steffanino; W: William James Kennedy; P: Frank Avianca, Steve Bono, Francis D. Poeta; C: Joe Spinell, Rebeca Yaron, Patrick Askin, Susan Bachi, Martha Somoeman

This was Joe Spinell's final film appearance before his unexpected death in 1989. Here, he plays an insane undertaker with a taste for murder and necrophilia. When his nephew (Askin) discovers his secret, he sets out to cover his tracks by killing anyone who threatens his extracurricular activities.

The film was never officially "finished," but two different versions (under alternate titles) have circulated on video for several years. Screenwriter Kennedy appears as a cop in the film, and worked regularly as an actor on several soap operas. Producer Steve Bono worked on several Bryanston films, including *Lord Shango* (1975). Avianca was previously known as rock singer "Frankie Sardo" in the 1950s (he opened for Buddy Holly on the disastrous "Winter Dance Party" tour) before moving into the night club business, acting, and producing. (Code Red)

Weasels Rip My Flesh (1979)

D: Nathan Schiff; W: Nathan Schiff; P: Nathan Schiff; C: John Smihula, Fred Borges, Fred Dabby, Jody Kadish, Steven Kriete, Edward Schiff

Radioactive waste dumped into a hole by a couple of kids turns a pair of weasels into giant, killer monsters. Cops with impressive mustaches (a Schiff signature) try to stop them.

High school student Nathan Schiff made his first Super 8 feature (named after the Frank Zappa song and inspired by H.G. Lewis movies) with a mere $400 and buckets of gory pluck. A well-received screening at Schiff's high school encouraged him to move on to more ambitious projects, the next one being *Long Island Cannibal Massacre* (1980). Although never officially released on VHS, Image released this film and the bulk of Schiff's other work on a series of DVDs, complete with director commentaries and a selection of Schiff's other adolescent Super 8 experiments. (Image)

Werewolf of Washington (1973)

D: Milton Moses Ginsberg; W: Milton Moses Ginsberg; P: Nina Schulman, Stephen A. Miller (AP); C: Dean Stockwell, Katalin Kallay, Henry Ferrentino, Thayer David, Clifton James, Biff McGuire, Michael Dunn

Reporter Stockwell is bitten by a werewolf while on assignment in Hungary, then returns to the U.S. to serve as the President's press secretary in this weird, funny take on the Watergate scandal. Michael Dunn appears as a mad scientist. Some footage was shot in Washington, D.C., but most of the film was made in Long Island.

Although characters in the film are obviously modeled on actual members of the Nixon administration, Ginsberg conceived and filmed *Werewolf* before the facts of the Watergate scandal were made public.

Ginsberg had previously directed *Coming Apart* (1969) with Rip Torn, and later made short films and documentaries. (Alpha/Shout Factory)

NORTH CAROLINA

Alien Outlaw (1985)

D: Phil Smoot; W: Phil Smoot; P: Phil Smoot, George B. Walker (EP), John G. Wolfe III (AP); C: Stephen Winegard, Kimberly Mauldin, Stuart Watson, Lash LaRue, Sunset Carson, Kari Anderson

Traveling show-woman and gunslinger Kari Anderson teams up with Lash LaRue to fight off a trio of alien invaders.

One of two films directed by Smoot (the other was *The Dark Power*, 1985), a producer and production manager who worked for Earl Owensby. This was the last film for old-time western actors LaRue, Sunset Carson, and "Wild" Bill Cody. (VCI)

Another Son of Sam (*Hostage*, 1977)

D: Dave Adams; W: Dave Adams; P: Dave Adams, Gene Cale, Christy Dimon, Carl Jones, Jerry Kool, Rozella Langston, Donnie Rucks, Ron Sherrill; C: Russ Dubuc, Joe Artero, Pam Mullins, Cynthia Stewart, Robert McCourt, John Harper, Larry Sprinkle, Bill Brown

A lunatic escapes from a mental hospital, kills a few people, then makes his way to a girl's dormitory where he holds some women hostage until the SWAT team arrives.

Adams (who also handled the crude editing) was a stunt man who had worked on *Trucker's Woman* (1975) and William Grefé's *Whiskey Mountain* (1977). He changed the title of this film (originally called *Hostage*) after the Son of Sam murders made the news. Several members of the cast were local TV news personalities. Filmed in Belmont and Charlotte, North Carolina.

Axe (*Lisa, Lisa*, 1974)

D: Frederick R. Friedel; W: Frederick R. Friedel; P: Irwin Friedlander (EP), J.G. Patterson Jr.; C: Leslie Lee, Jack Canon, Ray Green, Frederick R. Friedel, Douglas Powers, Frank Jones

Friedel's most well-known feature (bewilderingly retitled *California Axe Massacre* at one time) is about a trio of hoodlums (including the director) who get more than they bargain for when they take over a remote farmhouse inhabited by a strange young woman and her paralyzed grandfather.

Makeup man Worth Keeter and production manager Phil Smoot sometimes worked for local producer Earl Owensby. Cinematographer Austin McKinney had worked with David L. Hewitt, and later served as a visual effects cinematographer on *Galaxy of Terror* (1981), *Jaws 3-D* (1983), *The Terminator* (1984) and *Night of the Comet* (1984). J.G. "Pat" Patterson was responsible for *The Body Shop* (1973).

Friedel also directed *The Kidnapped Coed* (1976) and the comedy *My Next Funeral* (2000). His first two films were distributed by Harry Novak's Box Office International Pictures. (Something Weird)

The Body Shop (*Doctor Gore*, 1972)

D: J. G. Patterson Jr.; W: J.G. Patterson Jr.; P: J.G. Patterson, Jr., Craig Keller (EP), Jack Keller (EP); C: J.G. Patterson, Jenny Driggers, Roy Mehaffey, Linda Faile, Jan Benfield, Jeannine Aber

William Girdler provided the music for this film, which was shot in Charlotte and Asheville, North Carolina, by Junius Gustavious "Pat" Patterson, Jr., a magician, special effects artist and horror host from Gastonia.

In this film, Patterson (as Don Brandon) plays a plastic surgeon attempting to reanimate his dead wife (and create the "perfect woman" in the process) using parts from young women he's kidnapped with the help of hunchbacked assistant Greg.

Patterson produced the film through his Charlotte-based company, Metrolina Motion Pictures Corp. He later directed *The Electric Chair*, a gory courtroom drama released in 1977. He also served as assistant director on Donn Davison's *Obscenity* (1970), worked on *Blood Feast* (1963), *Two Thousand Maniacs!* (1964), *The Gruesome Twosome* (1967), *She Devils on Wheels* (1967), *Preacherman* (1971) and *Three on a Meathook* (1973), and produced *Axe* (1974). He died of cancer in 1975.

H.G. Lewis provided an introduction for the original video release of *The Body Shop*, which had a limited theatrical run in North Carolina in the early 1970s. The *Doctor Gore* version was "presented" by Jeffrey Hogue, also the distributor (through Majestic International Pictures) of *Blood Beast of Monster Mountain* (1965) and Girdler's *Asylum of Satan* (1971), as well as the current owner of the Charles Atlas, Ltd., company. (Something Weird)

Carnival Magic (1982)

D: Al Adamson; W: Mark Weston, Bob Levine, Elvin Feltner; P: Elvin Feltner, Bob Levine (AP); C: Don Stewart, Jennifer Houlton, Howard Segal, Regina Carrol, Joe Cirillo, Mark Weston

This low-budget family-oriented fantasy was one of director Al Adamson's last films. Soap opera star Stewart (who was on *The Guiding Light* for many years) is a carnival magician with real powers who works with a super-intelligent talking chimp. A jealous animal trainer kidnaps the chimp and tries to sell him to a research lab.

Adamson (son of former cowboy actor and film distributor Victor Adamson) and his partner Sam Sherman operated Independent-International Pictures in the 1960s and 1970s, and were responsible for a number of crazed horror and exploitation pics, including *Satan's Sadists* (1969), *Dracula vs. Frankenstein* (1971), and *Blood of Ghastly Horror* (1972), most of them featuring Adamson's wife, actress Regina Carrol. He made one last feature in Utah, *Lost* (1983), before retiring from the film business. He was murdered in 1995.

Cirillo was a regular on *Eischied*. Feltner also produced the West Virgina film *Teen-Age Strangler* (1964). Feltner was also a film collector and distributor, and by the mid–80s had amassed a library of several thousand titles. *Carnival Magic*, long thought lost, was located in Feltner's storage facility in Florida and restored for a special edition DVD in 2011. (Cultra)

The Dark Power (1985)

D: Phil Smoot; W: Phil Smoot; P: George B. Walker, Phil Smoot, Lash La Rue (EP), John G. Wolfe III (AP); C: Lash LaRue, Anna Lane Tatum, Cynthia Bailey, Mary Dalton, Paul Holman, Cynthia Farbman

College kids move into an old house where a quartet of superhumanly strong Toltec Indian zombies are about to rise from their graves in this gory film from Earl Owensby associate Phil Smoot. Lash La Rue (as a forest ranger) comes to their rescue, fending off the evil spirits with his whip.

Smoot was married to actress Mary Dalton. He most recently acted as producer on *Pucked* (2006), and was line producer on *The Gravedancers* (2006). (VCI)

A Day of Judgment (1981)

D: C.D.H. Reynolds; P: Earl Owensby; C: William T. Hicks, Harris Bloodworth, Robert Bloodworth, Brownlee Davis

A small town that has strayed from the ways of the Lord gets a visit from a vengeful Grim Reaper in yet another historical epic from Owensby's E.O. Corporation. The tagline on the movie poster was a play on the ad campaign for Halloween: "The Night HE Came to Collect His Own."

Director Reynolds also worked on Al Adamson's *Carnival Magic* (1981).

Death Screams (*House of Death*, 1982)

D: David Nelson W: Paul C. Elliot; P: Ernest Bouskos, Charles Ison; C: Susan Kiger, Martin Tucker, William T. Hicks, Jennifer Chase, Jody Kay, John Kholer

Standard slasher flick about a crazy killer offing teens during a town carnival, notable primarily because it was directed by former "Ozzie and Harriet" star David Nelson.

Cinematographer Darrell Cathcart also worked on *Final Exam* (1981) and a bunch of Earl Owensby films. Susan Kiger was a Playboy Playmate who had also worked in porn. Monica Boston, who plays one of the teenagers in this film, represented North Carolina in the Miss World-America pageant in 1980. Hicks was in *A Day of Judgment* (1981).

A Day of Judgment (1981) was one of several films produced by Earl Owensby's E.O. Corporation (courtesy Fred Adelman).

Dogs of Hell (*Rottweiler*, 1982)

D: *Worth Keeter;* W: *Thom McIntyre;* P: *Earl Owensby;* C: *Earl Owensby, Bill Gribble, Robert Bloodworth, Kathy Hasty, Ed Lillard, Jerry Rushing*

Shot in North Carolina and Georgia, this was the first of several Stereovision 3D movies Owensby produced. Rottweilers trained as bloodthirsty hunters by the U.S. Military escape from their kennels and terrorize a small town. Owensby plays the sheriff.

Owensby's other 3D efforts included *Tales of the Third Dimension* (1984), *Chain Gang* (1984), *Hit the Road Running* (1983), *Hyperspace* (1984), and *Hot Heir* (*The Great Balloon Chase*, 1984). According to an article in *Fangoria*, Owensby originally planned to make ten 3D movies. (Titanium Imageworks/Earl Owensby Studios)

Final Exam (1981)

D: *Jimmy Huston;* W: *Jimmy Huston;* P: *John L., Chambliss, Myron Meisel, John L. Chambliss (EP), Lon J. Kerr (EP), Michael Mahern (EP), Carol Bahoric (AP), Todd Durham (AP);* C: *Cecile Bagdadi, Joel S. Rice, Ralph Brown, DeAnna Robbins, Sherry Willis-Burch, Timothy L. Raynor*

Campus slasher film made by associates of Earl Owensby at the E.O. Studios in Shelby, North Carolina, and at Isothermal Community College. A pudgy killer arrives at Lanier College to kill a bunch of frat boys, screaming women and the bow-hunting football coach.

Huston also directed *Dark Sunday* (1976), *Death Driver* (1977), and *Seabo* (1978) for Owensby, as well as *My Best Friend is a Vampire* (1988). Joel S. Rice, who plays "Radish" in this film, and who clearly served as the partial inspiration for Jamie Kennedy's character in *Scream* (1996), is now a busy TV producer. Assistant director Charles "C.D.H." Reynolds directed *A Day of Judgement* (1981). (Code Red)

The Kidnapped Coed (*Date with a Kidnapper/The Kidnapped Lover/House of Terror*, 1976)

D: *Frederick R. Friedel;* W: *Frederick R. Friedel;* P: *Frederick R. Friedel, Irwin Friedlander (EP);* C: *Jack Canon, Leslie Rivers, Gladys Lavitan, Larry Lambeth, Jim Blankinship, Susan McRae*

Another interesting, oddball Friedel production. *Axe* star Canon kidnaps a teenage girl (Rivers) for ransom. After they are attacked by some hoodlums at a hotel, the two of them hit the road and develop a peculiarly close relationship.

In 2007, Friedel re-edited *Axe* (1974) and *Kidnapped Coed* into a new film called *Bloody Brothers*, which recast Canon's characters as twins. He also made a film called *Squish!* (2007) with his wife, Jill Jaxx. (Something Weird)

www.jilljaxxenterainment.com   www.squishthemovie.com

Killer! (1989)

D: *Tony Elwood;* W: *Mark Kimray;* P: *Tony Elwood, Tony Locklear, Skip McPhail, Jr. (EP);* C: *Duke Ernsberger, Andy Boswell, Mark Creter, Keith Liles, Terry Loughlin*

A mad killer with a mother complex slices his way through the supporting cast of this low-budget film that includes several homages to Sam Raimi and *The Evil Dead* (1981). Shot on Super 8 for $9,500 in Gastonia, North Carolina

Elwood (a North Carolina native) had worked on *The Dark Power* (1985), *Evil Dead II* (1987) and *Dracula's Widow* (1989). He later directed *Road-Kill U.S.A.* (1998) and *Cold Storage* (2006). (Synthetic Fur Productions)

www.tonyelwood.com

The Mutilator (1985)

D: Buddy Cooper, John Douglass; W: Buddy Cooper; P: Buddy Cooper; C: Matt Mitler, Ruth Martinez, Bill Hitchcock, Connie Rogers, Frances Raines, Morey Lampley, Ben Moore

Gory slasher flick (originally titled *Fall Break*) about a kid who accidentally kills his mother. Years later, the boy and his friends head to a beach house for vacation and are stalked by his vengeful father.

Director/writer/producer Cooper was an attorney who financed the film with his own money and a loan from Wachovia Bank. The film was edited by uncredited future Oscar winner Hughes Winborne (*Crash*, *Sling Blade*). Actor Matt Mitler was also in *Breeders* (1986) and *Deadtime Stories* (1986). Ben Moore, who plays a cop in the film, was in *Two Thousand Maniacs!* (1964) and several other H.G. Lewis films.

The snappy theme song "Fall Break," which was available as a 45rpm single, was performed by Peter Yellen and the Breakers. Composer Michael Minard wrote the song with Artie Resnick, who had co-written the Drifters' hit "Under the Boardwalk." Filmed in Morehead City, North Carolina

Tales of the Third Dimension (1984)

D: Tom Durham, Worth Keeter; W: Tom Durham, Worth Keeter; P: John Brock, Earl Owensby, Charles Heath; C: Robert Bloodworth, Kevin Campbell, William T. Hicks, Kate Hunter, Terry Laughlin

Omnibus horror-comedy made in 3D by the Earl Owensby organization. The stories include a vampire couple adopting a baby; grave robbers stealing from wealthy corpses; and a Christmas-set tale about a murderous grandmother. A rotting corpse named Igor provides the introductions to the stories.

Owensby followed with his final 3D film, *Hyperspace* (1984), a *Star Wars* spoof with Alan Marx, Paula Poundstone, Chris Elliot and Robert Bloodworth. (Titanium Imageworks)

The Mutilator (1985) was made by North Carolina lawyer Buddy Cooper (courtesy Fred Adelman).

Wolfman (1979)

D: *Worth Keeter;* W: *Worth Keeter;* P: *Earl Owensby, Martin Beck (AP);* C: *Earl Owensby, Kristina Reynolds, Julian Morton, Sid Rancer, Ed Grady, Richard Dedmon*

This was the first horror film to come out of Earl Owensby's E.O. Corporation in North Carolina. The actor/producer had previously made the action films *Challenge* (1974), *Death Driver* (1977) and *Seabo* (1978).

In this period film, Owensby is Colin Glasgow, who returns to his family mansion after his father dies. Once there, he falls victim to a family curse that causes him to turn into a werewolf, which has something to do with a conspiracy between a devil-worshipping priest and Glasgow's conniving relatives.

This was a fairly ambitious undertaking, and Owensby managed to get most of the costumes and period locations correct (although modern power lines are still visible in some scenes). However, Owensby himself is hard to swallow as the cursed hero (he's much better as an ass-kicking action star), something Owensby himself has acknowledged in interviews.

Owensby made his money in the pneumatic tool business, then built a large studio complex in Shelby, North Carolina, in the 1970s where he made his own films (typically car-chase pictures with Owensby in the lead role) and rented space to outside productions. He went head-to-head with both the Screen Actors Guild and the MPAA over wages and ratings, and even testified before a Congressional subcommittee investigating MPAA ratings practices. Owensby was also a Sunday school teacher and ran unsuccessfully for the North Carolina State House of Representatives.

Worth Keeter directed several other Owensby films, including *Lady Grey* (1980), *Living Legend: the King of Rock and Roll* (1980), *Dogs of Hell* (1982), *Hit the Road Running* (1983), *Hot Heir* (1984), *Tales of the Third Dimension* (1984), and *Chain Gang* (1984), and has since gone on to work on the various incarnations of *Mighty Morphin Power Rangers*. (BCI/Earl Owensby Studios)

www.earlowensbystudios.com

NORTH DAKOTA
(None)

OHIO

Beyond Dream's Door (1989)

D: *Jay Woelfel;* W: *Jay Woelfel;* P: *Dyrk Ashton, Susan Resatka (AP), Scott Spears (AP);* C: *Nick Baldasare, Jorge Aguirre, Dianna Ashton, Scott Bauer, R. Michael Bell*

A psychology student experiences terrifying nightmares because an inter-dimensional monster is trying to use his dreams to as a gateway to our world.

Influenced by both H.P. Lovecraft and *Nightmare on Elm Street* (1984), *Beyond Dream's Door* gained a small following after its direct-to-video release, and has received fairly good reviews in the years since. Woelfel shot the film in 16mm around the Ohio State University campus on a budget of $40,000. He later moved to California where he directed a segment of the shot-on-video anthology *Things* (1993), and has continued to work as a director, writer, editor and composer. In 2008, he shot the horror film *Closed for the Season* at the abandoned Chippewa Lake amusement park near Medina, Ohio. (Cinema Epoch)

www.jaywoelfel.com

The Dead Next Door (1988)

D: J.R. Bookwalter; W: J.R. Bookwalter; P: J.R. Bookwalter, Jolie Jackunas, Scott Plummer (AP), Sam Raimi (uncredited EP), Michael Todd (AP); C: Pete Ferry, Bogdan Pecic, Michael Grossi, Jolie Jackunas, Floyd Ewing, Jr., Jon Killough, Scott Spiegel, Bruce Campbell (voice)

A government-backed "Zombie Squad" searches for a cure to the zombie plague that has overrun the planet in this homage to George Romero's living dead films.

The debut feature of director/producer Bookwalter was shot in Akron (and Washington, D.C.) with a six-figure budget from Sam Raimi (credited here as "The Master Cylinder"), and has sometimes been touted as the most expensive Super 8 movie ever made. It built a loyal following over the years, particularly among like-minded independent filmmakers. Raimi cohort Scott Spiegel appears in the film, and Bruce Campbell dubbed a few of the voices.

Bookwalter followed up with two 16mm films (*Skinned Alive*, 1989, and *Robot Ninja*, 1990), then produced and directed a series of shot-on-video horror and science fiction movies and started his own video distribution company. He later relocated to California and worked for Charles Band at Full Moon, but has since returned to Ohio. (Anchor Bay)

www.tempevideo.com

Left: Beyond Dream's Door (1989) was filmed near the Ohio State University campus (courtesy Fred Adelman). *Right: The Dead Next Door* (1988), an Akron zombie film financed by Sam Raimi (courtesy J.R. Bookwalter).

Homebodies (1974)

D: *Larry Yust;* W: *Howard Kaminsky, Bennett Sims, Larry Yust;* P: *Marshal Backlar, James R. Levitt (EP);* C: *Douglas Fowley, Ruth McDevitt, Frances Fuller, Paula Trueman, Ian Wolfe, Kenneth Tobey*

When a group of senior citizens learn they'll be evicted from their apartment building to make way for a new high-rise complex, they begin murdering construction workers and developers in order to halt the project. This quirky film doesn't quite hit all its marks, but still remains a unique example of a multi-layered black comedy in a market that was increasingly dominated by teenage body count movies and flicks about demented hillbillies.

Stanford graduate Larry Yust is the son of Walter Yust, the editor-in-chief of the 14th edition of the Encyclopedia Britannica. The younger Yust got his start working in the Army Signal Corps' Army Pictorial Service, and made educational and dramatic films for Encyclopedia Britannica from the 1950s through the 1970s. His first feature film was an adaptation of *Trick Baby* (1970), a novel by former pimp Iceberg Slim. After *Homebodies*, he made only one other feature, *Say Yes* (1986).

McDevitt played Emily on the short-lived "Kolchak: The Night Stalker" series. Producer Backlar later opened a restaurant in Paris called Marshal's Bar & Grill. *Homebodies* was distributed by AVCO Embassy, and premiered in Cincinnati (where it was filmed) in August 1974.

Homebodies (1974) was filmed in a rapidly gentrifying section of Cincinnati.

Robot Ninja (1990)

D: *J.R. Bookwalter;* W: *J.R. Bookwalter;* P: *J.R. Bookwalter, David DeCoteau (EP);* C: *Michael Todd, Bogdan Pecic, Maria Markovic, Bill Morrison, James L. Edwards, Jon Killough, Burt Ward, Linnea Quigley*

A comic book artist adopts the persona of his own superhero

creation to take on a gang of murderers and rapists in this gory sci-fi/action film. Bookwalter considers this one of his worst films.

Former "Batman" star Burt Ward puts in a brief cameo with Linnea Quigley, and Bookwalter, Scott Spiegel and David DeCoteau all make appearances as well. (Tempe)

Skinned Alive (1989)

D: Jon Killough; W: Jon Killough; P: J.R. Bookwalter, David DeCoteau (EP), Michael Tolochko (EP); C: Mary Jackson, Scott Spiegel, Susan Rothacker, Floyd Ewing, Jr., Lester Clark

Killough, an actor in *The Dead Next Door* (1988), directed the second of J.R. Bookwalter's Ohio-based productions, and one of his last shot-on-film projects for several years. An alcoholic ex-cop takes on a family of foul-mouthed, psychotic killers (owners of "Crawdaddy's Traveling Tannery") in this horror-comedy hybrid. Producer Bookwalter appears as a Jehovah's Witness. Killough also wrote Bookwalter's *Galaxy of the Dinosaurs* (1992). (Tempe)

The Wednesday Children (1973)

D: Robert D. West; W: Robert D. West; P: Homer Baldwin, Cal Clifford; C: Marji Dodril, Donald E. Murray, Tom Kelly, Carol Cary, Al Miskell, Robert West

After suffering from rather banal neglect at the hands of their parents, a group of children are taught how to "transfer" the adults out of their lives by a creepy (and demonic) church janitor. Filmed in Wadsworth, Ohio.

According to an article in the Cleveland *Plain Dealer*, the late West was the program manager at local radio station WJW, a professor at John Carroll University and a Universalist-Unitarian minister (he later taught film and television courses at Kent State University, and plays a minister in the film). Producer Homer Baldwin (who died in 2009) was a former mailman and custodian at Wadsworth High, who later became a cable commissioner and producer for local channel WCTV. With music from Tom Baker and Dene Bays, who also provided tunes for Robert Emery's *Ghetto Freaks* (1970).

OKLAHOMA

Alien Zone (*House of the Dead/Zone of the Dead*, 1978)

D: Sharron Miller; W: David O'Malley; P: Art Leonard (EP), William Jackson; C: John Ericson, Ivor Francis, Judith Novgrod, Charles Aidman, Bernard Fox, Richard Gates, Elizabeth MacRae

Low-budget anthology filmed in Ponca City, Yale and Stillwater, Oklahoma. A philandering businessman at a plumbing convention gets lost on his way back to his hotel, and takes shelter from a rainstorm at a funeral home, where the mortician (Francis) spins four yarns about some of his recent customers. The stories: A schoolteacher who hates children is terrorized in her home by masked youngsters; a strange man films himself killing the women he brings home; an American and British detective (Aidman and Fox) compete to be the world's leading criminologist; and a thoughtless man is trapped and tormented inside an abandoned building.

According to a 1978 *Boxoffice* article about the film, producers Leonard (a "retired Hollywood filmmaker") and Jackson (an Oklahoma State University broadcasting and film instructor) shot the movie as *Five Faces of Terror*, with the help of non-unionized OSU broadcasting students, for $685,000. It was financed by Enid, Oklahoma, businessmen Leroy and Marvin Boehs. California technician Harry Woolman handled the special effects.

Director Sharron Miller was an Oklahoma native (and OSU grad) who worked on *The Life and Times of Grizzly Adams* and later directed episodes of dozens of TV series, winning an Emmy and a DGA Award along the way.

The movie premiered as *Alien Zone* in Stillwater in November 1978, with the producers and other "honored guests" arriving in a mock funeral procession.

Blood Cult (1985)

D: Christopher Lewis; W: Stuart Rosenthal, James Vance; P: Linda Lewis, Jill Clark (AP), Bill F. Blair (EP); C: Juli Andelman, Charles Ellis, James Vance, Bennie Lee McGowan, Peter Hart, David Stice, Fred Graves

A killer butchers women at a college campus with a meat cleaver to provide sacrifices for a dog-worshipping group of cultists. This nine-day wonder (originally conceived as a Buster Crabbe vehicle) was marketed as the first film made specifically for the direct-to-video market, and was one of the most successful and well-known shot-on-video horror films.

Producer Bill Blair was the founder of United Entertainment and VCI Home Video, which distributed this film.

Christopher Lewis is the son of actress Loretta Young and producer Tom Lewis. A USC grad, his first film script, *All the Kind Strangers*, was turned into a Movie of the Week in 1969. He worked in Tulsa, Oklahoma, as a TV news reporter, and later served as the co-host of the local version of *PM Magazine*. Lewis and his wife Linda formed United Entertainment Pictures in conjunction with United Home Video to release straight-to-video movies, *Blood Cult* being the first. He also directed the sequel to this film, *Revenge* (1986) as well as *The Ripper* (1985), and now produces TV programs and documentaries through his company The Entertainment Group. (VCI)

www.tegclassictv.com

Blood Lake (1987)

D: Tim Boggs; W: Doug Barry; P: Doug Barry; C: Doug Barry, Angela Darter, Mike Kaufman, Andrewa Adams, Travis Krasser, Christie Willoughby

Awful shot-on-video horror from United Home Video about partying teens being terrorized by a relentless killer.

Director Tim Boggs worked on *Offerings* (1989), and has since had a lengthy career as a dialogue and sound editor.

Demon from Devil's Lake (1964)

D: Russ Marker; W: Russ Marker, Don Phillips; P: Don Phillips; C: Dave Heath, James Britton, Stan Knight, Leta Disheroon, Charles Andrews, Charles Young, Barbara McClure

A rocketship crashes into Lake Texoma and unleashes some sort of mutant monster in this unfinished film that was set to be Marker's follow-up to *The Yesterday Machine* (1963).

The cast list above was culled from a June 17, 1964, *Variety* notice about the film. According to the article, tryouts were held at the Southeastern State College, with 19 students cast in minor speaking roles. James Britton was Marker's brother.

According to Marker, production ceased when the producers ran out of money; however, an online post by producer Phillips' wife indicated that the movie was nearly completed, and then handed over to Larry Buchanan.

Marker later used the same premise for *Night Fright* (1967), directed by Buchanan collaborator James Sullivan.

The Last Slumber Party (1988)

D: Stephen Tyler; W: Stephen Tyler, Jim Taylor; P: Jill Clark, Bill F. Blair (EP), Betty S. Scott (EP); C: Jan Jenson, Nancy Mayer, Joann Whitley, Danny David, Stephen Tyler, David Whitley

Jumbled, direct-to-video slasher from VCI (shot on 16mm), with teenagers being killed by a scalpel-wielding mental patient decked out in a surgical mask and scrubs. Music by FirstStryke. (VCI)

Mutilations (1986)

D: Lawrence Thomas; W: Lawrence Thomas; P: Paul Cowdin, Lawrence Thomas; C: Al Baker, John Bliss, Bill Buckner, Shelly Creel, Matthew Hixenbaugh, Katherine Hutson

An astronomy professor takes a group of students to investigate a meteor crash linked to some cattle mutilations, and they encounter giant, stop-motion alien monsters that have arrived to take over the planet.

The special effects team also worked on *Revenge* (1986) and *Terror at Tenkiller* (1986).

Offerings (1989)

D: Christopher Reynolds; W: Christopher Reynolds; P: Christopher Reynolds; C: Loretta Leigh Bowman, Elizabeth Greene, G. Michael Smith, Jerry Brewer

A *Halloween* knock-off in which a shy boy is disfigured and put into a coma after neighborhood bullies toss him down a well. Years later, he returns to kill his former tormentors, leaving their body parts as "offerings" to a girl who was nice to him. (Madacy)

Revenge (1986)

D: Christopher Lewis; W: Christopher Lewis; P: Linda Lewis, Bill F. Blair (EP), Jill Clark (AP); C: Patrick Wayne, John Carradine, Andrea Adams, John Bliss, Fred Graves, Josef Hanet

The third film in Lewis's direct-to-video trilogy, and a sequel to *Blood Cult* (1985). The cult from the first film is still active, and the brother of *Blood Cult*'s hero (Patrick Wayne, son of John Wayne) has come to investigate his sibling's death. (VCI)

Offerings (1989) was one of the better Oklahoma-lensed slasher films (courtesy Fred Adelman).

The Ripper (1985)

D: Christopher Lewis; W: Bill Groves; P: Linda Lewis, Bill F. Blair; C: Andrea Adams, Tom Savini, Tom Schreier, Wade Tower, Mona Van Pernis

When a college professor puts on an antique ring, he is possessed by the spirit of Jack the Ripper (Tom Savini). This was the United/VCI group's shot-on-video follow-up to *Blood Cult*. Savini has publicly apologized on several occasions for his participation in the film. (VCI)

Terror at Tenkiller (1986)

D: Ken Meyer; W: Claudia Meyer; P: Ken Meyer, Bill F. Blair (EP); C: Dale Buckmaster, Stacy Logan, Michelle Merchant, Kevin Meyer, Michael Shamus Wiles

Another 16mm direct-to-video horror from the VCI/United Home Video family, this time featuring college girls vacationing at a lake where a crazed, harmonica-playing handyman named Tor kills people. (VCI)

Left: Revenge (1986) was the shot-on-video follow up to *Blood Cult* (1985) (courtesy Fred Adelman). *Right:* VCI/United Entertainment released a series of cheap horror films in the 1980s, including *Terror at Tenkiller* (1986) (courtesy Fred Adelman).

OREGON

Deafula (1975)

D: Peter Wolf Wechsberg; W: Peter Wolf Wechsberg; P: Gary R. Holstrom; C: Peter Wolf, Lee Darel, Dudley Hemstreet, Gary R. Holstrom

Director/star Wolf/Wechsberg is a minister's son (and theology student) who transforms into a big-nosed vampire in the only horror film ever made entirely in sign language. Wechsberg (who is deaf) and producer Gary Holstrom worked together at a media center for a regional financial institution, and formed a company called SignScope to release educational films for deaf schools. When *Deafula* was exhibited, there was also a voice track for hearing audiences. Wechsberg, who was born in England, also directed *Think Me Nothing* (1975) and *I Love You, But* (1998), both in sign language. He previously toured with the National Theatre of the Deaf, created a TV news program in sign language, and made documentaries and commercials. He continues to work as a director and cinematographer, and still operates SignScope from a studio in Camarillo, California

www.signscope.biz

Sasquatch, the Legend of Bigfoot (1977)

D: Ed Ragozzino; W: Ed Hawkins, Ronald D. Olson; P: John Fabian, Ronald D. Olson; C: George Lauris, Steve Boergadine, Jim Bardford, Ken Kenzle, William Emons, Joe Morello, Lou Salermi

One of several pseudo-documentary bigfoot flicks that were released in the wake of *The Legend of Boggy Creek* (1972). *Sasquatch* is about a group of researchers (led by an Indian guide and a Gabby Hayes–style mountain man) who venture into the Oregon wilderness and are attacked by a pack of angry bigfeet. Along the way, they also encounter mountain lions and bears.

Producer Ronald Olson was actually a dedicated bigfoot researcher who founded the Eugene-based North American Wildlife Research Company in the 1970s. His father founded American National Enterprises, a Salt Lake City–based film distribution company that specialized in nature documentaries. Olson and ANE later made a 20-minute documentary based on the original Roger Patterson bigfoot film, but it would be several years before Olson made his own contribution to sasquatch cinema, which his family four-walled across the country. A soundtrack was also released.

Olson and his father also built the "Bigfoot Trap," a popular tourist attraction near Applegate Lake, in 1974. Originally designed to capture a live bigfoot, it mostly drew curious bigfoot devotees. In 2006, volunteers from the U.S. Forest Service's Passport in Time program restored the structure, which had been damaged in a storm.

Olson now operates two Lube It USA stores in Eugene. Director Ragozzino was an actor and voice-over artist; he died in 2010. (RetroMedia)

Unhinged (1982)

D: Don Gronquist; W: Don Gronquist, Reagan Ramsey; P: Don Gronquist, Dale Farr (EP), Dan Biggs (AP); C: Laurel Munson, Janet Penner, Sara Ansley, Virginia Settle, John Morrison

Three women on their way to a rock concert crash their car during a thunder storm and find themselves in the home of a man-hating old woman and her daughter. A cloaked killer picks them off one by one.

Although almost completely forgotten now, this film made the U.K. "video nasties" list when it was originally released. The DVD includes a TV interview (conducted by a local Portland station during the film's production) with a visibly nervous Gronquist and Sara Ansley.

Gronquist produced *Stark Raving Mad* (*Rockaday Richie and the Queen of the Hop*), a take-off on the Charles Starkweather murders that was made in the early 1970s but not released until 1983. He later directed *The Devil's Keep* (1995), and at one point operated a restaurant called Dazzle Dogs and Super Soups. Producer Biggs made *Shadow Play* (1986), also filmed in Portland. (IndieDVD)

PENNSYLVANIA

4D Man (1959)

D: Irvin S. Yeaworth, Jr.; W: Jack H. Harris, Theodore Simonson, Cy Chermak; P: Jack H. Harris, Irvin S. Yeaworth, Jr.; C: Robert Lansing, Lee Meriwether, James Congdon, Robert Strauss, Edgar Stehli, Patty Duke

Lansing is a scientist who is transformed into a "4D man" who can pass through solid objects. The process rapidly ages him, but he is able to rejuvenate himself by draining the lifeforce out of other people.

This was the Yeaworth/Harris team's second sci-fi feature, and was followed by *Dinosaurus!* (1960). (Image)

The Blob (1958)

D: Irvin S. Yeaworth, Jr.; W: Kay Linaker, Irvine H. Millgate, Theodore Simonson; P: Jack H. Harris, Russell S. Doughten, Jr. (AP); C: Steve McQueen, Aneta Corsaut, Earl Rowe, Olin Howlin, John Benson, George Karas

A gelatinous mass from outer space terrorizes a small town in one of the most well-known '50s schlock sci-fi flicks ever made.

The Blob was a collaboration between distributor Jack H. Harris and a religious film company, Good News Productions in Chester Springs, Pennsylvania. That partnership, called Valley Forge Films, also made *4D Man* (1959).

Religious filmmakers in Pennsylvania were responsible for both *4D Man* (1959) and *The Blob* (1958) (courtesy Fred Adelman).

Producer Russell Doughten went on to make *A Thief in the Night* (1972), one of the most influential Christian films ever released, along with its sequels. Yeaworth later made *Dinosaurus!* (1960), then returned to religious filmmaking (as well as theme park design). He died in a car accident in Amman, Jordan, in 2004. (Criterion)
www.rdfilms.com

Bloodeaters (*Toxic Zombies*, 1980)

D: Charles McCrann; W: Charles McCrann; P: J. William Lee (AP), Charles McCrann; C: Charles McCrann (as Charles Austin), Beverly Shapiro, Dennis Helfend, Kevin Hanlon, Judith M. Brown, Pat Kellis, John Amplas

Cheap, tongue-in-cheek zombie flick about a bunch of marijuana growers who get doused with an experimental herbicide by the DEA and turn into homicidal, knife-wielding zombies. They terrorize and kill various campers and hillbillies, and chase a young girl and her mentally disabled brother (a guy in overalls who acts like Lenny from *Of Mice and Men*). The film opens with a girl giving herself a sponge bath out of a bucket in the middle of the woods, and ends with the terrifying sneeze of a gas station attendant. With bad acting, okay gore effects, Romero regular John Amplas as a federal agent, horrible Polish jokes, and gratuitous giblet throwing.

Director McCrann was a Princeton and Yale Law School graduate. This was his only film; it aired several times on cable as *Toxic Zombies*. McCrann later became a vice president at financial services conglomerate Marsh & McLennan Companies, and died in the World Trade Center attack in 2001.

The Crazies (1973)

D: George Romero; W: Paul McCollough, George Romero; P: A.C. Croft; C: Lane Carroll, Will MacMillan, Harold Wayne Jones, Lloyd Hollar, Lynn Lowry, Richard Liberty

This was Romero's return to form after the disappointments of *There's Always Vanilla* (1971) and *Hungry Wives* (1972). The military quarantines a small town after an experimental biological weapon is accidentally released, but has to fight off the infected citizens who have been turned into homicidal maniacs by the contagion.

Pennsylvania was once again attacked by zombies in *Bloodeaters*, a.k.a. *Toxic Zombies* (1980) (courtesy Fred Adelman).

The film had a brief and unsuccessful run in 1973, but received a wider re-release in 1976. After this, Romero's next several films were made for his new company, Laurel Entertainment, including *Martin* (1977), *Dawn of the Dead* (1978), *Knightriders* (1981), *Creepshow* (1982), and *Day of the Dead* (1985). A remake was released in 2010. (Blue Underground)

Effects (1980)

D: Dusty Nelson; W: Dusty Nelson, William H. Mooney; P: John Harrison (EP), Pasquale Buba; C: Joe Pilato, Susan Chapek, Tom Savini, John Harrison, Bernard McKenna, Debra Gordon

A cameraman and special effects artist (Pilato) believes the low-budget horror film he has been hired to work on is actually a snuff film.

Shot on 16mm in Pittsburgh with a number of veterans of George Romero films, *Effects* had a brief release in 1980 before its distributor went bankrupt, finally surfacing on DVD in 2005. Producer Buba worked as an editor on most of Romero's films, and Harrison (who also plays the insane director) was the "screwdriver zombie" in *Dawn of the Dead*. He has gone on to direct a number of television series and movies. Star Pilato is better known for his role as the foul-mouthed Col. Rhodes in *Day of the Dead*. (Synapse) www.dustynelson.com

George Romero returned to form with *The Crazies* (1973) (courtesy Fred Adelman).

FleshEater (1988)

D: S. William Hinzman; W: S. William Hinzman, Bill Randolph; P: S. William Hinzman, David Gordon (EP), Simon Manses (AP); C: S. William Hinzman, John Mowod, Leslie Ann Wick, Kevin Kindlin, Charis Kirkpatrik Acuff

Hinzman, the graveyard zombie from *Night of the Living Dead* (1968), directed and starred in this film, which (not surprisingly) is about flesh-eating zombies on the loose in rural Pennsylvania.

Vincent D. Survinski here recreates his role from *Night of the Living Dead* as a gunman in a local posse. Hinzman also reprised his zombie role in a TV commercial for GoodFellas Brick Oven Pizza. He died in 2012. Filmed in Beaver Township, Pennsylvania. (Media Blasters)

Girls School Screamers (1986)

D: *John P. Finegan;* W: *John P. Finegan, Katie Keating, Pierce J. Keating;* P: *James W. Finegan, Jr., John P. Finegan, Pierce J. Keating, Michael Herz (EP), Lloyd Kaufman (EP);* C: *Mollie O'Mara, Sharon Christopher, Mari Butler, Beth O'Malley, Karen Krevitz*

Star students from an all-girl college go to a spooky old mansion to catalog an art collection donated to the school by a dead millionaire. The house turns out to be haunted, and the girls and their nun chaperone are terrorized and killed.

Finegan also wrote, produced and appeared in *Blades* (1989), another Troma film from New Jersey. (Troma)

Heartstopper (1989)

D: *John A. Russo;* W: *John A. Russo;* P: *Charles A. Gelini, Robert A. Donell (EP);* C: *Kevin Kindlin, Moon Unit Zappa, Tom Savini, John Hall, Tommy Lafitte, Michael J. Pollard*

A vampiric doctor put to death in 1776 is resurrected in modern-day Pittsburgh, then falls in love with a museum curator (Zappa) and encounters a copycat vampire killer (actually one of his descendents).

Based on Russo's novel *The Awakening*. (Media Blasters)

Hungry Wives (*Season of the Witch/Jack's Wife*, 1972)

D: *George A. Romero;* W: *George Romero;* P: *Nancy Romero, Gary Streiner, Alvin Croft (EP);* C: *Jan White, Raymond Laine, Ann Muffly, Joedda McClain, Bill Thunhurst, Neil Fisher*

This was Romero's second attempt to move away from *Night of the Living Dead* (1968) territory after making the romantic comedy *There's Always Vanilla* (1971). White plays an unhappy housewife trapped in a loveless marriage with her uncommunicative husband. After a visit with the neighborhood tarot reader, she finds solace in witchcraft. (Anchor Bay)

The Majorettes (*One by One*, 1986)

D: *S. William Hinzman;* W: *John Russo;* P: *John Russo, J.C. Ross (EP);* C: *Kevin Kindlin, Terrie Godfrey, Mark V. Jevicky, Sueanne Seamens, Denise Huot, Carl Hetrick, Russell Streiner*

Members of a squad of majorettes are systematically killed by a psycho in hunting garb in this late-entry slasher film.

Heartstopper (1989), based on John Russo's novel *The Awakening* (courtesy J.R. Bookwalter).

This was the first directorial effort from Hinzman (the cemetery zombie in *Night of the Living Dead*, 1968) who went on to direct *FleshEater* (1988). Russo originally adapted and sold the screenplay as a novel. (Media Blasters)

Malatesta's Carnival of Blood (1973)

D: *Christopher Speeth*; W: *Werner Liepolt*; P: *Richard Grosser, Walker Stuart*; C: *Janine Carazo, Jerome Dempsey, Daniel Dietrich, Lenny Baker, Herve Villechaize, William Preston*

Surreal film about a family searching for their missing son at a mysterious carnival staffed by ghoulish cretins who eat human flesh and watch silent horror films.

The art design on this peculiar film was done by a group called Alley Friends, a gaggle of green-minded architects who specialize in developments created from recycled materials.

Speeth studied film at the Annenberg Center of the University of Pennsylvania, and has since moved on to documentary filmmaking. Long thought lost, *Malatesta* resurfaced in 2003 when the director released a DVD. (Windmill Films)

www.malatestascarnival.com

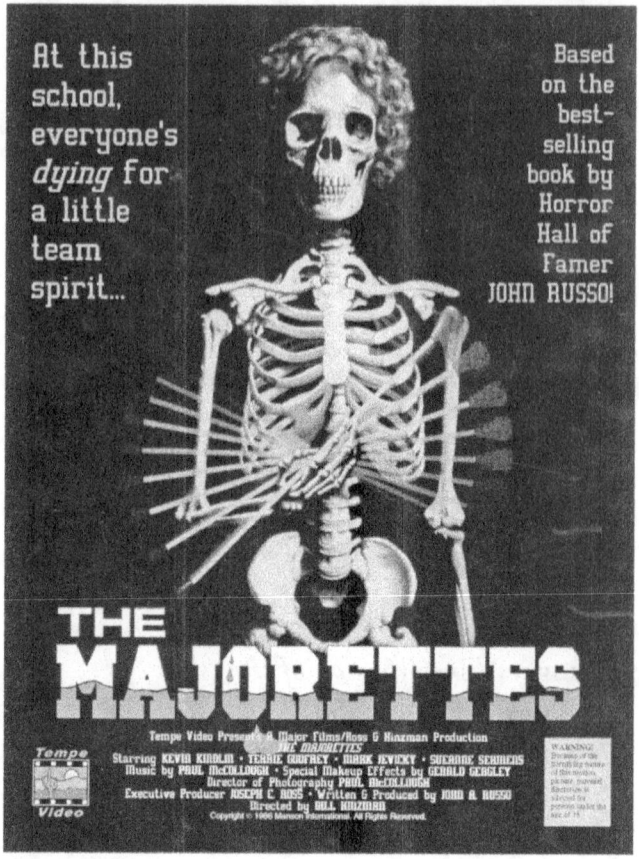

Night of the Living Dead veterans John Russo and Bill Hinzman reteamed for *The Majorettes* (1986) (courtesy J.R. Bookwalter).

Midnight (1982)

D: *John Russo*; W: *John Russo*; P: *Donald Redinger, Samuel M. Sherman (EP)*; C: *Melanie Verlin, Lawrence Tierney, John Hall, Charles Jackson, John Amplas, Lachele Carl*

Verlin, after escaping an attempted rape by her stepfather (Tierney), runs away from home and is picked up hitchhiking by couple of college kids. The trio find themselves trapped in an out-of-the-way small town populated with threatening hillbillies and devil worshippers.

This was based on Russo's novel, and distributed by Sam Sherman's Independent-International Pictures. Russo directed a shot-on-video pseudo-sequel called *Midnight 2* (1993) produced by Ohio filmmaker J.R. Bookwalter.

Elements of this film's plot also turn up in Rob Zombie's *House of 1,000 Corpses* (2003). (Lions Gate)

Night of the Living Dead (1968)

D: *George Romero*; W: *John Russo, George Romero*; P: *Russell Streiner, Karl Hardman*; C: *Duane Jones, Judith O'Dea, Karl Hardman, Marilyn Eastman, Keith Wayne, Judith Ridley*

The movie that launched a thousand inferior zombie films. The dead inexplicably rise and begin chowing down on the living, while a group of survivors take refuge in a remote farmhouse.

Romero and his cohorts operated a commercial film business in Pittsburgh called Latent Image, and decided to pool their money and make a cheap, black-and-white horror movie. The film suffered distribution problems and received mostly horrible reviews, including a scathing piece by Roger Ebert that criticized its packaging as a kiddie matinee. Over time, the film built a significant cult audience, but Romero was unable to benefit directly because (due to an oversight) the movie was never properly copyrighted and slipped into the public domain. Romero's two follow up films, *There's Always Vanilla* in 1971 (the production of which caused a rancorous implosion at Latent Image) and *Hungry Wives* (*Season of the Witch*, 1972) failed to generate much of an audience, so he soon returned to straight horror with *The Crazies* (1973), *Martin* (1977), *Dawn of the Dead* (1978) and *Day of the Dead* (1985).

Night was remade by Tom Savini in 1990, then revisited more pointlessly by Jeff Broadstreet in 2006 (in 3D). Several colorized versions of the film have also been released, and John Russo created a modified version in 1999 with newly filmed scenes and a different soundtrack. (Elite)

John Russo and Sam Sherman teamed up for the rural cult film *Midnight* (1982) (courtesy Fred Adelman).

Primal Scream (1987)

D: William Murray; W: William Murray; C: Kenneth McGregor, Sharon Mason, Julie Miller, Jenny Albert, Stephen Caldwell, Stephen Emhe

This futuristic sci-fi mystery is about a private detective investigating a mining company's interest in a new element called Hellfire that can cause people to burst into flames when it's injected into their bodies. Shot in New York City and Pennsylvania.

Splatter Farm (1987)

D: P. Alan (John Polonia, Mark Polonia, Todd Michael Smith); W: John Polonia, Mark Polonia; P: J.K. Farlew; C: Marion Costly, John Polonia, Mark Polonia, Todd Michael Smith, Todd Rimatti, Jeff Seddon

    Here we have a shot-on-video gore film made by teenagers that pretty much looks exactly like you'd think it would, but with slightly better-than-expected special effects and a creepy undercurrent of incest. The Polonias play two twins who spend the summer with their elderly aunt and her dimwitted farm hand Jeremy, who turns out to be a murderous looney with a penchant for necrophilia. Chock-full of gross-out moments that leave nothing to the imagination, this was given a surprisingly rich "special edition" DVD treatment by Camp Motion Pictures in 2007.

    The Polonias continued to make cheap horror films, the most recent of which was *Splatter Beach* (2007). They often collaborated with Jon McBride (director of *Cannibal Campout*, and *Woodchipper Massacre*, both 1988) and Todd Michael Smith (who played Jeremy in this film). Smith has also directed a number of low-budget films, and has a Web site: www.toddmichaelsmithfanclub.com. Mark Polonia works at Mansfield University in Pennsylvania. John Polonia died in 2008. (Camp)

RHODE ISLAND
(None)

SOUTH CAROLINA

Voodoo Dawn (1990)

D: Steven Fierberg; W: Jeffrey Delman, Evan Dunsky, Thomas Rendon, John Russo; P: Steven D. Mackler, Pat Troise (AP), Bernard E. Goldberg (EP); C: Raymond St. Jacques, Theresa Merritt, Gina Gershon, J. Grant Albrecht, Kirk Baily, Tony Todd

    An evil voodoo priest (Todd) creates an army of zombie field workers and kills people to steal their body parts.

    Based on a novel by John Russo. Director Fierberg had worked primarily as a cinematographer. Jeff Delman directed *Deadtime Stories* (1986). This was one of St. Jacques' last two films before his death in 1990.

SOUTH DAKOTA
(None)

TENNESSEE

Dear Dead Delilah (1972)

D: John Farris; W: John Farris; P: Jack Clement, Susan Richardson (AP); C: Agnes Moorehead, Will Geer, Michael Ansara, Dennish Patrick, Patricia Carmichael, William Kerwin

Farris, author of *The Fury*, wrote and directed this film around the same time his novel *When Michael Calls* was adapted for television. *Delilah* is about a mad killer roaming the halls of an old mansion, searching for Agnes Moorehead's fortune.

In past interviews, Farris has said that the budget for this film was between $200,000 and $225,000, and that the script was better than the movie. Originally, Farris and his partner Jack Clement had planned to make two films back-to-back. The second script Farris wrote was a vampire story that he eventually turned into the 1990 novel *Fiends*.

Clement worked at Sun Records and wrote songs for Elvis, Jerry Lee Lewis and Johnny Cash. With music by Tennessee native (and Sun recording artist) Bill Justis. This was Moorehead's final film.

Demon Queen (1986)

D: Donald Farmer; W: Donald Farmer; P: Donald Farmer, David Reed, Sterling Bingham; C: Mary Fanaro, Clifton Dance, David Blood, Rick Foster

Donald Farmer's debut shot-on-video gore opus stars Mary Fanaro (of *Truth or Dare*, 1986) as a vampire succubus who kills men she picks up in bars.

Farmer was a political reporter with the *Nashville Tennessean* and worked at Tennessee's WCET-TV. He also wrote for *Fangoria* and launched his own fanzine, *The Splatter Times* ("A decidedly unsavory publication..."). After establishing himself with *Demon Queen*, he went on to direct *Cannibal Hookers* (1987), *Scream Dream* (1989), *Vampire Cop* (1990), and more than a dozen other features.

The Evil Dead (1981)

D: Sam Raimi; W: Sam Raimi; P: Robert G. Tapert, Sam Raimi (EP), Bruce Campbell (EP), Gary Holt (AP); C: Bruce Campbell, Ellen Sandweiss, Richard DeManincor, Betsy Baker, Theresa Tilly

Five people staying in a remote cabin accidentally unleash creepy demons that kill and/or possess them in this scary, fast-paced and imaginative debut feature from Sam Raimi. Filmed mostly in Tennessee and partly in Michigan.

Sam Raimi's *The Evil Dead* (1981) was filmed in Tennessee and Michigan.

Michigan native Raimi and his high school friends Rob Tapert and Bruce Campbell had previously made a number of short films, including a horror movie called *Within the Woods* (1978) that they used as a promo to raise seed money from local business owners to film *Evil Dead*. The movie was popular in Europe and received an endorsement from author Stephen King before being picked up in the U.S. by New Line. It became a huge cult hit, with its crawling, low-angle camera moves copped by hundreds of other low-budget horror films. Although his follow-up, *Crimewave* (1985), flopped, Raimi scored with *Evil Dead II* (1987), *Darkman* (1990), and *Army of Darkness* (1992), eventually graduating to a number of middling studio productions like *The Quick and the Dead* (1995) and *The Gift* (2000) before launching the *Spider-Man* franchise in 2002.

Raimi also served as the uncredited executive producer of J.R. Bookwalter's *The Dead Next Door* (1988). (Anchor Bay)

I Was a Zombie for the F.B.I. (1982)

D: Marius Penczner; W: Marius Penczner; P: Marius Penczner, John Gillick, Nancy Donelson, Len Epand; C: Larry Raspberry, John Gillick, James Raspberry, D.M. Coger, Richard Crowe, Laurence Hill, Christina Welford

Black-and-white homage to 1950s sci-fi films about aliens trying to conquer Earth by using a popular cola to zombiefy people. Two FBI agents (played by the Raspberry cousins) stumble upon the plot while tracking down a pair of escaped convicts.

Made for $27,000 with help from Memphis-area film students, this film was only shown in 1985 on the old "Night Flight" cable program. Its first official video release came via the 2005 Rykodisc DVD, which included enhanced visual effects and a remastered soundtrack. The film was also cut by nearly 30 minutes, which greatly improved its previously sluggish pacing.

Director/writer Penczner was a member of Black Oak Arkansas in the mid–1970s, and later directed music videos and commercials. Part of the funding for *Zombie* came from prize money he received after winning an Emmy for one of his short films. He now operates a media consulting business (People By Penczner), and worked on campaigns for Bill Clinton, Al Gore and John Edwards. Larry Raspberry was the lead singer of The Gentrys ("Keep on Dancing"), a band that also included future professional wrestling manager Jimmy Hart. He still performs with the Gentrys and his later band, The Highsteppers. The stop-motion Z-Beast monster (created by Bob Friedstand) was later used in the ZZ Top video "TV Dinners," which Penczner directed.

In an article in *Spin* magazine in 1985, Bob Dylan listed this film as a movie he wished he had been in, along with *Raintree County* (1957) and *Ben Hur* (1959). (Rykodisc)

home.earthlink.net/~lraspberry/   *www.penczer.com*

Lord Shango (*Soulmates of Shango/The Color of Love*, 1975)

D: Ray Marsh; W: Paul Carter Harrison; P: Steve Bono, Ronald Hobbs, Ann Kindberg (AP), Vincent Albert DiStefano (AP); C: Marlene Clark, Lawrence Cook, Wally Taylor, Avis McCarther, John Russell

Strife between Christians and a Yoruba cult in Tennessee leads to murder, infidelity, and the possible reincarnation of an African deity in this Bryanston film. A soundtrack was also released.

Clark appeared in a number of blaxploitation-era films, including *Ganja & Hess* (1973), *Black Mamba* (1974), *The Baron* (1977), and Jack Hill's *Switchblade Sisters* (1975). Marsh directed *The Last Porno Flick* (1974, also produced by Bono), worked on *Jack the Ripper Goes West* (1974, another Bryanston film), and is still active as an assistant director. Screenwriter Harrison was a playwright who taught at Howard University and Columbia College, and directed the Melvin Van Peebles' play "Ain't Supposed to Die a Natural Death" at the State University of California in Sacramento in the early 1970s. He also wrote the script for *Youngblood* (1978).

The Monster and the Stripper (*The Exotic Ones*, 1968)

D: Ron Ormond; W: Ron Ormond; P: Ron Ormond, June Ormond; C: Wm. Austin, Ron Ormond, Kathy Clifton, Georgette Dante, Ronald Drake, Lynn Fontane, Sleepy LaBeef, June Ormond, Tim Ormond

A rare T&A/horror flick from Southern auteur Ron Ormond, which also happened to be the last of his exploitation quickies before he found God and started making equally deranged religious films. A sleazy strip club owner named Nemo (Ormond himself) decides to capture a local swamp monster that's been killing livestock and terrorizing local farmers. The Swamp Thing (played by giant rockabilly singer Sleepy LaBeef) puts up a fight—at one point ripping off a man's arm and beating him to death with it—but is eventually displayed, King Kong–style, at Nemo's club. As you can probably guess, this is destined to end in tears, mostly produced by a stripper whose breast is ripped off of her body.

This was shot partly in New Orleans and partly in Tennessee. LaBeef wound up in the movie because he was Ormond's neighbor.

After the success of this film, Ormond turned his operation over to religious filmmaking, teaming with Southern evangelist Estus Pirkle to produce a jaw-dropping bit of anti-communist religious propaganda called *If Footmen Tire You, What Will Horses Do?* (1971). They followed that up with *The Burning Hell* (1974), but Ormond eventually split with Pirkle after a financial dispute. Ormond then teamed with another minister, John Rice, for *The Land Where Jesus Walked* and *The Grim Reaper* (1976), which featured Jack Van Impe and Jerry Falwell. Ormond died in 1981.

www.sleepylabeef.com

A poster for Ron Ormond's ridiculous *The Exotic Ones* (a.k.a. *The Monster and the Stripper*, 1968).

Scream Dream (1989)

D: Donald Farmer; W: Donald Farmer; P: Donald Farmer (EP), Barney Griner, Bob Allison; C: Carol Carr, Melissa Moore, Nikki Riggins, Jesse Raye

A demon possesses the female singer of a rock band in Farmer's third film. Moore went on to a lengthy career in cheap movies, and even appeared in a comic book. Farmer followed this with *Vampire Cop* (1990), which was shot in Florida and Georgia.

TEXAS

The Abomination (1986)
D: Bret McCormick; W: Bret McCormick; P: Bret McCormick, Matt Devlen, Marie Skyler (EP); C: Scott Davis, Jude Johnson, Blue Thompson, Brad McCormick, Suzy Meyer

Cody (Davis) and his mother (Johnson) cough up malevolent tumors that multiply and turn into a grotesque, undulating heap of teeth and viscera that might have something to do with the Antichrist. This Super 8 film (shot in Poolville, Texas) was McCormick's first feature after participating in the *Tabloid* (1985) anthology, and was shot back-to-back with *Ozone! Attack of the Redneck Mutants* (1986). McCormick was married to actress Blue Thompson, and continued making low-budget horror and action films in Texas until 1997. (Muther Video)

The Amazing Transparent Man (1960)
D: Edgar G. Ulmer; W: Jack Lewis; P: Lester D. Guthrie, Robert L. Madden (EP), John Miller (EP); C: Marguerite Chapman, Douglas Kennedy, James Griffith, Ivan Triesault, Boyd "Red" Morgan, Carmel Daniel

A safecracker is busted out of prison by a scientist and rendered invisible so that he can steal radium. One of two sci-fi films made in Texas by Miller Consolidated Pictures (MCP) using imported Hollywood talent. The other was *Beyond the Time Barrier* (1960), on which producer Lester Guthrie served as production manager. MCP originally distributed the films (Ulmer's last American productions), which were later picked up by American International Pictures.

MCP was formed by John Miller, Mike Miller, and Robert Madden, and exploitation legend Kroger Babb served as the company's vice president and general manager at one point. (Robert O'Donnell, head of Texas-based Interstate Theaters, was also linked with the company.) (Mill Creek)

The Amazing Transparent Man (1960) was one of two films made in Texas by Edgar G. Ulmer (courtesy Fred Adelman).

The Aurora Encounter (1986)

D: Jim McCullough Sr.; W: Jim McCullough Jr., Melody Brooke; P: Jim McCullough Sr., Jim McCullough Jr., M.N. Sanousi (EP), Fred T. Kuehnert (EP), Phil Flora (AP); C: Jack Elam, Peter Brown, Carol Bagdasarian, Dottie West, Charles B. Pierce, Mickey Hays, George "Spanky" McFarland, Mindy Smith

An alien (Hays) lands in 19th Century Texas and befriends a cantankerous old timer (Elam). This was based on an allegedly true incident that made the Dallas newspapers in 1897: An air ship was reported to have crashed in Aurora, Texas, and the townspeople buried a small creature found with the ship in the local cemetery. The Texas Historical Commission placed a plaque at the cemetery commemorating the event, although the incident was likely a publicity hoax.

Mickey Hays (who died in 1992) suffered from Progeria, a genetic disease that causes rapid aging, resulting in his odd appearance. His role in this film came through the Make a Wish Foundation. Jack Elam had previously been in the McCulloughs' *Creature from Black Lake* (1976). This was the last film appearance for both country singer Dottie West and former Little Rascal Spanky McFarland. Watch for *Boggy Creek* creator Charles B. Pierce as a preacher.

The McCulloughs made a handful of feature films after this, including *Video Murders* (1988), *Where the Red Fern Grows: Part 2* (1992), and *The St. Tammany Miracle* (1994) with Joy Houck, Jr. Producers Kuehnert and Sanousi also helped finance *The Outing* (1987). (Anchor Bay)

Beyond the Time Barrier (1960)

D: Edgar G. Ulmer; W: Arthur C. Pierce; P: Robert Clarke, Robert L. Madden (EP), John Miller (EP); C: Robert Clarke, Darlene Tompkins, Vladimir Sokoloff, Boyd "Red" Morgan, Arianne Arden, Stephen Bekassy, Jack Herman

Astronaut Robert Clarke makes his way through post-apocalyptic Texas in *Beyond the Time Barrier* (1960) (courtesy Tom Weaver).

In this take on *The Time Machine*, a test pilot in an experimental jet flies through a time warp and lands back on Earth in a post-apocalyptic future where humans have been turned into sterile, mute mutants because of radiation from atomic bomb testing. Shot at the Texas State Fairgrounds in Dallas, this served as a companion film to Miller Consolidated Pictures' *The Amazing Transparent Man*.

Clarke was the star and creative force behind *The Hideous Sun Demon* (1959). He made one other film with Miller Consolidated, *A Date with Death* (1959), shot in New Mexico and distributed on the same bill with *Sun Demon*.

Russ Marker, who has a small part in this film, acted in a lot of Texas-made movies, and wrote *The Yesterday Machine* (1966) and *Night Fright* (1967). Jack Herman was also in *The Yesterday Machine* and Larry Buchanan's *The Naked Witch* (1964). (Sinister Cinema)

The Black Cat (1966)

D: Harold Hoffman; W: Harold Hoffman; P: Patrick Sims; C: Robert Frost, Robyn Baker, Sadie French, Scotty McKay, Bill Thurman, George Russell, Annabelle Weenick

Mid-century Texas-sleaze take on Poe, with Frost as a nutty playboy with father issues who assaults his wife and kills the pet cat she presents him for their anniversary (after gorily gouging out its eye). He's committed to an asylum, gets released, and spends most of his time drinking at a bar where the members of the house band all wear eye patches.

Both Bill Thurman and Annabelle Weenick were regulars in the films of Larry Buchanan and S.F. Brownrigg. Hoffman also directed *Sex and the Animals* (1969) and wrote several Larry Buchanan films. *The Black Cat* was produced by Falcon International Corp., which was also responsible for *Free, White and 21* (1963), *Under Age* (1964), *The Trial of Lee Harvey Oswald* (1964) and *Sex and the Animals*. (Something Weird)

Blood Suckers from Outer Space (1984)

D: Glen Coburn; W: Glen Coburn; P: Gale Boyd Latham; C: Glen Coburn, Robert Bradeen, Big John Brigham, Laura Ellis, Dan Gallion, Christine Crowe, Christopher Heldman, Dennis Letts

A strange alien gas turns the residents of a small town into chatty, fast-moving, flesh-hungry zombies. It's cheap and the acting is bad, but most of the gags in this horror-comedy work pretty well, including a scene where Coburn's zombiefied aunt and uncle try to talk him and his leading lady into staying for "dinner."

The late Dennis Letts, who plays General Sanders, was a prolific actor and a professor at Southeastern Oklahoma State University. Coburn co-wrote and directed Bret McCormick's *Tabloid* (1985) and directed *Among the Dead* (*Hollywood Deadbeat*, 1995), a gloomy film about a low-budget director sinking into depression. He also worked as a journalist and commercial photographer, as well as at Morgan Creek Productions and Propaganda Films. (Media Blasters)

Bloodsuckersfromouterspace.com

Creature of Destruction (1967)

D: Larry Buchanan; W: Tony Huston; P: Larry Buchanan, Edwin Tobolowsky (AP); C: Les Tremayne, Pat Delaney, Aron Kincaid, Neil Fletcher, Annabelle Weenick, Roger Ready, Byron Lord

This remake of *The She-Creature* (1956) was Buchanan's next-to-last AIP TV project. A hypnotist (Tremayne) reverts his assistant (Delaney) into her prehistoric form: a bug-eyed, murderous sea monster.

Delaney was a regular in Buchanan films and was married to screenwriter/actor Tony Huston (a.k.a. Enrique Touceda), who later made films with Anthony Cardoza in California. He now works as an attorney in Los Angeles, specializing in real estate law. Byron Lord, who played the monster in the film, also donned the critter suit in *Night Fright*. (RetroMedia)

Curse of the Swamp Creature (1966)

D: *Larry Buchanan;* W: *Tony Huston;* P: *Larry Buchanan, Edwin Tobolowsky (AP);* C: *John Agar, Francine York, Jeff Alexander, Shirley McLine, Cal Duggan, Bill McGhee, Roger Ready, Bill Thurman, Tony Huston, Annabelle Weenick*

A mad doctor trying to discover the secret of evolution turns a man into an amphibious monster (that looks like the critter in *The Creature Walks Among Us*, 1956) after a trio of criminals (who've just murdered an oil executive) and an innocent geologist (Agar) stumble upon his remote laboratory. This was one of Buchanan's AIP TV projects (not a remake, but it's kind of like *Voodoo Woman*, 1957). The same monster mask later turns up in *Creature of Destruction* (1967) and *It's Alive!* (1969).

Buchanan regular Jeff Alexander was also in *The Black Cat* (1966) and *Horror High* (1974). (Elite Entertainment)

Don't Look in the Basement (*The Forgotten*, 1973)

D: *S.F. Brownrigg;* W: *Tim Pope;* P: *S.F. Brownrigg, Walter L. Krusz (EP);* C: *Bill McGhee, Rosie Holotik, Jessie Lee Fulton, Gene Ross, Annabelle Weenick, Jessie Kirby, Camilla Carr*

The new nurse at a remote asylum discovers that the crazy, bug-eyed inmates have taken over. This film used the "It's only a movie..." tagline that had been popularized by Wes Craven's *Last House on the Left* (1972).

Arkansas-born Sherald "S.F." Brownrigg made military training films and worked in the sound department at Dallas-based Jamieson Film Company. He met Larry Buchanan in the 1950s and worked with him on a number of films, including *The Naked Witch* (1964), *High Yellow* (1965) and *Zontar: The Thing from Venus* (1966). *Basement* was his first feature. After he stopped making films in the 1980s (the last one was *Thinkin' Big*, 1986), he worked in television (usually on hunting, fishing or golf programs) and served as president of Century Studios in Dallas. In a 1990 interview with *Fangoria*, he claimed he was planning to make a sequel to Tod Browning's *Freaks* (1932). He died in 1996.

One of his sons, Tony Brownrigg, is an actor and cameraman. Another son, Stacy, is a sound mixer (and worked on the most recent *Texas Chain Saw Massacre* films).

Most of the cast worked steadily in both Brownrigg and Larry Buchanan films. Holotik appeared in *Horror High* (1974) and later married Dallas Cowboy Charlie Waters. She now sells real estate in Texas. McGhee was one of the first black actors in Texas to become a member of SAG. (VCI)

Don't Open the Door! (1975)

D: *S.F. Brownrigg;* W: *Frank Schaeffer, Kerry Newcomb;* P: *S.F. Brownrigg;* C: *Susan Bracken, Larry O'Dwyer, Gene Ross, Annabelle Weenick, Hugh Feagin, James N. Harrell*

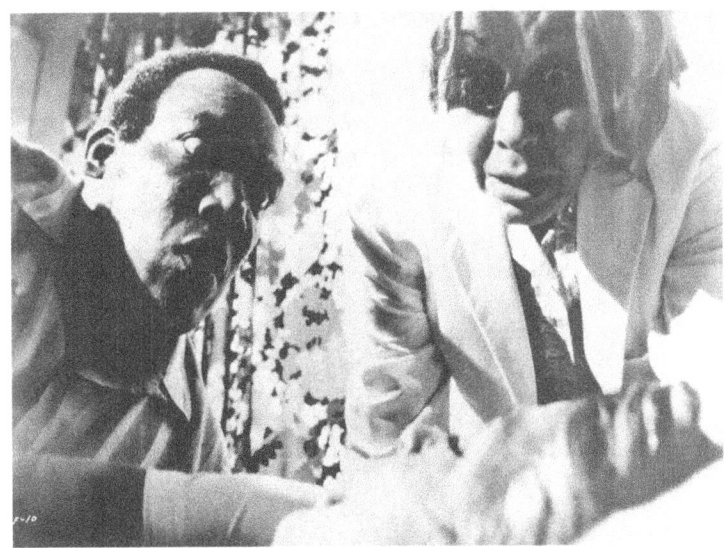

Bill McGhee and Annabelle Weenick in S.F. Brownrigg's *Don't Look in the Basement* (1973).

The Brownrigg players return in this slow-moving, but still eerie, tale about a young woman (Bracken, looking a bit like Rosie Holotik from *Don't Look in the Basement*) who moves back into her childhood home to take care of her grandmother. While creepy locals lurk around the house hoping to buy it from her, a cross-dressing psycho takes up residence in the attic and torments her with increasingly perverse phone calls.

Although it bears a 1979 copyright notice, *Don't Open the Door!* was made in 1973 as *Don't Hang Up*, and according to a 1990 article in *Fangoria* about Brownrigg, it was first released as *Season for Murder*. Former pro football player Langdon Viracola released the film in 1979 through his Capital Films Corp., and gave himself a producer credit in the press materials.

This was one of two films Brownrigg made with funding from *Breakfast at Tiffany's* producer Martin Jurow (the second was *Keep My Grave Open*). Larry Stouffer (*Horror High*) also worked on the film. Susan Bracken is the daughter of actor/comedian Eddie Bracken. (VCI)

Dungeon of Harrow (*Dungeons of Horror*, 1964)

D: Pat Boyette; W: Pat Boyette, Henry Garcia; P: Russ Harvey, Don Russell, Henry Garcia (EP), Fraser MacMillan (AP), Robert O'Donnell (EP); C: Russ Harvey, Helen Hogan, William McNulty, Michele Buquor, Maurice Harris, Eunice Grey, Lee Morgan

Don't Open the Door! (1973), one of S.F. Brownrigg's weird, stylish Texas horror films.

Two shipwreck survivors (Harvey and Morgan) wash up on an island and are taken captive by the sadistic Count de Sade (McNulty), who keeps his leprous wife locked up in the dungeon. This overlong, talky film is still strangely watchable thanks to its languid, almost hallucinatory pacing and one great shock sequence.

Boyette (who died in 2000) was a TV newscaster who later became a successful comic book artist. He made only two other films as director, *The Weird Ones* (1962) and *No Man's Land* (1964), but he wrote David L. Hewitt's oddball moonshiners-versus-bikers flick *The Girls from Thunder Strip* (1968). The man playing the pudgy "demon of the mind" that torments the Count was Texas horror host Joe Alston, who worked with Boyette. (Alpha/Mill Creek)

Enter the Devil (*Disciples of Death*, 1972)

D: Frank Q. Dobbs; W: David S. Cass Sr., Frank Q. Dobbs; P: Michael F. Cusack; C: Joshua Bryant, Irene Kelly, Davd S. Cass Sr., John Martin, Robert John Allen, Happy Shahan

Anthropologist Irene Kelly and sheriff's deputy Josh Bryant discover that a robed, knife-wielding Penitente cult called the Disciples of Death have been sacrificing people in the desert. The film also features an abandoned mercury mine, racist rednecks at a hunting lodge, death-by-rattlesnake, and a woman being burned alive. The heroine (Kelly) doesn't show up until half way through the movie. This played theaters as late as 1977, usually on double bills with imported horror films like *Beyond the Door* (1974).

Dobbs was a prolific producer and writer in Texas, and worked on a number of TV and theatrical films before his death in 2006. He also directed *Hotwire* (1983) and *Uphill All the Way* (1986), an action/comedy starring Roy Clark, Mel Tillis, Sheb Wooley, Frank Gorshin, Glen Campbell and Burl Ives. His final film as director was a TV project called *Hard Ground* (2003) with Burt Reynolds and Bruce Dern. Writer/actor Cass was also a stuntman (he doubled Robert Mitchum and Burt Lancaster) and second-unit director. Happy Shahan, who plays the missing motorist from the beginning of the film, sings the theme song. (Something Weird)

The Eye Creatures (1965)

D: Larry Buchanan; W: Al Martin, Robert J. Gurney Jr., Paul W. Fairman (short story); P: Larry Buchanan, Edwin Tobolowsky (AP); C: John Ashley, Cynthia Hull, Warren Hammack, Chet Davis, Bill Peck, Tony Huston

This was the very first film Larry Buchanan shot as part of his deal with American International Pictures to direct color remakes of their old sci-fi titles. The films were used to pad out AIP's TV syndication package. In this case, Buchanan tackles *Invasion of the Saucer Men* (1957) with the help of his usual cast and crew, augmented by beach party refugee John Ashley. The monsters are white, lumpy creatures with gaping mouths that have sometimes been described as resembling the Michelin Tire Man (I don't see it). S.F. Brownrigg was the editor. (RetroMedia)

Forever Evil (1987)

D: Roger Evans; W: Freeman Williams; P: Jill Clark, Bill F. Blair (EP), Mark V. Patton (EP), Hal Payne (AP), Rolf D. Reichardt (EP), Betty S. Scott (EP); C: Red Mitchell, Tracey Huffman, Charles L. Trotter, Kent T. Johnson, Diane Johnson, Howard Jacobsen

After surviving the slaughter of his brother and friends at the hands of some kind of demonic force, Marc (Red Mitchell) teams up with a cop and a photographer to find out exactly what happened in this Lovecraft-inspired film that apes parts of *The Evil Dead* (1981). It includes a surprisingly graphic sequence in which the lead character's dead girlfriend rips a fetus out of her stomach.

Producer Jill Clark also worked on *Blood Cult* (1985), *Revenge* (1986), and *The Last Slumber Party* (1988), while executive producer Blair was the founder of United Entertainment and VCI Home Video, which distributed this film. Mitchell (who died in a car accident in 1994) was also in *The Outing* (1987). Writer Freeman Williams (a.k.a. Dr. Freex) had acted in a Super 8 project for Evans called *The Jet Benny Show* (a hodge-podge of Jack Benny jokes and Flash Gordon space adventures) in 1986 and now runs The Bad Movie Report Web site (*www.stomptokyo.com/badmoviereport*), where you can read an 18-chapter account of the making of *Forever Evil*. (VCI)

Future-Kill (1985)

D: Ronald W. Moore; W: Ronald W. Moore, Edwin Neal, Gregg Unterberger, John H. Best; P: John H. Best, Gregg Unterberger, Don Barker (EP), Ronald W. Moore (AP), Edwin Neal (AP), Terri Smith (AP); C: Edwin Neal, Marilyn Burns, Gabriel Folse, Wade Reese, Barton Faulks, Rob Rowley

In some unspecified future time, garrulous fraternity members are sent into a city inhabited by anti-nuclear activist mutants (?) to kidnap a gang leader, and find themselves hunted by crazy cyborg Edwin Neal (who played The Hitchhiker in *Texas Chain Saw Massacre*). H.R. Geiger supplied the poster art for this low-budget Austin film. (Subversive)

The Giant Gila Monster (1959)

D: Ray Kellogg; W: Ray Kellogg, Jay Simms; P: Ken Curtis, B.R. McLendon, Gordon McLendon (EP); C: Don Sullivan, Fred Graham, Lisa Simone, Shug Fisher, Bob Thompson, Ken Knox

A giant lizard munches on the citizens of a rural Texas town. Heroic wannabe rock star/auto mechanic Don Sullivan helps local teens fight the monster after singing a series of maudlin folk/rock tunes (which Sullivan wrote) to his crippled sister.

Ken Knox (here playing a gregarious DJ) was an actual Texas disc jockey who worked for uncredited executive producer Gordon McLendon. Knox was also in *Beyond the Time Barrier* (1969) and Ray Kellogg's *My Dog, Buddy* (1960). Distributed by the McLendon-Radio Pictures Distributing Company.

R&B singer Joe Johnson recorded a song called "The Gila Monster" that appears to have been inspired by this film. (Alpha/Mill Creek/Goodtimes)

Highway to Hell (1990)

D: Bret McCormick; W: Gary Kennamer; P: Bret McCormick; C: Benton Jennings, Richard Harrison, Blue Thompson

An escaped killer hunts down the cop who put him in prison.

Busy actor Benton Jennings is the son of William Bryan Jennings, who played a cop in *Manos: The Hands of Fate* (1966). McCormick continued directing low-budget films well into the 1990s, including *Blood on the Badge* (1992), *Armed for Action* (1992), *Children of Dracula* (1994), *Bio-Tech Warrior* (1996), *Time Tracers* (1997) and *The Protector* (1999).

Honeymoon Horror (1982)

D: Harry Preston; W: L.L. Carney (story), Harry Preston (as Deanne Kelly); P: Nick Calpeno, Norman Brown (EP), Ken Chock (EP), Michael Wyckoff (EP); C: Paul Iwanski, Bob Wagner, Cheryl Black, Philip Thompson, James Caskey, Bill Pecchi, Michael Wycoff

Baffling slasher movie about couples visiting Honeymoon Island and being stalked by a mad killer who may or may not be the first husband of the woman who owns the place (she burned him alive when he found out she was cheating on him), or possibly the "retarded" caretaker.

This was shot at the Austin Patio Dude Ranch in Grapevine, Texas. It was one of the first direct-to-video movies purchased by Sony and allegedly grossed millions worldwide. The sequences with the comic sheriff were added later by Malcolm Whitman. Bill Pecchi, the sheriff in those scenes, appears to have worked as a grip or camera operator on a number of films, including *Hells Angels on Wheels* (1967), *Beware! The Blob* (1972), and *The Bad Pack* (1998).

Director Harry Preston (nee Harry Pimm) was born in South Africa and moved to the U.S. in the late 1940s. He worked in the Dallas film and TV industry for several years before becoming an author. He continued to write screenplays, operate a literary agency, and teach screenwriting at Richland College until his death in 2009. He also directed the unreleased film *Blood of the Wolf Girl* (1989) about a pudgy stripper who transforms into a werewolf. One of his books, *Shot in Dallas*, is a murder mystery about the making of a low-budget horror film.

Horror High (1974)

D: Larry Stouffer; W: Jack Fowler (J.D. Feigelson); P: James P. Graham; C: Pat Cardi, Austin Stoker, Rosie Holotik, John Niland, Joye Hash, Jeff Alexander, Calvin Hill, D.D. Lewis, Mean Joe Greene, Craig Morton

Somewhat ahead-of-its-time teen revenge take on *Dr. Jekyll and Mr. Hyde*, with a gawky science geek (Cardi) using his chemistry experiment to turn himself into a snarling, clawed monster.

Director Stouffer worked uncredited on a number of S.F. Brownrigg films, and Holotik was the lead actress in *Don't Look in the Basement* (1973). Niland, Greene and most of the actors playing the policemen were pro football players. Producer James Graham was an oil executive.

"Jack Fowler" is actually screenwriter J.D. Feigelson, who later wrote the excellent TV movie *Dark Night of the Scarecrow* (1981). Additional sequences featuring Vernon's absentee father were added later by director/composer Donald Hulette on behalf of Crown International when the film was distributed to television as *Twisted Brain*.

The film was adapted as a musical by playwright Jeff Kilgore in Mansfield, Ohio, in 2007 (Pat Cardi attended the opening performance), and Stouffer announced plans to remake the film in 2008. (Rhino/BCI/Code Red)

In the Year 2889 (1967)

D: *Larry Buchanan*; W: *Harold Hoffman*; P: *Larry Buchanan, Edwin Tobolowsky*; C: *Paul Petersen, Quinn O'Hara, Charla Doherty, Neil Fletcher, Hugh Feagin, Max W. Anderson, Bill Thurman, Byron Lord*

Post-apocalyptic survivors are attacked by cannibal mutants in Buchanan's minimalist remake of *Day the World Ended* (1955). It's dull, but may be one of the director's most coherent films.

Petersen was an original Mouseketeer and starred on *The Donna Reed Show*. O'Hara appeared in *The Ghost in the Invisible Bikini* (1966). Hoffman wrote several other Buchanan films, and wrote and directed *The Black Cat* (1966). Byron Lord once again plays the monster. (RetroMedia)

Keep My Grave Open (1976)

D: *S.F. Brownrigg*; W: *F. Amos Powell*; P: *S.F. Brownrigg, Richard H. Pew (EP)*; C: *Camilla Carr, Gene Ross, Stephen Tobolowsky, Ann Stafford, Sharon Bunn, Chelcie Ross, Annabelle Weenick, Bill Thurman, Jessie Lee Fulton*

Camilla Carr plays a crazy woman who may or may not be living with her incestuous brother in an old mansion while a sword-wielding killer slashes his way through the cast.

Originally shot in 1974 as *At the Stroke of Murder*, this was one of two films Brownrigg made with financing from Martin Jurow, the producer of *Breakfast at Tiffany's* (1961), *The Pink Panther* (1963) and *Terms of Endearment* (1983), who had at that point relocated to Dallas. It had additional theatrical runs in 1977 (through Flora Releasing) and 1980 (via Wells Films).

Busy character actor Stephen Tobolowsky is a third cousin of Larry Buchanan's frequent producer, Edwin Tobolowsky. F. Amos Powell also wrote the ridiculous *Demonoid: Messenger of Death* (1981). Executive producer Pew owned the Hilton Inn in Dallas. Larry Stouffer was the assistant director. (Alpha)

The Killer Shrews (1959)

D: *Ray Kellogg*; W: *Jay Simms*; P: *Ken Curtis, Gordon McLendon*; C: *James Best, Ingrid Goude, Ken Curtis, Gordon McLendon, Baruch Lumet, Judge Henry Dupree, Alfredo DeSoto*

Research scientists and a cargo ship captain (Best) are trapped on an isolated island with a horde of giant, poisonous, man-eating shrews (actually dogs in long-haired costumes).

Director Ray Kellog was the head of the special effects department at 20th Century–Fox. He also directed *My Dog Buddy* (1960) with much of the same cast and crew, and *The Green Berets* (1968). Baruch Lumet was the father of director Sidney Lumet. Swedish actress Ingrid Goude was a runner-up in the 1956 Miss Universe Pageant and had at one time been under contract at Universal. Ken Curtis was better known as Festus on *Gunsmoke*, but started his career as a singer for Tommy Dorsey. When he made this film, he was married to John Ford's daughter.

Killer Shrews was one of two films (along with *The Giant Gila Monster*) made in Texas by producer and co-star Gordon McLendon for his Hollywood Pictures Corp. company. At the time, these were touted as the first feature-length films made in Dallas, as well as the first to premiere (in Dallas) as a double-feature.

Texas millionaire McLendon is credited with popularizing the Top Forty radio format, was the first broadcaster to do play-by-play recreations of baseball games, and also owned a chain of drive-in theaters. He built Cielo Studios near Denton, Texas, and originally planned to make a whole series of films there. He also ran unsuccessfully for governor and the U.S. Senate, was implicated in the book *Deadly Secrets* (by conspiracy theorists Warren Hinckle and William Turner) as having a peripheral role in the Kennedy assassination, and produced the Sylvester Stallone film *Victory* (1981). The trailer for *Killer Shrews* features McLendon (in character) delivering a lengthy lecture on the eating habits of poisonous shrews. Actor James Best and his wife produced a sequel, *Return of the Killer Shrews*, in 2011. (Alpha/Mill Creek/Goodtimes)

Manos: The Hands of Fate (1966)

D: Harold P. Warren; W: Harold P. Warren; P: Harold P. Warren; C: Tom Neyman, Harold Warren, John Reynolds, Diane Mahree, Jackey Neyman, William Bryan Jennings

A vacationing family gets lost in Texas and winds up trapped at the home of the mysterious Master, his gaggle of ghostly brides, and creepy servant Torgo in this hypnotically dull film.

Although it was briefly mentioned in Harry and Michael Medved's *Golden Turkey Awards* books, *Manos* didn't achieve true infamy as one of the worst movies ever made until it appeared on an episode of *Mystery Science Theater 3000*, prompting a whole new flurry of interest that resulted in several articles and even a documentary (*Hotel Torgo*, 2004), as well as a lot of misinformation about the film.

Warren is usually described as a fertilizer salesman, but articles in the local El Paso newspaper indicate that he was manager of American Founder's Life Insurance Company. According to legend, he made a bet with Oscar-winning screenwriter Sterling Silliphant (whom he met while appearing in a walk-on part on an episode of *Route 66*) that he could make a horror film on a tiny budget.

Before moving into the insurance business, however, Warren had worked as a nightclub comedian, appeared in summer stock in Pennsylvania, community theater in Savannah, and with a professional theater company production of *Auntie Mame* in Houston. According to an article in the *El Paso Herald-Post* in 1967, he also wrote a musical comedy for the stage called *Chaos in Khaki* in 1949.

The film received a gala premier at the Capri Theater in El Paso, but otherwise had very limited distribution. Memorable Torgo actor John Reynolds (who was supposed to be a satyr in this film, hence his peculiar walk) killed himself a few months after production ended.

Jennings was an El Paso attorney. The little girl in the film, Jackey Neyman, is now a painter. Her father, Tom Neyman (who played The Master), was active in El Paso theater before and after *Manos*.

After *Manos*, Warren wrote the script for an unmade follow-up called *Satan Rides a Bike*. In later years, he sometimes sported the red and black Manos robe at Halloween parties. He died in 1985. (Rhino/Alpha/Shout! Factory)

Mark of the Witch (1970)

D: Tom Moore; W: Mary Davis, Martha Peters; P: Mary Davis, Thomas W. Moore, Patty McKiernan (AP), R.B. McGowen Jr. (EP); C: Marie Santell, Robert Elston, Anitra Walsh, Darryl Wells, Gary Brockette, Barbara Brownell, Lawrence DuPont

Taking its cues from *Black Sunday* (1960), *Horror Hotel* (1960) and the then-contemporary craze for witchcraft among college students, *Mark of the Witch* is about a cute co-ed (Walsh) who becomes possessed by the vengeful spirit of a dead witch (Santell). She's come back to take revenge on the descendants of the people who burned her at the stake.

Mary Davis also wrote S.F. Brownrigg's *Scum of the Earth* (1974). She was a former advertising executive who served as vice president of Presidio Productions. Producer R.B. McGowan wrote and produced *Quadroon* (1972). Actor Gary Brockette appeared in *The Last Picture Show* (1971) and

While professor Robert Elston looks on, college students Barbara Brownell, Darryl Wells and Anitra Walsh prove once again that playing with an Ouija board is never a good idea in *Mark of the Witch* (1970).

Encounter with the Unknown (1973), and has also worked as a director. Tom Moore was a prolific producer in the Texas/Arkansas/Louisiana area. He directed *Return to Boggy Creek* (1977), and also worked on *Horror High* (1974) and *The Town That Dreaded Sundown* (1976). (RetroMedia/Code Red)

Mars Needs Women (1967)

D: Larry Buchanan; W: Larry Buchanan; P: Larry Buchanan, Edwin Tobolowsky; C: Tommy Kirk, Yvonne Craig, Warren Hammack, Tony Huston, Larry Tanner, Pat Delaney, Byron Lord

Another of Buchanan's AIP TV projects, this one featuring fallen Disney star Tommy Kirk as the leader of a band of Martians who have come to Earth looking for females to mate with. It's a semi-remake of AIP's *Pajama Party* (1964), which also featured Kirk as a befuddled alien.

This was one of two films Kirk made with Buchanan, the other being the Arkansas-lensed *It's Alive!* (1969). (MGM)

Mongrel (1982)

D: Robert A. Burns; W: Robert A. Burns; P: John Jenkins, Lin Sutherland; C: John Dodson, Catherine Molloy, Andy Tienann, Terry Evans, Mitch Pileggi, Aldo Ray

The tenants in a run-down rooming house torment each other until one of them dies accidentally. The other tenants are then killed one by one by some sort of growling beast. This is the only feature directing credit for Robert Burns, who got his start as the art director on *Texas Chain Saw Massacre* (1974) and later worked on a number of other horror films, including *Tourist Trap* (1979), *The Howling* (1981) and *Re-Animator* (1985). He committed suicide in 2004 after being diagnosed with cancer.

The Nail Gun Massacre (1985)

D: Terry Lofton, Bill Leslie; W: Terry Lofton; P: Terry Lofton; C: Rocky Patterson, Ron Queen, Beau Leland, Michelle Meyer, Sebrina Lawless, Mike Coady

Proving that no power tool is safe in the hands of a Texan, *The Nail Gun Massacre* combines the rape-revenge plot of *Sudden Impact* (1983) with gratuitous sex, amateur acting, and a killer in a motorcycle helmet armed with a portable pneumatic nail gun who makes cheesy, echo-voiced wisecracks. Director/producer Lofton had worked for Warner Brothers on *The Dukes of Hazzard*, and made this film thinking it would sell well in the burgeoning direct-to-video market of the mid–1980s. (Synapse)

The Naked Witch (1964)

D: Claude Alexander, Larry Buchanan; W: Claude Alexander, Larry Buchanan; P: Claude Alexander; C: Libby Hall, Robert Short, Jo Maryman, Denis Adams, Charles West, Jack Herman, The Der Saengerbund Childrens Choir

"Filmed in Texas — Exactly Where it Happened!" Part horror film, part nudie-cutie, part travelogue, *The Naked Witch* follows the standard witch movie template of a student (Short) who travels to a Germanesque village in Texas to research the history of witches. He pulls the stake from the corpse of an executed witch, who springs back to life in the form of naked, nubile Libby Hall (who was also in *Common Law Wife*, 1963). Gary Owens opens the film with a lengthy narration about the history of witchcraft while the camera pans across a painting by Hieronymus Bosch.

The Naked Witch was shot at a cost of $8,000 in Luckenbach, Texas (presumably before the arrival of Waylon and Willie and the boys), a small town founded by German immigrants. The film is often confused with an Andy Milligan film made during the same period with the same title. Producer Claude Alexander was involved in a car accident in 2002 that killed his then-girlfriend Peggy Moran, an actress who had appeared in *The Mummy's Hand* (1940). (Something Weird)

Night Fright (*The Extra-Terrestrial Nastie*, 1967)

D: James Sullivan; W: Russ Marker; P: Wallace Clyce, Jr.; C: John Agar, Carol Gilley, Ralph Baker Jr., Dorothy Davis, Bill Thurman, Roger Ready, Darlene Drew, Russ Marker

This crazy alien invasion movie could easily be mistaken for a Larry Buchanan film, and may have only been released to television. A space capsule full of test animals that have been exposed to radiation crashes in the woods in rural Texas, unleashing a giant, gorilla-like monster. The film has the same storyline as Russ Marker's *The Demon of Devil's Lake*, an unfinished project that Marker had started in Oklahoma a few years earlier.

James Sullivan was a production manager and cinematographer who worked on several Larry Buchanan films, and is credited as an editor on *Manos: The Hands of Fate* (1966). His last credits include *Lethal Seduction* (1997) and *A Matter of Honor* (1995) for director Fred P. Watkins. Sullivan died in 2005.

Sullivan and producer Wallace Clyce also made a cheap western called *Fair Play* (1972). (Alpha/Mill Creek)

The Outing (*The Lamp*, 1987)

D: Tom Daley; W: Warren Chaney; P: Warren Chaney, Deborah Winters (AP), Fred T. Kuehnert (EP), M.S. Sanousi (EP); C: Deborah Winters, James Huston, Andra St. Ivanyi, Scott Bankston, Red Mitchell, Andre Chimene, Damon Merrill

An evil genie is unleashed from a magic lamp, first by a trio of murderous thieves, and then by a group of brainless teens who break into a museum to spend the night.

The Outing was financed by the producers who made *The Aurora Encounter* (1986). Screenwriter Chaney, a former magician who also worked on "The Fall Guy" TV series, is married to actress Deborah Winters, who now sells real estate. Winters, the daughter of actress Penny Edwards, appeared in *Blue Sunshine* (1976), *Tarantulas: The Deadly Cargo* (1977), and *The Winds of War* (1983).

Tom Daley also directed the Julie Brown music video "Homecoming Queen's Got a Gun." Robert Burns was the production designer, and David L. Hewitt's Hollywood Optical Company handled some of the visual effects. Filmed at the Houston Museum of Natural Science.

Ozone! Attack of the Redneck Mutants (1986)

D: Matt Devlen; W: Brad Redd; P: Bret McCormick, Matt Devlen, Marie Skyler; C: Scott Davis, Barbara Dow, Lorraine Dowdy, Richard Hawk, Brad McCormick, Rhonda Rooney, Blue Thompson

Chemical contamination and ozone depletion turn the residents of a small town into cannibalistic zombies. This was shot back-to-back with McCormick's *The Abomination* (1986). Devlen also directed a portion of *Tabloid* (1985), and has continued working as a producer in California. (Muther Video)

Scary Movie (1990)

D: Daniel Erickson; W: Daniel Erickson, David Lane Smith, Mark Voges; P: Keith Brunson, Daniel Erickson, Helen Rockenbaugh, Edward A. Ihle (AP), Mike Tolleson (EP); C: John Hawkes, Jason Waller, Suzanne Aldrich, Virginia Pratt, Mark Voges, Butch Patrick

Obsessively fearful and paranoid Warren (Hawkes) believes that an escaped homicidal maniac has taken up residence in a charity-run haunted house at Halloween.

Scary Movie received the Silver Award at the Houston International Film Festival. Director Daniel Erickson previously made a short film called *Mr. Pumpkin* (1986) that featured Robert A. Burns, and now directs music videos and commercials.

Hawkes had been in *Heartbreak Hotel* (1988) and *Rosalie Goes Shopping* (1989), and has had a successful career as a character actor in films like *Congo* (1995), *From Dusk Till Dawn* (1996), *Rush Hour* (1998), and *American Gangster* (2007).

Keith Brunson was a weatherman in Austin, and executive producer Mike Tolleson was a local entertainment attorney.

www.ericksonfilms.com/scarymovie.htm

Scum of the Earth (*Poor White Trash Part 2*, 1974)

D: S.F. Brownrigg; W: Mary Davis, Gene Ross; P: S.F. Brownrigg; C: Norma Moore, Gene Ross, Ann Stafford, Charlie Dell, Camilla Carr, Joel Colodner, Hugh Feagin

After her new husband is hacked to death by a mysterious axe murderer, a frantic woman (Moore) takes shelter in the remote cabin of the Pickett family, an incestuous clan of nutty rednecks led by Brownrigg regular Gene Ross. Moore soon finds herself trapped between the loony hillbillies and the shadowy murderer who has tracked her down.

After a lackluster run under its original title, distributor M.A. Ripps retitled it to make it look like a sequel to *Poor White Trash* (itself a retitling of *Bayou*, 1957). *Scum of the Earth* was also the title of a 1963 H.G. Lewis film about the nude modeling racket.

Stepsisters (*Hands of Blood*, 1974)

D: Perry Tong; W: Perry Tong; P: Perry Tong, George Tregre (EP); C: Hal Fletcher, Bond Gideon, Sharyn Talbert, Byron Wolfe, Sandy Pinkard, Linda Patterson, George Rodgers

Here's an odd, cheap, psycho-sexual soap opera distributed by Independent-International Pictures. Marital dysfunction takes a murderous turn when an alcoholic charter pilot (Fletcher) has an affair with his wife's stepsister (Talbert) and plots to kill his equally unfaithful spouse. Shot over six days in Weatherford, Texas, for $17,000.

Actress Bond Gideon was later on *Petticoat Junction* and *The Young and the Restless*. Hal Fletcher also worked in theater, and made 850 appearances opposite Martha Raye in *Everybody Loves Opal*. Sandy Pinkard later became a successful country songwriter ("Coca Cola Cowboy," "You're the Reason God Made Oklahoma") and is now one half of the novelty act Pinkard and Bowden.

Tong (who was from Fort Worth) and George Tregre made another film around the same time called *Slick Silver* (1974) about a couple of Southern con men that co-starred Bill McGhee. Tong ran Universal Amusements Production Company, and later directed *Flesh, Sea and Symphony* (1993) and *Mermaids at War* (1994). He also wrote a novel called *The Brutus Incident* in 1973. (Image)

The Texas Chain Saw Massacre (1974)

D: Tobe Hooper; W: Kim Henkel , Tobe Hooper; P: Tobe Hopper, Lou Peraino, Kim Henkel (AP), Jay Parsley (EP), Richard Saenz (AP); C: Marilyn Burns, Allen Danziger, Paul A. Partain, William Vail, Teri McMinn, Edwin Neal, Jim Siedow, Gunnar Hansen, John Dugan

A family of grave-robbing, cannibalistic crazies waylay and kill a group of kids on their way to visit their grandfather's Texas farm.

Easily one of the most successful and influential regional horror films of all time, *The Texas Chain Saw Massacre* launched the career of Tobe Hooper and the set a new standard for deranged redneck cinema. The film was very loosely based on the exploits of serial killer Ed Gein.

The creepy house was decorated by Texan Robert Burns, who became a prolific art director specializing in grime and decay on such films as *Tourist Trap* (1979), *The Hills Have Eyes* (1977), *Don't Go Near the Park* (1981), *The Howling* (1981), *Blood Song* (1982), *Microwave Massacre* (1983), and *Re-Animator* (1985). He also directed the Austin-lensed *Mongrel* (1982). Actor John Larroquette provided the opening narration.

The film was distributed by Bryantson Pictures, a company run by alleged mobster Lou "Butchie" Peraino (an associate of New York's Colombo crime family) that was formed, in part, to launder proceeds from *Deep Throat* (1972) and other pornographic films that the Peraino family was involved in.

Austin native Hooper, who had previously shot a number of documentaries and commercials, made a feature in 1969 called *Eggshells* (about a hippie commune dealing with the supernatural) that saw a limited release. While a teenager in Baton Rouge, he also made some amateur 16mm films, including something called *The Heir of Frankenstein* that was featured in a *LIFE* magazine spread in 1959.

Hooper followed up with *Texas Chainsaw Massacre 2* (1986), while Jeff Burr helmed *Leatherface: Texas Chainsaw Massacre III* (1990). Screenwriter Kim Henkel took the reins for *The Return of the Texas Chainsaw Massacre* (1994). The original was

Marilyn Burns in *The Texas Chain Saw Massacre* (1974).

The Weird Ones (1962)

D: Pat Boyette; W: Pat Boyette; P: Pat Boyette; C: Mike Braden, Rudy Duran, Lee Morgan, Phylis Warren, Henry Garcia, Bill McNulty

According to the AFI Catalog, *The Weird Ones* is about a space creature called an Astronik who arrives on Earth to "terrorize and murder women." A pair of press agents try to stop him with the help of a "Cosmos-Cutie."

This is a lost film (shot in San Antonio) from Pat Boyette, who also made *Dungeon of Harrow* (1964) and a war film called *No Man's Land* (1964). All copies of the film and related promotional materials were apparently destroyed in a garage fire, although a few posters have since surfaced.

The Yesterday Machine (1966)

D: Russ Marker; W: Russ Marker; P: Russ Marker, Dan W. Holloway (EP); C: Tim Holt, James Britton, Jack Herman, Ann Pellegrino, Olga Powell, Charles Young, Linda Jenkins, Bill Thurman, Robert Kelly

Herman stars as a crazed ex–Nazi scientist who wants to restore the Third Reich using a time machine.

This was Russ Marker's second film after the unfinished *The Demon from Devil's Lake* (1964), and was shot partly at the Studio Recording Office, operated by the film's musical director, Nick Nicholas. Marker wrote the song performed by Ann Pellegrino. Robert "Bob" Kelly was a local rockabilly singer/songwriter who also performed some songs in *Demon of Devil's Lake*, and penned "Git It" for Gene Vincent. James Sullivan, who directed Marker's *Night Fright* (1967), was the production manager. This was the first (and probably last) production from Texas-based Carter Films.

Zontar the Thing from Venus (1966)

D: Larry Buchanan; W: Hillman Taylor, Larry Buchanan, Lou Rusoff; P: Larry Buchanan, Edwin Tobolowsky (AP); C: John Agar, Susan Bjurman, Tony Huston, Pat Delaney, Neil Fletcher, Andrew Traister, Bill Thurman

This may be the most notorious and, dare I say, beloved of Larry Buchanan's AIP-TV projects. A loose remake of *It Conquered the World* (1956), *Zontar* is about an alien from Venus who arrives on Earth, shuts down all machinery, and enslaves the human race with the help of some flying bat creatures. John Agar, riding a bicycle, once again defends humanity (or Texas, at least).

Buchanan made this film with his usual Texas crew, including frequent collaborators S.F. Brownrigg, Annabelle Weenick, and Jim Sullivan. Hillman Taylor also wrote *Encounter with the Unknown* (1973). Producer Ed Tobolowsky was an anti-trust attorney who once appeared before the U.S. Supreme Court, representing Dallas theater owners who were challenging a municipal movie classification ordinance.

Zontar served as inspiration for a Church of the Subgenius newsletter, and was parodied on "SCTV." (RetroMedia)

UTAH

The Boogens (1982)

D: James L. Conway,; W: Thomas C. Chapman, Jim Kouf (as Bob Hunt), David O'Malley; P: Charles E. Sellier, Jr.; C: Fred McCarren, Rebecca Balding, Anne-Marie Martin, Jeff Harlan, John Crawford

Cincinnati-based Taft Broadcasting purchased Utah-based Sunn Classic Pictures in 1981, and one of the first films produced after the acquisition was this oddball horror picture. Sunn, a subsidiary of the Schick Razor Company, was best known for creating and distributing the *Grizzly Adams* series, and for producing a group of popular pseudo-documentaries with either biblical or paranormal themes, like *In Search of Noah's Ark* (1976) and *The Mysterious Monsters* (1976).

This film concerns a horde of toothy, turtle-like creatures released from an abandoned mine. Rebecca Balding (who was married to Conway) was on *Soap*, and the rest of the cast worked primarily in television. Conway also helmed *In Search of Noah's Ark*, *The Lincoln Conspiracy* (1977), *Hangar 18* (1980) and Sunn's TV version of *The Fall of the House of Usher* (1982) with Charlene Tilton. He has since worked primarily on various *Star Trek* series and *Charmed*.

Producer Charles Sellier was one of the founders of Sunn, and also served as head of production and president of the company. Sellier and Robert Weverka originally wrote *The Boogens* as a novel, and it was then revised multiple times by the three screenwriters. Sellier resigned from Taft in 1982, and directed the controversial *Silent Night, Deadly Night* (1984). He died in 2011.

The Boogens (1982), a Utah film made by the same folks who brought us *In Search of Noah's Ark* (1976) and *Silent Night, Deadly Night* (1984) (courtesy Fred Adelman).

Taft Broadcasting was founded by members of the politically prominent Taft family in Ohio (descendents of President William Howard Taft). In addition to radio and television stations, the company also owned the Hanna-Barbera library.

sunnclassicpicturesinc.com

Don't Go in the Woods (1981)

D: James Bryan; W: Garth Eliassen; P: James Bryan, Suzette Gomez, Roberto Gomez, William Stockdale (AP); C: Jack McClelland, Mary Gail Artz, James P. Hayden, Angie Brown, Tom Drury, Ken Carter, David Barth

Bloody, violent rural slasher film about a hairy, forest-dwelling killer who mutilates and murders a parade of oddball campers. Incredibly cheap, but self-conscious enough to lightly mock genre conventions — characters are introduced only to be killed off a few minutes later (including a man inexplicably struggling to make his way through the woods in a wheelchair).

Bryan had previously made a number of sexploitation pictures and hardcore pornos (as Morris Deal) in California before relocating to Utah to work as a sound effects editor for Sunn Classics (initially on the *Grizzly Adams* series). He also directed *The Executioner, Part II* (1984), *Hell Riders* (1984), *Lady Streetfighter* (1980) and a handful of adult films before retiring in the 1990s. (Code Red)

The Returning (*Witch Doctor*, 1983)

D: Joel Bender; W: Patrick Nash; C: Gabriel Walsh, Susan Strasberg, Victor Arnold, Ruth Warwick, Rick Barker

After their son is killed in a car accident, a couple (Walsh and Strasberg) discover that his spirit (and the spirits of some Native American warriors) have been linked to a rock the boy collected on a trip to the desert. The father becomes possessed by the spirits and begins acting violently, trying to take revenge on the driver who killed his son.

Bender was a film historian who had previously directed *Gas Pump Girls* (1979), later wrote Roberta Findlay's *Tenement* (1985), and went on to work on the *Mighty Morphin Power Rangers* TV series. He directed *The Cursed* in 2010. Music by Henry Manfredini.

joelbender.com

Don't Go in the Woods (1981), James Bryan's bloody and silly Utah slasher film (courtesy Fred Adelman).

Savage Water (1979)

D: Paul W. Kener; W: Kipp Boden; P: Paul W. Kener, Raymond H. Smith (AP), Lonnie R. Fausett (AP); C: Bridget Agnew, Ron Berger, Gill Van Wagoner, Pat Corner, Dewa DeAnne, Gene Eubanks, Paul Kener, Clayton King

Deliverance-inspired film about a group of river rafters being stalked and butchered by a mysterious killer.

This was the final and (with a reported budget of $500,000) most ambitious of the four films mounted by Paul Kener's Talking Pictures Inc.

Screenwriter Boden was an actual Utah river-runner. Kener's wife Karen and her band the KC Classics sang the song "Sherrie" in this film, while Doug Warr provided the folky theme song.

In 1984, Kener and Smith announced that Kener would direct a Ted Bundy biopic (*The Obsession of Ted Bundy*) that was set to star former *Brady Bunch* cast member Barry Williams.

The Varrow Mission (*TeenAlien*, 1978)

D: Peter Semelka; W: Ed Yeates, Sherma Yeates; P: Catherine Crofts, James Crofts (EP); C: Vern Adix, Michael Dunn, Keith Nelson, Dan Harville, Mike McClure, Judy Richards, Dale Angell

Aliens living in an abandoned mill disrupt a haunted house (or in the lexicon of the film, a "spook alley") set up by a bunch of teenagers trying to win a Halloween contest. It's extremely cheap, but kind of charming if you think of it as an extended episode of *Scooby Doo*. The bulk of the cast and a significant portion of the crew were local teenagers, most of whom were not paid for their services and who won their roles through a local radio station contest.

Czech-born director Semelka was a cameraman at KSL-TV Channel 5 at the time, and is still active in the Salt Lake City filmmaking community. Ed and Sherma Yeates are married, and Ed Yeates works as a health and science reporter at KSL-TV in Salt Lake City.

VERMONT

Dark August (1976)

D: Martin Goldman; W: J.J. Barry, Martin Goldman, Carole Shelyne; P: Martin Goldman, Marianne Kanter; C: J.J. Barry, Carole Shelyne, Kim Hunter, Frank Bongiorno

A man accidentally runs over a young girl with his car, and has a curse placed on him by her grandfather.

Barry was a regular on *Laugh-In*; Shelyne (his wife) was on *Here Come the Brides* and appeared as a dancer on *Shindig!* (she was the one who always wore glasses). Producer Kanter acted in and produced the Florida film *Blood Rage* (1987). Goldman previously directed the Fred Williamson film *The Legend of Nigger Charley* (1972).

VIRGINIA

Mutants in Paradise (1984)

D: Scott Apostolou; W: Scott Apostolou; P: William Moses, Peter M. Hargrove (AP), Brian Cartier (AP); C: Brad Greenquist, Robert E. Ingham, Ray "Boom Boom" Mancini, John Gamble, Edith Massey, Skipp Sudduth, Anna Nichols

Sci-fi comedy about scientists turning a geek into a superman who has to fight some Russian spies. Apostolou wrote this $60,000 send-up of *The Six-Million Dollar Man* as part of an independent studies project while a student at the University of Virginia.

Anna Nichols was on the soap opera *One Life to Live*. Associate producer Peter Hargrove worked for J.P. Morgan and in the cable industry, directed music videos and worked at Troma before founding Hargrove Entertainment. This was the final film appearance of Edith Massey, who worked frequently with Baltimore-based director John Waters. Filmed in Charlottesville, Virginia.

www.hargrovetv.com

The Redeemer: Son of Satan! (*Class Reunion Massacre*, 1978)

D: *Constantine S. Gochis;* W: *William Vernick;* P: *Stephen M. Trattner (EP), Sheldon Tromberg;* C: *Damien Knight, Jeanetta Arnette, Nick Carter, Nikki Bathen, T.G. Finkbinder, Christopher Flint*

Six former classmates show up for their high school reunion, only to find the school building empty and the janitor dead. A mysterious killer with an obnoxious voice and two thumbs on one hand (Finkbinder) kills them all as an act of religious retribution for their selfish, sinful lives (lust, gluttony, vanity, etc.). This has something to do with a fire-and-brimstone priest (again, Finkbinder) and a mysterious kid who rises out of a lake and hops on a church bus. With listless disco dancing and a sword-wielding, life-size marionette.

According to Finkbinder, director Gochis was an editor at NBC. Finkbinder later became a high school teacher. Sheldon Tromberg owned the distribution company Box Office Attractions in the 1960s. He and Trattner (both of whom taught film courses at Georgetown University) were the founders of TNT Productions, which made this film and the North Carolina flick *Teenage Graffiti* (1977), and later optioned Les Whitten's novel *The Alchemist*. Filmed in 1976 around the Staunton Military Academy in Staunton, Virginia. (Code Red)

WASHINGTON
(None)

WEST VIRGINIA

Chillers (1988)

D: *Daniel Boyd;* W: *Daniel Boyd;* P: *Daniel Boyd;* C: *Jesse Emery, Marjorie Fitzsimmons, Jonathan Wolf, Bradford Boll, Tom McGee*

Five people stuck at a remote bus terminal relate their nightmares to each other in this horror/comedy anthology filmed near Charleston, West Virginia. Includes stories about a haunted swimming pool, a homicidal Scout troop leader, an ancient Aztec deity, a man who can bring the dead back to life through a newspaper, and a woman who falls in love with a blood-sucking TV news anchor.

Director/producer Boyd is a communications professor at West Virginia State College who had previously made short films and documentaries, and partly financed this 16mm film with state grants. He also made the sci-fi comedy *Invasion of the Space Preachers* (1990) and *Paradise Park* (1991), which featured country singer Johnny PayCheck. In 1994, Boyd (who also briefly worked as a professional wrestler) established the Paradise Film Institute at his college to support filmmaking in West Virginia, and taught filmmaking in Tanzania as a U.S. Fulbright scholar. He continues to make documentaries for television.

Actors Tom McGee, John Riggs and Laurie Pennington also appeared in *Space Preachers*. Special effects artist Glen Harless attended mortuary school. (Troma)

www.danielboyd.com

Invasion of the Space Preachers (*Strangest Dreams*, 1990)

D: Daniel Boyd; W: Daniel Boyd; P: Daniel Boyd, David Wohl; C: Jim Wolfe, Guy Nelson, Eliska Hahn, Gary Brown, Jesse Johnson, John Riggs, Daniel Boyd, Delores Boyd, Barney the Squirrel

A dentist, an accountant and a shapely alien bounty hunger take on intergalactic evangelists who have turned the backwoods residents of West Virginia into mindless automatons. (Troma)

Teen-Age Strangler (1964)

D: Ben Parker; W: Clark Davis; P: Clark Davis, Elvin Feltner; C: Bill Bloom, John Humphries, Jo Canterbury, John Ensign, Rick Harris, Stacy Smith, Jim Asp

A psychotic killer stalks women in a small town, strangling them and leaving their bodies marked up with lipstick.

Filmed in Huntington, West Virginia, *Strangler* gained a cult audience years later when it appeared on an episode of *Mystery Science Theater 3000*. The film was put together by local businessmen, who hired New York director Ben Park to helm it. Herschell Gordon Lewis later released it on a double bill with is own *A Taste of Blood* in 1967. The musical number "Yipes Stripes," sung by the Huntington Astronauts, is a highlight, along with instrumental tracks from Danny Dean and the Daredevils.

Director Park, who died in 1983, had directed several short documentaries as well as *A Modern Marriage* (1950), which was re-released several years later as *Frigid Wife* with new footage. He also directed *The Invisible Avenger* (*Bourbon Street Shadows*, 1958) and *The Shepherd of the Hills* (1964). Feltner produced Al Adamson's *Carnival Magic* (1981), which was shot in North Carolina. Clark Davis was an executive at local WHTN-TV. Local sheriff (and former Huntington mayor) Harold Frankel also appears in the film.

Teen-Age Strangler later received a much-ballyhooed state premiere in 1991, along with newspaper coverage and a cast reunion, after being written up in *Psychotronic* magazine. (Something Weird)

WISCONSIN

The Alpha Incident (1978)

D: Bill Rebane; W: Ingrid Neumayer; P: Bill Rebane, Barbara Rebane (EP), Michael D. Graves (EP), Woody Jarvis (AP), Herbert L. Cohan (AP); C: Stafford Morgan, John Goff, Carol Irene Newell, George "Buck" Flower, Ralph Meeker, Paul Bentzen, John Alderman

After the complicated filming of *The Giant Spider Invasion* (1975), Rebane scaled back to shoot this low-key sci-fi thriller about an alien microorganism that contaminates the inhabitants of a remote railroad station. If they fall asleep, the virus makes their heads explode in pretty gruesome fashion. The minimal action takes place within the confines of the railroad office, where characters needle each other before dropping dead, and in an anonymous office where government scientists and officials first plan to cure, then kill, the infected protagonists.

Screenwriter Neumayer (*The Capture of Bigfoot*) is Rebane's cousin. According to *Boxoffice* magazine, Rebane announced two other horror films in 1977 (also scripted by Neumayer) called *The Maggots* and *Mind Blower* that were apparently never produced. (Mill Creek)

Blood Beat (1985)

D: Fabrice A. Zaphiratos; W: Fabrice A. Zaphiratos; P: Helen Boley, Henri Zaphiratos; C: Helen Benton, Terry Brown, Dana Day, James Fitzgibbons, Claudia Peyton

A family spending the holidays in Wisconsin is terrorized by the glow-in-the-dark ghost of a Samurai warrior.

Blood Beat has one of the most mysterious pedigrees of any film in this book: made in Wisconsin, edited in Paris, and directed by the exotically named Fabrice Zaphiratos, whose only other known credit was the French film *La grande frime* (1977). Producer Henri Zaphiratos (father of Fabrice) was a French filmmaker and novelist who began his career in the early 1960s with the film *Les Nymphettes* (1960).

Blood Harvest (*Nightmare*, 1987)

D: Bill Rebane; W: Ben Benson, Emil Joseph; P: Leszek Burzynski; C: Tiny Tim, Itonia (Cari) Salchek, Dean West, Lori Minnetti, Peter Krause, Frank Benson

Rebane's late-in-the-game slasher entry includes a frightening and compelling performance by weirdo singer Tiny Tim. Salchek is a college student who returns home to discover her banker parents have gone missing after foreclosing on several local farms, and that a masked killer is on the loose.

Salchek barely wears pants after the first 20 minutes of the film, and appears topless and nude in several sequences (a rarity in a Rebane movie). There are lots of long, slow sequences of people walking around and talking on the phone, but falsetto-voiced Tiny Tim steals the film as the brother of Salchek's

The Alpha Incident (1978), Bill Rebane's least ridiculous horror film (courtesy Fred Adelman).

childhood boyfriend, decked out in a quilted suit and clown make-up and calling himself The Magnificent Mervo. He sings, peeks through windows, and talks to himself in what is easily the most compelling performance ever by any actor in a Bill Rebane film.

Unlike Rebane's other mostly TV-friendly films, *Blood Harvest* is thick with nudity, gore and a significant amount of kink. The RetroMedia DVD of this film (which has the onscreen title of *Nightmare*) also includes an interview with Tiny Tim and footage of a children's show pilot he filmed with Rebane. This was Rebane's final horror film. He followed it with *Twister's Revenge!* (1987).

Peter Krause later became a star on *Sports Night*, *Six Feet Under* and *Parenthood* (RetroMedia).

Blood Hook (1987)

D: *Jim Mallon;* W: *Larry Edgerton, John Galligan;* P: *David Herbert;* C: *Mark Jacobs, Lisa Todd, Patrick Danz, Sara Hauser, Christopher Whiting*

For those of you wondering what the guys from *Mystery Science Theater 3000* did before they were semi-famous, series co-creator Jim Mallon (the voice of Gypsy) directed this slasher spoof (produced as *Muskie Madness*) about a psychotic killer terrorizing an annual fishing contest, landing his victims with giant hooks.

Mallon and Herbert financed the film by selling $5,000 shares to investors (including their parents). MST3K writer/producer Kevin Murphy was a grip on this film (which was distributed by Troma), and wrote the music. Mallon also directed *Mystery Science Theater 3000: The Movie* (1996). Filmed in Hayward, Wisconsin (Troma).

Bog (1983)

D: *Don Keeslar;* W: *Carl Kitt;* P: *Michelle Marshall, Clark L. Paylow (EP);* C: *Gloria DeHaven, Aldo Ray, Marshall Thompson, Ed Clark, Don Daniel, Leo Gordon, Thomas "Jeff" Schwaab*

A bog monster, awakened by dynamite fishing, starts killing people while a biologist (DeHaven) and sheriff (Aldo Ray) investigate. The bog monster, a bug-eyed man-fish type critter, tries to impregnate its victims with its eggs. Gordon plays an ichthyologist, and DeHaven also appears (under heavy make-up) as an old crone who lives in the woods.

Bog was filmed in 1978 near Harshaw, Wisconsin. Keeslar was a Canadian filmmaker who served as president of Ontario Film Productions during the 1960s.

Blood Hook (1987), an early feature by *Mystery Science Theater 3000* regular Jim Mallon (courtesy Fred Adelman).

The Capture of Bigfoot (1979)

D: *Bill Rebane;* W: *Ingrid Neumayer, Bill Rebane;* P: *Bill Rebane, Peter Fink (EP), M. Dan Stroick (EP), Elwyn O. Jarvis (AP), William D. Cannon (AP);* C: *Janus Raudkivi, Randolph Rebane, Stafford Morgan, Katherine Hopkins, Otis Young, John Goff, George "Buck" Flower, John Eimerman, Wally Flaherty*

Rebane enters the then-lively sub-genre of albino bigfoot movies with this tale of a game warden and a greedy businessman racing to capture a white yeti that's been terrorizing a logging community. The film includes lots of bigfoot attacks, a young boy who befriends the beast, snowmobile chases and even an Indian mystic. Watch for the teen party sequence in which badly dressed youngsters bump and grind to generic disco music (which, as everyone knows, was a required scene in all albino bigfoot movies). (RetroMedia)

The Demons of Ludlow (1983)

D: Bill Rebane; W: William Arthur, Alan Ross; P: Bill Rebane, Barbara J. Rean (EP), Cheri Caffaro (AP), Alan Ross (AP); C: Paul von Hausen, Stephanie Cushna, Carol Perry, James "Hambone" Robinson, C. Dave Davis, Debra Dulman

Slow-moving tale of a haunted piano that unleashes murderous demons in the village of Ludlow during its 200th anniversary celebration.

The film was shot in the same locations with some of the same cast as Ulli Lommel's *The Devonsville Terror* (1983), on which Rebane had an associate producer credit.

This was the second film that *Ginger* (1971) star Caffaro made with Rebane. They later collaborated with young filmmaker James Ali on the obscure *Evil Secrets* (2004), which was based on a novel by James Gordon White, screenwriter of *The Incredible 2-Headed Transplant* (1971). (Mill Creek)

The Game (1984)

D: Bill Rebane; W: William Arthur, Larry Dreyfus; P: Bill Rebane, Alan Rainer; C: Tom Blair, Jim Iaquinta, Carol Perry, Stuart Osborne, Donald Arthur, Debbie Martin

Three aging, bored millionaires lure nine people to a secluded resort with the promise of $1,000,000 if they can face their fears during an elimination contest. A shadowy killer then starts murdering the contestants in this talky, low-key film. (Mill Creek)

The Giant Spider Invasion (1975)

D: Bill Rebane; W: Robert Easton, Richard L. Huff; P: Bill Rebane, Richard L. Huff, William W. Gillett, Jr. (EP), Dick Plautz (AP), Jack Willoughby (AP); C: Steve Brodie, Barbara Hale, Alan Hale, Jr., Robert Easton, Leslie Parrish, Kevin Brodie, Tain Bodkin

This film, about a "miniature black hole" that unleashes an army of killer spiders (and one giant spider built on the chassis of

Bill Rebane's most boring movie? *The Game* (1984) (courtesy Fred Adelman).

a Volkswagen), may be Rebane's most beloved film. It was also one of the hardest for Rebane to complete, primarily because his special effects team was drunk for much of the shoot, and his two screenwriters did not get along. According to Rebane, former Madison, Wisconsin, Mayor William Dyke helped arrange the financing.

A comic book was given away to promote the film, and was reprinted for RetroMedia's original DVD release of the movie. In 2008, Rebane auctioned off the original VW spider chassis on eBay; in 2011, he adapted the film as a musical. (RetroMedia)

Invasion from Inner Earth (1974)

D: Bill Rebane; W: Bill Rebane; P: Bill Rebane; C: Paul Bentzen, Debbi Pick, Nick Holt, Karl Wallace, Robert Arkens

An alien disease is wiping out the Earth's population, and a group of people in a remote cabin spend the majority of the film talking to each other about what might be going on. This was Rebane's return to filmmaking after selling his initial Chicago-lensed project, *Terror at Halfday*, to Herschell Gordon Lewis (who retitled the film *Monster A Go-Go*, 1965).

After he made *Halfday*, Latvian-born Rebane went to work for Studio Bendestorf in Germany (helping them with foreign co-productions) before setting up a corporate and industrial film studio in Wisconsin. He directed another eight films there through 1987 before his Shooting Ranch Motion Picture Studios in Gleason went out of business.

Rebane was the American Reform Party's Wisconsin gubernatorial candidate in 2002 (he had previously run in 1979). He later became involved in a lengthy legal dispute with Fred Olen Ray over the DVD distribution of *The Giant Spider Invasion* (1975) and *Blood Harvest* (1987). (Mill Creek)

www.billrebanenews.com

The Giant Spider Invasion (1975) featured a massive arachnid built on a Volkswagen chassis (courtesy Fred Adelman).

Rana: The Legend of Shadow Lake (1975)

D: Bill Rebane; W: Lyoma Denetz, Jerry Gregoris, Mike Landers; P: Bill Rebane, Jerry Gregoris, Cheri Caffaro (AP), Jochen Breitenstein (AP), Joost van Oosterum (EP), Larry Dreyfus (EP); C: Karen McDiarmid, Alan Ross, Brad Ellingson, Glenn Scherer, Julie Wheaton, Jerry Gregoris

Rebane's entry in the 1970s cycle of 1950s-style guy-in-a-rubber-suit films. A part-frog/part-man creature guards a stash of gold from greedy loggers while terrorizing a forest ranger, his son and a paleontologist. Most of the film is presented as a convoluted flashback.

Producer Gregoris plays Charlie, a crazy old coot who knows the secrets of the lake. The DVD is retitled *Croaked: Frog Monster from Hell*. (Troma)

WYOMING

Wendigo (1978)

D: Rodger Darbonne; W: Rodger Darbonne, Algernon Blackwood (short story); P: Paul W. Kener, Raymond H. Smith, Lonnie R. Fausett (AP), Frank Roberts (AP); C: Van Washburn Jr., Victor Lawrence, Ron Berger, Carole Cocherelle, Cameron Garnick, Frank Lansing, Robert Steffen

A group of hunters arrives at an ancient Indian burial ground and are terrorized by an evil spirit (the Wendigo) guarding a buried treasure.

Filmed in Teton National Park, *Wendigo* was initially distributed by Dallas Farrimond of Filmbrokers. Kener (who served as director of photography on the film) also directed *Savage Water* (1979) in Utah.

Utah native Kener had a degree in cinematography, and served as a cameraman on the film *Toklat* (1971). His company, Talking Pictures Inc. (originally Filmmakers Studio), was based in Riverton, Utah, and specialized in commercials and educational films. Prior to *Wendigo*, Kener and his partners also made *One Second from Eternity*, a documentary about racing on the Bonneville Salt Flats, and a streaking movie called *The Streak Car Company* (1974).

Although Kener is frequently listed as the director of *Wendigo*, a 1977 *Boxoffice* article confirms that Rodger Darbonne (who appeared in Kener's *Streak Car*) was the director. Darbonne, an actor and songwriter, died in 1994.

Select Bibliography

Buchanan, Larry. *It Came from Hunger! Tales of a Cinema Schlockmeister*. Jefferson, NC: McFarland, 1996.

Craig, Rob. *The Films of Larry Buchanan: A Critical Examination*. Jefferson, NC: McFarland, 2007.

Curry, Christopher. *A Taste of Blood: The Films of Herschell Gordon Lewis*. London: Creation Books, 1999.

Donahue, Suzanne, and Mikael Sovijärvi. *Gods in Polyester, or, a Survivors Account of 70's Cinema Obscura*. Amsterdam: Succubus Press, 2004.

Friedman, David F. *A Youth in Babylon: Confessions of a Trash Film King*. Buffalo: Prometheus Books, 1990.

Gallagher, John Andrew. *Film Directors on Directing*. Westport, CT: Praeger, 1989.

Juno, Andrea, and V. Vale. *Incredibly Strange Films*. San Francisco: RE/Search Publications, 1986.

King, Stephen. *Danse Macabre*. New York: Berkley, 1981.

Landis, Bill, and Michelle Clifford. *Sleazoid Express: A Mind-Twisting Tour Through the Grindhouse Cinema of Times Square*. New York: Simon & Schuster, 2002.

Macor, Alison. *Chainsaws, Slackers and Spy Kids: Thirty Years of Filmmaking in Austin, Texas*. Austin: University of Texas Press, 2010.

McDonough, Jimmy. *The Ghastly One: The Sex-Gore Netherworld of Filmmaker Andy Milligan*. Chicago: A Cappella, 2001.

Monaco, Paul. *History of the American Cinema: The Sixties*. New York: Charles Scribner's Sons, 2001.

Newman, Kim. *Nightmare Movies*. New York: Harmony Books, 1989.

Palmer, Randy. *Herschell Gordon Lewis, Godfather of Gore: The Films*. Jefferson, NC: McFarland, 2006.

Rockoff, Adam. *Going to Pieces: The Rise and Fall of the Slasher Film*. Jefferson, NC: McFarland, 2002.

Thrower, Stephen. *Nightmare USA*. Guildford: Fab Press, 2007.

Vogel, Harold L. *Entertainment Industry Economics: A Guide for Financial Analysis*. Cambridge: Cambridge University Press, 1986.

Von Doviak, Scott. *Hick Flicks: The Rise and Fall of Redneck Cinema*. Jefferson, NC: McFarland, 2004.

Weaver, Tom. *Return of the B Science Fiction and Horror Heroes*. Jefferson, NC: McFarland, 1999.

_____. *Science Fiction and Fantasy Film Flashbacks*. Jefferson, NC: McFarland, 1998.

_____. *Science Fiction Confidential: Interviews with 23 Monster Stars & Filmmakers*. Jefferson, NC: McFarland, 2002.

Weldon, Michael J. *The Psychotronic Encyclopedia of Film*. New York: Ballantine Books, 1987.

_____. *The Psychotronic Video Guide*. New York: St. Martin's Griffin, 1996.

Young, Clive. *Homemade Hollywood: Fans Behind the Camera*. New York: Continuum, 2008.

Interviews

Adlum, Ed. Telephone interview, December 2007.

Barton, Donald. Telephone interview, October 2008.

Bookwalter, J.R. Telephone interview, June 19, 2008.

Burrill, Robert. Telephone interview, July 2006.

Folse, Martin. Telephone interview, January 9, 2009.

Ginsberg, Milton Moses. Telephone interview, September 2008; email interview, October 2008.

Grefe, William. Telephone interview, March 2008.

Jackson, Lewis. Telephone interview, December 2008.

Marker, Russ. Telephone interview, May 20, 2009.

Morgan, Robert W. Telephone interview, July 2008.

Rahner, Tom. Telephone interview, October 2008.
Salzer, Albert J. Telephone interview, March 28, 2007.
Stouffer, Larry. Telephone interview, July 2007.

Web Sites

Researching this book would have been significantly harder were it not for the great blogs, Web sites, and message boards where I was able to dig up new information, bounce ideas off of other researchers and fans, and generally waste hours and hours of my time doing everything except finishing this book.

The AVManiacs/DVDManiacs, www.avmaniacs.com
Ballyhoo Motion Pictures, ballyhoomotionpictures.blogspot.com
The Basement Sublet of Horror, www.basementsubletofhorror.com
The Classic Horror Film Board, monsterkidclassichorrorforum.yuku.com
Critical Condition, criticonline.com
The Dead Next Door—The Blog! regionalhorrorfilms.blogspot.com
The Latarnia Forums, thelatarniaforums.yuku.com
RetroMedia, www.retromedia.org
RetroRama, www.crazedfanboy.com
Something Weird, www.somethingweird.com
Tempe Entertainment, www.tempevideo.com
Temple of Schlock, templeofschlock.blogspot.com/
The Unknown Movies Page, www.badmovieplanet.com/unknownmovies/

Index

Numbers in ***bold italics*** indicate pages with photographs.

Abby 11, 207, 212, ***212***, 213
The Abomination 296, 307
Adams, Dave 273
Adamson, Al 231, 237, 274, 275, 314
Adler, Joseph 199
Adlum, Ed 11, 17–28, ***18***
Agar, John 99, 306, 309, 109, 117, 177
Albright, Carlton J. 209, 222, 236
Alexander, Claude 306
Alice, Sweet, Alice 5, 232, ***232***, 244, 247, 260
Alien Dead 187, 189
The Alien Factor 219, 222, 240
Alien Outlaw 273
Alien Space Avenger 234, 242, 269
Alien Zone 281
The Alpha Incident 314, ***315***
Alston, Joe 300
The Amazing Transparent Man 113, 296, ***296***, 298
The Amazing Transplant 243
American International Pictures 8, 25, 177, 179, 212, 215, 296, 298, 299, 301, 305, 309
Amplas, John 287, 290
Another Son of Sam 273
Apostolou, Scott 312
Arngrim, Stefan 252
Arnold, Mal 187
Aschbrenner, Scott 197
Ashe, Richard 242
The Astrologer 243
Asylum of Satan 212, ***213***, 274
Attack of the Beast Creatures 181
Attack of the Killer Refrigerator 222
The Aurora Encounter 297, 307
Axe 273, 274, 276

Backwoods 209
Baldwin, Homer 281
Ballard, John 239
Ballis, Socrates 90, 194
Banned 243
Bansbach, Richard 175
The Barbaric Beast of Boggy Creek Part II 176
Barracuda 187
Barry, George 13, 224
Barton, Donald 28–39
The Basement 47, 233

Basket Case 243, ***244***, 270
Basket Case 2 176, 230, 244, 254
Bateman, Kent 256
Battle for the Lost Planet 230
The Beast from the Beginning of Time 13, 210
The Beast That Killed Women 187
The Beautiful, the Bloody and the Bare 244
Bechard, Gorman 182, 186
Behind Locked Doors 245
Bender, Joel 271, 311
Best, James 227, 303
Beware: Children at Play 233
Beyond Dream's Door 278, ***279***
Beyond the Time Barrier 108, 113, 296, 297, ***297***, 302
Bigfoot 17, 56, 119, 120–126, 128, 176, 178, 179, 189, 204, 214, 217, 223, 228, 265, 285, 316
Bishop, Jenifer 90, 122, 144, 196
The Black Cat 298, 303
Black Devil Doll from Hell 5, 10, 206, 208
Blade 205, 245
Blades 181, 199, 233, 240, 289
Blair, Bill F. 282, 283, 284, 301
The Blob 47, 286
Blonde on a Bum Trip 17, 19, 24, 258
Blood 245
Blood Bath 245
Blood Beat 314
Blood Circus 219, ***220***
Blood Cult 10, 42, 282, 283, 284, 301
Blood Feast 1, 2, 3, ***5***, 187, 196, 274
Blood Freak 188
Blood Harvest 315, 318
Blood Hook 316, ***316***
Blood Lake 282
Blood of the Wolf Girl 302
Blood Rage 184, 188, 205, 312
Blood Sisters 246, ***246***
Blood Stalkers 119, ***119***, ***126***, 119–129, ***128***, 188, ***189***, 196
Blood Suckers from Outer Space 298
Blood Sucking Freaks 193, 246, ***247***
Bloodeaters 287, ***287***
Bloodrage 246
Bloody Brothers 276
The Body Shop 274

Bog 316
Boggs, Tim 282
Bohus, Ted A. 221, 222, 237, 239
The Boogens 309, ***310***
The Boogeyman 220
Bookwalter, J.R. 10, 11, 39–55, ***40***, ***45***, ***53***, 223, 233, 236, 279, 280, 281
Boyd, Daniel 313, 314
Boyette, Pat 300, 309
Bradford, Samuel 217
Brain Damage 247, 268, 270
The Brain Leeches 189
The Brain Machine 142, 226
The Brain That Wouldn't Die 244, 245, 247, ***248***
Brassloff, Stanley H. 272, 245
Bravman, Jack 19, 23, 24, 258
The Brides Wore Blood 130–134, ***133***, 289
The Brother from Another Planet 248
Browning, Ricou 31, 194
Brownrigg, S.F. 144, 149, 150, 299, 301, 303, 307
Bryan, James 310
Bryantson Pictures 184, 245, 260, 272, 294
Buchanan, Larry 11, 108, 110, 116, 150, 177, 229, 282, 298, 299, 301, 303, 305, 306, 309
The Burning 299, 261
The Burning Hell 7, 295
Burns, Marilyn 301, 308, ***308***
Burns, Robert 306, 307, 308
Burr, Jeff 204
Burrill, Robert 11, 12, 14, 158–174, ***159***, ***166***

Caffaro, Cheri 242, 317, 319
Campbell, Bruce 43, 224, 279, 293
Cannibal Campout 181, 186, 292
The Capture of Bigfoot 314, 316
Cardenas, Hernan 194
Cardone, J.S. 205
Carlton, Rex 247
Carnage 249
Carnival Magic 274, 275, 314
Carnival of Blood 249
Carnival of Souls 3, 4, 5, 210
Carr, Camilla 299, 303, 307

323

Carradine, John 200, 220, 262, 267, 283
The Carrier 224, **224**
Case of the Full Moon Murders 185, 190, 236
Casey, Thomas 192, 200
Catalanotto, Joe 58, 60, 218
The Chair 234
The Children 222
Children Shouldn't Play with Dead Things 32, 190, **190**
Chillers 313
Christion, Vaughn 240
Christmas Evil 96–108, **97, 106**, 234, 272
Cirile, Jim 243
Clark, Bob 190, 191
Class of Nuke 'Em High 234, 243
Claws 175
Coburn, Glen 298
Cohen, Gary 10, 241
Coleman, David 227
Color Me Blood Red 191
Colt, Zebedy 234
Conway, James L. 309
Cooper, Buddy 277
Copperhead 13, 228
Corso, John 219
Cramer, Massey 199, 204
Craven, Wes 152, 184
Crawford, Wayne 187, 192, 193, 200
The Crazies 287, **288**
Creature from Black Lake 140, 214, **215**
Creature of Destruction 177, 298, 299
Cribben, Mik 233
Crow, Dean 209
Crypt of Dark Secrets 214
Cunningham, Sean S. 184, 190, 235
The Curse of the Living Corpse 181, **182**, 210
Curse of the Screaming Dead 221
Curse of the Swamp Creature 299
Curtis, Jack 253

Daley, Tom 306
Damiano, Gerard 260
Danna, Ernest 250
Darbonne, Rodger 319
Dark August 312
The Dark Power 275, 276
The Day It Came to Earth 177
A Day of Judgment 275, **275**
Day of the Reaper 191
The Dead Come Home 249
The Dead Next Door 39, **45**, 39–46, **53**, 279, **279**
Dead of Night 191
The Dead One 214
Deadtime Stories 182, 230, 264, 277, 292
Deafula 285
Dear Dead Delilah 292
Death Bed: The Bed That Eats 13, 224

Death Collector 182
Death Curse of Tartu 76, 81, **81**, 84, 192
Death Screams 275
DeCoteau, David 45, 47–51, 222, 228, 236, 280, 281
DeGaetano, Michael A. 176, 205
The Degenerates 250
Delman, Jeffrey 182, 264, 292
del Mar, Glauco 260
Demon from Devil's Lake 108, 115, 282, 306
The Demon Lover 225, **225**
Demon Lover Diary 225
Demon Queen 293
The Demons of Ludlow 317
Deranged 250, **250**
Deubel, Robert 236
The Deviators 96, 98, 272
The Devil Inside 234
Devil's Due 250
The Devil's Mistress 242
The Devil's Sisters 82, 192
Devlen, Matt 296, 307
Disconnected 182
The Disturbance 192
Dobbs, Frank Q. 300
Dogs of Hell 276
Dohler, Don 10, 219, 221, 222, 240
Don't Go in the House 251
Don't Go in the Woods 310, **311**
Don't Look in the Basement 2, **6**, 149, 299, **299**
Don't Open the Door! 50, 299, **300**
Doom Asylum 199, 235, 254
Doran, Thomas 269
Doughten, Russell S. 286
Downe, Allison Louise 187, 193
Dracula Exotica 251
Drady, Curt 203
Dragula 245, 251
The Driller Killer 251, **251**
Dubois, Jean-Claude 192
The Dukes of Hazzard (TV) 135, 141, 142, 204, 306
Duncan, John 226
Dungeon of Death 235
Dungeon of Harrow 300
Dunlap, Jack 176
Dunn, Michael 69, **70**, 273
Durham, Tom 277
Durston, David E. 256

Echoes 252
Effects 288
Elam, Jack 141, 180, 214, 297
Ellison, Joseph 251
Elwood, Tony 45, 276
Emery, Robert J. 199
Encounter with the Unknown 177, 309
Enter the Devil 300
Erickson, Daniel 307
Evans, Roger 301
Evers, Jason 175, 187, 244, 247
The Evictors 215, **216**
The Evil Below 192

The Evil Dead 3, 4, 41, 293, **293**
The Eye Creatures 301

Farmer, Donald 10, 206, 293, 295
Farris, John 292
Faulkner, Brendan 269
Favorite, Robert R. 189
Fear No Evil 252, **252**
Feazell, Jim 178
Feigelson, J.D. 152, 302
Feltner, Elvin 275, 314
Ferrara, Abel 251
Fiend 221
Fierberg, Steven 292
Final Exam 275, 276
Findlay, Michael 17, 19, 25, **26**, 258, 265
Findlay, Roberta 17, 25, 243, 246, 257, 258, 261, 263, 264, 271
Finegan, John P. 233, 289
Fisher, Tom 181
555 5, 90, 206
Flanagan, Neil 245, 256, 265, 271
The Flesh Eaters 253, **253**
Flesh Eating Mothers 253, 269
Flesh Feast 192, 199, 200, 201
FleshEater 288
Flink, Richard S. 80, 196, 200
Flower, George "Buck" 314, 316
Folse, Martin 55–62, 218
Forced Entry 235
Forever Evil 301
4D Man 286, **286**
Frankenhooker 235, 244, 254
Frankenstein Meets the Space Monster 184, 254, **254**
Friday the 13th 2, 235
Friedel, Frederick R. 273, 276
Friedman, David F. 1, 187, 191, 202
Friedman, Richard 199, 235
Frumkes, Roy 270
Future-Kill 301

Gaffney, Robert 254
The Galaxy Invader 221
The Game 317, **317**
Ganja & Hess 255, 271
Garrett, Tom 182
Geek Maggot Bingo 255
Gershuny, Theodore 266
The Ghastly Ones 255, 256, 259
Ghoul School 46, 47, 49, 233, 236, **236**
Giannone, Joe 261
The Giant Gila Monster 302
The Giant Spider Invasion 317, **318**
Gillis, Jamie 250, 243, 251, 261, 262
Ginsberg, Milton Moses 63–75, **63, 74**, 273
Girdler, William 11, 203, 207, 212, 213, 274
Girls Nite Out 236, **237**
Girls School Screamers 199, 233, 289
Glickenhaus, James 243, 244, 254
Gochis, Constantine S. 313

God's Bloody Acre 9, 187, 193, ***193***, 200
Goldman, Martin 312
The Gore Gore Girls 207
Graverobbers 256
Green, Joseph 245, 247
Grefé, William 6, 11, 76–96, ***77***, 119, 192, 194, 196, 200
Grinter, Brad F. 84, 86, 188, 192, 199, 200
Grissmer, John 184, 188, 205
Grizzly 175, 203
Grizzly Adams (TV) 282, 310, 311
Gronquist, Don 285
Gross, Jerry 24, 184, 187, 194, 256, 272
Grossman, Douglas 256
The Gruesome Twosome 193, 274
Guest, Cliff 192
Gunn, Bill 255
Guru the Mad Monk 256

The Hackers 226
Haig, Roul 218
Haines, Richard W 234, 242, 268
Hancock, John D. 185
Hansen, Gunnar 225, 232, 308
Hanson, David W. 226
Harris, Jack H. 286
Hart, Dillis L. 211
Harvey, Herk 13, 210
The Haunted 176, 206
Hawkes, Steve 188
Hayes, Lance D. 210
The Headless Eyes 255, 256
Heartstopper 50, 289, ***289***
Hell High 256
Henenlotter, Frank 243, 244, 247, 254
Herz, Michael 234, 238, 241, 247, 254
Highway to Hell 302
Hilliard, Richard 183, 185
Hilligoss, Candace 181, 210
Hiltzik, Robert 267
Hinzman, S. William 288, 289
Hobart, Doug 81, ***81***, 189, 192, 193, 199, 200
Hoffman, Harold 298, 303
Hogue, Jeffrey 274
Holotik, Rosie 144, 145, 149, 177, 299, 302
Homebodies 11, 280, ***280***
Honeymoon Horror 6, 302
The Hook of Woodland Heights 222
Hooper, Tobe 308
Hopper, David 227
Horror High 144–157, ***147***, ***151***, ***154***, ***157***, 302
The Horror of Party Beach 79, ***79***, 183, ***183***, 254
Houck, Joy, Jr. 58, 135, 136, 142, 176, 214, 216, 218, 226, 297
Houck, Joy, Sr. 8, 60, 135, 136, 178
The House That Cried Murder 184, 188, 205
Hungry Wives 289, 291

Hurley, James F. 207, 208
Huston, Jimmy 276

I Drink Your Blood 194, 256, 272
I Eat Your Skin 79, 194, 257
I Spit on Your Grave 2, 3 184
I Was a Teenage Zombie 254, 257, 268
I Was a Zombie for the F.B.I 294
If Footmen Tire You, What Will Horses Do? 7, 295
Igor and the Lunatics 257, 269
Impulse 77, 81, 90, 92, 95, 119, 120, 121, 125, 194
In the Year 2889 303
Invasion from Inner Earth 318
Invasion of the Blood Farmers 17, 18, 19–25, 257
Invasion of the Space Preachers 3, 14
Iselin, Alan V. 181, 183, 184, 254
Island Claws 194, ***195***
It's Alive! 177

Jackson, Donald 225
Jackson, Lewis 96–108, 234, 272
Jamieson Film Company 8, 145, 146, 148, 152, 299
Janie 5, 258
The Jar 181
Johnsen, Sande N. 244
Jones, Brian Thomas 264

Kalmanowicz, Max 222
Kanefsky, Rolfe 271
Kaufman, Charles 238
Kaufman, Lloyd 234, 238, 241, 257, 267, 271, 289
Keen, Chuck D. 175
Keep My Grave Open 150, 300, 303
Keeslar, Don 316
Keeter, Worth 274, 276, 277, 278
Kelleher, Ed 20, 24, 27, 257, 261, 264, 265
Kellogg, Ray 302, 303
Kener, Paul W. 311, 319
Kerwin, Harry 82, 187, 192, 193, 196
Kerwin, William 82, 125, 187, 193, 194, 196, 200, 201, 202, 292
The Kidnapped Coed 276
Killer! 276
The Killer Shrews 4, 303
Killing Spree 195
Killough, Jon 47, 279, 280, 281
King Kung Fu 210
The Kirlian Witness 258
Kirtman, Leonard 234, 249
Kiss of the Tarantula 203
Kissinger, Charles 203, 212
Korzeniowsky, Waldemar 234
Koz, Wally 10, 206

Lady in White 5, 258
LaLoggia, Frank 5, 252, 258
Lamberson, Greg 208
Las Vegas Bloodbath 229
Las Vegas Serial Killer 229, 242

Last House on Dead End Street 259, ***259***
The Last House on the Left 2, 3, 5, ***6***, 184
Last Rights 237
The Last Slumber Party 283, 301
Leahy, Tom 210, 211
Legacy of Horror 259
Legacy of Satan 260
Legend of Blood Mountain 199, 204
The Legend of Boggy Creek 140, 178
Leroget, Ferenc 262
Leslie, Bill 306
Let's Scare Jessica to Death 72, 185, ***186***, 271
Lewis, Christopher 282, 283, 284
Lewis, Herschell Gordon 1, 77, 187, 191, 193, 201, 202, 207, 208, 314, 318
Lewnes, Pericles 186
Lieberman, Jeff 205, 245
Liquid Sky 260, ***261***
Loch Ness Horror 229
Lommel, Ulli 220, 317
Long Island Cannibal Massacre 260, 272
Lord Shango 272, 294
Love After Death 260
Love Goddesses of Blood Island 196
Lowry, Lynn 256, 287
Lurkers 257, 261
Lustig, William 262
Luther the Geek 209

Madame Zenobia 261
Madman 249, 261
Mahon, Barry 187, 214, 265
The Majorettes 50, 289, ***290***
Mako: The Jaws of Death 77, 93, 119, 120, 122, 189, 196, ***196***
Malanowski, Tony 221, 222
Malatesta's Carnival of Blood 290
Mallon, Jim 316
Malvasi, Dennis 249
Maniac 262
Manos: The Hands of Fate 5, 12, 302, 304, 306
Mardi Gras Massacre 214, 215, ***217***
Mark of the Witch 304, ***305***
Marker, Russ 11, 108–118, 282, 298, 306, 309
Mars Needs Women 305
Marsh, Ray 294
Martin, Bob 247, 255
Martin, James Aviles 253, 257
Mason, Connie 187, 202
Maylam, Tony 249
McBride, Jon 50, 51, 181, 186, 292
McConnell, Arn 265
McCormick, Bret 296, 298, 302, 307
McCullough, Jim, Jr. 140, 214, 215, 217, 218, 297
McCullough, Jim, Sr. 140, 214, 215, 218, 297
McGhee, Bill 214, 299, ***299***, 308
McKeown, Douglas 239
McLendon, Gordon 302, 303

Meeks, Trent 192
Meyer, Irwin 194
Meyer, Ken 284
Michalakis, John Elias 257, 268
Midnight 290, **291**
Miller, Sharron 281
Miller Consolidated Pictures 296, 298
Milligan, Andy 235, 239, 245, 249, 250, 251, 255, 256, 259, 265, 271
The Milpitas Monster 12, **15**, 158–174, **159**, **163**, **164**, **166**, **169**, **172**
Mishkin, Lew 249, 256
Mishkin, William 239, 245, 249, 271
Mitler, Matt 182, 230, 277
Mongrel 305
Monster a Go-Go 207, 318
The Monster and the Stripper 295, **295**
Monster of Camp Sunshine (or, How I Learned to Stop Worrying and Love Nature) 262
Moore, Ronald W. 301
Moore, Tom 153, 178, 179, 304
Morgan, Robert W. 11, 119–129, **119**, **128**, 188, 196
Moss, Jim 251
Mother's Day 238, 261
Mountaintop Motel Massacre 215
Multiple Maniacs 221
Munger, Chris 203
Muro, James Michael 270
Murray, William 291
Mutant War 230
Mutants in Paradise 312
Mutilations 283
The Mutilator 277, **277**
Mysterious Planet 230
Mystery Science Theater 3000 (TV) 35, 37, 177, 202, 304, 314, 316

The Nail Gun Massacre 306
The Naked Witch (New Jersey) 239
The Naked Witch (Texas) 306
Natas: The Reflection 176
Nelson, David 275
Nelson, Dusty 288
The Nest of the Cuckoo Bird 196
The Nesting 262
Neubeck, Jack 22, 28, 257, **258**, 265
Night Fright 109, 116, 282, 298, 306, 309
Night of Bloody Horror 135–140, **137**, **140**, 216
Night of Horror 222
Night of the Bloody Transplant 226
Night of the Living Dead 2, 3, 4, 5, 137, 138, 256, 288, 290
Night of the Strangler 135, 139, 216
Night of the Zombies 262, 263, **263**
Night Screams 211
A Night to Dismember 261, 263
Nightbeast 222, 240
Nizet, Charles 229

Nuchtern, Simon 264, 266
Nude on the Moon 197, **197**, 202

O'Dwyer, Larry 150, 299
Offerings 282, 283, **283**
The Offspring 204
Olson, Ronald D. 285
The Oracle 263
O'Rawe, Timothy 47, 233, 236
Ormond, Ron 7, 295
Ormsby, Alan 190, 191, 200
The Orphan 239
The Outing 297, 301, 306
Owensby, Earl 6, 273, 274, 275, 276, 277, 278
Ozone! Attack of the Redneck Mutants 307

Paris, Domonic 237
Parker, Ben 314
Parolini, Billy 257
Patterson, J.G. "Pat" 194, 214, 274
Payton, Leland 278
Penczner, Marius 294
Phantom Brother 263
Pierce, Charles B. 176, 177, 178, 179, 215, 297
Pierson, R.E. 175
Pinion, Charles 201
Pintoff, Ernest 245
Piper, Brett 10, 50, 230, 231
Plone, Allen 211
Plutonium Baby 264
Polonia, John 10, 51, 55, 292
Polonia, Mark 10, 51, 292
Poor Pretty Eddie 7
The Premonition 227
Preston, Harry 302
Primal Scream 291
Prime Evil 291
The Prowler 239, 246
The Psychic 207, 208
Psycho from Texas 5, 178, **179**
Psychomania 185
Psychos in Love 186
The Psychotronic Man 208

Ragozzino, Ed 285
Rahner, Tom 11, 130–134, 189
Raiders of the Living Dead 231, **231**
Raimi, Sam 39, 41, 43, 46, 224, 279, 293
Ramirez, Alfred 197
Rana: The Legend of Shadow Lake 319
Ray, Aldo 176, 305, 316
Ray, Fred Olen 95, 130, 187, 189, 200, 318
Rebane, Bill 207, 314, 315, 316, 317, 318, 319
The Redeemer: Son of Satan! 313
Redneck Zombies 186
Reed, Joel M. 245, 246, 262
Rejuvenatrix 264
Return of the Aliens: The Deadly Spawn 221, 237, 239
Return to Boggy Creek 178
The Returning 311

Revenge 283, **284**
Revenge of Bigfoot 179
Reynolds, Christopher 283
Richichi, Salvatore 229, 241, 242
Riffel, James 249
The Ripper 282, 284
Ritter, Tim 10, 191, 195, 201
Roberts, Robert L. 270
Robinson, Chris 77, **84**, 88, 199, 200
Robot Ninja 39, 46, 47, 280
Romero, George 10, 41, 287, 289, 290
Romine, Charles 245
Rondinella, Thomas R. 199, 233, 240
Ross, Gene 150, 177, 299, 303, 307
Russo, John 182, 289, 290, 291, 292
Rutt, Todd 265

Salzer, Albert 11, 135–144, 216, 218
Santa Claus Conquers the Martians 264
Santo Gold 219
Sarno, Jonathan 258
Sasqua 223
Sasquatch, the Legend of Bigfoot 285
Satan Place: A Soap Opera from Hell 197
Satan's Children 6, 197
Savage Water 311, 319
Savini, Tom 191, 236, 239, 249, 262, 284, 288, 289
Savino, Michael 222
Sayles, John 248
Scalpel 205
Scarecrows 9, 198, 198, **199**
Scared Stiff 199, 235
Scary Movie 307
Schiff, Nathan 260, 271, 272
Schnitzer, Robert Allen 227
Schwartz, David 229
Scott, Channon J. 223
Scream, Baby, Scream 199
Scream Bloody Murder 199
Scream Dream 295
Screams of a Winter Night 217
Scum of the Earth 304, 307
Sear, Walter E. 243, 246, 261, 263, 264
Seeds 265
Seeman, Ed 261
Seidelman, Arthur Allan 252
Sell, Jack M. 208
Sellier, Charles E. 309
Semelka, Peter 312
The Sex Killer 265
Shadows of the Mind 265
Shallow Grave 198, 199
The Shaman 182, 233, 240
Sheets, Todd 10, 228
Sherman, Samuel M. 231, 290
Shock! Shock! Shock! 257, 265
Shock Waves 191, 200
Shriek of the Mutilated 5, 17, **23**, 25–27, 265, **266**

Silent Death 240, **240**
Silent Madness 266, **266**
Silent Night, Bloody Night 266, **267**
Skinned Alive **40**, 46, 47–50, 281
The Slayer 205
Sleepaway Camp 267
Slime City 257, 268, **268**, 270
Smith, Todd Michael 292
Smoot, Phil 273, 275
So Sad About Gloria 179, **180**
Sole, Alfred 232
Something Weird 208
Sometimes Aunt Martha Does Dreadful Things 193, 200
Sotos, Jim 235
Southern Shockers 13, 227, **227**
Speeth, Christopher 290
Spelson, Peter 208
Spiegel, Scott 43, 48, 49, 279, 281
Spinell, Joe 190, 262, 272
Splatter Farm 10, 51, 292
Splatter University 257, 268, **268**
Spookies 240, 269, **269**
Squirm 205, 245
Stanley 77, 82, **84**, 88, **89**, 90, 200
Stanley, Michael 181
Steckler, Ray Dennis 229
Stepsisters 307
Sting of Death 76, 89, 82, 200
Stouffer, Larry 144–157, 300, 302, 303
Street Trash 269, 270, **270**
Styles, Richard 199
Sullivan, James 108, 116, 282, 306, 309
Sweet Savior 270
Szarka, William 262, 263, 264

Takakjian, Glenn 237
Tales from the Quadead Zone 207, 208, **209**
Tales of the Third Dimension 277
A Taste of Blood 196, 201, 314
Taylor, Hillman 177, 309
Teen-Age Strangler 274, 314
Teen Vamp 217
Tenement 271
Tenney, Del 79, 181, 182, 183, 185, 194, 254
Terror at Tenkiller 284, **284**
Terror in the Swamp 55–62, **59**, 218
The Texas Chain Saw Massacre 2, 3, 5, 308, **308**
There's Nothing Out There 271
They Don't Cut the Grass Anymore 271

A Thief in the Night 287
Thies, Christopher 223
Thomas, Lawrence 283
Thomason, Harry 177, 179
Three on a Meathook 213
Thurman, Bill 111, 118, 142, 177, 214, 215, 216, 298, 299, 303, 306, 309
Tierney, Lawrence 204, 239, 247, 258, 290
Tong, Perry 307
Torture Dungeon 271–272
Toscano, Bruce 181
The Town That Dreaded Sundown 179, 218, 303
The Toxic Avenger 241, **241**
Track of the Moon Beast 11, 242
Transformation (A Sandwich of Nightmares) 96, 99, 272
Travis, Bernard 265
Troma 186, 210, 221, 233, 234, 238, 241, 246, 250, 267, 269, 271, 289, 316
Truth or Dare? A Critical Madness 201
Turner, Chester Novell 207, 208
Turner, Dean 175
Twice Under 209
Twisted Illusions 201
Twisted Issues 201
Two Girls for a Madman 272
Two Thousand Maniacs! 202, **202**, 277
Tyler, Stephen 283

UFO: Target Earth 176, 205
Ulmer, Edgar G. 114, 296, 297
The Undertaker 272
Unhinged 285
United Home Video 10

Valley of Blood 175
Vampire Cop 206
The Varrow Mission 312
VCI Home Video 282, 283, 284, 301
Veau, Mark 222
Video Murders 218
Video Violence 10, 229, 241
Video Violence 2 ... The Exploitation 242
Vincent, Chuck 250
Voodoo Dawn 182, 292
Voodoo Heartbeat 229
Voodoo Swamp 214

The Wacky World of Dr. Morgus 218

Wanzer, Orville 242
Warren, Harold 12, 304
Waters, John 7, 97, 105, 108, 207, 221
Watkins, Roger Michael 259, 265
Weasels Rip My Flesh 272
Webster, Nicholas 264
Wechsberg, Peter 285
The Wednesday Children 281
Weenick, Annabelle 177, 298, 299, **299**, 303, 309
The Weird Ones 300, 309
Weis, Jack 214, 215
Wendigo 319
Werewolf of Washington 63–76, **63**, **74**, 75, 273
Wesley, William 198
West, Robert D. 281
Weston, Armand 262
White, Nathan J. 224
Whitson, Gary 235
Wiederhorn, Ken 200
Wiezycki, Joe 197
Wild Women of Wongo 202
Wilkins, Bob **159**, 161, 165, 167
Williams, Bert 196
Wilson, James L. 217
Winterbeast 50, 223, **223**
Wishman, Doris 197, 202, 243, 263
The Wizard of Gore 208
Woelfel, Jay 278
Wolcott, James L. 202
Wolfman 278
Women and Bloody Terror 135, 138, **141**, 218
Woodchipper Massacre 10, 51, 86
Wynkoop, Joel D. 195, 201

Yakub, Michael 240
Yeaworth, Irvin S., Jr. 286
The Yesterday Machine 108–115, **110**, **112**, **115**, 309
Yust, Larry 280

Zaat **9**, 28–39, **29**, **34**, **36**
Zacherle, John 247, 254, 255
Zaphiratos, Fabrice A. 314
Zarchi, Meir 184
Zedd, Nick 255
Zito, Joseph 239, 246
Zombie Rampage 228, 246
Zontar the Thing from Venus 177, 299, 309
Zwick, Joseph Ryan 219

www.ingramcontent.com/pod-product-compliance
Lightning Source LLC
Chambersburg PA
CBHW080758300426
44114CB00020B/2749